Preface

The atmosphere of educational reappraisal and change which was evident at the time the first edition of this book was published has intensified over the past seven years, necessitating this revision. Change in elementary school education, particularly in the curriculum of the school, assumes proportions of fundamental reform; the elementary school is truly an institution in transition. All persons who would work in it are required to understand what is happening and what the alternatives are for the future if the possibilities for change that are all around us are to be directed ultimately to the benefit of the children. This book addresses itself primarily to the person now in preparation for elementary school teaching or only recently launched in his teaching career. At the same time, an elementary educator who has not had the opportunity to maintain familiarity with the overall curriculum over the past several years will find it useful in gaining perspective on the current scene.

Part 1 focuses on the changing elementary school, includes sufficient history to help the reader to sense the magnitude and direction of the present change effort, locates the forces at work for change, and then illustrates the way in which these forces are influencing goals, curriculum, instruction, and school organization.

Part 2 devotes a chapter to each of the major programs within the elementary school curriculum, calling attention especially to the changing nature of them.

Part 3 focuses on the role of the teacher who implements the changing curriculum, with attention to planning for instruction, using materials and technology in teaching, evaluating pupil progress, and managing the human relations component that is involved in teaching. The intent is to inform the reader about the changing nature of elementary school education and to help him to sense the reasons for much that is happening. It is hoped that the reader will be able not only to comprehend what is occurring but be able to participate constructively and effectively in the improvement efforts that inevitably will continue over the next decade.

Special appreciation is expressed to Professors Louise L. Tyler, Alice Miel, Henry J. Otto, Theodore Manolakes, H. Orville Nordberg, Phyllis

Henry, Harold S. Drummond, and Margaret Lynch for their careful reading of the manuscript, wholly or in part, and for their helpful suggestions for its improvement. The authors are indebted also to the several authors, publishers, and school districts who have granted permission to quote from their publications.

Recognition is also given to the many unnamed colleagues and students with whom the authors have had rich associations since the first edition and who have contributed greatly, though perhaps unknowingly, to this second edition.

G. W. S.
M-M. S.

9,45

995
01

DATE DUE

NOV 0 1 1985			
DEC 2 3 1991			
OCT 2 0 1992			
MAR 2 2 1997			
MAR 2 9 2011			
GAYLORD			PRINTED IN U.S.A.

*The Changing Curriculum
and the Elementary Teacher*

Second Edition

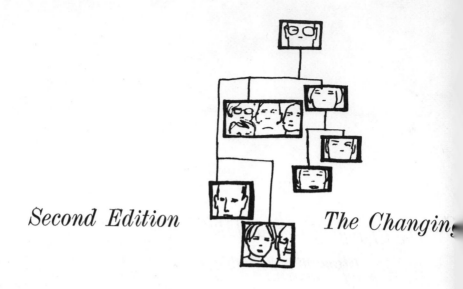

The Changing

Wadsworth

Curriculum and the Elementary Teacher

G. Wesley Sowards and Mary-Margaret Scobey

FLORIDA STATE UNIVERSITY   SAN FRANCISCO STATE COLLEGE

Publishing Company, Inc., Belmont, California

The Changing Curriculum and the Elementary Teacher, 2nd
Edition by G. Wesley Sowards and Mary-Margaret Scobey

Second printing: August 1969

© 1968 by Wadsworth Publishing Company, Inc., Belmont,
California.

L. C. Cat. Card No.: 68-18425
Printed in the United States of America
by American Book–Stratford Press, Inc.

Contents

The Changing
Elementary School

Part 1

*This is a time of great change in elementary education.
The elementary school teacher must recognize the forces
of change, understand the new priorities in programs, and
learn to work with the new curricular and instructional
arrangements. He must consider the school as it has been,
as it is now, and as it may become. Thus, this book opens
with a brief overview of the history of elementary education in the United States. It continues with descriptions
of the major ideas which have influenced curriculum planning and instruction to the present time, the forces which
are at work to bring about change, the goals for elementary education, some new approaches to curriculum
planning, and some new organizational arrangements
through which teachers may implement the school experience for the pupil.*

The Elementary School: A Changing Institution

1

At the present time about 36,000,000 children attend elementary schools in the United States.[1] This figure accounts for about 70 percent of the five-year-olds and almost 99 percent of the six-to-thirteen-year-olds that could be enrolled. The great majority of these children, about 30,500,000 of them, attend public elementary schools. This book is a statement about public elementary school education in recognition of the extent to which the American people have accepted the free, tax-supported "common" school for their children.

One major reason that the elementary school has been able to retain the confidence and support of the people over the years has been its demonstrated responsiveness to the changing nature of the American scene. Over the years almost everything about elementary school educa-tion has changed—and then has changed again. In some periods educators and laymen have exerted great effort to bring about extensive change. They have raised basic questions about a guiding philosophy for child education, or an appropriate curriculum for the school, or an effec-tive methodology for instruction, or a useful organizational plan for deploying pupils and teachers.

The elementary school is now in a period of major change. This change effort, which began around 1955, embraces the curriculum, instruction, and school organization. Many elementary schools are testing one or another of seemingly equally promising "new" ways of going about some particular aspect of their work. In some schools pilot projects have been set up to put an emerging conceptualization to a developmental test. A "new" mathematics, a "different" science, an i/t/a approach to

---

[1] U.S. Department of Health, Education, and Welfare, Office of Education, OE–10030–65: (1) Projections of Educational Statistics to 1974–75, 1965 Edition, (2) "Back to School Statistics," American Education (September 1966), pp. 2–23.

reading, a teaching team, a "head start" class—all of these developments point to the elementary school as a changing institution.

In commenting recently on some contemporary issues in elementary education, the Educational Policies Commission had this to say:

> The elementary school, here defined as a school extending through the sixth grade, has responded to the 20th century with many changes. The content of instruction has expanded. Teaching procedures have shifted from a heavy reliance on rote learning of printed materials to a wider variety of approaches. Instructional materials such as textbooks and supplementary reading materials, films, sound recordings, maps, and models have increased dramatically in variety, quality, and availability. Elementary-school buildings have been better designed for serving children. School services have been extended. The kindergarten, merely an experiment a century ago, has been increasingly accepted as a part of elementary education. . . .
> The elementary school continues to change today, for it must strive incessantly to take account of social change and to improve its effectiveness. In changing it must pay due regard to the role which it alone can play, and to the growing body of knowledge about children and about learning.[2]

THE FOUNDATION AREAS
AS DATA SOURCES

Change is a response to forces or circumstances. We can identify forces for change in elementary school education by examining the following data sources:

1. The social, political, and economic scene.
2. The human organism.
3. Man's accumulating knowledge (the disciplines).

These sources have always influenced the development of elementary school education. The first two of them have been referred to as *foundation areas of education* since about 1930. The clear identification of man's organized knowledge, that is of the disciplines, as a *foundation* area has come about since 1950. Organized subject matter has always had a major influence on curriculum development. But the disciplines are now often being looked to first for new answers to old and persistent curriculum questions; they are the focal point for many of the curriculum improvement projects in elementary education. It is their *direct* and *deliberate* utilization for answers to curriculum and instruction planning tasks that is different.

---

[2] Educational Policies Commission, *Contemporary Issues in Elementary Education* (Washington, D.C.: NEA, 1960), pp. 2–3.

Recent publications from the Center for the Study of Instruction (NEA) identify the same three major data sources for decision-making in curriculum planning: society, the learner, the discipline.[3] Together these foundation areas, or data sources, have formed and continue to form a kind of triangle against which educational choices can be cast and decisions contemplated. And these sources continuously change. The social, political, and economic scene is a changing one. Values which guide behavior are susceptible to change. Investigators provide new evidence about the human organism and its possibilities for learning. The rapid expansion of knowledge in the humanities and sciences is some-times called an "explosion." Thus the elementary school must change if it is to remain an effective place for the education of children. The relevance of its programs of instruction and the acceptability of its procedures for work must be reestablished from time to time.

Thus, these data sources influence what is taught, when it is taught and the way it is taught, as well as the organizational arrangement in which the teaching is done.

SOME ESSENTIAL DEFINITIONS

At this point some definitions will help to facilitate communication. The definition we are using for *curriculum* is as follows:

> The curriculum is the school's plan for the intentional modification of pupil behavior in the direction of agreed-upon educational goals.

We define *instruction* as follows:

> Instruction is that total set of actions involved in the implementation of the curriculum.

One might say that where curriculum development stops, instructional planning begins. Teaching is, in a sense, the presentation of the curriculum plan to children—and learning is their response to that which is presented. When we see evidences of behavior in children consistent with the intentions of the plan, we say that both learners and teachers are successful. And we say that the curriculum plan is effective.

Curriculum development, then, is the working out of a plan in the first instance. It may be concentrated on a particular area of instruction, such as arithmetic. Or it may encompass several areas in an attempt to work out an overall design that will relate the areas to each other and into

---

[3] NEA Project on Instruction, *Deciding What to Teach* (Washington, D.C.: NEA, 1963), Preface, p. 2.

some meaningful, viable whole. Curriculum development calls for decisions as to which subject matter, method, and material will be utilized in what combination to try to insure that pupils will develop the behaviors called for by the stated goals. Choices made by the planners help to determine the actions of the teachers and of the pupils. The accepted plan may specify how the time available for instruction will be distributed and what facilities will be required to accomplish the job.

THE CURRENT SITUATION

Changes must be made in the elementary school curriculum when one or more of the following conditions prevail:

1. When educational goals are revised sufficiently to call for new means of achieving them.
2. When the changing nature of man's knowledge brings about obsolescence in the content of the school's program.
3. When the present curriculum provides for instruction that is ineffective in modifying the behavior of most pupils or of particular subpopulations of pupils.

All of these conditions prevail at the present time. They serve to motivate current reexaminations of elementary school education. Planners are changing programs and procedures extensively in light of current social circumstances, rapidly accumulating additions to human knowledge, and more complete understandings of child growth and development.

The elementary school, of course, has been developed and is maintained by society to minimize the factor of chance with respect to certain aspects of the education of children. School is only a part of the total education of a child. Family life educates; neighborhood and community living educate; the church educates; the Girl and Boy Scouts educate; the mass media educate; and so on. But the elementary school is expected to make a particular contribution to the education of the child. It would appear that present circumstances signal for change in that contribution for the well-being of both the individual and the larger society.

CHANGE OVER TIME

Change takes place over time—and evolution has characterized educational change more than has revolution. Therefore, an understanding of present events calls for some insight into the past of the elementary school. Elementary school education as we know it today is a combination of long and firmly established programs and procedures, embellished by a residual from two earlier major efforts, both since 1900, to bring about change in the enterprise. Careful and painstaking effort lies ahead if the major transformation of which many elementary school educators speak is to come about. Persistence is called for if we are now to maintain a sensible and timely relationship between the needs of the individual and of society and the school.

We have come a long way since the Massachusetts educational acts of 1642, which required town officials to compel parents to provide elementary instruction for their children, and those of 1647, which required each town of fifty families to provide an elementary school teacher and each town of one hundred families to establish a Latin grammar school. These actions, according to Cubberley, set the "cornerstone of our American state school system."[4]

The remainder of this chapter is devoted to a brief overview of the development of the elementary school from about 1650 to 1950. There exists a vast store of historical literature to which one can turn for a more detailed account of these years. But even this general survey-like statement reveals many of the changes that have taken place as the elementary school has striven to be in and of the society which has supported it.

Elementary School Education in the 1600's

The elementary schools that were provided in New England in 1650 were essentially the *dame school* and the *writing school* that had been known in England. In the dame schools, some women in the community would gather a few children into their homes for instruction. They would teach the children the alphabet and the beginnings of reading while they went about their usual chores. This approach was brought to New England, where the curriculum went beyond the alphabet and reading to include some spelling and certain moral and religious precepts. Some schools attempted to teach writing and arithmetic, but as a rule these subjects were reserved for the more advanced town schools. The dame school experience marked the end of formal education for most girls at this time, and their program might be broadened, therefore, to include sewing and knitting. Boys, once they could handle words of two or three syllables, could go on to the town reading and writing school. Small had this to say about the dame school:

> The dame school was a necessity of the times. Boys were not generally admitted to the master's school until they could "stand up and read words of two syllables and keep their places"; girls were not

---

[4] Ellwood P. Cubberley, *The History of Education* (Boston: Houghton Mifflin Company, 1920), p. 366.

admitted at all. The teaching of the simple rudiments was made a family, not a public matter. . . . The floor was scoured to whiteness and covered with the finest sand. Here instruction in arithmetic was oral, Miss Betty making the figures on the sanded floor with her rod, . . . and her pupils, with their square pieces of birch bark and bits of charcoal, copying the sums she gave them. . . . The children, having walked long distances, were made very comfortable at the long recess, as their dinners were many times frozen, and sometimes their food required cooking. Miss Betty was devoted in her care for them in preparing their frugal repast. Apples were roasted and nuts were cracked in profusion, and then with their old fashioned games they had an enjoyable time.[5]

From these beginnings the typical elementary school, devoted to "the three R's," took shape in this country. One teacher handled the instruction for all children. The educational system was financed almost exclusively from tuition fees paid by parents, although such fees were often waived for the children of poor families who could not afford to pay. The school might be housed in the teacher's home, in the church, in the town meetinghouse, or in any available building.

In the Southern Colonies a pattern of aristocracy dominated life, and education was no exception; schooling was a private affair. Parents who were financially capable made provision for the education of their children. The Southern Colonies looked upon free education as charity education, for the poor only. The church was influential in education in the South, and the aims of education and the content of the curriculum were much the same as they were in New England.

The Middle Colonies in the 1600's were sparsely populated, with many diverse religious and civil groups; there was no unified demand for education and schools. Too, these colonies were in great part commercial ventures, and the companies involved were more concerned about goals other than universal education. State and civil control over schools was secondary to private and religious control. The curriculum was usually limited to instruction in reading, writing, and some very simple arithmetic, with emphasis throughout on religion.

Elementary School Education in the 1700's

During the 1700's the elementary school began to be the typical beginning school experience for children, combining in a single institution that which the dame school and the writing school had provided separately before. The elementary school was concerned primarily with

---

[5] W. H. Small, *Early New England Schools* (Boston: Ginn and Company, 1914), pp. 162–164, as quoted in Henry J. Otto, *Elementary School Organization and Administration* (New York: Appleton-Century-Crofts, Inc., 1954), pp. 1–2.

teaching children reading, writing, and eventually, the fundamentals of arithmetic. Religion was still a prime concern in the schools at the beginning of the century, and almost all of the reading material used in the schools dealt with religious matters. A good example of the concern with religion is the *New England Primer,* a reading book used almost universally in the elementary school during this period. Butts's description of the content of this reader is revealing:

> It commonly contained the alphabet in capital and small letters; lists of syllables; and lists of words emphasizing moral concepts, for example, abusing, bewitching, confounded, drunkenness, faculty, godliness, impudent, everlasting, fidelity, glorifying, and humility. Then came the famous woodcuts illustrating the letters of the alphabet and accompanied by religious and moralistic rhymes, many of them reflecting the gloomy outlook of Puritanism. The reading material followed, usually under such headings as "The Dutiful Child's Promises" and "An Alphabet of Lessons for Youth," and including the Lord's Prayer, the Apostles' Creed, the Ten Commandments, the names of the books of the Old and New Testaments for memorizing, religious verses and stories, and finally the Westminster Catechism.[6]

Later in the 1700's, in response to the mood of the times, revised editions of this *New England Primer* included patriotic sentiments and a good deal of secular material. Again from the work of Butts, note the following:

> For example, the early rhyme describing the letter K and expressing loyalty to the king of England had read, "Our King the Good, No man of blood." After the Revolution, patriotism became the motif: "Kings should be good, Not men of blood," "The British Kings, Lost states thirteen," or "Queens and Kings, Are gaudy things." Other changes reflected patriotic and nationalist sentiments; "Whales in the sea, God's voice obey" became "Great Washington brave, His country did save." . . . practical values of learning to read began to replace its use in reading the Bible. For example, the *New England Primer* exhorted pupils in the following manner: "He who ne'er learns his A.B.C. Forever will a blockhead be. But he who learns his letters fair Shall have a coach to take the air."[7]

Even the arithmetic taught in most of the town elementary schools after about 1725 was related to religious training, since the learning of numerals was considered preparation "for the ready finding of any Chapter, Psalm, and Verse in the Bible." It was at a later time that different ends were sought through arithmetic instruction. Spelling, related to the

---

[6] R. Freeman Butts, *A Cultural History of Education* (New York: McGraw-Hill Book Company, Inc., 1947), p. 373.

[7] Butts, p. 373.

instruction in reading, came to be a regular part of the elementary school curriculum about the middle of the century. History, geography, and science as such were not included in the program.

One teacher handled the teaching in an elementary school, and the individual method of instruction was used. Pupils were called up, one by one, for recitation, and a poor performance was very likely to result in the use of "the rod" as a spur to learning. Class methods of instruction were not prevalent until the next century.

A most interesting description of an elementary school program in the period after the Revolution is cited by Edwards and Richey:

> The schoolhouse chimney was of stone, and the fireplace was six feet wide and four deep. The flue was so ample and so perpendicular that the rain, sleet, and snow fell directly to the hearth. In winter the battle for life with green fizzling fuel, which was brought in lengths and cut up by the scholars, was a stern one. Not unfrequently the wood, gushing with sap as it was, chanced to let the fire go out, and as there was no living without fire, the school was dismissed, whereat all the scholars rejoiced.
>
> I was about six years old when I first went to school. My teacher was "Aunt Delight," a maiden lady of fifty, short and bent, of sallow complexion and solemn aspect. We were all seated upon benches made of slabs—boards having the exterior or rounded part of the log on one side. As they were useless for other purposes, they were converted into school benches, the rounded part down. They had each four supports, consisting of straddling wooden legs set into auger holes.
>
> The children were called up one by one to Aunt Delight, who sat on a low chair, and required each, as a preliminary, "to make his manners," which consisted of a small, sudden nod. She then placed the spelling-book before the pupil, and with a pen-knife pointed, one by one, to the letters of the alphabet, saying, "What's that?"
>
> I believe I achieved the alphabet that summer. Two years later I went to the winter school at the same place kept by Lewis Olmstead—a man who made a business of ploughing, mowing, carting manure, etc., in the summer, and of teaching school in the winter. He was a celebrity in ciphering, and Squire Seymour declared that he was the greatest "arithmeticker" in Fairfield Country. There was not a grammar, a geography, or a history of any kind in the school. Reading, writing, and arithmetic were the only things taught, and these very indifferently—not wholly from the stupidity of the teacher, but because he had forty scholars, and the custom of the age required no more than he performed.[8]

In the late 1700's the requirement for elementary school teaching was the ability to teach reading, writing, and simple arithmetic. Certificates to

---

[8] Newton Edwards and Herman Richey, *The School in the American Social Order* (Boston: Houghton Mifflin Company, 1947), pp. 116–117.

teach were issued only to those who clearly were religious persons, of "sober and good conversation," with the minister usually being the person authorized to issue the certificate. Ministers were also expected to supervise both school and teacher to see that the school adhered to its expected role. Other prominent citizens often assisted in the supervision.

The New England Colonies were setting the pace in education during the 1700's. Development of schools was slow in the Middle Colonies, with a tendency to keep education free of state control or support. Education at private expense and under private control was characteristic of the Southern Colonies, consistent with the Southern social order. The nearest approach to a public school system in the South before the Revolution was found in the elementary schools maintained by the Society for the Propagation of the Gospel in Foreign Parts. These were charity schools whose chief purpose was religious training, but who also provided instruction in reading, writing, and simple arithmetic.

Elementary School Education in the 1800's

The distinctive pattern of American public schools was truly taking form in the 1800's. The European system, a two-track affair that tended to perpetuate separate schools for upper and lower social classes, was rejected. The idea that everyone should go as far as his talents would permit was being accepted. The school system was increasingly tax-supported and secular in its control. Another essential ingredient to the realization of basic purposes was added through the idea of compulsory school attendance. The first law requiring school attendance was set down by Massachusetts in 1852. All other states except those in the South had taken a similar step by 1900. The school, as we know it, was beginning to take shape. As the enrollment in the elementary schools increased, its organization, its procedures, its curriculum, and even its purposes for being were reexamined and revised.

Purposes of elementary school education. At the beginning of the nineteenth century, the goals of primary school education were much the same as they had been earlier: to develop literacy and sound moral character. An adequate elementary school program at this time was outlined in a *Code of Regulations* issued by a Connecticut Association for the Improvement of Common Schools. As quoted in Edwards and Richey, the code in part had this to say about the program:

> In the morning, the Bible may be delivered to the head of each class, and by them to the scholars capable of reading decently or looking over. This reading with some short remarks, or questions, with the morning prayer, may occupy the *first half hour*. The second may

be employed in hearing the morning lessons, while the younger classes are preparing to spell and read. The third in attention to the writers. The fourth in hearing the under classes read and spell. The fifth in looking over and assisting the writers and cipherers. The sixth in hearing the under classes spell and read the second time; and receiving and depositing pens, writing and reading books. . . .

In the afternoon one half hour may be employed in spelling together, repeating grammar, rules of arithmetic, and useful tables, with a clear, and full, but soft voice, while the instructor prepares pens, writing books, &c. The second and third half hours in hearing the under classes and upper classes read. The fifth to hearing the under classes read, and spell the second time. The sixth in receiving and depositing the books, &c. as above.[9]

As the century progressed, purposes other than the development of literacy and moral character began to be felt in the elementary school program. Citizenship education became a larger concern, and the growing commercial and industrial activity in the various states made the development of commercial and industrial skills a necessity among workers. Thus, certain social and practical educational aims emerged.

An expanded curriculum. From about 1825 to the end of the Civil War in 1865 the elementary school curriculum expanded considerably. The primary purpose of the school remained that of developing literacy among children, and the curriculum comprised work in reading, writing, spelling, and eventually the rules of grammar, rhetoric, and composition. Arithmetic was next in importance because of its practical application in daily affairs and because of its value to straight thinking and mental discipline. Next in importance was a social studies program restricted to some study of history and geography. Massachusetts passed laws late in the 1820's requiring that geography be studied in elementary schools; Vermont passed similar legislation with respect to American history about this same time. Later in the nineteenth century the study of government was added to social studies. A program in science, or nature study, began to take form late in the 1800's, and drawing, music, and physical education were given some very limited attention. The earliest instruction in science was restricted to the object study approach, becoming much more nature study oriented by the end of the century. Drawing was first quite formal or draftsman-like and only later did freehand drawing become popular. Music was mostly singing and choral work. Physical education was offered in only a few places and not until the latter part of the century. None of these latter subjects was very widely developed at the end of the 1800's.

New organization and methods. With the growth of public education came a swelling elementary school enrollment. The one-room school, with

---

[9] Edwards and Richey, p. 388.

a single teacher responsible for the work of a highly varied age group on an almost individual basis, began to feel the pressures. Two developments that resulted from the increased enrollment still characterize elementary school education today: (1) the elementary school became a graded school, with children of the same age grouped together for instruction, and (2) practices and procedures were developed that would allow a single teacher to work with a class group rather than with individuals. By the end of the Civil War there were usually two elementary schools in a community—a Primary School, comprising grades one through four, and a Grammar School, comprising grades five through eight. By the end of the century the most common unit was an eight-year, graded elementary school, in which teachers were using methods that enabled them to work with large numbers of children at the same time.

Beginnings of teacher preparation. The combination of an expanded curriculum, the graded school, and the class method of instruction necessitated a new kind of specialization in American elementary education. The normal school was developed to give the rudiments of professional preparation to elementary school teachers. The normal school usually admitted students directly from elementary school graduation, and as late as 1900 the most common requirement for admission was only two years of high school work. The course of study in the normal school usually covered two years, with focus on the elementary school subjects and special emphasis on a given grade level for each candidate. There was some work in philosophy, psychology, and history of education, and a laboratory experience of some sort was usually provided, similar to present-day observation and student teaching programs.

European influences. All during these years certain voices from Europe had great effect on education in America. The work of three Europeans—Pestalozzi, Froebel, and Herbart—received the most attention. Pestalozzi's ideas on both the content and method of elementary education were evident. His concern for the practical in education was appealing, and his ideas on a psychological rather than a singularly logical approach to organized subject matter appealed to many. Froebel, a student of Pestalozzi, was primarily concerned with preschool children and established the kindergarten in Germany. By 1900 there were some 4,500 kindergartens, mostly private, operating in the United States. Herbart developed a science of teaching through "the five formal steps" that was widely accepted as the basic approach for planning and executing a lesson.

As the nineteenth century closed, a subject matter program embracing language, arithmetic, history, geography, civics, some science or nature study, and a small measure of music, art, and physical education was usual in the elementary schools. Some schools offered instruction in the manual and domestic arts in the upper grades, but not on an extensive scale. Great differences existed, of course, between the programs of schools in the growing urban centers and of those in rural America. The typical elementary school found in the United States in the closing years of the 1800's is vividly described by Reisner as follows:

> The effect of all the factors surrounding the graded school of the generation following the Civil War was to develop a school machine. In contrast with the school conditions of a generation preceding there was a great deal more material included in the graded course of instruction, but the quality of teaching and learning was improved hardly at all. From the lowest grade to the highest the pupils followed an endless succession of book assignments which they learned out of hand to reproduce on call. The chief end of pupils was to master skills and learn facts as directed by a teacher who in turn was under the automatic control of a printed course of study, a set of textbooks, and the necessity of preparing her class to pass certain examinations on the contents of a specific number of printed pages. From the standpoint of discipline the physical cruelties of the earlier day had to a large degree disappeared, but the control exercised over the pupils was at least negative. The business of the school being what it was, any movement, any conversation, any communication, were out of order. The spirit of control was military and repressive, not constructive and cooperative. Long rows of seats, military evolutions of classes, stated appearances for recitations, with the rest of the school time devoted to narrowly prescribed exercises, had for their moral equivalent being quiet, industrious at assigned tasks, and submissive to the rule of the drill-sergeant in skirts who unflinchingly governed her little kingdom of learn-by-heart-and-recite-by-rote.[10]

ELEMENTARY EDUCATION 1900–1950

It was inevitable that a young nation with a distinctly new concept of public education should eventually develop an educational point of view unique and indigenous to the American scene. By the beginning of the twentieth century this development was beginning to take form. Two voices in particular were making themselves heard. One was that of G. Stanley Hall, a teacher and researcher at Johns Hopkins University, who investigated much and wrote a great deal on the psychological aspects of the educative process. He turned the attention of elementary educators from a single concern for subject matter to the need for the careful study of child development. His ideas were often controversial, but his influence was no less significant.

The other voice was that of John Dewey, probably the most influen-

---

[10] Edward H. Reisner, *The Evolution of the Common School* (New York: The Macmillan Company, 1935), pp. 427–428.

tial thinker and writer on education that America has produced, whose ideas have stimulated supporters and critics alike to reach for a better quality school experience for children. It was in the early 1900's that Dewey began to speak out on educational matters and to demonstrate to society his conception of sound elementary education.

The rapid changes that occurred in American life generally from 1900 to 1950 made their impact on American education as a whole and on elementary education specifically. The consistent movement of the period toward political, economic, and social reforms prompted educational change. Early in the century it became evident that a deeper interest in children and youth was developing, along with a greater desire to meet certain responsibilities toward them. The shift of our economy from an agrarian base to an industrial one put new educational demands on the schools. And our increased national wealth made it possible to finance education more generously than ever before. All of these developments took place within the larger framework of World War I, the Roaring Twenties, the Great Depression, and World War II.

Legislation and Education

The legal authority of the state with respect to the schools was now well established; boards and departments of education operated at the state level in all states. By 1918 every state had passed legislation making school attendance compulsory for some stipulated period of time, usually through an eight-year elementary school experience as a minimum.

A law passed by the State of Oregon in 1922 led to the clarification of the rights of the state with respect to private and parochial schools that had continued to operate in many communities as the public school system had grown. The Oregon law required children and youth between certain ages to attend a public school. In an appeal it was struck down by the United States Supreme Court, reaffirming the right of the states to require education but not the exclusive use of the public schools. It was decided that the state was within its rights to inspect and to supervise all schools, public and private, to see that they were meeting minimum acceptable standards for education, but the right of private and religious schools to exist alongside public schools was guaranteed.

Traditions Challenged

During the first decade of the 1900's newer philosophies of education, increased knowledge about child growth and development, altered statements of the proper aims of education, and newer conceptions of the curriculum arose; and all of these had a greater effect on elementary school education than on any other segment of the school system.

It was John Dewey who was most critical of the traditional elementary school as described above in the Reisner quotation. Dewey could not accept this approach to education; he thought its content and its methodology were inconsistent with both a growing democracy and the nature of children. His own words best express this point:

> The traditional scheme is, in essence, one of imposition from above and from outside. It imposes adult standards, subject matter, and methods upon those who are only growing slowly toward maturity. The gap is so great that the required subject matter, the methods of learning and of behaving are foreign to the existing capacities of the young. They are beyond the reach of the experience the young learners already possess. Consequently, they must be imposed, even though good teachers will use devices of art to cover up the imposition so as to relieve it of obviously brutal features. . . . Moreover that which is taught is thought of as essentially static. It is taught as a finished product, with little regard either to the ways in which it was originally built up or to changes that will surely occur in the future. It is to a large extent the cultural product of societies that assumed the future would be much like the past, and yet it is used as educational food in a society where change is the rule, not the exception.[11]

Dewey saw the school as an institution to be used for social progress and reform, and he saw in America a great challenge to link school and society in a way yet unrealized. His conception was bold, it was new, and it was provocative. He operated a laboratory school at the University of Chicago as a demonstration of his ideas at the beginning of the century, and continued his writing and teaching at Columbia University after 1904. Spurred by his ideas, a different approach to the education of children was being talked about, written about, and experimented with in a few private schools. This new approach came to be called Progressive Education, and with it was ushered in one of the most controversial and exciting periods in the history of the elementary school. Here was a conception of education that put the experiences of learners, rather than organized subject matter, in the center of the educative process. Dewey's ideas were supported indirectly by the research in psychology of Robert Thorndike at Columbia University, whose findings questioned the rationale basic to much of the methodology and content of the then typical elementary school program. This child-centered approach to curriculum development was challenged in the 1930's by a group of educators who contended that the educational process was basically a social one, and that progressive education, as it had developed and was being practiced,

---

[11] John Dewey, *Experience and Education* (New York: The Macmillan Company, 1938), pp. 4–5.

did not give sufficient attention to the problems of society. These two opposing ideas are still identified as fundamental issues in modern theory of elementary school education.

Attempts to Individualize Instruction

A growing awareness of individual differences led to considerable efforts in the early 1900's to individualize instruction within a grade group. For example, the Winnetka plan of the 1920's instituted an arrangement whereby a certain number of projects or units in each subject were assigned to each grade level, but a student was allowed to work his way through at his own rate so long as he mastered the subject matter. The XYZ plan, another approach to this problem of individual differences, attempted to use intelligence tests to divide students into grade groups of similar aptitude and ability. Thus, the bright were not to be held back by the slow, the slow were not to be discouraged and frustrated by the bright, and the curriculum was to be adjusted to the varied needs of these different groups of students. In these and similar ways elementary educators tried to individualize instruction within the traditional framework of the graded school and the class method of instruction. This concern with the individual is, of course, still very much with us.

Growth of Early Childhood Education

The provision of a free school experience for children younger than first graders was widely discussed in the early 1900's, and the establishment of nursery schools and kindergartens was accelerated. A strong assist came from the federal government during the depression period of the 1930's. By 1940 some 625,000 children were enrolled in public kindergartens, and another 40,000 were attending private ones.[12] The White House Conference on Children in a Democracy, held in 1940, recommended the public support of nursery schools, and attention was focused on the nursery school in the early 1940's, when great numbers of men and women were drawn into military service or industry, and family life was disrupted accordingly.

Clearly the development of both the kindergarten and the nursery school was largely due to the division of mothers' time between jobs in industry and child-rearing at home, coupled with the importance that child specialists attached to organized educational opportunities for all children in their early years.

---

[12] Butts, p. 629.

As the end of World War II was anticipated, there was an expressed concern that the nation think again about its domestic well-being. Education, especially in the elementary school, was given increased attention. After a period of study in the late 1940's the Educational Policies Commission issued a report entitled *Education for All American Children*. In this statement an attempt was made to project goals for elementary education in the immediate postwar years, and to set down some guidelines for the development of the elementary school in the 1950's. A few selected recommendations from that report are interesting to consider at the present time:

> Educational services of the public schools should include kindergarten and nursery school ages.
>
> Children should spend, as a rule, two or three years with the same teacher.
>
> Class size should be greatly reduced to an average of twenty pupils.
>
> Each teacher should be free to utilize cooperative teacher-pupil planning in selecting and adapting the activities suggested in courses of study.
>
> The appraisal of results should be in terms of the behavior of children, as well as in terms of what they know and what they can do.
>
> Skill in reading, writing, and arithmetic should be a major objective.
>
> Habits of good workmanship should be emphasized.
>
> Critical thinking and constructive discussion should be encouraged.
>
> Programs of citizenship education should endeavor to develop sturdy independent initiative while at the same time emphasizing social responsibility and cooperative skills.
>
> Small business enterprises should be established and operated by the school as a means of training children in economic skills.[13]

Other recommendations were made that touch on every aspect of the operation of the elementary school—its administration, pupil personnel services, teaching staff, school and class organization, and school buildings.

THE ELEMENTARY SCHOOL 1950–1955

By 1950 elementary school education was a vast enterprise. More than 30,000,000 children were being taught by almost 1,000,000 teachers. As a consequence of population shifts and a sharply increased birth rate

---

[13] Educational Policies Commission, *Education for All American Children* (Washington, D.C.: NEA, 1948).

in the 1940's the elementary schools of many communities were operating with double and even triple shifts. Both teachers and classrooms were in short supply, though there were encouraging signs of progress in overcoming both of these problems.

The elementary school in the 1950's was a varied school. In rural America there were still many small elementary schools of one, two, and three rooms, which provided the first six or eight years of education for children. In the suburbs and in small cities an elementary school system was developing which was characterized by units enrolling from 350 to 500 children and including grades kingergarten through six. In the great cities there were a growing number of large elementary schools which enrolled from one to two thousand children. The goal was to provide essentially the same education for all of these children, and in general the same kinds of things were going on in all of these schools.

In both rural and urban areas the elementary school had retained its image as a neighborhood institution, close to parents and children alike. Parents increasingly understood the significance for their children of this first sustained out-of-family experience. And, in the more limited sense of school success, they realized that a sound beginning to what was to become a long school experience helped to insure a satisfactory ending. The school and the parents valued close family-school communication.

Children, too, had strong feelings for *their* school, *their* teachers, *their* principal, and so on, and saw the school as a neighborhood center. After-school playground programs, evening Boy and Girl Scout meetings, and neighborhood association meetings, all held at the school, completed this picture. Clearly, in 1950–1955 the American people were comfortable with the neighborhood elementary school concept.

The curriculum of the elementary school in 1950–1955 continued to include programs of instruction in the English language arts, in arithmetic, and in social studies. Some science was taught, usually programmed as a part of the social studies and often designated to include health education. Music and art were in the curriculum, as was physical education. Industrial arts and homemaking programs were more the exception than the rule. Instruction in foreign language was clearly the exception. The usual pattern of organization was for one teacher to teach all or almost all of these subjects to a given group of pupils, usually about 30 to 35 children of the same age. There had been little or no experimental or developmental curriculum work done in the past decade, and whatever ingenuity was being applied to problems in elementary education in 1950–1955 was more likely to be in relation to the earlier mentioned areas of teacher and classroom shortage.

The debate over the quality of elementary school education offered in the nation's public schools had been picked up again in 1950–1955.

Bestor wrote of *Educational Wastelands;*[14] Lynd wrote of *Quackery in the Public Schools;*[15] and Smith wrote of *The Diminished Mind.*[16] But a new dimension was evident in the statements issued by most responsible critics of the enterprise. These statements made it increasingly clear that the United States of America, and indeed the whole world, had entered into a new era. It was argued that what had been an effective and acceptable sort of school effort in the past would not be so in the future. The situation was related to much more than just improved methodologies with greater school achievement as a result. It embraced that most fundamental of questions—what does it mean to be educated in our time? The stage was set for the next great round of change in elementary school education. Signs were emerging that purposes, curricula, methods, materials, equipment, organizational schemes, and even school buildings themselves were to be subjected to a careful and complete reexamination.

An overview of the development of elementary education in the United States from Colonial times to 1955 has been presented here. The elementary school has been shown to be a changing institution almost from its inception. But special attention must be given to change by looking at the history of elementary education from the standpoint of the major sets of ideas which have dominated curriculum planning and instruction at various periods in the past. These sets of ideas are, of course, still very much with us today, and reference to them is not just a simple historical exercise. In the next chapters we will examine them as the rather complete systems which they purport to be, and then see their influences in the current curriculum improvement effort.

RECOMMENDED READINGS

BRUBACHER, JOHN S. *A History of the Problems of Education* (second edition). New York: McGraw-Hill Book Company, Inc., 1966.

BUTTS, R. FREEMAN, and LAWRENCE CREMIN. *A History of Education in American Culture.* New York: Holt, Rinehart and Winston, Inc., 1953.

COMMAGER, HENRY STEELE. *Our Schools Have Kept Us Free.* Washington, D.C.: NEA, 1962.

CREMIN, LAWRENCE A. *The American Common School: An Historic Conception.* New York: Bureau of Publications, Teachers College, Columbia University, 1951.

---

[14] Arthur Bestor, *Educational Wastelands* (Urbana: University of Illinois Press, 1953).

[15] Albert Lynd, "Quackery in the Public Schools," *Atlantic Monthly,* Vol. 185 (1950), pp. 33–38.

[16] Mortimer B. Smith, *The Diminished Mind: A Study of Planned Mediocrity in Our Public Schools* (New York: Henry Regnery Company, 1954).

EDWARDS, NEWTON, and HERMAN RICHEY. *The School in the American Social Order*. Boston: Houghton Mifflin Company, 1947.

GROSS, RICHARD E. *Heritage of American Education*. Boston: Allyn and Bacon, Inc., 1962. (See especially Chapters 11 and 12.)

NATIONAL SOCIETY FOR THE STUDY OF EDUCATION. *The Changing American School* (Sixty-fifth Yearbook, Part II). Chicago: University of Chicago Press, 1966. (See especially Chapters 1–6.)

REISNER, EDWARD H. *The Evolution of the Common School*. New York: The Macmillan Company, 1935.

SHANE, HAROLD G. (editor). *The American Elementary School* (Thirteenth Yearbook of the John Dewey Society). New York: Harper & Row, Publishers, Inc., 1953.

Curriculum Planning: A History of Competing Ideas

2

At the outset let us restate the definition for the curriculum that is used in this book:

> The curriculum is the school's plan for the intentional modification of pupil behavior in the direction of agreed-upon educational goals.

Let us remind ourselves, too, of the more explicit questions for which answers must be provided in the process of planning a curriculum for use in the school:

What shall we teach? (The selection of subject matter.)
How shall we teach? (The choice of method and material.)
When shall we teach? (Grade placement and continuity.)
How shall we know how well we have taught? (Evaluation techniques and processes.)

The preceding chapter gave a general overview of the development of the elementary school. No attempt was made to recount the several points of view which have become identified as relatively complete and consistent systems of thought for use in undertaking the curriculum development task. As conceptual tools these points of view direct attention to critical decision points in curriculum planning, and they help to identify those elements of design with which any plan must come to grips. The system chosen by a planner influences the total curriculum rationale that is finally developed. Each system also suggests a way to view the nature of instruction and the role of the teacher and of the pupil. These competing sets of ideas, when described, tend to trichotomize education into subject matter, children, and society.

Any student of the current situation needs the help that some understanding of these points of view can furnish.[1] First let us describe two patterns for developing the curriculum plan which take as their point of departure organized subject matter. These are the *separate subjects* pattern, and the *broad fields* pattern. Next we will describe two approaches to curriculum planning which were developed as parts of major reform movements in an earlier day, as responses to what were perceived as limitations in curriculum plans that were aligned too completely with organized subject matter. The first of these, the *activity* or *experience* curriculum, took the child and his interests and concerns as its point of departure. The second, the *core* curriculum, took society and its arrangements and problems as a point of departure. The intent is to make clear the nature of the educational ideas embodied in these two twentieth-century reform movements. At the same time it will be argued that neither had the effect of replacing "subject" thinking to the extent which their developers had hoped they would.

Chronology is important to the matter of past efforts for reform in elementary education. The points in time at which attention has been given to major change in the curriculum bear a close relationship to happenings in the wider society. Social forces inspire and support new ways of viewing the elementary school program, just as an increased level of professional skill improves curriculum planning. The diagram will help to establish the time relationship between these competing curriculum points of view and will point up the relationship between major events in society and the emergence of new views about the curriculum.

THE SEPARATE SUBJECTS CURRICULUM

The separate subjects pattern[2] was the first general approach taken to curriculum planning in the elementary school. Because most people understand this traditional kind of curriculum, it continues to influence planning. This pattern is not a complete system of thought about curriculum planning which was developed and then applied as a system to curriculum development many years ago. It is, rather, an analytical description of the curriculum that developed as schools were formed. It

---

[1] Harold Rugg, *Foundations for American Education* (New York: Harcourt, Brace & World, Inc., 1947), pp. 700–708; B. O. Smith, W. O. Stanley, and J. H. Shores, *Fundamentals of Curriculum Development* (revised edition) (New York: Harcourt, Brace & World, Inc., 1957), pp. 225–228; F. Stratemeyer and others, *Developing a Curriculum for Modern Living* (New York: Bureau of Publications, Teachers College, Columbia University, 1957), Chapter 4.

[2] Henry J. Otto, "Comparison of Selected Organization and Administrative Practices in 286 Public Elementary Schools and Forty-Six Campus Demonstration Schools," *Journal of Educational Research* (October 1947), pp. 81–87; Smith, Stanley, and Shores, *Fundamentals*, Chapters 10 and 11.

A CULTURAL-CURRICULUM TIME LINE

	1700	1800	1900	1910	1920	1930	1940	1950	1960	1970	1980
	End of Colonial America; founding of independent nation	Expanding westward; saving the Union; reconstruction	General growth and consolidation; World War I		Roaring Twenties	Depression	World War II; the Cold War	UN-Korean action; more Cold War	Outer Space exploration; Cybernetics; Viet Nam War; Civil Rights efforts		?
	Separate subjects curriculum pattern used throughout										?
			Ideas emerge for the activity curriculum		Period of widest use of the activity curriculum		Continued to influence practice in these years		Less influence but still identifiable in practice		?
					Broad fields curriculum ideas emerge		Becomes a strong influence on practice		The dominant curriculum pattern followed		?
					Core curriculum ideas emerge		Period of widest use of core curriculum	Continued to influence practice	Less influence but still identifiable in practice		?

began to be studied for what it was in the early 1900's, chiefly by those who had misgivings about it. The distinguishing characteristics that have come to be associated with this curriculum plan need to be considered here.

Subjects as Organizing Centers

When this curriculum pattern is used, instruction is planned and given by subjects; the scope of the curriculum is the number of subjects to be taught. Each is allotted time during which the focus of instruction is on that particular subject, be it arithmetic, handwriting, history, or reading. Varying amounts of time are allotted to different subjects on the basis of two criteria: (1) a consideration of which subjects are most important to the child's education, and (2) evidence of the best length of time for instruction in a certain area, with attention to the maturity level of children.

The Role of Organized Subject Matter

From this point of view, the *sine qua non* of education is the study of organized subject matter, the collected and categorized experience of the human race. To be educated is to know this cultural heritage, and the function of the school is to pass it on to children. It is held that this system maintains the culture, and makes collected information available to each succeeding generation in meeting current problems. Therefore, the mastery of subject matter becomes a very important end in itself, as do such skills as reading, handwriting, spelling, and arithmetic computation.

The Selection and Grade Placement of Subject Matter

Organized subject matter must be allotted year by year for study in the elementary school, if this pattern is to be followed. All subject matter cannot be studied; the bulk would simply be too great. Therefore, the selection of subject matter of most worth from each content area is an important task. This selection is generally made by experts from each area of study.

After the general content has been selected, the subject matter must be arranged over the elementary school years. Specific amounts of it must be allocated to particular grade levels. In this process, at least two sorts of forces are at play. First, each area of subject matter has an internal logic which is a primary factor in determining the way it should be studied in school, and which in turn determines the curriculum sequence; chronology is centrally important in history, arithmetic is developed along a scheme of prerequisite learning of simple to complex processes, reading is learned by a controlled increase in total vocabulary, and so on. Second, scientific inquiries have aimed at identifying the optimum chronological or mental age for meeting certain subject matter learnings. These studies have some influence on the points at which content is assigned for study.

The Predetermined Nature of the Curriculum

When the separate subjects pattern is used, the curriculum is almost completely predetermined for the child. When he comes to the school in any given year, his teacher knows precisely what he is going to study and when he is going to study it.

Learning and the Role of the Teacher

The subject approach to curriculum tends to support a teaching-learning relationship in which the teacher shows and tells and explains and the child watches and listens and remembers. The teacher must be well-informed. His teaching procedures are heavily influenced by his showing, telling, and explaining role. The child is a more passive participant in the learning situation.

Textbooks and Other Instructional Materials

In this approach to curriculum planning, the textbook is seen as the major instructional tool. Experts can make available the most valuable content in a given subject by preparing textbooks to be used in the classroom. Furthermore, the subject matter in textbooks, singly and in series, can be carefully arranged in light of both the difficulty and the logic of the subject involved, to insure proper sequence. It can be designed to serve directly as an assistant to the teacher as he shows, tells, and explains. In the textbook the child has a source of reference and review as he attempts to remember and to reproduce. Other audio-visual aids supplement the textbook.

Evaluation of Learning

The major focus in evaluation is on the degree to which a child has understood, remembers, and can reproduce or repeat the subject matter or skill learnings that have been attempted. Most of the evaluation procedures employ paper and pencil, and the child is asked periodically to give written evidence of the fact that he is learning. There is a heavy premium put on memory, of course, and in certain situations speed of recall or skill performance also becomes important in the evaluation of learning.

A Critique of the Separate Subjects Curriculum

This has been a most widely used and an often debated approach to curriculum planning. It is supported by many different persons for a variety of reasons. Some see in this point of view real assurance that the cultural heritage will be known by children, and that it will be used to the maximum in the education of the young. Others support it because the "logical" elements in it appeal to them. The curriculum can be planned carefully, subject matter arranged year by year with great care, well ahead of the actual instructional situation. Still others are attracted to the conception of the role of the teacher and the place assigned to the learner in the classroom. A description of this relationship seems to "make sense." And so it goes.

But this approach to curriculum planning has had many sharp critics, too. A variety of weaknesses have been identified by school persons. Let us consider the most important of these here.

Too fragmented a learning arrangement. This plan results in a high degree of fragmentation. Every subject has its time and place, separate and distinct from any other. The critics point out that clear relationships exist between many of the various branches of human knowledge, and that these connections are important to make if learning is to serve the individual as well as it might. They see in this separate subject arrangement an approach to learning that works against recognition of relationships.

Too passive a learning experience. Others have taken the position that the passive role assigned to the child and the showing, telling, and explaining role assigned to the teacher in the classroom simply do not agree with the evidence in learning. The child is seen as an active, goal-seeking organism, with personal interests, curiosities, and concerns, who needs to be an active participant in teaching-learning enterprises. This view suggests that the showing, telling, and explaining of the teacher should be held to a very minimum, so as not to interfere with the child's efforts to learn. To assign the child to a sitting and listening role in the main seems to go against the learning process as it is coming to be understood, as well as the basic nature of childhood itself. Furthermore, this particular approach to the teaching-learning enterprise puts the child in the position of always dealing with the end-products of inquiry and largely ignores the processes by which knowledge is accumulated and by which people learn. Thus, he has little occasion for finding things out for himself, and little opportunity to learn the processes of problem solving.

Too logical and predetermined. The logical arrangement of subject matter and the predetermined plan for learning have met with criticism, too. The general feeling expressed is that this plan introduces unnecessary and unwise elements of fixity and order into the curriculum. The argument is supported by evidence from the psychology of learning to the effect that, for learning purposes, a logical order of content is not always the best order. Instead, a psychological order of subject matter, or the development of a way through to a given learning goal which is the result of teacher-pupil interaction and planning, is often called for. It is felt that the internal systems of logic identifiable in the various separate subjects do not have to be followed as stringently in curriculum planning as this point of view suggests. And, to predetermine the school experience in such a complete and comprehensive way keeps both teachers and pupils from capitalizing on the developing situations around them in the interests of reaching educational objectives.

Too verbal an experience. Criticism has been leveled, too, at the extent to which this approach to curriculum planning tends to restrict the school experience to a verbal one. Armed with evidence from learning theory and child development, critics have raised questions about the limitations inherent in such an approach to learning with children. They feel that the evidence suggests the need for a variety of approaches to learning in addition to highly verbal ones, and they see little reason to expect such variety to be used within this curriculum model.

Too limited evaluation efforts. Lastly, there are those who see the approach to evaluation in this curriculum pattern as being quite limited, and the evidence collected for use in evaluation as being very meager. They question the heavy reliance on paper-and-pencil devices that this curriculum plan supports, to the exclusion of other sources of evidence of learning. And they argue that the end result is a tendency to disregard educational objectives in areas other than intellectual development.

THE BROAD FIELDS CURRICULUM

Supporters of the subject-centered approach to curriculum planning were not insensitive to the questions that were leveled at the separate subjects pattern. As a result, in the 1920's and 30's, they made efforts to revise that pattern to meet many of the most serious criticisms of it. Out of these efforts came the broad fields pattern of curriculum planning.[3]

Broad Fields as Organizing Centers

As the responsibilities of the school grew and as the programs of study multiplied, the list of subjects that children were being asked to study in the elementary school approached the ridiculous. Each school day was a series of short, separate periods of instruction. To meet this situation, some educators began to organize content from related subjects into broad fields. For example, the separate subjects of history, geography, and civics were grouped together into one broad field known as the social studies. There was an attempt to fuse their subject matter into one course. The broad field still remained as an organized field of knowledge, but the resulting structure reduced fragmentation and permitted more latitude in instruction. Thus, we have seen the emergence of broad fields such as general science, social studies, and language arts to be utilized as organizing centers for the curriculum in many elementary schools.

The Role of Organized Subject Matter

The role of organized subject matter remains much the same in the broad fields pattern of curriculum as in the separate subjects pattern. The intent is to pass on selected portions of the cultural heritage. Instruction still takes place within these broad fields of subject matter. Some of the relationships between separate areas of subject matter are more readily grasped, of course. For instance, when the United States is studied in a way that relates its geography, its history, and its government in one learning unit, certain relationships that might be obscured by a separate subject organization come to light.

The Predetermined Nature of the Curriculum

The broad fields pattern retains the characteristics of preplanning that were found in the separate subjects approach. Sequences are still laid out in advance, assignments of subject matter are still made grade by

---

[3] Smith, Stanley, and Shores, *Fundamentals*, pp. 255–262; Rugg, *Foundations*, pp. 708–714; Henry Harap, "A Survey of Courses of Study Published in the Last Two Years," *Journal of Educational Research* (May 1935), pp. 641–656; Otto, "Comparison"; J. Wayne Wrightstone, *Appraisal of Newer Elementary School Practices* (New York: Bureau of Publications, Teachers College, Columbia University, 1935).

grade, and the child comes to school with his curriculum already determined for him.

Learning and the Role of the Teacher

The basic methodology in the broad fields curriculum is, again, not unlike that of the separate subjects curriculum. The teacher is still committed to a showing, telling, and explaining role; the child is committed in the main to a listening, watching, and remembering role. With the program fixed, and the subject matter of most worth already selected, a more dynamic methodology seems to be unnecessary.

Textbooks and Other Instructional Materials

The textbook is the major instructional tool in the broad fields curriculum. The development of broad fields of study has put new demands on writers and publishers. For instance, the planning of a series of textbooks for use in the social studies program calls for content from three areas to be skillfully woven into one textbook series. Similar tasks must be accomplished in the area of science. In the broad field of the language arts, separate materials are retained for reading, spelling, handwriting, and oral and written expression. Of course, many audio-visual aids are used in the broad fields pattern to help the teacher to show, tell, and explain.

Evaluation in the Broad Fields Curriculum

The general approach to evaluation in the broad fields curriculum is not much different from what it was in the separate subject setting. Priority goes to techniques that will give evidence of subject matter achievement, and paper-and-pencil devices are relied upon rather heavily. There is some greater possibility to test for certain cause-effect relationships, in addition to simple recall tasks.

A Critique of the Broad Fields Curriculum

The attempts at reorganizing the content from highly related separate subject areas into broad fields of study have been partially successful in meeting the criticisms of the extreme fragmentation of the separate subjects approach. The broad fields organization should help the child to become aware of important relationships between the various areas of human knowledge.

Concerns over the arrangement of content. Some subject specialists have attacked the idea of the broad fields arrangement because they feel that the child gets too little knowledge about any one field of study. They argue that not enough history, or geography, or civics, for instance, can be put into a social studies course. Also, some specialists feel that to destroy the internal logic that is unique to each of the subjects, and to attempt to replace it with some sort of manufactured internal structure, is not defensible. They argue that an experience with the logic of a subject is as important as an experience with the content.

A high level of generalization. Some educators question the tendency to deal with generalizations in the broad fields pattern. They point to the great amount of experience necessary for the emergence of meaningful generalizations, and to the development of concepts used in generalizations. They fear that a teacher might be tempted to use generalizations as a way of covering more content, and that he might accept from the child simple verbalizations that have little meaning for him.

Yet the broad fields pattern has become one of the preferred ways of organizing the curriculum in the elementary school. As recently as 1960 it was reported that this was the most common way for the curriculum of the elementary school to be organized.[4] It seems to have been accepted as a way of reducing the unacceptable features of the separate subject pattern, while still retaining many of the characteristics of subject-centered planning which appeal to many school people, and to much of the public.

THE ACTIVITY CURRICULUM

You will recall from Chapter 1 that the closing years of the nineteenth century saw the emergence of some revolutionary ideas concerning the role of the school in society and the nature of the school experience itself. The schools operated by John Dewey at the University of Chicago and J. L. Merriam at the University of Missouri in the opening years of the twentieth century were the forerunners of the activity curriculum theory.[5]

---

[4] Stuart E. Dean, *Elementary School Administration and Organization: A National Survey of Practices and Policies* (Washington, D.C.: U.S. Department of Health, Education, and Welfare, 1960).

[5] Smith, Stanley, and Shores, *Fundamentals,* Chapters 12 and 13; Rugg, *Foundations,* Chapter 17; Ellsworth Collings, *An Experiment with a Project Curriculum* (New York: The Macmillan Company, 1923); Arthur T. Jersild and others, "An Evaluation of Aspects of the Activity Program in the New York City Elementary Schools," *Journal of Experimental Education* (December 1939), pp. 166–207; National Society for the Study of Education, *The Activity Movement* (Thirty-Third Yearbook, Part II) (Bloomington, Ill.: Public School Publishing Company, 1934); Harold Rugg and Ann Shumaker, *The Child-Centered School* (New York: Harcourt, Brace & World, Inc., 1928).

Activities and Impulses as Organizing Centers

The activity approach uses activities and impulses of children as the organizing centers of the curriculum in place of subjects. Dewey, in his early school, tried to use four child impulses—the social impulse, the constructive impulse, the investigative impulse, and the expressive impulse—as the centers around which learning experiences would be organized. Merriam's school replaced subjects with four categories of activities: observation, play, stories, and handwork. Within these activity areas, the selection of content for study is a matter of determining the points at which children, in growing up and probing their culture as they do, have encountered things that they want to know more about.

The Role of Organized Subject Matter

In the activity curriculum, organized subject matter is used as a learning resource. Rather than starting out in the elementary school to cover subject matter as an end in itself, the child becomes aware of organized subject matter and learns to use it when he needs it. Because the child has varied interests, he will study a great deal of the cultural heritage. Direct teaching of such skills as reading and arithmetic computation will be related to his emerging realization that he must develop these important skills.

Grade Placement and Continuity

In the activity curriculum the ordering of content is psychological rather than logical. That is, history is studied when children become interested in the past, and their interests might depart greatly from the strict chronology of a given historical period. In arithmetic children are taught what they need at a given time and in relation to a developing learning enterprise. In reading, the logic of the controlled vocabulary is displaced by an experience approach in which children learn to read through using the words involved in what they are doing.

The Emergent Nature of the Curriculum

The activity curriculum is not determined in advance, but emerges from week to week over the school year. While the teacher may anticipate that the class will be interested in and want to study some particular thing, and plan for it accordingly, he would be bound to give this up when an actual contact with the class indicates a different concern. To the degree that there is a spread of interests in the group the teacher is asked to develop learning enterprises around these varied interests. In other words, common learning experiences call for expressed common interests.

Learning and the Role of the Teacher

In the area of methodology, the position is taken that the learning situation in the classroom ought to approach a problem-solving situation as much as possible. The starting point is the teacher's commitment to work with the expressed interests of children. The teacher is the guide and facilitator in helping to implement the children's learning. He tells and shows and explains very sparingly, supplying needed information himself when this seems to be the only sensible way to supply it, or demonstrating something that is vital to the problem-solving sequence as it is developing. There is to be a great deal of discussion between the teacher and the class throughout the total learning sequence, including the original determination of important interests. Teacher-pupil planning is central to the activity curriculum. The child is expected to demonstrate initiative and responsibility in relation to his own learning, not to sit and be told.

Textbooks and Other Instructional Materials

The typical textbook is not the useful tool in the activity curriculum that it is in the subject curriculum. The most useful printed materials are those that are designed expressly to be used as resources, rather than as total learning experiences. Needed is a wide range of materials, broad enough to be of use to the wide variety of interests that are assumed to be operating in the class group. The teacher will have to prepare some instructional materials himself, since children may develop interests that lead them far afield of the usual printed materials available at a given grade level. Children learn, too, in many ways other than by reading printed materials. They should have access to a wide selection of audio-visual aids, realia, artifacts, sets of tools, and a variety of art materials. Children use dramatic play for learning in certain settings, too.

Evaluation of Learning

Evaluation in the activity curriculum is necessarily very broad. The commitment is to the total development of the child, that is, his social, emotional, and physical well-being as well as his intellectual develop-ment; the instructor attempts to collect evidence in terms of the child's total progress. In addition to paper-and-pencil tests he must use a wide variety of procedures—interest inventories, attitude scales, sociometric techniques, simple projective instruments, and other devices. He will also collect evidence by observation and conversation, and attempt to analyze this information in relation to pupil development.

A Critique of the Activity Curriculum

The activity curriculum is the most controversial point of view that has been advanced in curriculum planning. It has been argued in educational circles since its early development. The public has a tendency to blame any lacks in the results of education on the use of these ideas in developing the curriculum. As a theory, it was developed at a time when it seemed that the dynamic sort of society that was emerging in the United States called for a kind of education that was itself more dynamic. In the minds of those who developed these ideas was a concept of the role of the school in society different from that which had long existed. They felt that the typical school situation was too far removed from society and life as it was being lived, and they hoped to bridge this gap with a different type of school experience. Also, they were rather sure that the emerging information on child growth and learning called for ways of teaching that were not found in the subject-centered classroom.

From the outset the activity curriculum had outspoken and militant critics. Subject-centered advocates saw in it nothing but chaos and superficiality in learning. It struck at the very heart of all that they held to be important. Another group of persons, though interested in moving the school curriculum away from a simple subject-centered structure, took exception to the activity curriculum for other reasons.

A misunderstood concept of interest.　These latter critics of the activity curriculum felt, among other things, that the theory placed too great a reliance on the present interests of children. While these critics did not deny the fact that interest was an important ingredient in learning, they felt that this theory tended to be extreme, and in error in its concept of child interests. They took the position that interests are learned, just as so much of human behavior is learned, and that the school ought to be as much a developer of new interests as a follower of already existing ones. They believed that the school experience is as responsible for helping children to probe their culture systematically as it is for helping them to understand those aspects of the culture that they have happened to experience.

A lack of social consciousness.　Along with the above came the criticism that the activity curriculum was so committed to the interests of the individual that it overlooked the interests of society. These critics felt that the welfare of the individual is inextricably involved in the welfare of the group, and that the school has an obligation to help children to become aware of, and predisposed to consider, the larger social setting in which they live as well as their own individual concerns. The social unrest during the Coolidge administration and the Great Depression of 1929 and the early 1930's gave added support to this idea.

A need for a curriculum framework. The emergent nature of the activity curriculum was also a most debatable aspect of it. As educators analyzed some of the general patterns of experience that were developing in the school lives of children in progressive schools, many began to doubt the usefulness of the activity curriculum. They saw what they considered to be some very trivial activities developed under the banner of child interest, and they saw what they considered to be indefensible repetitions and omissions in experience. They felt that until some sort of general framework was established in a school and some agreements were reached as to the general focus of experiences from year to year, this situation would not be corrected. These ideas, naturally, were in basic conflict with the activity point of view.

Too passive a role for the teacher. Many critics believed that in the activity curriculum the teacher was too passive a participant in the learning enterprise. It was their impression that teacher-pupil planning was very often simply pupil planning. It appeared that teachers were hesitant to take an active part in much of the classroom program, and were vague and undecided on the limits that the activity curriculum placed on their role. The critics believed, generally, that the teacher could and should play a decisive role in the classroom and yet not maintain autocratic control.

THE CORE CURRICULUM

In the early 1930's the core curriculum[6] began to take form. It would be a mistake to picture this pattern as an attempt to evoke a compromise between the two subject matter approaches and the activity curriculum. It was born, rather, of a feeling of urgency among some educators that

---

[6] Smith, Stanley, and Shores, *Fundamentals,* Chapters 14 and 15; Rugg, *Foundations,* Chapter 18 and pp. 714–716; Oric L. Frederick and Lucille J. Farquear, "Areas of Human Activity," *Journal of Educational Research* (May 1937), pp. 672–679; Virginia State Board of Education, *Tentative Course of Study for Virginia Elementary Schools, Grades 1–7,* Bulletin, Vol. xix, No. 5 (Richmond, Va.: The Board, 1937); Santa Barbara County, Calif., *Santa Barbara County Curriculum Guide for Teachers in Elementary Schools,* Vol. ii (Santa Barbara, Calif.: Schauer Printing Studio, 1940); Santa Barbara County, Calif., *Santa Barbara County Program of Curriculum Development,* Vol. vii (Santa Barbara, Calif.: Schauer Printing Studio, 1942); Roland C. Faunce and Nelson Bossing, *The Core Curriculum* (Englewood Cliffs, N.J.: Prentice-Hall, Inc., 1951).

the school's maximum contribution as an agency of society was not being realized. This point of view toward curriculum planning developed initially in the same period as the Great Depression with its myriad social problems and issues. While the core protagonists did not close their eyes to psychology, they insisted that the philosophical and social foundations of education also be used in arriving at a defensible overall pattern of curriculum.

Basic Human Activities as Organizing Centers

As a curriculum model, the core position rejects both the ideas of using subjects or broad fields and of using children's interests and impulses as organizing centers. Rather, it takes the position that "basic human activities," sometimes referred to as "areas of living," should be used as the centers around which curriculum is planned and instruction takes place. These areas of basic human activities are variously identified by anthropologists and sociologists. A typical and widely used list of these would be as follows:

1. Protecting and conserving life, resources, and property.
2. Producing, distributing, and consuming goods and services.
3. Transporting people and goods.
4. Communicating ideas and feelings.
5. Providing education.
6. Providing recreation.
7. Organizing and governing.
8. Expressing spiritual and esthetic impulses.
9. Creating new tools and techniques.[7]

The core curriculum uses these areas of basic human activities as the organizing centers for the curriculum. It is felt that subjects themselves are too restrictive and categorical, and that the impulses or interests of children are too vague. The use of basic human activities introduces the kind of order that closely resembles life as it has been and is being lived, and the use of these activities as the scope of the curriculum should help to relate school to society.

A Central Role for Values

Values are central to this point of view toward curriculum development. Proponents believe that a person's behavior is fundamentally

[7] From a projection of an integrative-core curriculum prepared by Paul R. Hanna, School of Education, Stanford University.

influenced by his commitment to values, and that the social problems that people face are, in most instances, to be finally solved by the application of values. Therefore, one finds in much of the writing on the core curriculum a heavy and obvious commitment to bring values more consciously into the school curriculum, and to push more school studies to the question of "what ought to be," rather than leaving them at the descriptive stage of "what is."

The Role of Organized Subject Matter

The core curriculum is basically committed to the idea that organized subject matter is best viewed in school as a resource to which one goes with problems, concerns, and questions. It obviously rejects the concept of a subject-centered curriculum. It is closer to agreement with the position taken in the activity theory. There is no denying the relevance of much of the organized cultural heritage to the basic human activities. Many of our organized disciplines are closely related to the activities, as economics and the production, distribution, and consumption of goods and services. But the starting point is to be an area of activity, not a subject.

Grade Placement and Continuity

The questions of grade placement and continuity are answered in core theory by a combination of psychological and sociological information. The child will best understand, and will accomplish more meaningful learning, if in the early years of the elementary school the focus of attention is on life close to him. Therefore, the basic human activities are studied in situations that are near and intimate, such as the home, the neighborhood, the school, and the local community. In the intermediate grades the child can begin to understand places and people farther removed from him, and the focus of his attention swings to the state, the nation, other countries, and other continents. Some core theorists have used the generic term *community* in relation to continuity, and see the matter of sequence as the act of focusing on ever larger "communities of men" sequentially in the elementary curriculum. Others feel that a job well done within the confines of the local community through about grade three should mean that any other community group, large or small, past or present, near or far, can be studied with profit in any of the intermediate years.

A General Framework for Curriculum

The core approach to curriculum planning utilizes a broad and general preplanned framework. It cannot accept either the completely predetermined structure of the subject-centered patterns, or the completely emergent concept found in the activity curriculum. The core pattern takes the position that some advanced planning is necessary in a school. Only in this way can assurances be given that the experience will be truly a cumulative one, free of unnecessary repetitions and unwise omissions. And only in this way can society be assured of consistent social direction in the school experience. A framework might be built around the basic human activities within some given community of men at a particular grade level. Given this, the teacher is to be left free to develop the learning experience in the most efficient way he sees. He can be as creative and imaginative as possible in the development of the learning enterprise itself.

Learning and the Role of the Teacher

Core theory asks that the teaching-learning situation be developed consistent with available information on child growth and development and learning. The child is an active participant in the learning he is to accomplish, helping to plan for it, helping to guide and direct it, and helping to evaluate progress. The teacher shows, tells, and explains only when necessary in the interests of improved problem solving. At the same time, the teacher must play a *decisive* role in the classroom, working actively to support and sustain the learning experience.

Textbooks and Other Instructional Materials

There is a clear recognition in this position that children learn in a variety of ways, and that a variety of instructional materials and resources must be available. Printed materials are considered important, but their use should be within the "resource and reference" idea. Additionally, a wide array of audio-visual aids, a careful utilization of community resources of people and places, opportunities to construct and to process raw materials, and the use of dramatic play would be central in the development of learning units.

Evaluation of Learning

The approach to evaluation taken in the core pattern is broad and comprehensive. It recognizes important purposes in addition to intellectual development, and calls for the collection and interpretation of a wide range of information accordingly. Paper-and-pencil tests will be used, along with many other instruments and techniques, such as attitude scales, interest inventories, sociometric devices, simple projective tests, and the like. Teacher judgment, based on careful observations and intimate associations with pupils, counts heavily, too. Attempts to assess progress are focused on the group as a group, as well as on each individual.

A Critique of the Core Curriculum

Poor substitute for subjects. Persons with continuing commitments to subject-centered structures have seen this pattern simply as a poor substitute for the well-organized and easily identifiable subject and broad field patterns. They believe that both the child and the teacher will perform more efficiently by utilizing subjects or broad fields as organizing centers rather than basic human activities.

Too logical and mechanical. Those educators with heavy allegiance to the activity curriculum see in the core position an attempt to introduce an undesirable kind of preplanning and fixity into the elementary school curriculum again. They perceive the arrangements by which grade emphases are determined and questions of continuity are resolved as being extremely mechanical and logical. Some have criticized the core pattern for being unduly sympathetic with a kind of "cultural determinism" in human development. Generally, they take the position that many of the dynamic aspects of the educative process and the nurturing of individual uniqueness and creativeness are reduced unduly in the interests of the demands of society.

A questionable role for the school. There are persons who cannot support the core position because of the implied role for the school in the society with which it is identified. In its formative years, the core pattern was associated with social reconstructionist ideas in education. That is, proponents believed that the school was going to have to play a much more vital role in *leading* in social reconstruction instead of simply *following.* The suggestion was not an "educational revolution" as some have interpreted it, but it did mean that the value dimension in society should become a matter for conscious attention in school, and that value change and value conflict had to be recognized in school studies. The early core protagonists felt that only through the study of controversial issues could the school help to equip the upcoming generation with the insights and understandings, and the predispositions to action, that were demanded by the times.

Of course, for the school experience to be conceived in such a way has always been debatable in American society. Many persons believe that the school should remain aloof from this kind of social argument, while the larger society struggles with important matters. Such a concept becomes even more controversial when it is applied to elementary school children. This is a time, in the view of many, to build basic skills of literacy, and to begin to build socially useful concepts and generalizations of many kinds. But it is not the time to focus on complex and controversial situations in society. Of course, as the core concept has been applied to the elementary school, the extremes of it have been tempered. The central importance of values has not been discarded, but the focus of attention is on helping children to be aware of values, to understand them, and to be able to identify them in practice. In the process the children may become aware of inconsistencies and a lack of completeness in application of these values, but this is not a major focus of study at this level.

This is, then, a description of the ideas which have controlled the development of the elementary school curriculum in the past. It is clear that these ideas are competitive. No one of these curriculum patterns can be found being followed in a pure and complete way in an elementary school today. Rather attempts have been made to take the most attractive components of any one of these points of view and to adapt them to another. In any case, these are the ideas which had been developed for use by curriculum planners at the time the current improvement effort was begun in the middle 1950's. They should be kept in mind as we examine current developments in curriculum and instruction.

RECOMMENDED READINGS

ALCORN, MARVIN D., and JAMES M. LINELY (editors). *Issues in Curriculum Development*. New York: Harcourt, Brace & World, Inc., 1959.

BODE, BOYD. *Progressive Education at the Crossroads*. New York: Newsom and Company, 1938.

COLLINGS, ELLSWORTH. *An Experiment with a Project Curriculum*. New York: The Macmillan Company, 1923.

CREMIN, LAWRENCE A. *The Transformation of the School: Progressivism in American Education 1876–1957*. New York: Alfred A. Knopf, Inc., 1961.

DEWEY, JOHN. *Experience and Education*. New York: The Macmillan Company, 1938.

HANNA, PAUL R. "Society–Child–Curriculum," in Clarence W. Hunnicutt (editor). *Education—2000 A.D.* Syracuse, N.Y.: Syracuse University Press, 1956.

MAYHEW, KATHERINE, and ANNA EDWARDS. *The Dewey School*. New York: Appleton-Century-Crofts, Inc., 1936.

RAGAN, WILLIAM B. *Modern Elementary Curriculum* (third edition). New York: Holt, Rinehart and Winston, Inc., 1966. (Chapters 1 and 6.)

RUGG, HAROLD, and ANN SHUMAKER. *The Child-Centered School.* New York: Harcourt, Brace & World, Inc., 1928.

SAYLOR, J. GALEN, and WILLIAM M. ALEXANDER. *Curriculum Planning for Modern Schools.* New York: Holt, Rinehart and Winston, Inc., 1966. (Chapters 8–11 especially.)

SMITH, B. O., W. O. STANLEY, and J. H. SHORES. *Fundamentals of Curriculum Development* (revised edition). New York: Harcourt, Brace & World, Inc., 1957. (See Part IV.)

WRIGHTSTONE, J. W. *Appraisal of Newer Elementary School Practices.* New York: Bureau of Publications, Teachers College, Columbia University, 1935.

Elementary Education: Forces for Change

3

The forces for change in elementary school education have been located in (1) social, political, and economic matters at home and abroad, (2) biological and psychological studies of the human organism, and (3) the academic disciplines themselves. We have said that, while these foundation areas have always contributed to change, some developments in them, at this time, carry a kind of special urgency for consideration by those engaged in elementary school education. Only by considering them can educators plan an elementary school curriculum that is relevant to life as it is and as it is becoming. Let us identify specifically some of the current happenings in each of the broad areas.

This will be a very selective presentation. The more inclusive way in which elementary school education embraces and utilizes a "sociology of education," a "psychology of education," and "organized subject matter" in accomplishing its purposes comes to the elementary educator through extended study of the vast literature available in relation thereto. We will deal only with selected items from each that are literally forcing themselves on the school as invitations for change and which serve to demonstrate well the relationship referred to above.

SOCIAL CHANGE AND ELEMENTARY EDUCATION

Social change has been a part of the American scene from the beginning—and as such has always carried with it implications for the nature of elementary school education. Some matters at this particular period tend to dominate much of people's thinking. The public expects all appropriate social institutions, including the elementary schools, to contribute what they can in helping society to cope with current situations.

Nothing is more characteristic of our time than its scientific-technological orientation. The research laboratory continues to be a frontier in America. Engineers have been inventive in applying the fruits of science to our lives. The evidence of technology is everywhere, in transportation, in communication, in medicine, in agriculture, in housing, in food processing, and so on. Man's successes in outer space are current reminders of the power and possibility in our science. Even though Americans have been aware for some time of the progress made in science and technology, they are now seeing new dimensions to this progress which are moving them to a deeper and wider examination of this whole phenomenon. More than a decade ago David Sarnoff wrote prophetically as follows:

> The dominant physical fact in the next quarter-century will be technological progress unprecedented in kind and in volume. In relation to the total history of the human race, the last hundred years have been no more than a split second. Yet they have compassed more technological achievement than the millennia that preceded. . . .
> It is not a case of continued increase . . . but of continued acceleration of increase. We need only project the curve into the future to realize that we are merely on the threshold of the technological age.[1]

Sarnoff's point has to do with more than the gadgets or devices that technology provides. It has to do with the growing realization in society of the extent of its dependence on and its commitment to science. Most of the problems of our society have been shaped and formed in part by science, and their solutions depend upon science.

A technological society calls for an effective educational system. Every reasonable step must be taken to insure a continuing supply of highly capable scientists and engineers. For the elementary school this means a new kind of concern for an appropriate experience with mathematics and science for children—an experience that will help to introduce them to technology as a part of their general culture, and that will also begin to capture the attention of some students toward mathematics and science as eventual careers.

Drive for Civil Rights

There is a concerted effort under way in the United States to gain a full measure of civil rights for people who have at best lived on the edge

---

[1] David Sarnoff, "The Fabulous Future," *Fortune* (January 1955), pp. 82–83, 114–118.

of society for many years. In the main this drive is concerned with the Negro population, though it touches on other minority populations as well. People of minority groups are pressing for access to jobs, to housing, and to public facilities. Many cannot yet vote freely. Access to the public schools has been at the very top of the list since the Supreme Court decision of 1954 calling for an end to "equal but separate" educational systems.

The forces that have been set in motion will not rest until discriminatory practices of the past have been resolved. Progress has been made, but much remains to be done. Legislation has been passed at the state and national levels to help Negroes especially to take their places in society. But the tensions that have developed as a consequence of civil rights actions are quite formidable and we can look ahead to a difficult path to a solution.

Education is essential to progress. Along with the achievement of "rights" in a legal sense must come the development of skills and understandings that will help to insure the exercise of "rights" in a real sense. For instance the legal right to a job must be matched with the development of skills that will enable one to hold a job. Curriculum changes are called for that will contribute to improved intergroup understanding. Human relations skills become a matter of concern in a very specific way. The application of the democratic ethic in dealing with all people must be understood. The location of school buildings and the establishment of attendance areas need to be decided, in part, with the goal of increased contact between whites and minority groups in mind. Civil rights problems cannot be solved in the school alone. But society does look to the school as one likely place where something significant can be done.

A War on Poverty

Closely aligned to the civil rights issue, but going beyond it to embrace the poor of all races, is the renewed concern in this country to wage war on poverty. Most people believe that ways must be found to help poor people to share more realistically in the great wealth of this nation. In spite of the nation's general economic well-being, too many of its people live on the very edge of subsistence at best. This segment of the society is concentrated in some rural areas and in crowded neighborhoods in the cities.

Again, though the problem is many-sided, the schools are being looked to for a large part of the solution to it. Society expects the school to organize itself in such a way as to be more effective in educating the children of the poor. No longer will it suffice for school people to say that a child is not doing well because of being underprivileged in his general out-of-school life experience. Rather they will be expected to describe what it is that they are doing with and in the school as a consequence of this disadvantagement to help to insure the educational success of the child. The elementary school is expected to take steps to break the pattern of very low achievement in school in childhood. Unless the pattern is broken, a failure syndrome may become well established by the end of the elementary school years. This then culminates too frequently in the youthful school drop-out, the unemployable young adult, and repetition of the cycle in the next generation.

This is the context out of which such things as compensatory education and Head Start programs are developing. The concept of the National Teacher Corps stems from this general concern. These and other educational developments will be discussed in more detail later. But, clearly, the elementary school has its role to play in helping to improve the lot of the poor people of this nation by becoming more effective with their children.

A Concern for Stability in International Relations

The desire for better relations between nations and the search for a basis for a lasting peace in our time continues to be a matter of highest priority. The shifts in power in the world which have come about in this extended post-World War II period continue to put great strains on international politics. The Free World and the Communist World search for acceptable ways to accommodate to each other. The dissolution of colonial empires in Asia and Africa have highlighted the plight of the underdeveloped nations of the world as they press for assistance toward a better life for their people. The aspirations of the people of Latin America have risen. Over all of the unrest hang the awesome nuclear military capabilities of the United States and of the Soviet Union, while other ambitious nations press hard to develop their own arsenals of advanced weapon systems. People watch the uneasy course of "small wars" as tensions break out into armed conflicts, and they make clear their fears of another worldwide military confrontation.

Through it all the United Nations remains intent on becoming a more substantial force for peace in the world, and its use of discussion and debate has been extended to include the placement of troops in the field to maintain an uneasy peace in a few of the more sensitive spots in the world. There is the European Common Market and some hopeful moves toward an even more completely united Europe. The interdependence of the economy of much of the world may contribute significantly to stability in world affairs in the future. Scientific information is increasingly exchanged across national boundaries; international scientific meetings are regularly scheduled. Art, music, and the theater become tools for understanding as a part of international cultural exchange programs that are able to penetrate both the "iron" and the "bamboo" curtains. International travel is more convenient and less costly with each passing year, and both formal exchange programs and casual vacation trips enable people to see more of their world.

In this area, too, the people look to their schools for help. Today's children are seen as tomorrow's citizens and the feeling is growing that they be helped to know the world not only as it is but as it could become. Differences among people need to be understood and accepted. A major thrust is being made to accommodate the curriculum to international phenomena and to improve our instructional practices and procedures for intercultural education. Because of this expansion, the social science component in the curriculum is in need of new ideas. There is increasing support for foreign language teaching in the elementary school.

The Matter of Values

Amid all the social, political, and economic change in our lives there is placed an inevitable strain on values. The values of a culture are those things which people accept as worth striving for, those norms which give direction to behavior as choice is contemplated. The gulf between the ideal and the manifest values in American culture has long been a reality of life, and the school is caught up in a conflict as it tries to decide toward which it will orient its efforts. Often the school promotes both—as in cooperation and competition—and may not take a firm stand for either. In a time of great cultural change the matter of values becomes even more confused; traditional values are challenged by new life situations and are changed or reinterpreted. The emergence of the United States as a highly industrialized, affluent society has put a great strain on the values of the Puritan ethic, which were established in a much different set of circumstances. Abstinence is challenged by a need to consume goods and services; frugality is challenged by credit and installment buying; a willingness to wait for the future is replaced by enjoyment of the present. People are seeking freedoms that seem to others to border on license.

The conflicts which become evident as the traditional rubs against the emergent in values place very real stresses on the school as an institution to pass on the cultural heritage, and on the teacher as an agent for cultural transmission. Not only does the school as an educational institution become confused over the direction it should take; classroom teachers find themselves unintentionally passing along to students a great deal of confusion and conflict as they themselves strive for some sort of synthesis between the "old" and the "new" in values.

Values are central to the determination of society to reduce cultural alienation for minorities and to bring them into the mainstream of American life. A sensitive part of any such effort has to do with a clash between the values dominant in the general society and those held by the minority groups themselves. The Negro who has lived a long life of discrimination has almost certainly developed a value system consistent with his experiences. The poor family that has lived with the minimum of goods, services, and housing has developed a value system appropriate to those circumstances. The educator finds himself confronted with a communication problem as he strives to understand and be effective with children from these minority groups. Values constitute a subculture difference of crucial importance; school and teacher must strive for empathy with their client group if they are to be effective at all.

Social Circumstances:
A Force for Change

There are many significant aspects of the current and emerging social scene—urbanization, impact of mass media, population movements, increase in leisure time, growth of organizations, changes in family life, religious developments, etc.—that have not been discussed here but that must be reckoned with in educational planning. Our purpose has been to illustrate the relationship between the school and society, and to establish a sense of expectation for social change to be an identifiable force for curriculum change in the elementary school. Curriculum decision-making does call for a "sociology of education"; current social, political, and economic information must be used deliberately as a data source. What has gone before is not to be ignored. He who overlooks history is often destined to relive it. But the curriculum must not be limited by history. The focus is on the future we wish to build on the present which we now have.

THE CHILD AND CHANGE IN
ELEMENTARY EDUCATION

Planning for curriculum and instruction in the elementary school will always be influenced in a major way by the nature of children. Understanding their general pattern of growth and development and their propensity and capacity for learning helps planners to decide what is possible of accomplishment and what limits must be set on expectancies.

From the early efforts of William James to the present, psychologists have learned a great deal about children and about their learning. Specialists in human biology have contributed additional information. As discoveries are made, beliefs are altered, concepts are refined, generalizations are restated—and the result on educational practices is to open doors to new possibilities in curriculum or methodology or to raise questions about familiar ways of doing things. One result of the current feelings of urgency for improvement in educational effectiveness has been to attract the attention of psychologists and biologists anew to the problems of learning, and to cause the elementary educator to reexamine the data available to him.

Here, as with social change, we shall direct attention to selected items that carry a certain priority in decision-making in elementary education at this time. The knowledge that is accumulating on these items contributes to the urgency for change in elementary school education.

Intelligence

Because the elementary school is a place for learning, teachers and administrators have felt a great need to understand the nature of intelligence. Investigators shed more light on this subject from year to year. Most useful has been the successful attempt to differentiate between *intellectual ability* (the collective mental power a child possesses in some pattern and amount) and *tested intelligence* (a measurement of how well or how much this ability is functioning for a given child at a particular time in his life). A concept of fixed intelligence is giving way to one of variability. We have come to conceive of intellectual ability for any given individual as having an upper limit set as a consequence of heredity. When we test a person's intelligence we collect evidence of the extent to which he is successful in doing a particular set of tasks. From this evidence we infer the amount of intellectual ability the child has, adding strength to our inference by reference to the performances of many other children of the same age on the same test. But we do not stop with this.

Fortunately we have studies which demonstrate ever more conclusively the influence of the environment on the development and functioning of intellectual ability. The extent and quality of encounters with the environment become all-important. We realize more clearly, too, that the items included on any intelligence test presume a kind of experiential background for the child being tested. This information can keep us from making errors in judgment about children and in the actions we take in their behalf in school. A child may score low on an intelligence test because of a lack in intellectual ability, or he may score low only because of a lack in experience.

Recently there has been increased attention to the cruciality of the quality of experiences which children have at various ages in relation to the realization of their full intellectual potential. These studies point up the importance of mental stimulation in the early years from about three to eight. Bloom has published a report on this issue that is intriguing. He says:

> . . . it is possible to say, that in terms of intelligence measured at age 17, at least 20 percent is developed by age 1, 50 percent by about age 4, 80 percent by about age 8, and 92 percent by age 13. Put in terms of intelligence measured at age 17, from conception to age 4, the individual develops 50 percent of his mature intelligence, from age 4 to 8 he develops another 30 percent, and from ages 8 to 17 the remaining 20 percent.
>
> . . . This would suggest the very rapid growth of intelligence in the early years and the possible great influence of the early environment on this development.[2]

As we come to understand intelligence and its development in these terms, practices in elementary education tend to change. Decisions about the ages at which the school experience will begin and the values to be placed on early childhood education are influenced greatly. Also, the school experience begins to be viewed in part as a way to help the pupil to develop more of his intellectual potential as well as a place in which to use an already developed part of it. It also helps the elementary educator to see in somewhat different terms the inability of some children to be successful with the usual set of school-prescribed tasks.

Readiness

Curriculum planners often must decide when particular things will be taught to pupils in the elementary school. Such decisions are usually based upon pupil readiness. We have come to differentiate between physical maturation as a biological process controlled by heredity and psychological maturation as a function of experiences which children undergo. We can have no effect on a child's heredity. But we know that psychological maturity develops from opportunities to learn, and that social maturity develops from opportunities to interact with people; and the school can take steps to provide for both. Of late there has been renewed speculation about the concept of readiness. Elementary educators are being urged toward more action in regard to readiness. In 1960 Bruner suggested that "any subject can be taught effectively in some intellectually honest form to any child at any stage of development."[3] In 1966 he wrote as follows:

> The "curriculum revolution" has made it plain even after only a decade that the idea of "readiness" is a mischievous half-truth. It is a half-

---

[2] Benjamin S. Bloom, *Stability and Change in Human Characteristics* (New York: John Wiley & Sons, Inc., 1964), p. 68.

[3] Jerome Bruner, *The Process of Education* (Cambridge, Mass.: Harvard University Press, 1960), p. 33.

truth largely because it turns out that one teaches readiness or provides opportunities for its nurture, one does not simply wait for it.[4]

In the same vein, Ausubel says:

> Pedagogically, therefore, recognition of the principles of readiness implies both that methods of teaching take account of general developmental changes in cognitive functioning, and that the curriculum be organized along sequential lines, i.e., that pupils acquire readiness for each new unit of subject matter as a result of mastering the preceding sequentially related unit.[5]

The consequence of this kind of thinking is to counsel the educator to take a more active role in fostering readiness by providing appropriate preparatory experiences as any given curriculum sequence moves along.

The school must not put undesirable demands on children, overtaxing their maturity and running the risk of harming developing structures and organs, or simply working from too far outside the experience of the child for the learning to have meaning. But at the same time the school must provide a rich and stimulating environment that will act as an invitation to a next step in learning. Thus decisions will continue to be made about the size of type in first reading books, or the use of phenomena in the immediate environment in early social studies or science programs, or the role of experience charts in early reading in relation to the readiness of particular children to profit accordingly. And head start programs will be used to supplement the limited experiences which some young children would otherwise have, while "follow through" programs will be used to sustain and reinforce gains made in these early years.

The idea of readiness to learn does, then, continue to be a useful concept. The curriculum planner takes it into account in setting out sequences of learning tasks. The teacher uses it diagnostically as he plans for the work of his class over the year. Thus, readiness is not being abandoned as an essential in learning, but it is being redefined in a more dynamic way than has been the usual practice.

The Self-Concept

Of late psychologists have extended their understanding of the self-concept, and have helped elementary teachers to see the significance of it in their work with children. The self-concept is defined as that set of inferences a person makes about himself on the basis of his experiences. Thus, a child begins to see in himself a certain degree of intellectual

---

[4] Jerome S. Bruner, *Toward a Theory of Instruction* (Cambridge, Mass.: The Belknap Press of Harvard University Press, 1966), p. 29.

[5] David Ausubel, *The Psychology of Meaningful Verbal Learning* (New York: Grune and Stratton, Inc., 1963), p. 112.

strength, or social competence, or physical skill, or a set of attitudes. In most instances the child tells himself what his characteristics are. In many instances others tell him about himself directly (as in comments) or indirectly (as in behavior toward him) in convincing terms, and he is persuaded to accept what is "said" as being an accurate description of himself.

Since the self-concept is a product of experience, and since a person has experiences over many years, there is reason to believe that the self-concept is susceptible to change over the years. There is also some reason to believe that a person eventually becomes fixed enough about his self-concept as to select experiences for himself whenever possible that are consistent with it. The consequences, thus, tend to confirm for the person the accuracy of his report to himself about himself and make change less likely to occur.

The young child comes to school with a developing self-concept already a part of his personal equipment. The beginning school experience undoubtedly is significant for the child from the standpoint of providing new tests for this developing self-concept. This widened experience may confirm the child's idea of himself, or it may introduce new information into his thinking that would change his ideas to some degree.

Success or failure with any of the wide variety of tasks which the school requires of the child becomes important information in relation to the self-concept. A child who has begun to doubt his intelligence may find confirmation that he is not very bright in the difficulties he has with his initial study efforts in school. He may actually try less to learn and in so doing seriously hamper his chances of success while at the same time contributing to greater doubts about his ability. Another child may find confirmation of his ability to get along well with people in the ease with which he makes new friends at school. He may become even more outgoing in his relations with others and confirm over and over for himself his social acceptability.

Thus, the early school years may be crucial for the self-concept. The level of confidence in and esteem for one's self that is developed in these initial years through successful experiences appears to be predictive of behavior in later years. The nature of the relationship that is developed between pupil and teacher, especially as this is viewed by the pupil, has an important impact on the self-concept.

Extending Understanding of Learning

An understanding of the learning process is central to the design and execution of educational experiences. Over the years many models have been presented that purport to describe the dynamics of the process. These are useful in helping the elementary teacher to conceptualize a learning event. Such constructs as rote learning, deductive learning, and inductive learning are used in the models. Furthermore, there are attempts to describe what is involved in the learning of concepts, of interests, of attitudes, of motor skills, and of generalizations.

Learning is sometimes called cognitive development. The theories of Jean Piaget have captured considerable attention in the current desires to understand the cognitive development of children.[6] He expounds a theory about children's thinking which may be summed up partially in these terms:

1. There are stages in the development of children's thinking about their environment and their reactions to it.
2. Children seem to move through three stages: the intuitive thought stage from about 4 to 7 years of age, the concrete operations stage from 7 to 12, the formal operations stage to about age 15.
3. Each of these stages has distinctive characteristics that set limits to the kinds of problems that children can readily deal with at any one of these stages.
4. Children find themselves dissatisfied with the explanations they have for problems at any of the lower stages; their dissatisfaction provides considerable motivation to move to the next higher stage until development is complete.
5. The human organism is a dynamic, seeking one; it is open to and ready for change; it explores and examines phenomena in the environment; it is self-regulating as it moves through the various levels of mental development.

Piaget suggests that logic appears rather late in the child's thinking. For instance, in the intuitive-thought stage he is often satisfied with incomplete, multiple, and contradictory explanations of events. Even in the middle childhood years, Piaget says, some children have difficulty in encompassing a whole problem and in considering all of the factors that need to be considered in solving it, and inconsistencies continue to appear in their explanations for happenings. No one knows how fixed these stages are or whether a teacher might accelerate a child through them. There is some reason to believe that the richer the environment in which the child is placed the more rapidly his cognitive powers will develop. There seems to be no escaping the sequence of development described by Piaget; there may be a way of pacing a child through it.

Concern over children's thinking has brought attention to processes and experiences which call upon the pupil to invent ideas, to test hunches, to make guesses, to ask questions, and so on. Much of what is being attempted in these efforts is referred to as "discovery" oriented learning for the pupil. The intent is to provide the minimum of direction

---

[6] Jean Piaget, *The Origins of Intelligence* (New York: International Universities Press, 1952).

over the pupil's learning, sufficient simply to enable him to arrive at his own explanations, conclusions, answers. This kind of learning closely resembles inductive learning. In inductive learning the pupil is helped to find for himself the rule or generalization that applies in a given situation. This is the opposite of deductive learning in which the rule or generalization is given to the pupil and he must find the situations in which it applies.

The teacher can think of the child as having a "data processing" capability. McDonald writes of "response systems" available in some form to the learner:

1. A motivational system: the capacity of the learner to select and seek goals. A major directive or orienting system, the motivational system accounts for variation in energy expended and the complex choices of approaching and engaging in learning experiences or of avoiding them.

2. A cognitive system: the set of responses by which the learner organizes and orders the stimuli around him. It also is the system by which he symbolically recalls or reinstates these stimuli and his conceptualizations of them. Finally, it is the system by which he interrelates his conceptualizations and solves problems.

3. An attitudinal system: the evaluative system of the person by which he judges the "goodness" or "badness," for him, of the stimulus information he receives.

4. A self system: a complex integration of concepts of oneself as a learner and an associated evaluation. We assume that the person "sees" himself in some way as a successful or not very successful learner, as having or not having certain learning capacities. This self-image determines his "openness" to learning, whether he will, for example, even participate in a learning experience.[7]

He then presents a symbolic model of the learner as follows:[8]

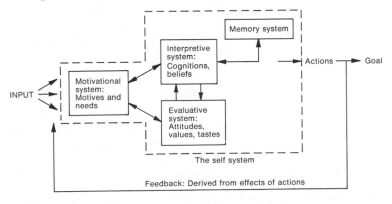

---

[7] Frederick J. McDonald, *Educational Psychology* (second edition) (Belmont, Calif.: Wadsworth Publishing Company, Inc., 1965), Chapter 3, pp. 76–77.
[8] McDonald, p. 77.

Much of the current effort to understand cognitive development and thinking processes finds its way to the very center of curriculum improvement projects.

Understanding of Children:
A Force for Change

Again the discussion here has been limited and selective. Beyond this lies a further vast body of literature—facts, concepts, and generalizations —that constitute a psychology of education for the elementary school. Undoubtedly this body of information helps us to be more sensible about our expectations for children and more effective in arranging learning situations for them. The sociologist and the anthropologist too are helping us to see child socialization, enculturation, and acculturation as processes with which the elementary school is inevitably involved.

Thus, we view the learner himself as a data source in curriculum and instructional planning, and new information about the learner is a force for change in educational arrangements and practices.

THE DISCIPLINES AND CURRICULUM
CHANGE

The disciplines, that is the subject areas, have always been a major influence on curriculum planning. In fact, in elementary education that influence has been seen by many as so overpowering that elementary educators have rallied around such slogans as "we teach children, not subjects" in an attempt to balance the data sources being used. But over the years the curriculum has been shaped in many ways by the subjects included therein.

At the present time it can be said that the disciplines as such are probably having more effect on the thinking of curriculum planners and on their products than at any time since about 1920. They are a strong force for change on the current scene.

Rapid Expansion of Knowledge

In great part the present preoccupation with the disciplines in curriculum planning stems directly from the rapid rate at which knowledge is expanding. Methods for the production of new knowledge are efficient as never before. An NEA report has described the accelerated rate with which knowledge is accumulating:

In the nearly 2000 years since the birth of Christ, there has been first a very slow and then a rapidly accelerating growth in the accumulation of knowledge. If this accumulation is plotted on a time line, beginning with the birth of Christ, it is estimated that the first doubling of knowledge occurred in 1750, the second in 1900, the third in 1950, and the fourth only ten years later, in 1960![9]

The consequences of the "knowledge explosion" go beyond coping with direct additions to knowledge. When new information challenges and displaces old information, a choice must be made as to which knowledge (in any given field) is of most worth. For the school this is a crucial matter, obviously. There is just so much time available in the classroom, and the goal is to invest it most wisely. Coverage of subjects in any detail is just not a tenable principle. The selection of material used calls for wise judgments about the amount of information and about the life-span of that information. Thus, our very affluence in knowledge serves to establish a certain priority on it as a force for change in curriculum reformulations.

A Respect for Knowledge

The growing respect for knowledge in our time serves to direct attention to subject matter as a point of departure in curriculum planning. The complex and demanding culture which we have developed puts a heavy premium on knowledge. Occupational training in most instances includes an ever-increasing intellectual component. Numerous careers call for extended periods of study and preparation. Enrollment in the graduate divisions of colleges and universities is at an all-time high. The general population understands increasingly the necessity of research efforts to its continued and improved well-being. Many parents sense that success for the generation of their children will be tied more than ever before to intellectual proficiency. In such a setting it is to be expected that the disciplines would be considered as a valuable and necessary data source for curriculum planning.

The Disciplines, Curriculum, and Instruction

There is considerable feeling, too, that *in* the disciplines we find answers to the kinds of questions which the curriculum planner and the teacher face in their respective roles. For instance, Phenix[10] comments that ". . . a discipline is knowledge organized for instruction." And he goes on to say: "The distinguishing mark of any discipline is that the

---

[9] NEA Project on Instruction, *Schools for the Sixties* (Washington, D.C.: NEA, 1963), p. 50.
[10] Phillip Phenix, "The Use of the Disciplines as Curriculum Content," *Educational Forum*, Vol. 26 (March 1962), p. 273.

knowledge which comprises it is instructive—that it is peculiarly suited for teaching and learning." Bruner has written also to this point and states that "the curriculum of a subject should be determined by the most fundamental understanding that can be achieved of the underlying principles that give structure to that subject."[11]

And Schwab writes persuasively of this matter as follows:

> . . . they [the disciplines] pose problems with which we in education must deal. The structures of the modern disciplines are complex and diverse . . . The diversity of modern structures means that we must look, not for a simple theory of learning leading to a one best learning-teaching structure for our schools, but for a complex theory leading to a number of different structures, each appropriate or "best" for a given discipline or group of disciplines. . . . they are necessary to teachers and educators; they must be taken into account as we plan curriculum and prepare our teaching materials; otherwise, our plans are likely to miscarry and our materials, to misteach.
> . . . they are necessary in some part and degree *within* the curriculum, as elements of what we teach. Otherwise, there will be failure of learning or gross mislearning by our students.[12]

Thus, in these and other writings of recent years the disciplines have been clearly identified as a basic data source for work in curriculum and instruction. And, to the extent that these expressed ideas open new ways for the educator to view the disciplines, they constitute a force for change in thinking about curriculum planning and the development of instructional strategies.

The society, the learner, and the disciplines have been identified as data sources for decision-making in curriculum planning. There has been no attempt here to be exhaustive in identifying specifics in these areas. We have called attention to selected matters that are but a small part of the total set of forces at work on both ends and means in elementary school education—a set of forces for change.

RECOMMENDED READINGS

Materials related to the psychological foundations:

CRONBACH, LEE J. *Educational Psychology* (second edition). New York: Harcourt, Brace & World, Inc., 1963.
HUNT, J. MC VICKER. *Intelligence and Experience*. New York: The Ronald Press Company, 1961.

---

[11] Bruner, *The Process of Education*, p. 31.
[12] Joseph Schwab, "The Concept of the Structure of a Discipline," *Educational Record*, Vol. 43 (July 1962), p. 197.

HURLOCK, ELIZABETH. *Child Development* (fourth edition). New York: McGraw-Hill Book Company, Inc., 1964.

MC DONALD, FREDERICK J. *Educational Psychology* (second edition). Belmont, Calif.: Wadsworth Publishing Company, Inc., 1965.

NATIONAL SOCIETY FOR THE STUDY OF EDUCATION. *Theories of Learning and Instruction.* (Sixty-Third Yearbook, Part I). Chicago: University of Chicago Press, 1964.

PRESCOTT, DANIEL A. *The Child in the Educative Process.* New York: McGraw-Hill Book Company, Inc., 1957.

RUSSELL, DAVID H. *Children's Thinking.* Boston: Ginn and Company, 1956.

STENDLER, CELIA B. (editor). *Readings in Child Behavior and Development.* New York: Harcourt, Brace & World, Inc., 1964.

STEPHEN, JOHN M. *The Psychology of Classroom Learning.* New York: Holt, Rinehart and Winston, Inc., 1965.

Materials related to the social foundations:

BELL, ROBERT H. *The Sociology of Education: A Source Book.* Homewood, Ill.: Dorsey Press, 1962.

CHILDS, JOHN L. *Education and Morals.* New York: Appleton-Century-Crofts, Inc., 1950.

CORWIN, RONALD G. *A Sociology of Education.* New York: Appleton-Century-Crofts, Inc., 1965.

DRUCKER, PETER. *Landmarks of Tomorrow.* New York: Harper & Row, Publishers, Inc., 1959.

HAVIGHURST, ROBERT J., and BERNICE L. NEUGARTEN. *Society and Education* (second edition). Boston: Allyn and Bacon, Inc., 1962.

HODKINS, HAROLD L. *Education in Social and Cultural Perspectives.* Englewood Cliffs, N.J.: Prentice-Hall, Inc., 1962.

NATIONAL SOCIETY FOR THE STUDY OF EDUCATION. *Social Forces Influencing American Education* (Sixtieth Yearbook, Part II). Chicago: University of Chicago Press, 1961.

NEA PROJECT ON INSTRUCTION. *Education in a Changing Society.* Washington, D.C.: NEA, 1963.

SCHULTZ, THEODORE W. *The Economic Value of Education.* New York: Columbia University Press, 1963.

SPINDLER, GEORGE. *Education and Culture.* New York: Holt, Rinehart and Winston, Inc., 1963.

Materials related to knowledge as a foundation area:

BRUNER, JEROME. *The Process of Education.* Cambridge, Mass.: Harvard University Press, 1961.

FORD, G. W., and LAUREN PUGNO. *The Structure of Knowledge and the Curriculum.* Chicago: Rand McNally & Company, 1964.

JENKINS, WILLIAM A. (editor). *The Nature of Knowledge*. Milwaukee: University Bookstore, 1961.

KING, ARTHUR R., and JOHN BROWNELL. *The Curriculum and the Disciplines of Knowledge*. New York: John Wiley & Sons, Inc., 1966.

SOWARDS, G. WESLEY (editor). *The Social Studies: Curriculum Proposals for the Future*. Glenview, Ill.: Scott, Foresman and Company, 1963. (See the paper by Arno Bellack.)

Elementary Education: Changing Goals

4

First, let us remind ourselves of the objectives that have been most commonly assigned to the schools for the past three decades. General goal statements provide overall descriptions of the behaviors which a society would like its members to demonstrate. A representative and widely used list of goals is contained in a statement which was published by the Educational Policies Commission in 1938. The Commission statement says that the overall objective "is the fullest possible development of the individual within the framework of our present industrialized democratic society. The attainment of this end is to be observed in individual behavior or conduct."[1]

Then the Commission statement outlines four categories of educational objectives, stating more specific goals for each. The total statement of objectives is as follows:[2]

The Objectives of Self-Realization

The Inquiring Mind. The educated person has an appetite for learning.

Speech. The educated person can speak the mother tongue clearly.

Reading. The educated person reads the mother tongue efficiently.

Writing. The educated person writes the mother tongue effectively.

Number. The educated person solves his problems of counting and calculating.

---

[1] Educational Policies Commission, *The Purposes of Education in American Democracy* (Washington, D.C.: NEA, 1938), p. 41.

[2] Educational Policies Commission, pp. 50, 72, 90, and 108.

Sight and Hearing. The educated person is skilled in listening and observing.

Health Knowledge. The educated person understands the basic facts concerning health and disease.

Health Habits. The educated person protects his own health and that of his dependents.

Public Health. The educated person works to improve the health of the community.

Recreation. The educated person is participant and spectator in many sports and other pastimes.

Intellectual Interest. The educated person has mental resources for the use of leisure.

Esthetic Interests. The educated person appreciates beauty.

Character. The educated person gives responsible direction to his own life.

The Objectives of Human Relationship

Respect for Humanity. The educated person puts human relationships first.

Friendships. The educated person enjoys a rich, sincere, and varied social life.

Cooperation. The educated person can work and play with others.

Courtesy. The educated person observes the amenities of social behavior.

Appreciation of the Home. The educated person appreciates the family as a social institution.

Conservation of the Home. The educated person conserves family ideals.

Homemaking. The educated person is skilled in homemaking.

Democracy in the Home. The educated person maintains democratic family relationships.

The Objectives of Economic Efficiency

Work. The educated producer knows the satisfaction of good workmanship.

Occupational Information. The educated producer understands the requirements and opportunities for various jobs.

Occupational Choice. The educated producer has selected his occupation.

Occupational Efficiency. The educated producer succeeds in his chosen vocation.

Occupational Adjustment. The educated producer maintains and improves his efficiency.

Occupational Appreciation. The educated producer appreciates the social value of his work.

Personal Economics. The educated consumer plans the economics of his own life.

Consumer Judgment. The educated consumer develops standards for guiding his expenditures.

Efficiency in Buying. The educated consumer is an informed and skillful buyer.

Consumer Protection. The educated consumer takes appropriate measures to safeguard his interests.

The Objectives of Civic Responsibility

Social Justice. The educated citizen is sensitive to the disparities of human circumstance.

Social Activity. The educated citizen acts to correct unsatisfactory conditions.

Social Understanding. The educated citizen seeks to understand social structures and social processes.

Critical Judgment. The educated citizen has defenses against propaganda.

Tolerance. The educated citizen respects honest differences of opinion.

Conservation. The educated citizen has a regard for the nation's resources.

Social Application of Science. The educated citizen measures scientific advance by its contribution to the general welfare.

World Citizenship. The educated citizen is a cooperating member of the world community.

Law Observance. The educated citizen respects the law.

Economic Literacy. The educated citizen is economically literate.

Political Citizenship. The educated citizen accepts his civic duties.

Devotion to Democracy. The educated citizen acts upon an unswerving loyalty to democratic ideals.

This statement provides, at a general level, a behavioral answer which the Commission would accept to the question of what it means to be educated in our society. The groups of objectives are spoken of in the report as "vantage points from which to study the purposes of education." The report also says that ". . . the school is only one of the many educational influences in these various fields of human life. Its responsibility extends to all of these areas, but in some areas the weight of education rests on the schools more exclusively than in others."[3]

---

[3] Educational Policies Commission, pp. 47–48.

The elementary school does not seek in any direct sense to contribute to the achievement of all of the goals included in the EPC statement just reviewed. Instead its curriculum is planned to include programs of learning directed to selected goals only. This selection is influenced by the nature of childhood in a developmental sense, and by the expectancies which our culture holds for children. For instance, on both counts it is considered to be unrealistic for the elementary school to direct its efforts to the selection of and preparation for an occupation.

Some years ago Kearney made a comprehensive study to ascertain the objectives allocated to the elementary school in the United States.[4] The following goals were most often cited:

1. *Physical Development, Health, and Body Care.* Physical development, health, and body care is a broad category as compared with the narrow conception of physiology and hygiene which it has replaced in the elementary school curriculum. Today it involves both health and safety. It includes individual health and the elementary aspects of public health. It includes physical education, personal grooming, safety, sportsmanship, and an understanding of growth and maturation. . . .

2. *Individual Social and Emotional Development.* This category includes material that is commonly associated with mental health, emotional stability, and the growth of personality [with] emphasis on such goals as understanding oneself and evaluating oneself. . . . In this area there is more difficulty in pointing out basic knowledge and skills than is true in some others, since the area itself is so much one of attitudes and interests. . . .

3. *Ethical Behavior, Standards, Values.* Ethical behavior, standards, and values are related to the observance of the moral law and the civil law. This area includes the observance of much that gains validity from the customs and mores of the culture. It involves sportsmanship, kindliness, helpfulness, and the problems involved in living in a society with other people. It is concerned with the integrity and honesty of people. . . .

4. *Social Relations.* This . . . is devoted to the individual as a person in his personal-social relations with others, when he has to consider the needs, interests, motives, convictions, and ideals of others with whom he associates in home, community, and place of work. . . .

5. *The Social World.* This . . . considers the child in a somewhat broader social setting than does . . . social relations. Here we set the goals for the child in terms of the structure and the institutions of our culture. The behavior of the child is considered in relation to community, state, and nation. Geography in its relation to man is

---

[4] Nolan C. Kearney, *Elementary School Objectives* (New York: Russell Sage Foundation, 1953), pp. 52–113.

in this background. Civics, elementary economics, government, and the traditional American way of life come in this area. . . .

6. *The Physical World (The Natural Environment).* In this . . . attention is centered on an enlarged concept of science, and reference is made to many aspects of the child's environment. Physical science problems, as well as the science that deals with plants and animals, are emphasized. Also stressed are learning to think scientifically and the use of *methods of science* in solving problems in science and problems in everyday living. Emphasis is on thinking that associates facts and relates them in various ways to form generalizations. . . .

7. *Esthetic Development.* In this . . . emphasis is placed on esthetic appreciation and expression. Though the primary emphasis here is on art, music, and the crafts, . . . many types of artistic and creative endeavor are mentioned. The moral, the intellectual, and the emotional aspects of esthetic development are all included. . . .

8. *Communication.* This . . . covers the wide variety of means by which man communicates with man. It emphasizes the mechanical and skills aspects of reading, writing, composition, correct usage, spelling, punctuation, speaking, and listening. It includes the use of the library and of references of various kinds. It includes group skills, such as conducting and participating in meetings. It stresses the various constructive uses to which communication skills must be put, if their mastery is to be of value. . . .

9. *Quantitative Relationships.* Here we find arithmetic and the elementary aspects of algebra and geometry. Here children are introduced to a great variety of measures by which man describes in quantities the things he finds in his world. This involves the ability to analyze and solve problems on the basis of the particular problem, the information needed to solve it, and how to get the information. Emphasis is placed on giving the child an understanding of how our number system works and why, so that he will have greater competence in using numbers. Since mathematics is the language of quantity, it could be included as another means of communication, but it is so important and specialized that it is considered separately.

Together, the report of the Educational Policies Commission and the Kearney report provide a useful base for the study and discussion of the objectives of education generally, and of elementary education specifically. In the main, other statements of purpose that might have been quoted here are very much like these.

A UNIQUE ROLE FOR THE SCHOOL

These statements range over a broad set of goals, including intellectual development, social competence, emotional and mental health, physical well-being, and general personality development. For a long time there has been divided opinion in society and within the education profession about this broad goal commitment. The EPC statement calls attention to the fact that institutions and agencies other than schools educate. It implies, too, that the school has a unique contribution to make to education. Planners have some disagreement about isolating this uniqueness, and it is precisely at this point that we are able to identify some change action at the present time.

Some educators feel strongly that the school should work at the development and modification of behavior along all of the dimensions cited in such goal statements as Kearney's. They reason that only in school will these behaviors become objects of deliberate concern. They doubt that either the spontaneity of general living or the efforts of other service agencies will be sufficient to do the job. Furthermore, they argue that the various aspects of human behavior are so interrelated that to work at one is inevitably to give attention to all anyway.

Other educators argue that a statement of goals such as those cited overextends the school and carries it into areas of behavior change where it cannot be effective and should not be responsible. These educators would like to sharpen the concept of "schooling" as only a part of "educating." They would press for agreement on the unique role and function of the school in the totality of education. And they would typically set a priority for the school on goals that have to do with intellectual or cognitive development.

This latter point of view has commanded serious attention in the years since about 1955. While the controversy is one of long standing, the launching of the original Sputnik satellite in 1957 brought a sharp focus to the argument again. Those people who considered the Russian launching a "defeat" for American science and engineering believed that the defeat was the inevitable consequence of our having allowed the school system to try to be all things to all pupils. It was charged anew by many that the schools were subordinating intellectual development to personal and social development—and by some that the schools were in fact anti-intellectual in their orientation. These arguments did not fall on deaf ears. There was enough latent concern in the society at large to cause laymen to be willing to listen and react to these charges sympathetically. And there were many school people who, under the growing pressures of responsibility and accountability for educational accomplishments, supported fresh attempts to reconsider the question of the limits which ought to be put on the school's role in its service to society.

A New Educational Policies Commission Statement

The Educational Policies Commission in 1961 issued a statement entitled "The Central Purpose of American Education." In part their statement was as follows:

Effective citizenship is impossible without the ability to think. The good citizen, the one who contributes effectively and responsibly to the management of the public business in a free society, can fill his role only if he is aware of the values of his society. Moreover, the course of events in modern life is such that many of the factors which influence an individual's civic life are increasingly remote from him. His own firsthand experience is no longer an adequate basis for judgment. He must have in addition the intellectual means to study events, to relate his values to them, and to make wise decisions as to his own actions. He must also be skilled in the processes of communication and must understand both the potentialities and the limitations of communication among individuals and groups.[5]

And they summarize:

Thus the rational powers are central to all the other qualities of the human spirit. These powers flourish in a humane and morally responsible context and contribute to the entire personality. The rational powers are to the entire human spirit as the hub is to the wheel.

These powers are indispensable to a full and worthy life. The person in whom—for whatever reason—they are not well developed is increasingly handicapped in modern society. He may be able to satisfy minimal social standards, but he will inevitably lack his full measure of dignity because his incapacity limits his stature to less than he might otherwise attain. Only to the extent that an individual can realize his potentials, especially the development of his ability to think, can he fully achieve for himself the dignity that goes with freedom.[6]

A teacher should read this statement in its entirety. The statement carries with it the expectation that the school will continue to work with students on a broad range of goals. It places a priority on the development of rationality and on thinking—and in the process on the intellectual development of pupils.

The Project on Instruction and Priorities

In 1963 the National Committee of the Project on Instruction expressed the following views:

[The essential objectives of the school program] must be premised on a recognition that education is a process of changing behavior and that a changing society requires that its members acquire the capacity for self-teaching and self-adaptation. Therefore, priorities in educational objectives need to be placed upon such ends as (a)

---

[5] Educational Policies Commission, *The Central Purpose of American Education* (Washington, D.C.: NEA, 1961), p. 6.
[6] Educational Policies Commission, *The Central Purpose*, p. 8.

learning how to learn, how to attack new problems, how to acquire new knowledge; (b) using rational processes and developing an abiding interest in learning; (c) exploring values in new experiences; (d) understanding concepts and generalizations; (e) competence in basic skills.[7]

They go on to say:

> The Commission recommends these objectives for schools in every community in every part of the United States. They might be considered the national objectives of the schools. How they are to be achieved in the school program will vary from one community to another, as will the degree of emphasis on social, physical, and vocational needs of learners. These objectives constitute general criteria for deciding what shall be included and excluded in planning the school program. They must be translated by each school system into more specific criteria . . .[8]

The report of the Project on Instruction dealt specifically with the matter of priorities in the school program, and with matters of "distinctive" versus "shared" responsibilities for education. Their recommendation was stated as follows:

> Priorities for the school are the teaching of skills in reading, composition, listening, speaking (both native and foreign languages), and computation . . . ways of creative and disciplined thinking, including methods of inquiry and application of knowledge . . . competence in self-instruction and independent learning . . . fundamental understanding of the humanities and the arts, the social sciences and natural sciences, and mathematics . . . appreciation of and discriminating taste in literature, music, and the visual arts . . . instruction in health education and physical education.
> Responsibilities best met by joint efforts of the school and other social agencies include development of values and ideals . . . social and civic competence . . . vocational preparation.
> The decision to include or exclude particular subjects or outside-of-class activities should be based on (a) the priorities assigned to the school and to other agencies; (b) data about learners and society and developments in the academic disciplines; (c) the human and material resources available in the school and community.[9]

Clearly these statements from the Project group recognize the existence of child and youth-serving agencies, other than the school, which can and do contribute to the education of children and youth. Too, these statements recognize the fact that not all communities are blessed with

---

[7] NEA Project on Instruction, *Deciding What to Teach* (Washington, D.C.: NEA, 1963), p. 92.
[8] NEA Project on Instruction, pp. 92–93.
[9] NEA Project on Instruction, p. 102.

the same number or quality of such agencies and services, and that the school must try to do for pupils what other agencies and services are unable to do. These Project statements call for an emphasis on intellectual development in the efforts of the school. And the position enunciated by the Project group complements in many ways the earlier cited statement from the Educational Policies Commission on the development of the rational powers of pupils.

A Priority on Goals in Elementary Education

Since 1957 the one major change that has come about in the goals of the elementary school is the greater priority placed on intellectual or cognitive development. Affective goals, the "feelings" aspect of being educated, have not been excluded from the school's commitments, but they are being given less attention.

For the elementary school this shift in goals means a program in which more attention is committed to the accomplishment of goals which have to do with subject matter learnings, and less attention to the more general goals of socialization. Obviously, in light of the history of elementary education and the commitments which many elementary educators hold, this shift meets some resistance and leads to some controversy.

The misgivings that some hold can be illustrated by reference to Havighurst's work on the identification of "developmental tasks" in our culture, specifically those of middle childhood, or the age range encompassed by the elementary school years. Such a task was defined as "a task which arises at or about a certain period in the life of the individual, successful achievement of which leads to his happiness and to success with later tasks, while failure leads to unhappiness in the individual, disapproval by the society, and difficulty with later tasks."[10] Havighurst went on to identify the developmental tasks of middle childhood as follows:

1. Learning physical skills necessary for ordinary games.
2. Building wholesome attitudes toward oneself as a growing organism.
3. Learning to get along with age-mates.
4. Learning an appropriate masculine or feminine social role.
5. Developing fundamental skills in reading, writing, and calculating.
6. Developing concepts necessary for everyday living.

---

[10] Robert Havighurst, *Human Development and Education* (New York: David McKay Company, Inc., 1953), p. 2.

7. Developing conscience, morality, and a scale of values.

8. Achieving personal independence.

9. Developing attitudes toward social groups and institutions.[11]

This conceptualization has been attractive and useful to elementary educators who are committed to teaching "the whole child." It has contributed additional understanding to those so committed, and support for their commitment, at least as they have interpreted the statement. They see in present events the possibility of too much stress being placed on intellectual development in the elementary school program.

This sort of reservation is reflected in the response which some elementary educators make to the possibility of teaching children to read in kindergarten, or to encounter other learnings at an earlier than usual point in the school experience—the response usually being that the fact that it can be done is not sufficient reason that it should be done. Some teachers argue that such early teaching constitutes undue and unwise pressure on children; they question the priority being placed on cognitive development in the elementary school.[12] The fact remains that special attention is being given to cognitive goals in the curriculum of the elementary school, and many efforts are being made to increase the effectiveness of the elementary school experience in the intellectual development of children. As a result it is probably true that affective goals are not receiving as much attention as they did before 1957.

In many communities there is a concerted effort under way to mobilize the totality of child- and youth-serving agencies found there for an improved total effort at child education. Many elementary school educators are reexamining their positions with respect to what the Project on Instruction report cited above refers to as "distinctive" and "shared" responsibilities for the school. The distinctive responsibilities of the elementary school usually have a heavy ingredient of intellectual or cognitive elements. In these matters the school as an institution and the teacher as a professional stand unique in society. At the same time it would be unfortunate for the idea of shared responsibilities to be translated into a "no responsibility" point of view for the elementary school in relation to affective development. A priority on the development of the intellect can be sensibly applied to the elementary school, with due consideration to the facts of childhood, and further to the facts of early childhood as compared to middle childhood. Applying this priority to the advantage of children is one of the real challenges to all elementary school educators at this time.

---

[11] Havighurst, pp. 28–40.

[12] Ronald C. Doll and Robert S. Fleming, *Children Under Pressure* (Columbus, Ohio: Charles E. Merrill Books, Inc., 1966).

Earlier in this chapter a statement of goals for American education was cited that had been published by the Educational Policies Commission. Lists such as this are published from time to time by public and private groups in an attempt to influence the goals which society will accept for its schools. None of these statements have power beyond the power to inform and to persuade. Schools do operate within limits set by laws in any particular state. But the objectives to be sought by any given public school system, and the priorities that are set among those objectives, are determined largely by the Board of Education in the local school district. Traditionally such an arrangement has been seen as a way of keeping the schools close to the people and as a way of insuring a proper goal focus for a school which would reflect the distinguishing characteristics and educational needs of the local community.

In recent years, however, there has been some shift in thinking on this matter. The people have come to perceive the United States itself as a community, albeit a national one. As a nation, the characteristics for community status have been identifiable in our midst for a long time. Consider the following:

> A community is any group or society of people who live in a definable geographic space, who possess sufficient historic values and customs in common to hold the society together, who face common problems, who have devised solutions (institutions, laws, customs) that are workable and somewhat unique to that community, who have developed means of communication throughout the community space, and who acknowledge membership in the group or society.[13]

Of late, Americans have spoken more acceptingly and more matter-of-factly of national needs, of national problems, and of national goals. The report of the President's Commission on National Goals is an especially good example of this development.[14] Thus, the fact of what might be called multiple but concurrent citizenship, in the local, the state, and the national community would appear to be accepted as such by growing numbers of people. The task of setting and accomplishing goals is more readily seen as a matter of finding ways of using the resources, human and otherwise, of all of these communities.

One consequence of the growth of national community feeling has

---

[13] Paul R. Hanna, in G. W. Sowards (editor), *The Social Studies: Curriculum Proposals for the Future* (Glenview, Ill.: Scott, Foresman and Company, 1963), pp. 54–55.

[14] The Commission, *Goals for Americans,* The Report of the President's Commission on National Goals (Englewood Cliffs, N.J.: Prentice-Hall, Inc., 1960).

been the realization on the part of most people that the accomplishment of almost all of the goals which they hold, for themselves as individuals and collectively as a nation, is intimately related to the quality of education which is provided for their children. Another consequence is that there are some basic changes in the way in which the people view the nation and accept a role for the national government in the affairs of the public school system.

One of these changes has been in the matter of deciding on educational goals to be achieved. While the state retains its legal authority and the local operating school district retains its delegated power to determine goals, the national dimension is receiving more and more attention. The development and acceptance of educational objectives in the locality has begun to include deliberate attention to their value and their necessity for the larger community.

Another consequence of the growth of national community feeling has been passing of educational legislation by Congress, with the support of the President, for school financing which has moved the national government into precollegiate education in this country on a scale undreamed of a few years ago.

A NEW IMPORTANCE FOR OBJECTIVES

Another noticeable development in relation to objectives in elementary school education is a renewed appreciation of their importance in any deliberate, intentional effort to modify behavior. The idea of elementary education as a goal-oriented enterprise is being reestablished. At the level of the society, goals serve to give some general sense of direction to the school's efforts to educate; at the levels of the school and of the classroom, goals serve to shape educational experiences.

The goal statement of the Educational Policies Commission is a rather general and abstract sort of behavioral profile. Society can express its intentions for education in this style. But this is not a very useful form in which to state objectives as a school system begins to plan in detail the nature of the curricular programs it will provide for its pupils, or when a teacher sits down to decide on the specific outcomes to be pursued in his classroom. A system-level curriculum guide must delineate the behaviors which students are expected to demonstrate both ultimately and at various major articulation points in the school system (at the end of the elementary school years, for instance). Classroom teachers must be able to state in detail the behaviors to be developed in their pupils. A consistency of effort must be evident across these statements, of course, from society to school system to classroom and back again, so that in the detailed planning necessary for operations the school does not unintentionally veer away from the ultimate intentions of society. Diagrammatically, this level-by-level expression of goals statements looks like this:

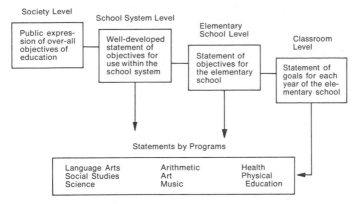

It is necessary, in turn, to refine the expression of any given objective appropriately at each of these levels, starting with the general way in which society will undoubtedly express it through to the specific way in which the teacher must express it. For instance, let us take the general goal that commits the school to "develop a sense of personal responsibility" in students. This calls for a definition, expressed in terms of behaviors, as to what personal responsibility is in our society. Even more delimiting, the elementary school educator must decide what this responsibility can be in behavioral terms for children as they live and work and play at school. The statement, once developed, can be used in two ways: (1) to direct the school's and the teacher's efforts and (2) to check with society as to the accuracy of the school's understanding of the way in which a trait like personal responsibility is defined behaviorally in the wider social setting.

For this goal, the following statement might be the result:

> The educated child demonstrates a developing sense of responsibility in all aspects of living. A responsible child (a) finishes schoolwork assigned to him for completion, (b) returns to the classroom equipment that he has taken out for use on the playground, (c) remembers to bring things from home to school, and vice versa, when the situation demands it of him, and (d) carries through on "classroom helper" assignments without constant reminders from the teacher.

A much longer list could be developed, obviously, but this should be sufficient to illustrate a behaviorally expressed statement. It suggests some of the things in which the children will have to be involved in order to become responsible; it also points to sources of data that the teacher can use to evaluate the development of a given child's "responsibility" behavior.

Or suppose the goal to be sought is the common one of teaching children to read. The school is more sure of its objective and the teacher is better served by a behavior statement such as the following:

> The educated child reads the mother tongue effectively. Such a child (a) discusses with understanding the content of what he has read, (b) reads with understanding both silently and aloud, (c) applies various word attack skills to new words, and (d) chooses to read at times when given a free choice of activity.

The school will be more sure of the set of behaviors it must help children to develop if an overall statement like this has been thought through. And the teacher is more likely to know what to do in the classroom to help children to become effective readers when there is this sort of behavioral statement available to guide the planning of classroom-level learning experiences, and to assess the effectiveness of the program once these experiences have been undergone by the pupils.

Thus, the ability to formulate objectives becomes for the elementary educator a matter of great importance. The task is not simple. Most educators need to improve their skills in this area. Too often the statements formulated identify only the general domain of behavior with which the goals are concerned, as, for instance, knowing, or appreciating, or valuing. Such a form is not very useful for either the planning of a curriculum or the designing of teaching strategies for goal accomplishment. This problem has been recognized for a long time, and many teachers have asked to have their schools' goals stated in behavioral terms. As yet schools have been able to come only part of the way in meeting this requirement.

Current efforts to develop competence in the formulation of objectives focus attention on the analysis of goals as such, and on the development of taxonomies for the classification of educational objectives. Illustrative of the attention to goal analysis is a recent statement by Mager.[15] He suggests three steps in formulating objectives that reveal the demands of the task very well. *First,* name the desired behavior, often called the *terminal behavior. Second,* specify the conditions under which the behavior may be expected to occur. *Third,* specify an acceptable level of performance. Such an approach to stating outcomes is more demanding than that which has typically been utilized in the elementary school and by the classroom teacher, though the specificity of it has always been implicit in what the school was assumed to be doing. Illustrations of the efforts to develop useful taxonomies of educational goals are to be found

---

[15] R. F. Mager, *Preparing Objectives for Programmed Instruction* (Palo Alto, Calif.: Fearon Publishers, Inc., 1961).

in the publications on cognitive and affective goals that are currently demanding the attention of many elementary school educators.[16] It is interesting to note the date of publication for the cognitive goal taxonomy, and the number of years that went by before it was taken very seriously.

The last word is not in on any of this, of course. There is a new sense of urgency about being clear on what it is that the school is actually trying to produce as behavior change in its pupils. And the work of the curriculum developer and the classroom teacher is coming to be judged more on the clarity and the specificity of the statement of outcomes toward which their efforts are to be directed. Clarity can do a great deal to make more effective the anticipatory sort of designing and planning that must be engaged in by the school and the teacher before instruction begins. Clarity of goals can be of great assistance to the evaluation effort after instruction has taken place.

OBJECTIVES AND CURRICULUM FUNCTIONS

Educational goals may be viewed from one other perspective, that of the "functions" they accomplish for the individual and for society. These goals can be classified as *general education* and *special education.*

General education is the effort that is made in school to insure that certain understandings, values, loyalties, attitudes, and skills (language and otherwise) are developed in every child to the limit of his potential for such development. Learnings so selected and specified are considered to be an expression of the essentials required for any person to live effectively in his own life and in relation to others in our society. Such learnings could be said to constitute a *common learnings* core which must be transmitted to each succeeding generation if our cultural heritage is to be preserved and continued.

Special education, on the other hand, refers to learning requirements —understandings, attitudes, and skills—that are imposed on the individual and must be mastered by him as he chooses to prepare himself to fill a specific position in society. These learning requirements are usually related to occupations, and they are seen as preparation for professional or vocational training. Such learning opportunities must be made available if society is to insure itself a continuing supply of doctors, lawyers, teachers, mechanics, plumbers, and so on.

An analogy from the field of physics may be helpful here. When a wheel is in motion, there are two opposing forces, centrifugal and

---

16 See B. S. Bloom (editor), *Taxonomy of Educational Objectives: Handbook I: Cognitive Domain* (New York: David McKay Company, Inc., 1956); and David R. Krathwohl (editor), *Taxonomy of Educational Objectives: Handbook II: Affective Domain* (New York: David McKay Company, Inc., 1964).

centripetal, that insure the form of the wheel by counteracting one another. Centrifugal force is directed, of course, outward from the center of the wheel. Centripetal force is directed in the opposite direction toward the center of the wheel. The equal but opposite directional pull of the forces results in the wheel's neither spinning apart nor collapsing inward. Applied to society and education, the elements of the analogy are easily identified; we can substitute society for the wheel, special education for centrifugal force, and general education for centripetal force. Thus the specializations that stem from a combination of the unique personal interests of individuals and the requirements of occupations in our culture are counterbalanced by strong common and shared understandings, values, and skills that are the possession of the vast majority of our people, and the "societal wheel" is helped to preserve its integrity accordingly. In curriculum planning this division of labor must similarly be attended to. Reference back to the EPC statement on educational purposes will demonstrate clearly this general–special education matter. According to the Kearney project on objectives, the elementary school is expected to contribute almost exclusively to general education. Special education does not really exist in the elementary school program. All pupils are offered essentially the same program of instruction. The realities of individual differences being what they are, there are some qualitative variations in programming and in how well things are learned. And there are variations in the enthusiasm with which various learning areas are approached by some pupils. But, in spite of differences in ability to learn and interest in learning, all children are involved with the language arts, mathematics, the sciences, the fine arts, and other subjects.

Thus, it is possible to interpret some of what was said early in this chapter about changes in the priority on objectives for the elementary school as constituting to some degree a change in the requirements and specifications for general education in our time. The reference to a willingness to think beyond the local community to the national community in setting goals for elementary education can be viewed as an attempt to think broadly about the nature of general education and an acceptable common learnings base for our time. The comments on a renewed concern for stating educational outcomes more precisely and in more detail can be seen as an effort to identify more surely the behaviors that are the components of this common learnings requirement that society would exact from its members.

RECOMMENDED READINGS

BLOOM, B. S. (editor). *Taxonomy of Educational Objectives: Handbook I: Cognitive Domain.* New York: David McKay Company, Inc., 1956.

EDUCATIONAL POLICIES COMMISSION. *The Purposes of Education in American Democracy.* Washington, D.C.: NEA, 1938.

HANNA, PAUL R. (editor). *Education, An Instrument of National Goals.* New York: McGraw-Hill Book Company, Inc., 1962.

JESSUP, JOHN K., and others. *The National Purpose.* New York: Holt, Rinehart and Winston, Inc., 1960.

KEARNEY, NOLAN C. *Elementary School Objectives.* New York: Russell Sage Foundation, 1953.

KRATHWOHL, DAVID R. (editor). *Taxonomy of Educational Objectives: Handbook II: Affective Domain.* New York: David McKay Company, Inc., 1964.

KRUG, EDWARD A. *Curriculum Planning* (revised edition). New York: Harper & Row, Publishers, Inc., 1957. (See especially Chapters 2 and 3.)

MAGER, R. F. *Preparing Objectives for Programmed Instruction.* Palo Alto, Calif.: Fearon Publishers, Inc., 1961.

SHANE, HAROLD G., and E. T. MC SWAIN. *Evaluation and the Elementary Curriculum* (revised edition). New York: Holt, Rinehart and Winston, Inc., 1958. (See especially Chapter 2.)

Curriculum and Instruction: Focus for Change

5

The determination of effective means for realizing agreed-upon goals is the challenge of curriculum planning; it is the challenge of instruction. A great deal has happened in the recent past and is happening now that is concerned with both of these matters. Here an attempt will be made to describe generally some of the changing aspects of curriculum building and of instructing.

A NEW SUBJECT-CENTEREDNESS

The elementary school curriculum is undergoing what will be called here a "new" subject-centeredness. The focus of current curriculum improvement projects is, in the main, on separate subjects; to some extent it is on groups of subjects, seen as broad fields. There is little in these current reform efforts that bears a strong resemblance to either the activity curriculum of the late 1920's and early 1930's, or the core curriculum of the late 1930's and early 1940's—both of which were reform movements in their own time.

Still, the spirit of this current movement is not to be described as an attempt to get back to something "good" in relation to curriculum and instruction which had escaped the schools in the aftermath of the earlier attempts at reform, though some people may see it that way. There is a great preoccupation at this time with the questions of "what knowledge is of the most worth?" and "how should it be arranged for instruction by the teacher and learning by the pupil?" There is always the risk that preoccupation with these questions could blind curriculum planners to some of the important realities of childhood, and of the relationship between school and society. But this need not necessarily be the case at all. Some observers of the current scene have suggested that the elementary school may be entering on an era of a new sort of "progressivism" in curriculum planning and in instruction. Others see in current happenings the abandonment of child-centered, society-centered, and subject-centered curriculum thinking, in which any one of these was typically pitted against the other two. They would suggest that we may have finally realized the limitations imposed upon curriculum planning by invoking this either-or sort of thinking and are now ready to plan the whole within the demands of the three parts.

It is too early to know just what the outcomes of all of this activity will be. It is true, however, that current curriculum impovement projects are focused on the school subjects; the point of departure for reform has been the school subjects. The crucial demand placed on the new elementary school educator is to develop an understanding of what this new subject-centeredness is all about, how it differs from former subject-centeredness in the curriculum, and where it would seem to carry the elementary school program in the future. But let us take a closer look at this development for what it is and what it may become.

SCHOOL SUBJECTS AND THE DISCIPLINES: STRUCTURE

At the close of the 1950's it was clear to most curriculum planners that the idea of "coverage" as a useful concept in relation to any of the subjects included in the school program was obsolete. In its place references were made increasingly to "selection" and to "sampling." Decisions would have to be made as to what, out of the extensive content of any given discipline, would be dealt with in the school curriculum. But the criteria for selecting content were not readily evident.

It was into this situation that the proceedings of the Woods Hole Curriculum Conference of 1959 were introduced. In a thought-provoking report of the conference, Jerome Bruner enunciated the position that the "curriculum of a subject should be determined by the most fundamental understanding that can be achieved of the underlying principles that give structure to that subject."[1] It was his feeling that adherence to this principle was responsible for the early successes of new curricula in mathematics and the sciences, and educators were urged to think in terms of the "structure" of the disciplines for the purposes of curriculum planning. This idea caught the imagination of curriculum planners; it has in fact become one of the key ideas in almost all of the curriculum

---

[1] Jerome Bruner, *The Process of Education* (Cambridge, Mass.: Harvard University Press, 1960), p. 31.

improvement projects that have been undertaken. It was an approach to dealing with the unlimited amount of subject matter that was being accumulated and the delimitations which the school inevitably must impose on the encounters which pupils will have with it.

In 1963 the Project on Instruction reported on discussions in a Disciplines Seminar it had sponsored in 1961. Three ideas came through forcefully in all presentations:

1. Much of what is being taught in the curriculum is woefully out of date.
2. The mere substituting of new content for old is not the answer to updating the curriculum.
3. Basic to each discipline are methods of inquiry and structures or systems by means of which the field is organized for discovery, accumulation, and communication of knowledge. Learning these methods and structures is necessary to understanding the field in any general or specialized way.[2]

May we call attention again to what Schwab had to say about the importance of the structures of the disciplines to education:

> . . . they [the disciplines] pose problems with which we in education must deal. The structures of the modern disciplines are complex and diverse . . . The diversity of modern structures means that we must look, not for a simple theory of learning leading to a one best learning-teaching structure for our schools, but for a complex theory leading to a number of different structures, each appropriate or "best" for a given discipline or group of disciplines.
> . . . they are necessary to teachers and educators; they must be taken into account as we plan curriculum and prepare our teaching materials; otherwise, our plans are likely to miscarry and our materials, to misteach.
> . . . they are necessary in some part and degree *within* the curriculum, as elements of what we teach. Otherwise, there will be failure of learning or gross mislearning by our students.[3]

In that same year Foshay, a well-known curriculum specialist, noted that "every academic school subject that we try to teach was originally based upon some discipline. . . . A school subject is a translation of a discipline into a pattern for learning." He went on to write at length as follows:

> . . . how good is the translation? Is the subject of mathematics as we conceive of it in school true to the discipline of mathematics as a

---

[2] NEA Project on Instruction, *Planning and Organizing for Teaching* (Washington, D.C.: NEA, 1963), pp. 16–17.

[3] Joseph Schwab, "The Concept of the Structure of a Discipline," *Educational Record*, Vol. 43 (July 1962), p. 197.

mathematician sees it? . . . In a good many cases our attempts to translate the discipline into viable subject matter that can be learned in school are mistranslation, in the sense that the learning method that we have developed has taken the place of the discipline. We have become subject-centered in fact; the subject is no longer relevant to the discipline. Our objection to the artificial and largely arbitrary nature of much school subject matter is derived from the fact that it is arbitrary, superficial material. It fails properly to represent the discipline out of which it came.

Listen to a series of charges. We have taught prosody in the name of poetry, thus killing an interest in poetry for ourselves and our descendants. We have taught grammar in the name of composition, destroying the possibility of a widespread ability to write good essays or even good expository prose. We have taught computation in the name of mathematics, and now we commonly say to one another, "The trouble is, the youngsters can do it, but they don't understand it." When we have taught phonics in the name of reading, we have produced in the early grades word-callers, not readers. We have taught place geography in the name of geography, almost killing this subject in the schools. No geographer says that this is what geography is. We have taught dates and battles in the name of history; I would say instead of history. An historian does not describe his discipline thus. Only in school do you get preoccupied with these matters—never again. We have taught facts and principles in the name of science; but science is a mode of inquiry, and the scientists now say what we are doing is not only out of date, but is not science.

The Physical Science Study Committee conceived a way of thinking of science that stems directly from the discipline, and that does not correspond to our tradition of subject matter in the schools. They have destroyed our subject matter; they could not modify it. They could not go gradually from where we are, for example, in physics in the secondary schools, to where they thought we ought to go. They had to destroy what we were doing and reconceive it from the bottom up.

Such reconceptions of the disciplines we mean to teach are the most important thing that is going on in education, because they are so fundamental. Such revision is very likely to go all the way through the subjects we teach.[4]

These selected quotations illustrate the seriousness with which scholars and curriculum planners have taken the concept of the structure of knowledge as a viable approach to program development. Much energy has gone and continues to go into efforts to identify these structures, i.e., those key concepts and the generalizations derived of these concepts which give power and meaning and identity to a particular discipline. Thus, the curriculum planner identifies such concepts as party

---

[4] Arthur Foshay, "Education and the Nature of the Discipline," in Walter B. Waetjen (editor), *New Dimensions of Learning* (Washington, D.C.: Association for Supervision and Curriculum Development, NEA, 1962), pp. 5–6.

and power in political science, energy and force in physics, scarcity and demand in economics, homeostasis and adaptation in biology, and social class and social mobility in sociology as he searches out the structure of any given field.

Some planners have worked at the matter of developing conceptual maps, as it were, of a given field of knowledge, identifying those concepts that have the most explanatory power for the field and calling attention to the relationships that exist among the concepts that account for the generalized ideas that are a part of the discipline. A "map" developed by Senesh in the field of economics illustrates this very well. It shows the concepts that Senesh feels combine to give economics, as a discipline, its character and its usefulness. And it points up, as one's understanding develops and permits him to move back and forth through the conceptual map, the dynamics that come into play in the phenomena under study.

This is, then, one aspect of the new subject-centeredness referred to earlier, namely trying to utilize the conceptual structure of the several fields of knowledge with which the school curriculum must deal as a way of economizing on learning for the pupil while at the same time adding power to that which is learned.

SCHOOL SUBJECTS AND THE DISCIPLINES: MODES OF INQUIRY

A second dimension to the structure of a field of knowledge is also of concern to current curriculum improvement projects. This is the method-ological dimension—the modes of inquiry used by scholars to extend and verify knowledge in the area. These modes of inquiry are as much a part of any given discipline as the dependable information which they have been able to yield over the years. Pupils need opportunities not only to become aware of and understand the conceptual dimension of a field of knowledge; they must also be made aware of and, as far as possible, skillful with the methodological dimension of the field. Awareness of the inquiry system in a discipline also adds to the meaning of the idea of the "expansion of knowledge" for the pupil. Such insight helps him to grasp the way in which new information as it becomes available strengthens already available information, or forces a reorganization of it, or displaces it. Thus, the fund of knowledge in any field is seen as a changing, not a static, phenomenon. The idea that each field tends to "renew" itself every five to fifteen years takes on added meaning.

Recognition of the inquiry dimension, and acceptance of the need to include experiences with inquiry procedures as a part of the curriculum, has brought attention to inquiry itself, to its scope and complexity. Illus-tratively, consider the following "groups of inquiries" as presented in a

THE FUNDAMENTAL IDEA RELATIONSHIPS OF ECONOMIC KNOWLEDGE

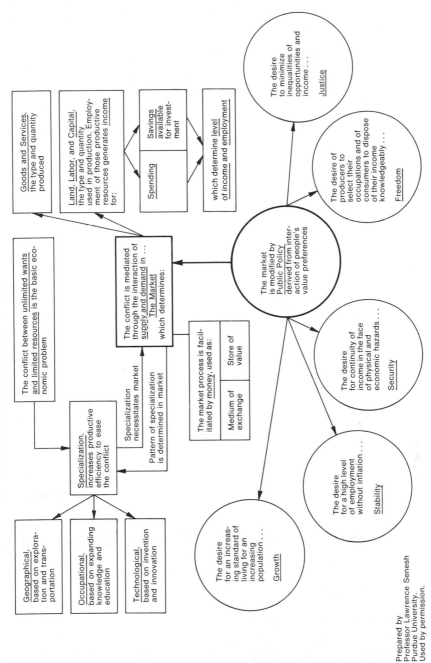

Prepared by
Professor Lawrence Senesh
Purdue University.
Used by permission.

paper by Schwab.[5] He first defines inquiry as ". . . a discipline's move-ment from a starting point and by a pathway to an appropriate end." Then he goes on to say:

The starting point, pathway and end are not always and every-where the same, however. They are radically different in the humani-ties as against the sciences, for example. Indeed, they cannot readily be described as separable into a mere three or four classes, but a rough grouping is helpful and I shall risk sloganeering by listing five of the radically different groups of inquiries which can take place.

(1) There is inquiry characteristic of the sciences. This is inquiry whose aim is to *understand* and whose dual starting points are a natural subject matter and a conception of it. A scientific inquiry, therefore, is a process which moves from a particular subject matter and a particular conception of it to an understanding of the subject matter. The process differs as the subject matter differs and as the conception of it differs.

(2) There is a second chunk of inquiries which belong to disci-plines which I shall call axiomatics. This group can be illustrated simply and properly and in ordinary language by saying: Mathematics is not a science; it has no subject matter; numbers have no existence; shapes have no existence; algebraic equations do not inhere in any matter—they are not discovered in that way. Rather, mathematics is the outcome of a process of exploiting a set of conceptions by means of an agreed-upon set of rules. Mathematics and many economic systems are of this sort—they are axiomatics, not sciences.

(3) Third, there is humane analysis. The inquiry of the humani-ties has as its outcome not understanding, as in the case of science, but *appreciation*, which means not mere liking, but grasping and adding to. In this kind of inquiry, the starting points are all the elements of which art objects are composed; in lyric poetry they are imagery, music, the sound of words and letters and even the look of them upon a page; in the case of the short story or drama or novel, the starting points are diction, characters, action and plot. The outcome is an appreciation of the artfulness with which these multitudes of elements fit one another.

There are two patterns of inquiry radically different from all of these, because the three groups just mentioned are in some sense inquiries *to* a principle (beginning with scattered parts, they end up in a formulation . . . a whole poem . . . a whole short story . . . a whole theory or some usable fraction of it. The other patterns are inquiries *from* a principle, and there are two of them:

(4) Call one of them *engineering*—this is the wide range of *application of principles*. To take just one example from this vast inquiry group, we know that bodies fall at a constant acceleration; what would be the terminal velocity of a particular falling body at a particular point? Finding the answer involves inquiry which identifies and applies various engineering principles.

[5] Joseph Schwab, "Teaching and Learning as Inquiry and the Contributions of Television," in Wilma McBride (editor), *Inquiry: Implications for Television* (Wash-ington, D.C.: NEA, 1966), pp. 19–20.

(5) The fifth pattern—the inquiry most vastly ignored by the schools—is the group called *prudence*. (Webster: cautious practical wisdom; good judgment; discretion.) This is an indispensable kind of inquiry for applying a *moral* principle or a value to a particular situation.

Reflection on this sort of analysis underscores the varied demands on planning which follow from a commitment to embrace as curriculum content the modes of inquiry of the subject matters included in the program of the elementary school. This becomes a necessary part of the development of the curriculum plan if we are to take seriously the matter of children as inquirers. It becomes crucial to any point of view which argues for the child to have the opportunity to be a scientist or a geographer or a historian as he undertakes his study of any of these fields of knowledge.

The goal envisioned is to equip the child with a kind of intellectual power, via a learned structure and inquiry process for each of the subjects, which enables him to comprehend better now, and which will enable him to exercise some appreciable control over his own subsequent learning in the future. The pupil is to be seen and treated as both a consumer and a producer of knowledge.

A SPIRAL CURRICULUM

One conception of the dynamics of such a curriculum plan over time in the school is referred to as the spiral curriculum. The general idea conveyed is that concepts and generalizations and processes of inquiry which are decided upon as being of central importance to a given field of knowledge would need to be dealt with again and again in new contexts from year to year. Each such turn of the spiral would give an opportunity for further depth of understanding and refinement of those knowledge and process elements which had been selected as constituting the structure of a given field.

Such a spiral-like perception recognizes the unwisdom of expecting children at very early ages to form "finished" concepts, for at these ages experience is meager. The spiral plan provides time for concepts to take on real meaning for the child. In fact, the energies of the school must be devoted to some extent to keeping open the matter of concept development and generalization building for the child so that he does not become satisfied with misconceptions that he does not recognize as such. In much the same way planners recognize that inquiry skills will improve over time, and they too are "revisited" and extended from year to year as they are used in new settings and for new purposes.

This spiral approach to the curriculum design will be evident in some of the project descriptions in Part Two that have to do with particular curriculum areas.

STRUCTURE, INQUIRY, AND CHILDREN

There is the question, of course, as to the feasibility of children accomplishing what this reformulated curriculum would have them do. At this point many curriculum improvement projects find it appropriate to include an experimental and research-oriented dimension to their work. A number of project planners have a less ambitious goal than that of developing an overall curriculum plan for a field. Instead they are investigating the feasibility of accomplishing particular kinds of learning in a field with a selected age group of pupils.

A reference was made earlier to a belief on the part of some learning psychologists that elementary school educators, under the influence of the concept of readiness, may tend to underestimate the ability of children to learn. Bruner hypothesized as follows: ". . . any subject can be taught effectively in some intellectually honest form to any child at any stage of development."[6] He went on to refer to the work of Piaget and other psychologists who have studied the intellectual development of children. He noted that research suggests that "at each stage of development the child has a characteristic way of viewing the world and explaining it to himself. The task of teaching a subject to a child at any particular age is one of representing the structure of that subject in terms of the child's way of viewing things."[7] Bruner's idea has spurred researchers to action. Since about 1960 a wide range of "feasibility" studies have been undertaken with elementary school age children as a sort of test of statements on readiness like the one quoted above. Studies have been undertaken in mathematics and in selected areas of the natural sciences where the attempt has been to try to teach to young children aspects of those subjects that were usually not attempted until the post-elementary school years. Some of these studies center on concept development per se, as in physics or astronomy.[8] Other efforts have centered on inquiry training.[9] Much remains to be done before there is sufficient evidence at hand to guide decision-making about a good deal of this development. But successes have been sufficient to encourage further efforts along these lines of research and experimentation and to hold final conclusions in abeyance accordingly.

---

[6] Bruner, *The Process of Education,* p. 33.

[7] Bruner, p. 33.

[8] Robert Karplus (Director), Science Curriculum Improvement Study (K–6) Dept. of Physics, University of California, Berkeley, Calif.; Myron Atkinson, Elementary School Science Project (5–8), University of Illinois, Urbana, Ill.

[9] J. Richard Suchman, "Inquiry Training in Science," *Science Teacher,* Vol. 27, No. 7 (November 1960), pp. 42–47.

Some elementary school educators are skeptical about this line of endeavor. They believe that evidence that something can be taught at a much earlier age than has normally been assumed does not constitute sufficient grounds for deciding that it will be taught then. They raise the complex and value-laden question as to what children should be learning as children, and they are not ready to say that a sort of "advanced" content in the subjects of the curriculum is necessarily the most acceptable answer. They are influenced in their position by the developmental task sort of analysis cited in the preceding chapter, and seek a balanced educational experience in the school that reflects an acceptance of some such broad task-oriented point of view. Others are hesitant, as was noted earlier, lest such heightened expectancies in the curriculum bring children under undue and unhealthy pressures for achievement that may harm them more than help them.[10]

Again it must be stressed that the final answer, to the extent that there ever is one, to all of this belongs to the future. Attention is directed in Part 2 of this book to what is going on in each of the several areas of the curriculum as new ideas are formulated and tested. The generally developmental character of much of this work is revealed in these descriptions. More has been done in some areas than in others. The investigators have unanswered questions which they keep before them in their work. From the investigations which are under way can come new conceptualizations of what education might be like, and badly needed additions to what is a rather meager research-based literature on most of these matters.

HOW MANY SUBJECTS?

There is another sense in which many elementary school curriculum specialists express concern over the current activity in curriculum planning projects. Almost all of the projects that are under way are focused on particular subject matter fields. To a great extent these are subject areas that have long been a part of the elementary school program. In some instances the projects are focused on a discipline that has not commonly been included in the elementary school curriculum. The concern expressed has to do with the entirety of the curriculum. If ultimately each discipline that might be included in the program actually pressed for inclusion there would simply not be time in the day or week to get the job done. There would be so many parts that there would not be a distinguishable and viable whole, and time for any one would be so limited as to be self-destroying for the disciplines and self-defeating for

---

[10] Ronald C. Doll and Robert S. Fleming, *Children Under Pressure* (Columbus, Ohio: Charles E. Merrill Books, Inc., 1966).

the pupil. Any great increase in the number of content areas that are to be included in the curriculum is just not feasible.

Thus, there is a need to think about ways of building relationships between and across curriculum areas. A persistent issue in curriculum planning is the design of daily and weekly learning schedules for pupils. Some planners take the position that any subject matter area that is to be included in the curriculum must have a time and place of its own so that its integrity as an area will be preserved and learned by the pupil. Other planners argue for a more holistic treatment in the curriculum of at least the major divisions of knowledge such as the natural sciences or the social sciences, especially at the level of initial elementary school experiences. People of this persuasion would expect the separate disciplines to be studied as unique and special fields later in the secondary school. Both of these points of view are clearly evident in the history of curriculum planning for the elementary school, and in fact much of the reform efforts of an earlier time placed this issue of the separateness, fusion, or integration of subject matter at the very center of their work.

The experimental projects dealing with structures of knowledge give support to thinking in terms of separate subject fields. But many of the participants in these projects are aware of the necessity of trying to relate one area to another, and they are aware of the gains that might well accrue to any two areas that can be related operationally. Some reference has been made to this matter as being of great importance for consideration in a sort of "second round" of reform effort in those subject areas that are farthest along in revising curriculum plans for their disciplines. For instance, curriculum leaders in mathematics and in science show some signs of being ready to talk in these terms in the not-too-distant future. There is some evidence of an almost prediscipline kind of thinking in the work of some curriculum project staffs. The stuff of the environment would be treated first in a rather undifferentiated way, with the various subjects which we have developed for categorizing it for ease of description, understanding, and further study being made known to pupils over a period of several years. This arrangement is most often put forth as a way of working in the primary school years, with the broad divisions of knowledge into the areas of the humanities, the natural sciences, and the social sciences being used and learned in the intermediate years of the elementary school. This system would then lead to programming in the secondary school years that would deal with certain of the specific disciplines in each of these broad areas as distinct fields of knowledge.

Again, there is much to be done before one or more possible solutions emerge to this problem. Perhaps it is understandable that in the initial years of intensive curriculum improvement work there would be a tendency for any given subject matter area to be a focus of study in and of itself. Especially might this be expected in an area that was seen by its supporters as being neglected by the school. Yet the whole-part dilemma needs to be recognized and dealt with.

SCHOLARS AS CURRICULUM PLANNERS

The leadership for curriculum change in the subject matter areas of the elementary school program has come to be vested, in the main, in scholars identified with a given discipline. From the turn of the century until about 1955, scholars had participated very little in precollegiate curriculum development, and almost not at all at the level of the elementary school. Educators had been increasingly responsible for this task since the early 1900's, in part because they believed that they could do the job effectively, and in part because it was difficult to capture the attention of scholars for work on the school curriculum, especially the elementary school curriculum. But, starting in the middle 1950's, mathematicians, biologists, chemists, economists, political scientists, linguists, musicians, and other experts became involved in curriculum improvement projects in relation to their particular disciplines. These experts usually work with learning psychologists and with outstanding classroom teachers on a team basis to design new curriculum programs. Such teams have worked mainly in the summers, while schools have been closed, to develop and write curriculum plans and to design instructional episodes and sequences that have seemed to show promise of accomplishing the learnings envisioned in the new plan. These summer products have then been tested in schools and classrooms across the country during the school year, with the results being fed back into the next summer's work of revising and extending the plan, and so on in the cycle. Perhaps another way to describe what has happened would be to suggest that a new kind of scholar-educator has emerged on the scene, one whose first identification and competence is with the discipline he represents, and who chooses to work at some of the knotty problems of curriculum improvement at the elementary school level. This procedure has meant and continues to mean that these interested scholars have a considerable amount to learn about children, and about the general capabilities and potential of the elementary school. But they give evidence of being determined to learn, and of being ready to find ways of engaging in a cooperative effort with others for the improvement of elementary school programs.

A NEW LOCUS FOR MAJOR CURRICULUM WORK

Another significant result of activities of the recent past has been to shift a great deal of the major effort in curriculum development to new locations. The work is increasingly done by project staffs housed on college or university campuses and in newly created nonprofit organizations designed specifically to carry out such developmental work. A good example of the former is the location of the headquarters staff of the School Mathematics Study Group first at Yale University and later at Stanford University. Illustrative of the latter is the organization known as Educational Services Incorporated, located at Watertown, Massachusetts, and operated as a nonprofit organization working on a variety of projects that focus on curriculum development and the improvement of instruction.

These procedures are a fundamental change in the way in which and the place where this sort of educational work is carried out. Since about 1920 the commitment to local curriculum development has characterized the schools' mode of operation to an ever-increasing degree. Such a commitment rested on several assumptions:

1. Curriculum work done at the local level would insure the highest validity for the product in terms of local educational needs and possibilities.
2. The professional competence of the local staff would be increased as a consequence of their being involved in this demanding development task.
3. The final product would be a curriculum understood by and accepted by the local staff, and both conditions were seen as crucial to its successful implementation in the schools.

However, there has been a developing tendency to question whether or not the local school district really had the resources, both human and fiscal, to carry out this task. The emergence of the new concerns over subject matter seen in the terms described earlier here has acted to sharpen this issue. The result has been to take steps to focus funds and scholarly talent into a few projects, under working conditions that make it possible to attract some of the best minds in the country to the task, and wherein proposals can be developed and plans produced for what are commonly referred to as "national" curriculums. These products are national in the sense that they are prepared for utilization in any school system in the country. Usually more than one project group is at work in any given subject matter area of the elementary school curriculum. Not only is this sort of multidevelopmental work seen as a way of encouraging healthy competition between project groups, but it is also seen as a way to provide competing and alternative curriculum plans for the schools who are the users of them, thus offering a choice at that level for use in light of particular and unique local school system conditions.

The curriculums are national in another sense, too. The money that is made available to underwrite the costs of these projects comes in the greatest part from federal sources and under terms of recently passed national legislation. The National Science Foundation has made available millions of dollars in the past decade for curriculum improvement work. The United States Office of Education awards money to underwrite research and development efforts in curriculum and instruction. Fiscally, then, there is a noticeable national dimension to current efforts to improve the curriculum of the elementary school.

Again, how this approach to nationwide planning will finally be accepted remains to be seen. But certainly there are a great number of such national projects under way across the country, with many of them concerned with the elementary school program. And a significant number of elementary schools across the nation are adopting programs, especially in science and mathematics, that have emanated from such project operations. This is a way of working at the task of curriculum development and at the task of instructional planning that will probably be with us for a long time.

TEACHERS AND TEACHING: INSTRUCTION

There are a number of consequences for teachers and teaching that accompany new developments in the elementary school curriculum. One has to do with the subject matter preparation of the classroom teacher. The generally accepted point of view is that elementary school teachers are going to have to have a nearly complete understanding of the structure, both conceptual and methodological, of the fields of knowledge with which they will work in the school. This is called for if they are to grasp the significance of and the rationale behind the curriculum designs they will be asked to accept. And this is called for in the instructional planning they will be expected to do. Thus, the "new mathematics" calls for more mathematical insight and skill on the part of the teacher, the "new science" calls for the same in the sciences, the "new language arts" calls for a grasp of linguistics, and so on.

The classroom teacher will also be called upon for greater understanding in the area of intellectual development and cognitive processes and skills. He will be expected to make this understanding operational in his plans for instruction.

Out of all this has to come a willingness to reexamine teaching and the role of the teacher in the context of what is coming to be accepted as an adequate school curriculum. One consequence of current curriculum developments is to bring to attention again the whole matter of specialization in elementary school teaching. The question is whether or not the effectiveness of the elementary school would be increased if some greater degree of specialism, drawn along either age levels, or types of students, or areas of the curriculum, or particular teaching modes, or a combination of these were accepted for elementary school teaching.

A more advanced instructional technology is emerging, too, for use in the classroom as a supplement to the usual textbook and simple audio-visual devices. The most advanced development is that which combines programmed instruction material with the computer into a computer assisted system. The pupil working with such a system needs little assistance from the teacher, and he is not affected by what other pupils are doing who are working at other stations of the same system at the same time. Such technologies suggest that many of the things which the teacher has had to do in the past may be done through computer assisted systems in the future. The result can be a nearly complete restructuring of the way in which the teacher will spend his time with pupils.

Gagne puts it this way:

> Specialization is doubtless inevitable in the educational system. What is left for the teacher to do? What priority should be given to the following six kinds of decisions, so far as the teacher's job is concerned? To answer this question, one must consider mainly the kinds of teacher functions that are most highly dependent on dynamic interpersonal relationships for their success. At the same time, functions of the teacher should be those that a moderately wise, mature, adult individual can be expected to perform without acquiring an impossibly great amount of specialized professional knowledge. Looked at from this point of view, the decisions for the teacher have something like the following priorities:

> 1. *Motivation*—No set of decisions are more clearly dependent on personal interactions with the student than are those concerned with motivation. The establishment and nurturing of personal goals and values, and the relation of these to more specific motives for achievement, can best be done by a person who occupies a position of authority in the everyday life of the developing individual. Specializing this function in the "guidance specialist" does not appear to be a direction of educational change that is likely to succeed in the long run. Every teacher should be a guidance specialist.

> 2. *Transferability of Knowledge*—To the extent that the teacher on the end of the log is considered to be discussing ideas (rather than instilling them), this is a classic teacher function. To some degree, and in suitable circumstances, other students can serve this function too. But whoever the participants may be, the refinement, qualification, and elaboration of acquired knowledge appears to be a process best conducted by interaction between people. The skillful teacher has learned a variety of techniques for conducting discussions that aid the generalizability of knowledge.

> 3. *Assessment*—The teacher should be the best-equipped person to know what questions to ask the student. Teachers need to take a great deal of the responsibility for this function, and need to learn

the techniques necessary to perform it well. To some degree, testing is necessarily a specialized function, and methods of testing are much in need of further development by specialists.

4. *Conditions for Learning*—Although the teacher should doubtless continue to have some part in determining the conditions of learning, there is a distinct possibility that predesign of these conditions will be found to be the more efficient procedure for many kinds of content. As a specialized function, the choice of learning conditions often requires the professional knowledge of the learning psychologist.

5. *The Structure of Knowledge to be Learned*—Determining learning structures has been a specialized function in which the teacher has played a minor role, for a number of years. (Exceptions occur in some instances of college instruction.) Ideally, it would seem reasonable for the learning structure of knowledge to be determined by people with professional "content" knowledge working together with educational psychologists.

6. *Learning Objectives*—These decisions are also in a sense "specialized" beyond the realm of teacher responsibility. Parents, scholars, community leaders—all have some part to play in the stating of objectives of instruction. But objectives must also be defined in terms of observable human performances, and this activity requires some specialized psychological knowledge.[11]

For elementary school teachers there is always a certain difficulty involved in grasping operationally the meaning of the term "predesigned" as it relates to teaching. The difficulty stems from their experiences as teachers and the conclusions they have drawn from these experiences about the way in which the teacher must always be ready to shift ground, to try it another way, in the give and take of the classroom. The facts of individual differences make further demands on the teacher to use a variety of method-material combinations in order to reach as many as possible of the pupils in the class. Still, there is every indication that certain questions are to be raised concerning "the extemporaneous" in teaching—in an effort to be more certain of the points in teaching at which improvisation is to be expected, encouraged, and seen as essential, and the limits within which it may realistically be expected to operate.

For instance, a curriculum sequence that has stood some kind of logical and/or psychological test of adequacy is likely to be presented as a predetermined set of experiences. The teacher will spend little time in planning with pupils the next most useful and legitimate step in a given unit of experience, but will instead ascertain how well the pupils have learned the material thus far in the predetermined sequence. Then he will

[11] From *The Conditions of Learning*, pp. 264–265, by Robert M. Gagne. Copyright © 1965 by Holt, Rinehart and Winston, Inc. Reprinted by permission of Holt, Rinehart and Winston, Inc.

plan the most effective ways of helping pupils to move into and through the next already-agreed-upon episode in the sequence. This procedure is hard for many elementary educators to embrace. The pedagogical point of view that is most widely accepted makes a great deal of the fact that effective teaching is quite situational—that what one does depends so much on "the terrain" (pupils), and too much predesign will restrict the acts of the teacher. The ultimate results may be that *planning for teaching* will be separated functionally from *engaging in teaching*, that designs for pupil learning will be separated from efforts to sustain pupil involvement in tasks that should yield learning, that systematic ways of getting feedback about the effectiveness of one's teaching (and pupils' learning) will be differentiated from the immediate teacher-to-pupil and pupil-to-teacher responses that are an essential part of keeping a learning encounter going once it has been launched.

Much of the talk about teachers and teaching is speculative at this time, to be sure. But it is clear that the need for more adequate instructional theory is revealed as the current curriculum reform movement runs its course.

CURRICULUM PLANNING AND PUPIL DIFFERENCES

Current curriculum improvement projects are finding that they have to come to grips with the realities of pupil differences. We have already indicated that a major question in much of this work is whether or not children can handle a concept-oriented and process-oriented curriculum. Will it hold their attention? Will they be motivated by it? Will they learn from it? Such questions as these need qualification. For instance, some well-conceived plans lead to certain consequences with bright children and to very different ones with slow-learning children. The challenge lies in deciding how to adjust these newer curricula to these definable sub-populations of pupils. Adaptation can mean many things—a slower pace through the same material to be learned, variations in the instructional media used to make information available to the learner, and so on. The reports to date on most of the newer curriculum plans do show differential results with various segments of the total pupil population. These reports support thinking which suggests that we need to know more about the results of teaching "this concept or skill to these pupils using this method/material for this period of time with these results." There is evidence being accumulated which shows that different types of children may have very different learning styles, and that educators will be more effective in their endeavors as they can be helped to understand these styles.

The Special Instance of Compensatory Education

One does find curriculum adjustment of a kind taking place and referred to as compensatory education. Generally, this adjustment is part of the effort of the school to be more effective with children who come to it from a life experience to date that can be described as "deprived" or "different." These children do not measure up to the expectancies teachers usually hold for language development and general experiential background of entering five- and six-year-old children, and for older children as well. Therefore, curriculum planning is attempted which will try to "compensate" for what amounts to major gaps in experience for children. The school takes responsibility in trying to provide for children that which they need experientially if they are to be successful with the kinds of things they will be asked to do in school. Planning the nature of such a program becomes a unique curriculum planning task. Implementing such a plan makes unique demands on the teacher. Major efforts are under way in most of our very large cities to meet this challenge and to develop effective "compensatory" curricula.

Beginning School at Four

One other significant development in elementary education at the moment is the growing belief that the program should be extended downward to include all children of the four- and five-year-old age groups. At the present time many five-year-olds do have a kindergarten experience, but attendance is not compulsory. Few four-year-olds have an organized school experience. In a recent Educational Policies Commission report entitled "Universal Opportunity for Early Childhood Education" the position is taken that school should begin at age four for all children.[12] The estimate is that presently 5 million of the 8.4 million four- and five-year-olds are not in school. We shall not consider here what such a development would call for in the sense of facilities and teachers. But clearly the logistics of such a move would be staggering. We do call attention to the task of deciding on a useful educational experience for very young children, as this age group becomes a part of the public school population. This task constitutes a real frontier in curriculum work and instruction. Teachers have had only limited experience with young children. And so often in the past early childhood education has been undertaken only secondarily for the child. The vast expansion of nursery schools during World War II came first as a way of releasing mothers to

---

[12] Educational Policies Commission, *Universal Opportunity for Early Childhood Education* (Washington, D.C.: NEA, 1966).

work in war industry and only second as a profitable experience for children. The job that lies ahead is a curriculum planning one which is consistent on the one hand with the nature of early childhood and on the other with the long-term goals of our educational system. At the moment some efforts are being made for particular subgroups of four-year-olds in such programs as Head Start.

Altogether then, curriculum change in the elementary school is renewed concern for the disciplines, and is attention to structure both conceptual and methodological. It finds the scholar at the very center of the effort to change the curriculum; it finds the national government ready to invest money in the developmental and experimental work to be done. It finds the role of the teacher being reexamined and changed as the curriculum changes. It touches virtually every part of elementary school education, and every category of pupil who comes to the school.

RECOMMENDED READINGS

ASSOCIATION FOR SUPERVISION AND CURRICULUM DEVELOPMENT. *New Insights and the Curriculum.* Washington, D.C.: NEA, 1963.

————. *Curriculum Change: Direction and Process.* Washington, D.C.: NEA, 1966.

BECK, ROBERT, WALTER COOK, and NOLAN KEARNEY. *Curriculum in the Modern Elementary School* (second edition). Englewood Cliffs, N.J.: Prentice-Hall, Inc., 1960.

BENJAMIN, HAROLD. *The Sabre-Tooth Curriculum.* New York: McGraw-Hill Book Company, Inc., 1939.

CHASNOFF, ROBERT E. (editor). *Elementary Curriculum, A Book of Readings.* New York: Pitman Publishing Corporation, 1964.

FLEMING, ROBERT (editor). *Curriculum for Today's Boys and Girls.* Columbus, Ohio: Charles E. Merrill Books, Inc., 1963.

GOODLAD, JOHN. *The Changing School Curriculum.* New York: The Fund for the Advancement of Education, 1966.

HAAN, AUBREY. *Elementary School Curriculum, Theory and Research.* Boston: Allyn and Bacon, Inc., 1961.

HASS, GLEN, and KIMBALL WILES. *Readings in Curriculum.* Boston: Allyn and Bacon, Inc., 1965.

HEATH, ROBERT. *New Curricula.* New York: Harper & Row, Publishers, Inc., 1964.

KING, ARTHUR R., and JOHN BROWNELL. *The Curriculum and the Disciplines of Knowledge.* New York: John Wiley & Sons, Inc., 1966.

LEE, MURRAY J., and DORRIS MAY LEE. *The Child and His Curriculum* (third edition). New York: Appleton-Century-Crofts, Inc., 1960.

NEA, CENTER FOR THE STUDY OF INSTRUCTION. *Rational Planning in Curriculum and Instruction.* Washington, D.C.: NEA, 1967.

NEA PROJECT ON INSTRUCTION. *Deciding What to Teach.* Washington, D.C.: NEA, 1963.

RAGAN, WILLIAM B. *Modern Elementary Curriculum* (third edition). New York: Holt, Rinehart and Winston, Inc., 1966.

SAYLOR, J. GALEN, and WILLIAM M. ALEXANDER. *Curriculum Planning for Modern Schools.* New York: Holt, Rinehart and Winston, Inc., 1966.

TABA, HILDA. *Curriculum Development, Theory and Practice.* New York: Harcourt, Brace & World, Inc., 1962.

School Organization: Focus for Change

6

A new surge of interest has developed in manipulating the way in which the elementary school is organized and operated to increase its educational effectiveness with children. Choices made about the curriculum carry consequences for the utilization of teachers, for the grouping of pupils, for the allotment of time, and for the design of the school plant itself. Teachers and pupils as such have to be taken into account in decisions about organizational design as well. For instance, the facts of individual differences among pupils affect the organization of the school quite directly.

In the main, current attention to structural change in the elementary school is focused on the following:

1. More effective ways of dividing children into groups to undergo instruction.
2. More effective ways of utilizing teachers to provide instruction.
3. More effective ways of regulating the progress of children through elementary school year by year.

These are not new foci for concern. Attempts to manipulate school organization arrangements for the more effective realization of educational goals have been frequent and persistent. But along with, and almost as a part of, the curriculum improvement effort has come this renewed interest in such matters. If organizational change continues to move in the direction it is currently going the teacher will find himself working in a considerably altered school setting and one that will make different demands on him and on his skill. Major points of focus for organizational change are pupil grouping and teacher utilization.

THE GRADED ELEMENTARY SCHOOL

The most persistent organizational idea in elementary education for the past one hundred years has been that of the graded elementary school. We speak of elementary schools as being made up of so many grades; we refer to teachers by the grade they teach; we refer to pupils by the grades they are in. This basic system of vertical organization for the elementary school took form in the United States before the middle of the nineteenth century. Meyer writes, "Classifying pupils in accordance with their years and their scholastic accomplishment, and arranging them in grades, each with its own master, had become familiar enough in the cities by the forties."[1] Nearly all elementary schools in the United States now follow this graded scheme to some degree.

Yet it is difficult to defend the graded elementary school in light of the realities of individual differences in children as we have come to understand them. Furthermore, the graded concept places restraints on people's thinking with respect to overall curriculum planning, and with respect to teaching as well. Other concepts, such as those of the ungraded elementary school and the open-ended curriculum, have come to the fore in recent years; their goals are to make possible continuous school progress for children. Before we examine these recent ideas, let us review briefly the most salient characteristics of the graded plan which they challenge.

The Graded School and the Curriculum

The graded school structure calls for the division of subject matter and skill learnings of various instructional areas, such as reading and arithmetic, into blocks of material for allocation to each grade level of the school. Curriculum guides outline the content to be dealt with in a particular year. School textbooks are developed in graded series. A teacher can focus his energy on increasing his power over the material for the grade to which he is assigned.

The Graded School and a View of Children

Proponents of the graded school concept make certain assumptions about children. First, they assume that a child at any given chronological age is, in the main, very much like any other child that same age. Thus, all children in an age group should be ready for and be able to cope

---

[1] Adolphe E. Meyer, *An Educational History of the American People* (New York: McGraw-Hill Book Company, Inc., 1957), p. 126.

equally well with the curriculum material assigned to a given grade. Implicit in the concept is the idea that the school experience will tend to make children more alike. Second, the assumption is made that there is a kind of developmental "evenness" within each child which makes it possible for him to do about the same quality of work in each of the various curriculum areas. Thus, grade groups brought together are approachable for teaching on a whole class basis. When a child does not succeed with the work assigned to the grade the teacher and parents may blame the child for lack of effort and attention. Altogether, the graded school concept tends to overlook much of the reality of differences among children and also within each child.

The Graded School and School Progress

Children enroll in school at about age six and are assigned to the first grade. The expectancy is that they will accomplish in one year whatever has been decided is first grade work. Attainment of the agreed-upon minimum standard for achievement in first grade leads to promotion to the second grade for the next year, and this process continues through six or eight years, depending on the number of grades into which the school is organized. It is assumed, of course, that achievement standards have been set at points that should match the learning ability of almost every child. Some modifications are made for children who consistently exceed these defined levels of achievement. They may be given "extra work" during the year, work that does not encroach upon the material of the next grade level, or they may be "double promoted" at the end of the year so that they can skip the next grade and move along accordingly. On the other hand, it is realized that some children will not reach the minimum acceptable standard for "passing" by the end of the school year. They are to be retained or "failed," and asked to repeat the work of the same grade again next year, on the assumption that the second time over the material will result in learning gains sufficient to win promotion. This possibility of being "held back" is considered to provide a constant source of motivation to spur children to apply themselves diligently to their school work.

CHALLENGES TO THE GRADED SCHOOL

The Challenge of Child Variability

With this description of the rationale for the graded school in mind let us consider some generalizations that Goodlad and Anderson derive from selected elementary school data on the ability and achievement of children. The data they examined gave support to the following:

1. Children entering the first grade differ in mental age by approximately four full years.
2. The achievement range begins to approximate the range in intellectual readiness to learn soon after first-grade children are exposed to reasonably normal school instruction.
3. Individual children's achievement patterns differ markedly from learning area to learning area.
4. The initial spread among pupils in intellectual readiness to learn (as determined by the M.A. factor)[2] grows still greater as children advance through their second year in school.
5. The spread in achievement in the various subject areas also grows greater, closely approximating the spread in mental age.
6. By the time children complete the fourth grade, the range in readiness to learn (as suggested by the M.A.) and in most areas of achievement is approximately the same as the number designating the grade level.[3]

It is this kind of evidence that calls for modifications in the assumptions that underlie the graded school structure. Curriculum planners and teachers simply cannot expect to find in reality what the scheme promises in theory.

The Challenge of Pupil Progress

Attention to the literature on the promotion-nonpromotion aspect of the graded school concept also reveals considerable evidence that contradicts the rationale upon which it is based. The major arguments offered in support of this regulatory idea are:

1. To repeat the work of a given school year will result in greater achievement on the part of the child the second time. Repetition will insure his being ready to cope successfully with the work of the next grade and to meet the expectations of the teacher at that level, and will eliminate the necessity of lowering standards in the next grade to the level of his inability.
2. The child's increased achievement during the repeated year will give him greater feelings of confidence and security, erasing for the

---

[2] M.A. (mental age) is one way of expressing the mental growth of children. By converting scores from intelligence tests to M.A. scores one gets an indication of the level of mental maturity that the child has reached. That is, a ten-year-old may have a mental age of twelve years, a level beyond his chronological age, or one of eight years, a level below his chronological age. M.A. may be divided by C.A. (chronological age) to determine an I.Q. (intelligence quotient) score. The I.Q. indicates rate of mental growth and relative brightness. For a more complete discussion see Arden M. Frandsen, *How Children Learn* (New York: McGraw-Hill Book Company, Inc., 1957), pp. 361–365.

[3] John Goodlad and Robert Anderson, *The Nongraded Elementary School* (New York: Harcourt, Brace & World, Inc., 1959), Chapter 1.

most part the discouragement and frustration that come from his not being able to do the work of the grade.

3. These two factors will combine to the advantage of the child in establishing friendships and close associations with other pupils in the class, contributing in the process to a more positive state of social and emotional adjustment.

A great deal of evidence has been gathered over the years on each of these points, and in almost every instance it throws grave doubts on the arguments stated above.

Nonpromotion and subsequent achievement. The studies that have been made in the area of nonpromotion and school achievement all indicate essentially the same thing, and their conclusions are in direct contradiction to the arguments above. These investigations all point to the following:

1. Children do not learn more by repeating a grade in the elementary school.
2. Children often learn less, that is, they show actual regression, after repeating the work of a given grade level.
3. Promoted low achievers generally do better in school than do their nonpromoted counterparts.[4]

In this same connection, the evidence that has been gathered does not lend support to the argument that the presence of these low achievers in the next higher grade operates to lower, generally, the work standards and the achievement in that grade. In fact, the data suggest, instead, that achievement is generally lower in the upper grades in districts that practice a high rate of nonpromotion and is higher in those districts that have a high rate of promotion.[5] In light of the evidence, then, it is difficult to reach any other general conclusion than that, insofar as achievement is

---

[4] See the following for a more extensive analysis of individual studies: Charles H. Keyes, *Progress through the Grades of City Schools* (New York: Bureau of Publications, Teachers College, Columbia University, 1911); Vivian Klene and Ernest Branson, "Trial Promotion versus Failure," *Educational Research Bulletin,* Los Angeles City Schools (January 1929); Grace Arthur, "A Study of the Achievement of Sixty Grade 1 Repeaters as Compared with That of Nonrepeaters of the Same Mental Age," *Journal of Experimental Education* (December 1936); Carleton M. Saunders, *Promotion or Failure for the Elementary School Pupil?* (New York: Bureau of Publications, Teachers College, Columbia University, 1941); William H. Coffield, "A Longitudinal Study of the Effects of Nonpromotion on Educational Achievement in the Elementary School," unpublished doctoral dissertation, State University of Iowa, 1954); William H. Coffield and Paul Blommers, "Effects of Non-Promotion on Educational Achievement in the Elementary School," *Journal of Educational Psychology,* Vol. 47 (April 1956), pp. 235–250.

[5] Walter W. Cook, *Grouping and Promotion in the Elementary Schools,* Series on Individualization of Instruction, No. 2 (Minneapolis: University of Minnesota Press, 1941).

concerned, the low-achieving child is more likely to do better work in school if he is promoted than if he is retained.

Nonpromotion and the self-concept. The second of the above generalizations suggests that low achievers, when allowed to repeat the work of a given grade, come out of the experience with greater feelings of confidence in themselves, with a more secure feeling generally, and with an improved attitude toward school and learning. Here, again, there is some evidence to throw doubt on this conclusion. One of the best analyses of the studies that have been done in this area is reported by Caswell and Foshay. Contrary to the above generalization, they concluded that the studies found more evidence of emotional depression and discouragement among the nonpromoted. Furthermore, they found that these studies indicated a sense of skepticism on the part of such pupils in their own ability, and a tendency to expect to fail in future school situations. Also, the general attitude toward school of pupils who are not promoted was found to deteriorate, with many of them seeking the first opportunity to withdraw from school permanently.[6]

These findings are consistent with the evidence generally reported by recent researchers in the areas of motivation, level of aspiration, and the self-concept. Failure does not seem to inspire future success in any general way, nor does it seem to help one to develop a realistic sense of one's own potentialities and limitations. Rather, discouragement, an unreal level of aspiration, and a tendency toward aggression are more likely to follow.[7] Thus, though more research evidence is needed on this point, it is difficult to support the idea that nonpromotion results in any general strengthening of character, or that it contributes positively to the mental health of the pupils involved.

Nonpromotion and personal associations. The last of the above generalizations suggested that the nonpromoted pupil, as a result of being retained and thus successful in school, would find himself better able to establish friendships in his new class group, and his social competency would increase. Let us look at some of the evidence that has been made available on this point.

One of the most complete studies on this matter was done by Sandin. Exploring this phenomenon of personal-social adjustment in connection with nonpromoted children compared with promoted ones, he found that:

---

[6] Hollis Caswell and Arthur Foshay, *Education in the Elementary School* (third edition) (New York: American Book Company, 1957), pp. 387–394.

[7] Kurt Lewin and others, "Level of Aspiration," in J. McV. Hunt (editor), *Personality and the Behavior Disorders* (New York: The Ronald Press Company, 1944), Vol. 1, Chapter 10.

1. Children retained more frequently preferred to find their friends among pupils from grades above their own.
2. The majority of retained students did not find ready social approval or acceptance among those regularly promoted.
3. Children retained were rated by other children more often as being unfriendly, cruel, and having a tendency to bully other pupils.
4. Retained children did not really "feel good" toward themselves and found it difficult to "feel good" toward others.[8]

Goodlad, too, has reported a study relevant to this matter. He equated a group of nonpromoted first graders with a group of children who were promoted to the second grade. Studying these children carefully over one school year, he concluded that the nonpromoted children, rejected by many of their peers at the beginning of the year, were even more rejected by the end. The promoted group, however, while starting the year in a sort of "neutral" position in their class, grew consistently in acceptance over the year to a level of normal expectancy. Again in agreement with other studies, he found the nonpromoted group consistently lacking in feelings of adequacy and rating themselves unliked and unwanted by their classmates. The promoted group felt better about themselves generally.[9] In light of these kinds of findings, it is difficult to support the idea of gains in the area of personal associations through the practice of nonpromotion.

The Challenge to Subject Matter Placement

Little discussion is needed here to throw doubts on the allotment of subject matter to various grade levels by following, in a strict sense, the graded school concept. No one would question that in an area such as arithmetic there are kinds of sequences to be dealt with in facing the problem of continuity in the curriculum, or that some arithmetic processes are actually more difficult than others. But, apart from a general framework for making year-by-year "expectancy" decisions, it is not possible to identify "third grade" or "fourth grade" arithmetic. The same is true of other subject matter areas. To say that children should achieve just so much as third, or fourth, or fifth graders is not possible. It is quite apparent that, in any group in any given year, there are many different "acceptable levels of achievement" that depend more on children than on logic.

---

[8] Adolph Sandin, *Social and Emotional Adjustments of Regularly Promoted and Nonpromoted Pupils*, Child Development Monographs No. 32 (New York: Bureau of Publications, Teachers College, Columbia University, 1944).

[9] John I. Goodlad, "Some Effects of Promotion and Nonpromotion on the Social and Personal Adjustment of Children," unpublished doctoral dissertation, University of Chicago, 1949.

It would appear, then, that (1) in the face of the obvious differences between pupils and the variable pattern within a given child, and (2) in light of the lack of evidence to support gains in achievement, renewed self-confidence, or more adequate social relations when children are retained, and (3) in light of the flexibility of standards for achievement that seems to be called for in the elementary school, we must conclude that the burden of proof is on those who would seek to retain the graded school concept in elementary education.

MODIFICATION IN PRACTICE WITHIN
THE GRADED SCHOOL STRUCTURE

The graded school is still the most common organizational arrangement utilized in elementary education. To ask about a child's school progress is to receive an answer in terms of the grade that he is in. To speak with a teacher about his assignment is usually to discuss the grade that he teaches. But there have been important modifications in the meaning of "grade" when defined by current school practices. Classroom groups continue to consist of children of like chronological age. But policies and procedures have been evolved that help to bring school practice into a position more consistent with the realities of children. In fact, these modifications are sufficient in many schools to make the label "graded school" somewhat of a misnomer.

A Less Rigid Assignment of Subject Matter

One evident characteristic of today's elementary school curriculum is a less rigid assignment of subject matter to particular grade levels. Decisions on allocation of material are made with attention to more factors than just the subject matter itself. While certain general expectancies are set down in grade level terms, there is usually an accompanying policy which states that some children will not yet be working "at grade level" while others will already have gone considerably beyond these preselected points of progress. The teacher is expected to be able to work with the curriculum of grades below and grades above the one to which he is assigned. Sequences are preserved for pupils, but the pupils' rate through them is variable.

Multiple-Text Teaching

Many of the textbooks that are made available for use in the elementary school continue to be published in graded series. Each series usually covers all of the grades of the elementary school. Teachers have had to be increasingly flexible about these series. A fourth grade teacher would probably have at least third, fourth, and fifth grade books in use in his classroom in each subject matter area. The use of multiple textbooks is consistent with the recognition of different achievement levels among children, regardless of grade level, and the acceptance of work being done at varying grade levels in the same classroom group. Similarly, and in keeping with the less rigid assignment of particular items of subject matter to specific grade levels, this same teacher might be using science or social studies books from more than one textbook series as well, in an attempt to supplement and extend the coverage in any single one. Multiple textbooks provide a richer opportunity for learning.

Attention to the Formation of Grade Groups

Children of like ages are still typically grouped together for instruction at each grade level. But in the elementary schools that are large enough to have more than one classroom group at a given grade level, a wider range of information than chronological age is used in assigning children to one rather than another group. A number of individual pupil traits ranging over learning ability, actual school achievement, social maturity, friendship patterns, and personal adjustment are taken into account. In part this broader base of information is used in recognition of the fact that educational objectives to be pursued go beyond academic achievement and should be reflected in group placement. This is also an effort to try to insure, through careful assignment, that each child will be in a situation in which he feels personally secure and adequate, the better to be able to attend to the tasks which the school puts before him and to use his ability to the fullest in the accomplishment of them.

Two terms need to be defined. A *heterogeneous* group of children is characterized by differences in age, ability, achievement, interests, and other qualities. A *homogeneous* group of children is characterized by similarity in one or more factors. Beginning in the 1920's efforts were made to solve the problem of pupil differences in the graded school by dividing children of a given grade into groups according to either ability or achieved learning. The intent was to present the teacher with pupils that could be taught more readily as a total class group. Though used in many schools over the years, homogeneous grouping practices have always been controversial.[10]

Some people argue that homogeneity is just not possible to achieve to any degree that would be very helpful to the teacher. They question seriously the general social and philosophic consequences of such divi-

---

[10] Douglas E. Lawson, "An Analysis of Historic and Philosophic Considerations for Homogeneous Grouping," *Educational Administration and Supervision,* Vol. 43 (May 1957), pp. 257–279.

sions among children during early socialization experiences. They argue further that the very fact of differences in a class group enriches and extends the learning experience for all members of the class, and that differences should be deliberately planned for in a group. Teachers are to be helped to develop ways of working within this setting. Over the years the supporters of heterogeneous grouping arrangements have prevailed. Still the idea of homogeneous grouping persists; some schools use it, and study of its effectiveness goes on. A recent report by Borg on this question will no doubt stimulate discussion again.[11] He compared pupils in intermediate grade groups in two school systems in which one practiced random (or heterogeneous) grouping and the other ability (or homogeneous) grouping. He concluded as follows:

1. Superior pupils achieved best in ability grouped classes but developed better study methods in randomly grouped ones. Those in ability grouped classes scored somewhat lower in sociometric status and in self-concept than did their counterparts in random grouped classes, perhaps reflecting a somewhat more generally healthy attitude. The overall treatment effects during the intermediate grades of the elementary school favor the ability grouping treatment slightly for superior pupils.

2. For average pupils there is nothing in terms of achievement upon which to choose between grouping treatments, though those in the random grouped treatment did have better study methods. Average pupils showed more favorable personality characteristics, higher self-concept scores, and fewer pupil problems in the random grouped situation. Only in sociometric status did the ability grouped treatment favor the average pupil. The needs of the average pupil are better met in the heterogeneous classroom group.

3. The achievement gains and study methods of slow pupils were slightly but consistently higher in the random grouped situation. Slow pupils did, however, make tremendous gains in sociometric status, and their attitudes toward school and teacher were more favorable in the ability grouped treatment. Self-concept data and personality information tended to favor the random grouped situation, though much less than for superior or average pupils. The ability grouping system, with the large gains in sociometric status, provides a more favorable environment for the slow pupil than does the random grouping treatment.

The conclusions that Borg drew from the study reflect the complexity of the matter, and point up especially the dilemma one faces in trying to provide for broad personal and social development as well as academic achievement. There has been some indication in recent years that homogeneous grouping practices based on ability and on achievement might

---

[11] Walter R. Borg, "Ability Grouping in the Public Schools: A Field Study," *Journal of Experimental Education,* Vol. 34 (1965), pp. 1–97.

be on the increase in elementary education, perhaps in response to the priority assigned to the cognitive development of pupils.[12] The Borg data remind us how carefully such decisions must be made.

The Use of Multiple Subgroups

For a number of years the necessity and the desirability of working with several smaller subgroups within the larger heterogeneous classroom group has been accepted in practice in the elementary school. Teachers tend to view efforts to work with all of the class at one time as generally undesirable. Participation for each child is too limited, and the teacher's opportunity for individual assessment and assistance is too difficult. Thus, for some subjects a teacher will form two or more learning groups which bring together children at similar achievement levels and/or with similar learning problems. The membership of these groups usually changes with the subject matter involved, because of the realities of differences within as well as among the children.

Subgroups are often used in social studies and in science as a way of differentiating assignments for pupils in light of their ability to perform while still relating their work to a larger classwide learning unit. A subgroup is sometimes formed as a vehicle for learnings that are not readily identified with a school subject but with other nonsubject learning goals. Children may be placed in such a subgroup, for instance, to learn how to join their efforts in the accomplishment of a common task, and to lead and to be led in the process.

Thus, the concept of multiple-group teaching as a procedure takes its place beside multiple-text teaching as a procedure for helping to remove some of the obstacles to learning inherent in the graded school structure.

More Enlightened Promotion Policies

There have been significant modifications in policy relating to the regulation of children's progress through the elementary school. The kind of evidence cited earlier in this chapter has weakened the generalizations that were once used so widely to justify promotion and retention. The concept of similar minimum grade standards for all pupils is gradually being replaced by a point of view that recognizes the individual nature of acceptable work levels for children. The unevenness of development within any one child and the irregularity of individual children's growth curves over the years of childhood have given support to this idea. Also,

---

[12] NEA Project on Instruction, *The Principals Look at the Schools, A Study of Selected Instructional Practices* (Washington, D.C.: NEA, 1962), p. 15.

the fact that the elementary school program is responsible for contributing to growth in areas in addition to intellectual development has made its impact on promotion-retention decisions. Such decisions are now much more likely to be made in light of all the needs of children and not just those in a single area of development.

The general result of these combined factors has been a greatly reduced incidence of retention in the elementary school. A careful assessment will, at times, indicate that a child should be retained because of a pattern of general immaturity, questionable achievement, and so on. Similarly, there will be some children who should be accelerated in some way in their placement in school. What is sought is a policy that will facilitate a concept of continuous progress for the child over a broad front of educational tasks. It should be noted that what is described here is not an endorsement for "automatic" or "social" promotion. It is for deliberated and considered promotion in the fullest sense of the term. What is desired is a reasoned decision about the year-by-year placement of children in school.

TOWARD A NONGRADED ELEMENTARY SCHOOL

At the present time there is a great deal of interest in and much writing about attempts to organize and operate nongraded elementary schools. It is argued that such an organizational scheme would serve better both children and society in helping to insure the accomplishment of educational objectives set for the elementary school. A nongraded school would find terms such as grade level, promotion, retention, or third grade work irrelevant and useless. Instead the design would provide for the continuous progress of children. In 1965 some 25 percent of all elementary schools reported some use of nongraded arrangements; this is up from 10 to 12 percent reported in 1960.[13]

Where people are committed to nongradedness they appear to be guided by propositions such as the following:

1. Skill and content learnings are made available to pupils on the basis of more than just year in school.
2. The acceptability of achievement or performance levels of pupils is measured against more than just year in school.
3. It is expected and accepted that an uneven and changing rate of progress will be reflected in the learning curves of pupils, and school arrangements are to be flexible and responsive to variability.

---

[13] NEA Research Division, *Nongraded Schools,* Research Memo 1965-12 (Washington, D.C.: NEA, May 1965). NEA Project on Instruction, *The Principals Look at the Schools,* p. 40.

4. Pupils are brought together into instructional groups on the basis of the likelihood that each will find it an advantageous setting in which to learn.
5. The control of pupils' progress through the school rests on efforts to sustain motivation and insure success in learning.

Intraclass Nongradedness

The modifications in the modern elementary school's approach to gradedness discussed earlier are in the direction of these propositions. When many of today's elementary schools are measured against the older and more narrowly conceived set of "graded" ideas they are more nongraded than graded even now. Perhaps the organization of these elementary schools at the present time can best be described by reference to an *intraclass* approach to the concept of nongradedness. Teachers try to differentiate the work assigned to pupils and the expectations held for them. The usual policy followed is to "start with each where he is and take him as far as possible" over the course of the school year. Certainly this is a kind of nongraded operation. At the same time it is a limited approach to the concept and it can be more completely realized if the elementary school goes beyond this intraclass nongraded arrangement.

Multiclass Nongradedness

The desire to realize even more the ideas embodied in the notion of continuous progress for pupils has motivated many schools and teachers to want to try to move beyond this intraclass approach to grouping to a multiclass approach as well and thus to a more complete nongraded school. The multiclass approach opens numerous new possibilities for consideration. It leads to interage groupings and to an adoption of flexibility in pupil assignment far beyond that usually contemplated. It also leads toward the definition of subdivisions within the elementary school that include several successive years rather than the usual single "grade" unit. Many elementary schools have organized nongraded primary units for which goals are stated for achievement by the end of the primary unit, and not year by year through it. Further, and in recognition of the differences among children, such plans usually include arrangements through which some pupils may complete the expectancies set for the primary unit in less time than the usual three years, while other pupils may need more time.

Year-by-year promotion or retention decisions give way to attention to the best class-group placement for a particular child at a particular time. Movement from one group to another may take place at the beginning of the school year or at any time when such a shift is seen as being in the best interests of the child. At the present time almost all of these so-called nongraded units terminate at the close of the primary years and a kind of promotion decision does have to be made that moves children out of the primary unit and on into the fourth grade. Usually in such schools the organizational base at that point returns to the intraclass approach to nongrading that was mentioned earlier, and pupils move along through "grades" four, five, and six. Thus, we find a mixed model of nongradedness readily identifiable in today's elementary school. A recent survey showed that about 80 percent of those elementary schools using nongrading were using it at the primary level only; another 10 percent were using the arrangements in the intermediate years as well.[14]

Curricular Nongradedness

It must be remembered, of course, that organizational nongrading is different from curricular nongrading. The curriculum must really be conceived in nongraded terms first, and organizational arrangements used in a school must be conceived in light of and in response to the curriculum plan itself. From the point of view of the curriculum there have been very clear limits on the nongrading that has been accomplished. In the main curricular nongradedness thus far has been restricted to the reading program. In reading, nongrading has come to mean the description of nine or more reading levels which pupils are to move through in the primary years at a pace which fits each pupil best. The assumption is that all pupils would have accomplished all defined levels before leaving the primary unit. At the end of each school year a record is made of the reading level that has been attained by a given child at that time and this record determines his starting point in the reading curriculum in the next school year. In some instances this same sort of "levels" breakdown is followed in mathematics and in selected aspects of the language arts program other than reading. Although this arrangement does reflect a certain kind of nongraded thinking, it may lead to a truncated rather than a continuous progress experience for the child. Levels expectancies can become much like grade expectancies.

Not many elementary schools have been successful in extending the nongraded concept into the social studies or science curriculum areas. The "levels" approach does not lend itself to such areas, and no one has yet decided just what a nongraded conceptualization in social studies or science would be. In the interim most schools expect the teacher to try to individualize instruction and thus nongrade the experience throughout the class in these areas within some unit-of-work setting. In some schools the interage groups that have been formed as basic classroom units for

---

[14] NEA Research Division, *Nongraded Schools*.

reading stay together as such for their work in these other curriculum areas. In others there is a tendency to regroup along single age lines for work in social studies or science, so that a "mixed" curriculum model combines with a "mixed" organizational one.

Because of the difficulty in developing nongraded curriculum sequences in the social studies and science, there is a danger that some schools may allow organizational arrangements to unduly determine what the school will be like, and curriculum plans will be subordinated to some already agreed-upon way of organizing for work. This would seem to be unfortunate; function would be determined by form, rather than the reverse. What is called for is continued attention to the way in which the total curriculum can be conceived for pupils so that they can make continuous and individualized progress through it. The demands which each curriculum area would put on organizational arrangements in the school would be faced as a next step.

To date the research evidence on the consequences of nongrading on pupil achievement is divided.[15] Some of the studies show a slight advantage in achievement for pupils in nongraded classes; others show an advantage for pupils in graded classes. Some studies show no significant differences at all. The evidence is about equally divided, too, on the extent to which teachers are attracted to nongradedness as a work setting. More research is called for on this matter. Researchers must take care that they make comparisons between truly graded and nongraded arrangements. We suspect that often what is actually being compared is one kind of nongrading (perhaps intraclass) with another (perhaps interclass) and that this fact contributes to the ambiguity of the findings.

As the nongraded school becomes a more general reality, the work of the teacher is affected. He must be a more competent diagnostician. He must understand the complete curriculum sequence in any given subject area; there is no second grade or third grade curriculum as such. He

---

[15] Studies that found nongradedness superior: R. H. Hart, "The Non-Graded Primary School and Arithmetic," *Arithmetic Teacher,* Vol. IX (March 1962), pp. 130–133; V. Ingram, "Flint Evaluates Its Primary Cycle," *Elementary School Journal,* Vol. LXI (November 1960), pp. 76–80; M. K. Siapski, "Ungraded Primary Reading Program: An Objective Evaluation," *Elementary School Journal,* Vol. LXI (October 1960), pp. 41–45; W. W. Hillson and others, "A Controlled Experiment Evaluating the Effects of a Non-Graded Organization on Pupil Achievement," *Journal of Educational Research,* Vol. 57 (July–August 1964), pp. 548–550.

Studies that found gradedness superior or not significantly different: R. F. Carbone, "A Comparison of Graded and Non-Graded Elementary Schools," *Elementary School Journal,* Vol. LXII (November 1961), pp. 82–88; K. D. Hopkins and others, "An Empirical Comparison of Pupil Achievement and Other Variables in Graded and Ungraded Classes," *American Educational Research Journal,* Vol. 2, No. 4 (November 1965), pp. 207–215; R. Kierstead, "A Comparison and Evaluation of Two Methods of Organization for the Teaching of Reading," *Journal of Educational Research,* Vol. 56 (February 1963), pp. 317–321.

must understand early childhood or middle childhood as age ranges rather than concentrating on any single age level. Perhaps the most fundamental way in which the work of the teacher is affected has to do with the fact that fewer teachers work alone in a nongraded school. Instead there is an almost inevitable sharing of information concerning any given child between two or more teachers. And it is almost inevitable that a child will be taught by more than one teacher. A special look needs to be taken at this aspect of the "new" in school organization for the effect it has on both the teacher and the pupil.

ASSIGNING AND UTILIZING TEACHERS

In the final analysis any curriculum plan is as effective as the teacher whose job it is to bring it to life in the classroom. The way in which elementary schools are staffed, then, has a great deal to do with the general effectiveness of the educational program. Over the years, elementary schools have been staffed in various ways. In the main, changes have centered on the question of whether one teacher or several specialists should be responsible for all of the learning experiences of a given group of children. The latter arrangement is referred to as *departmentalization,* and in it each teacher teaches only one or two subjects in which he is a specialist. The other scheme is most often referred to as the *self-contained classroom;* most elementary schools are staffed in this way at the present time. Interestingly, the development of the self-contained, or one-teacher-per-group, arrangement paralleled the growth of the graded elementary school. As the graded school concept spread after 1850 so did the single-teacher-per-class plan.[16] About 1900 some elementary school systems began to departmentalize the work of the upper grades again, and from that time until the 1930's there was a tendency for the practice of departmentalization to spread throughout the elementary school, sometimes even to the earliest grade levels.[17] Around 1930, however, the shift began to move in the other direction again. Increased insight into child growth and development, curriculum theories that placed great emphasis on the child, a different conception of the role of organized subject matter, and the development of learning schemes, such as the unit of work, that envisioned a much different use of time available in school, all combined to cast grave doubts on the wisdom of departmentalized arrangements in the elementary school years. Otto reported that by 1948 about a third of those districts still departmentalized said that it was definitely on the way out. Certainly the dominant pattern for

---

[16] Henry J. Otto, *Elementary School Organization and Administration* (third edition) (New York: Appleton-Century-Crofts, Inc., 1954), p. 25.
[17] Otto, p. 26.

staffing the elementary school in the 1940's and 1950's was the self-contained classroom.

At the present time this arrangement is again being reexamined for its effectiveness in the elementary school. For a number of reasons there are many elementary educators who question the wisdom and the feasibility of retaining the self-contained classroom as the setting in which teachers should work. Not the least of these reasons is the curriculum improvement movement itself. Many teachers believe that it is most unrealistic to expect any single teacher to be learned and skilled in all areas of the school curriculum, especially as these areas increase their scope. Many efforts are under way to test models of teacher utilization that have some sort of division of labor in teaching. As a prelude to examining these alternative plans let us consider in some greater detail the self-contained classroom concept which they challenge.

The Self-Contained Classroom Concept

The rationale behind the self-contained classroom is based on the one hand on evidence concerning the growth and development of children, and on the other, on preferred pedagogical schemes for using time and for arranging learning experiences in the classroom.

First and foremost in the minds of the early proponents of a return to the self-contained unit was to find a classroom staffing arrangement that would be more in agreement with developing insights concerning human growth. The departmentalized setup had tended to emphasize subject matter. What was sought was an arrangement that would emphasize children. It was felt important to begin to teach children first, and subject matter second, rather than vice versa. Here the self-contained classroom concept seems to fit. Teachers could be prepared as specialists who knew how to work with children; their subject matter preparation would be secondary. There was also considerable evidence from child development studies that suggested that children found it difficult to adjust to several different teachers over the course of a day's work. The information indicated that children fared best at school when they felt close to their teacher and when they felt that their teacher really knew and understood them. This evidence helped to establish great support for the self-contained unit.

Also, following the ideas on curriculum that emerged in the early 1920's, the tendency was to endorse and develop ways of organizing learning units in the elementary school that extended over fairly large blocks of time daily and crossed over subject matter lines as appropriate and necessary. Certainly, such approaches to learning did not fit well into the departmentalized arrangement.

There can be little doubt that the self-contained classroom staffing plan has made a significant contribution to improved elementary school education. There can be little doubt, either, that the self-contained classroom will continue to be used in many elementary schools for a long time to come. The undeniable strengths in the arrangement appeal to many.[18] Most educators do not want to go back to the departmentalized elementary school of an earlier time. Nevertheless there are increasing efforts to conceptualize and test other approaches to staffing arrangements. These approaches seek to avoid the classical model of departmentalization. They try, too, to retain some of the recognized strengths of the self-contained way of working. Let us here consider what these new proposals are like.

The Concept of Teaming

The central feature of the plans for teacher utilization that are emerging in a number of school systems is the concept of teaming.[19] In these plans two or more teachers become jointly responsible for the instruction of a proportionately larger group of pupils. Thus their combined talents and skills are brought to bear on the curriculum to be provided. They work together to develop plans for instruction, they determine together the best way in which their individual teaching competences can be used in the realization of their plans, and they jointly evaluate the progress made by the pupils. There is a great deal of communication between teachers in such teaming arrangements as they pool their knowledge of children and their knowledge of curriculum and instruction. In a sense this plan can be viewed as self-containment, but the unit consists of three or four teachers and seventy-five or one hundred children, rather than the more usual one teacher and twenty-five or thirty pupils.

In order that children will not have to make adjustments to several new teachers each year, and in an attempt to increase for teachers the utilization of the knowledge gained about their pupils, many of these teaming plans call for the same teachers to work with the same pupils for two or more years. For instance, a group of four teachers might be assigned to work with a group of one hundred pupils through their primary school years. The only new children in any one year would be the six-year-olds who would come into the group to replace the nine-year-

[18] See Alice Miel, "The Self-Contained Classroom: An Assessment," *Teachers College Record* (February 1958), pp. 282–291.
[19] See Judson R. Shaplin and Henry F. Olds (editors), *Team Teaching* (New York: Harper & Row, Publishers, Inc., 1964) for a series of essays on various aspects of this topic.

olds who would enter the fourth grade. Such an arrangement makes possible a kind of longitudinal experience with the group, and helps to keep the focus of attention on the children as they progress through the school. When this plan is used, the concept of nongraded pupil groups determines the vertical organization, and the concept of teaming for teaching determines the horizontal organization.

Ways of Organizing Teams

Some schools are attracted to a formal hierarchical kind of teaching team. In such an arrangement one teacher is designated as the continuing team leader, with responsibilities to coordinate and facilitate the work of the total team. Other team members may be referred to as master or senior teachers; one member may be an intern from a training institution who is participating in the team as a culmination of his preservice preparation for teaching; and still another member may be a paraprofessional, a teaching aide or a clerical assistant, who is expected to work under the guidance and direction of the other members of the team. In such a hierarchical team plan teaching responsibilities are somewhat differentiated, and teacher pay is differentiated accordingly. The leader is paid more, the neophyte is paid less, and the aide is paid at a nonprofessional rate. In fact, this possibility for career-level differentiation was the reason why many teachers gave early support to team teaching. It seemed to open up a way for a master teacher to stay in the teaching role and still progress toward increased responsibility and higher pay.

Other schools are attempting to operate a teaming approach to teaching within a less formal work structure. Referred to usually as cooperative teaching, the attempt is to allow the leadership role to shift from one teacher to another as a function of the task before the team. Such arrangements still often make a place for the intern and for the paraprofessional, but the teachers are all perceived as equals. Pay differentiation comes about only as a matter of seniority on the salary schedule.

Reasons for Teaming

Teachers support teaming for several reasons. To some teachers, the plan represents the acceptance of individual differences in teachers and the necessity to differentiate responsibilities in teaching accordingly. To other teachers it represents a way of realizing the career-levels concept in teaching. Still others see teaming and the use of "lead" teachers as the only viable way to insure that the new curricula that are developing will in fact be understood well enough and executed efficiently enough to be accepted by teachers and made worth while for pupils. A great many teachers see in the collegial relationship which such a teaming organization brings about a real hope for a continuing inservice stimulation for teachers. The belief is that teachers will be more likely to continue to grow and develop as teachers if they work closely with respected and accepted colleagues on a day-to-day basis. Some teachers value the fact that any particular pupil will have two or more adult teachers with whom he will work. He will have more than one "model" of behavior.[20] The team plan also helps to insure that each child will have at least one teacher with whom he relates easily and well, who may in turn be able to assist other team members in their approach to the child. One other advantage relates to the induction of new teachers into the profession. Under the self-contained concept, they are assigned, in the first year of teaching, the full responsibility for an age or grade group. Teaming makes it possible to limit the responsibility of the neophyte, and to induct him into the full responsibilities of teaching much more systematically.

In our judgment the concept of teaming for elementary school teaching will be utilized by many elementary schools for all of the reasons listed above. Similar ideas have been advanced before; consider for a moment these propositions set forth in 1929 by Hosic:[21]

1. A teacher can usually best assist in carrying out the purposes of an elementary school by undertaking not the whole but only part of the educational stimulation and guidance of individual pupils and groups of pupils.
2. Each teacher in the elementary school should plan and carry on her work cooperatively as a member of a group of teachers who have the same pupils in charge.
3. Every group of teachers in the cooperative plan of organization should be led by one of their own number, designated chairman, or group leader.
4. Each group leader or chairman should bear a portion of the responsibility for the supervision of the teaching done by the other members of his or her group.
5. Even though five teachers, more or less, share the work of guiding the activities of a group of children, as proposed in the Cooperative Group Plan, nevertheless each of them should bear special responsibility for the welfare of one portion of the group, that is, for a "class."

Dr. Hosic's plan went on to include specially equipped rooms for each teacher in line with his or her specialty, referred to as laboratories. The pupils were to move from place to place accordingly during the school

---

[20] See George D. Spindler, *The Transmission of American Culture,* Third Burton Lecture in Elementary Education, Graduate School of Education, Harvard University, 1959.

[21] James F. Hosic, *The Cooperative Group Plan: Working Principles for the Organization of Elementary Schools* (New York: Bureau of Publications, Teachers College, Columbia University, 1929).

day. As might have been expected, Hosic's ideas were not accepted in practice to any great extent at that time. But the situation seems to be particularly "right" now for such cooperative or teaming arrangements to be tested in the schools.

Research on Teaming

The research evidence to date on the consequences of teaming on both pupils and teachers is meager and divided.[22] Generally speaking, pupils report that they like it, but there is no consistent advantage in achievement that accrues to children taught by teams. Some of the studies favor teaming in their findings; others favor the self-contained arrangement. Teachers report that they enjoy working in a teamed organization. But it must be remembered that these reports are from teachers who stay with teaming and that data from those who transferred out for one or another reason are not readily available. All in all, it would appear that the evidence at this time is favorable enough to teaming to suggest that it will be developed more completely and become a viable and effective work arrangement. The evidence is not complete enough or strong enough to cause schools to abandon the self-contained classroom as a way of working. Children seem to learn about as well under one scheme as under the other. Some teachers prefer to work under one arrangement and some under the other. In the meantime critiques are available concerning teaming, and further studies will be done and reported in the literature to extend our understandings of the potential in the teaming concept.[23]

Teaming for teaching does put some additional demands on each teacher. He must be able to work cooperatively with colleagues in a very close way. He must be a skillful group member; he must be able to plan

---

[22] For more information see Ray F. Blake, "Small Group Research and Cooperative Teaching Problems," *National Elementary Principal*, Vol. 43 (1964), pp. 31–36; Harold S. Davis, *The Effect of Team Teaching on Teachers*, unpublished doctoral thesis, Wayne State University, 1963; Joseph Jackson, "Analysis of a Team Teaching and of a Self-Contained Homeroom Experiment in Grades Five and Six," *Journal of Experimental Education*, Vol. 32 (1964), pp. 317–331; Philip Lambert and others, "A Comparison of Pupil Achievement in Team and Self-Contained Organizations," *Journal of Experimental Education*, Vol. 33 (1965), pp. 217–224; Norwalk Board of Education, *The Norwalk Plan of Team Teaching, Fifth Report 1962–63* (The Board, 1963); Peter B. Shoresman, "A Comparative Study of the Effectiveness of Science Instruction in the Fifth and Sixth Grades under Two Different Patterns of Teacher Utilization and Pupil Deployment," unpublished doctoral thesis, Harvard University, 1963.

[23] Harold Drummond, "Team Teaching: An Assessment," *Educational Leadership*, Vol. 19 (December 1961), pp. 160–165; and Glen Heathers, "Research on Implementing and Evaluating Cooperative Teaching," *National Elementary Principal*, Vol. 44 (January 1965), pp. 27–33.

with others; he must be predisposed to share ideas, facilities, time, and even pupils. He must be secure in teaching in the presence of colleagues and find satisfaction in the reactions of others to his teaching. Coping successfully with some of these demands is a function of personality factors in the individual teacher. Other demands are related to new and additional professional skills that he must develop.

NEW OVERALL SCHOOL REORGANIZATION IDEAS

In addition to organizational matters internal to a given building unit, such as nongradedness and the teaming of teachers, there is the more inclusive matter of school organization at the system level itself. Here, too, we find new ideas emerging for discussion, and a few school systems testing such ideas in practice. We will consider them only briefly here.

One consideration is concerned with the already mentioned growing feeling that the elementary school experience should be extended downward to include children of four and five.

The other focus of thought has to do with whether or not the curriculum of the intermediate years of the elementary school, "grades" four, five, and six, is coming to be such that it calls for a specially organized school. Those who feel that it does are recommending the establishment of a new "middle" school that could be designed to meet the unique demands of curriculum implementation at that level. These new middle schools are usually seen as including what are now referred to as grades five though eight. They combine the last two years of the usual elementary school and the first two years of the usual intermediate school or junior high school.

In schools where this arrangement is being tested, the 4-4-4 plan is usually established: a lower elementary school of four years (grades one through four), a middle school of four years (grades five through eight), and a high school of four years (grades nine through twelve). Foremost among those school systems currently testing the potential in the scheme is New York City.

It is clear that if four- and five-year-olds are added to the compulsory school attendance group our organizational system will change. For instance, the above mentioned 4-4-4 plan would become either a 2-4-4-4 plan, or more likely a 6-4-4 arrangement, with the lower six-year elementary school including the age ranges four through nine.

Without further lengthy discussion of school organizational plans, this chapter has served to point out that the recent focus on curriculum improvement and change calls for new and more creative organizational plans for its realization.

These first six chapters should give you a background for considering the changing nature of the elementary school curriculum in the more specific sense of what it is coming to mean for the various areas of subject matter usually included in the elementary school curriculum. The next few chapters will deal with each of these major divisions of the curriculum in turn.

RECOMMENDED READINGS

ANDERSON, ROBERT H. *Teaching in a World of Change.* New York: Harcourt, Brace & World, Inc., 1966.

ASSOCIATION FOR CHILDHOOD EDUCATION INTERNATIONAL. *Grouping: Problems and Satisfactions.* Reprint Service Bulletin No. 26. Washington, D.C.: The Association, 1954.

ASSOCIATION FOR SUPERVISION AND CURRICULUM DEVELOPMENT. *A Look at Continuity in the School Program* (1958 Yearbook). Washington, D.C.: The Association, 1958.

————. *The Self-Contained Classroom.* Washington, D.C.: The Association, 1960.

ELSBREE, WILLARD, HAROLD MC NALLY, and RICHARD WYNN. *Elementary School Administration and Supervision* (third edition). New York: American Book Company, 1967. (See especially Chapters 13, 14, and 15.)

GOODLAD, JOHN, and ROBERT ANDERSON. *The Nongraded Elementary School* (revised edition). New York: Harcourt, Brace & World, Inc., 1963.

NEA PROJECT ON INSTRUCTION, *Planning and Organizing for Teaching.* Washington, D.C.: NEA, 1963.

NATIONAL SOCIETY FOR THE STUDY OF EDUCATION, *Individualizing Instruction* (Sixty-First Yearbook, Part I). Chicago: University of Chicago Press, 1962.

OTTO, HENRY J., and DAVID SANDERS. *Elementary School Organization and Administration* (fourth edition). New York: Appleton-Century-Crofts, Inc., 1964.

PETTY, MARY CLARE. *Intraclass Grouping in the Elementary School.* Austin, Tex.: University of Texas Press, 1953.

STODDARD, GEORGE D. *The Dual Progress Plan.* New York: Harper & Row, Publishers, Inc., 1961.

The Changing Elementary School Curriculum

The elementary school curriculum, conceived as an integrated, holistic plan for the education of children is composed of several distinct and systematic programs of instruction. In the last decade each of these program areas has undergone extensive change in overall design, and in content and methodology. In the following series of chapters each curriculum area is discussed. Particular effort is made to call attention to the nature of changes that have either been made or are being made in each program. The intent is to help the reader to grasp currently accepted practices and to anticipate possible future developments. In order, the chapters deal with language arts, foreign language, mathematics, science, social studies, health and physical education, and the fine arts.

Communication: Receptive Language Arts

7

Through the centuries communication has progressed from dependence on primitive gestures and simple noises to the development of spoken and written languages based upon complex combinations of sound and symbol.[1] Communication involves both expression and reception of ideas or feelings. Communication may evoke feelings of excitement or tranquility, sadness or humor, love or anger. People increase their understanding of themselves and others by communicating. They transmit their own feelings and ideas; they are receiving the same kind of information from others.

WHAT IS LANGUAGE?

Today the written word, changing with social and technological influences, takes various forms from poetry to novels, editorials to news reporting, comic strips to political cartoons, advertisements, pictures, and graphs. The spoken word comes to us in speeches, debates, sales talks, sermons, and conversations. The invention of the printing press and movable type in 1456 facilitated the spread of the written word. The invention of the telephone, the radio, and television have made possible almost instantaneous transmission of spoken words throughout the world.

Verbal language is not our only means of communication, for man also expresses ideas and feelings effectively though music, dance, drama,

---

[1] For further historical information on language and communication, see Joyce O. Hertzler, *A Sociology of Language* (New York: Random House, 1965), Chapters 1, 2, and 3; Mario Pei, *Language for Everybody* (New York: The Devin-Adair Company, 1957), Chapter 3; Mario Pei, *Voices of Man: The Meaning and Function of Language* (New York: Harper & Row, Publishers, Inc., 1962), Problems I and II.

and the graphic arts. And who among us misses the message of a fire siren, a traffic signal, school bells, the dollar sign, skull and crossbones, or an A on a composition?

Need for Communication

Communication is a vital need of man. The ability to express oneself in the spoken and written forms so that others may understand is almost as essential to modern life as sleeping and eating. It is the basis for thinking, for sharing, for creativity, and for survival.

Communication has patterned and held social groups together: world groups that speak similar languages are closely identified; teen-agers, seeking social identity, develop their own "language"; families, regional groups, and occupational groups may be identified by their particular means of communication. A group develops its language through words, phrases, and gestures that reflect common experiences, common thinking, and common purposes.

We transmit and preserve our way of life, our culture, through language, which makes possible the recording of experiences and ideas of men of the past. As our world has become smaller, the cultures of other peoples have become apparent and immediate through modern means of communication. Language barriers in themselves probably present the most complex of problems, because real communication involves being able to understand the fundamental thoughts, values, beliefs, and ideas of others.

Communication and Literacy

Although literacy is important, it is not by itself enough to meet the demands of communication for modern living. The arts of communication are more than verbal skills. Daily one sees pictures, cartoons, and illustrated charts that must be *interpreted*. Listening to radio and television requires skill in *discrimination*. Meeting and understanding people with differing life patterns demands *insight and knowledge*. In the past, *literacy* meant simply a minimal ability to read and write. The man of one hundred years ago was considered literate if he could read a little, write his name, and phrase a simple note or letter. Today the literate man must be able to do more. He must know something of the historical background of present-day life, something of human relationships, something of the mechanical processes of the tools he uses constantly, something of scientific facts. Without this knowledge, he cannot understand the information presented in newspapers, television programs, or the conversation of the teen-aged boy who lives next door. The literate man of today must distinguish among various values, grasp the total idea of an argument, evaluate the constant avalanche of propaganda. Thayer summarizes by saying, "In short, literacy involves a minimum degree of facility in finding one's way around in a world where communication through plural media is a condition of intelligent living."[2]

Not only must teachers understand the changing meaning of "arts of communication," they must constantly modify the curriculum so that these arts can be taught.

New Insights into Language

Language is under constant study, and through the diverse approaches of current scientific research we are gaining new insights into language as language. Cultural anthropologists are studying language as a mode of culture and with the sociologists are discovering the nature and function of language in the behavior of groups. Philosophers are clarifying the logic of language symbols. Psychologists are exploring the relation of thought to language and the means by which an infant learns language. Descriptive linguists, who make scientific analyses of the structure of our language, have accumulated much material now being utilized by educators.

Today we recognize language as a tool allowing man to accumulate and communicate experiences and concepts. This tool is a set of habitual rather than logical symbolic sounds and their written equivalents that have developed from the oral root. Sound determines the written symbols, and in some languages the written symbol is not yet utilized. Meaning is determined by usage; thus meaning and pronunciation may have individual as well as regional differences.

Linguistics. Educational literature has included considerable attention in recent years to the study of linguistics and its implications for teaching language to children.

Linguistics is the scientific study of language and speech. Our discussion will be limited to its applications in English. It seeks to discover and describe the objective structure of our language, its basic sound, words and sentence forms, and changes in function and meaning according to arrangement patterns. Linguistic vocabulary is specialized and complex.

Linguists search for the systematic, hierarchal organization of language by placing the parts in meaningful relation to the total structure. They identify the units and working processes of English, define prin-

---

[2] V. T. Thayer, *The Role of the School in American Society* (New York: Dodd, Mead & Company, 1960), p. 158.

ciples of operation, and identify the interrelation between these principles. They accept the idea that speech, and written language as the reiteration of speech in symbolic form, is composed of arbitrary symbols that evolve not through logical development but from the experience of the people and from habitual use in a social setting. They expect a constant, normal, and necessary change in language patterns.

Educators have been concerned with most aspects of the English language from the time Latin ceased to be the medium of communication in the schools. It is hardly surprising that many of their insights are in accord with the current perceptions of the scientific linguist, even though the two groups have developed markedly different vocabularies to express their knowledge. A study of linguistics has suggested to educators many subtle ways to improve aspects of the language arts program. It is a contributing factor to the selection of content and to sequential development. The greatest contribution of linguistics to education appears to be in calling educators' attention to important steps in the developmental sequence which have been slighted in the past.

Foreign language. With new insights into the structure and meaning of the English language, much thought has been given to the improvement of instruction in foreign language teaching.

When an individual learns a system of communication that is foreign to his own living situation and language patterns, the learning act is doubly complex. He learns that the sound system, meanings, and structure of the second language are in all ways different from those of his mother tongue and are *used in a different psychological and cultural setting.* Each language has its own structure system.

THE LANGUAGE PROCESSES

Four Related Language Processes

The totality of communication is taught in the modern elementary school through attention to four related language processes: the receptive (incoming) processes of *listening* and *reading,* and the expressive (outgoing) processes of *speaking* and *writing.* Reading is to writing as listening is to speaking. *Listening* and *speaking* are the primary communication processes, and *writing* and *reading* are secondary communication processes.

The interrelatedness of the four processes is illustrated by tracing their development as the young child initially learns language. First the infant *listens.* He listens to the sounds made by others, especially by his mother, who by means of words and arbitrary sounds communicates to him her love, her instructions, her anger. Through listening he begins to understand, and then to imitate, and soon to repeat the most common sounds. Thus listening is basic to oral language.

As the child practices imitating sounds, his speech becomes clear, his sentences lengthen, his vocabulary grows. His *speaking* ability increases steadily, stimulated by the many reasons he finds to communicate.

The child's next big step in the manipulation of language is learning to *read*. The reading program in school—based on oral vocabulary—is begun when children can handle an oral language with some fluency. The child associates abstract symbols with spoken words, and gradually achieves the ability to evoke meaning from printed symbols.

As a beginning is made in the reading process, the young child learns to *write* the same symbols he is learning to read. Skill in writing demands three kinds of learning: understanding the formation of the symbols (penmanship), understanding the formulation of the word (spelling), and understanding the design of the sentence (grammar).

Analysis of this normal development of language for a child reveals a recognized sequential relationship. Listening is preliminary to readiness for speech; fluency in speech becomes readiness for reading; the ability to read precedes readiness for writing. In recognition of this sequential relationship, teachers plan readiness activities. For example, as children read paragraphs within reading texts, they analyze the reasons why the author indented or set off one group of sentences from another group. When the child begins to write, his previous understanding of paragraphing makes his written organization more effective.

The four processes of language are also interrelated because of the nature of the thinking process. Language is important to thought for several reasons: (1) language is necessary to communicate one's thoughts to others; (2) communication is meaningless unless it reflects thinking; (3) the ideas of others stimulate reaction and more careful individual thinking; (4) most thinking is done with words, or the mental action of translating feeling or experience into word-symbols; (5) the ability to translate into words, or language symbols, improves the quality of thought. Because of these relationships between language and thinking, some linguists consider language a conditioner of thought as well as a means of expressing thought.

Each of the four language processes is involved in the whole of the communication act. Shane and others[3] tell us "All four of these components of communication are of equal importance. Each is like the leg of a chair. All four are needed to support a balanced language program."

---

[3] Harold G. Shane, Mary E. Reddin, and Margaret C. Gillespie, *Beginning Language Arts Instruction with Children* (Columbus, Ohio: Charles E. Merrill Books, Inc., 1961), p. 10.

Skill in the four language processes has become increasingly important to the educated person, and the school's language arts program seeks to help the child develop skill in these processes. They are basic to learning, to living with others, and to becoming a self-sufficient productive citizen. Literacy is almost a necessity in a world where an illiterate person has difficulty finding a job and meeting the demands of everyday living.

Receptive Language Arts

The receptive language skills, listening and reading, are intimately related. An analysis of the common processes in which the reader or the listener becomes involved reveals that both require comprehension by the receptor of another's vocabulary and unique grouping of words. Both demand assimilation of facts and ideas in terms of past experiences. Both necessitate interpretation which may involve some critical or creative action as in the following of directions. The ability to listen, to read, to follow the sequence of ideas, and to make inferences depends on one's level of language skill and verbal intelligence. Appropriate mental and experiential maturity and adequate vocabulary are required to develop readiness for and interest in the presented material.

Like reading, listening is used to gain information, to understand differences in situations, to explore issues and ideas, and to be entertained. As compared to personal or concrete experience, listening and reading are vicarious. Listening and reading *must involve response*. In some way there must be acceptance or rejection, action or reaction; that is, there is some thought or feeling about what has been heard or read. Listening and reading have several skills in common. Each demands the ability to follow sequence of ideas or a plot, to discriminate opinion from fact, and to make inferences from expressed ideas.

Listening and reading also differ in some respects. Whereas the reader proceeds at his own rate and may reread or refer to other sections of reading matter, the listener must accommodate his pace to the sounds to which he is listening. The pace in the listening process is that of the person speaking. The listener has little time for repetition or reflection; if he takes time to think his listening often ceases. Also, spoken material very often is not as well organized as written material. Thus listening demands greater alertness and more careful attention than reading.

Expressive Language Arts

Speaking and writing are closely related to listening and reading, for writing is a silent means of talking, and reading is the silent partner of listening.

Speaking and writing are the symbolic means of expression, involving the ability to put ideas together so that others receive the meaning. The purpose is to present material for consumption; the style may be direct and objective, or colorful and emotional. It is up to the expressor to choose his style and to use it effectively, in relation to his purposes and in recognition of his audience. He needs several powers and skills: use of an adequate and appropriate vocabulary, ability to challenge the interest of the audience, and clear and distinct organization of language. The writer or speaker must anticipate his audience; his explanations must be appropriate, his examples meaningful, his arguments persuasive.

The writer operates in a different manner from the speaker. Writing, of course, can be carefully evaluated and reviewed for fluency, meaning, and overall effectiveness before it is ever released. The speaker may write and analyze his written speech, but often, as in a conversation, he must judge his effectiveness as he analyzes the reaction of his listeners while he is speaking.

THE CHANGING LANGUAGE ARTS PROGRAM

Schools have drawn the four processes of language arts together into a practical program. Because of the changing curriculum in our schools, our recent knowledge from research about learning, and cultural changes, especially in modes of communication, the language arts program of today is different from that of years past. A number of changes can be identified:

1. Curriculum in the modern elementary school places emphasis upon reading and language, and its purposes go beyond instruction in grammar. Its stress is upon *meaning*. Language experiences are provided that are closely related to practical problems in meaningful situations from daily life. David H. Russell describes this more meaningful approach when he speaks of reading and writing activities:

> . . . Goals for reading and writing activities mean, of course, an increasing variety of good books in school libraries, classroom and daily activities, and increasing opportunities in writing for many purposes. It means planning in matching a boy and a book. But it means also a shift in group instruction from stress on the narrow mechanics of reading to emphasis on the place of reading materials in the life of the individual. It means the teacher asks questions not like, "What was the color of Bill's dog?" but "Was Bill the kind of boy you would like to have for a friend?" It means not hurrying to finish a story but stopping to savor what it tells us of courage or loyalty or justice or other lovely words of our language which we call values. If our children are to face the 1960's and 70's, they need some grasp of values

for their personal living and for a "lacework of coherence" in our culture. Reading and writing can help give this.[4]

2. No longer is language approached through unrelated rote instruction; modern methods do not dictate and regulate learning by text or teacher prescription alone. Experiences in penmanship, for example, are not confined to copying meaningless phrases. Instruction based on repetition and recall is provided through meaningful experiences that are varied, interesting, and challenging to children, and that stimulate action rather than passivity. Content for language comes not only from basic texts but also from other sources of subject matter as well as from the specific needs or weaknesses of the children. The interrelatedness of experience, content, and skills is recognized. Some skills may be useful for more than one area—skills such as the phonetic abilities that support and supplement both the reading and spelling programs.

3. Drill periods help only to develop and maintain skills, but language is made meaningful in practical situations. Usually drill periods are presented when a group of children have a special problem, or when special attention to one aspect of language will help them use skills more effectively. In everyday usage the clues for needed drills are observed. Continuing group experiences devoted to skills such as reading are part of the daily program.

4. Throughout the school day the arts of language are practiced in relation to other studies. Reading is necessary for research in social studies and science. Writing is used for record keeping, creative efforts, and many other tasks. Without attention to spelling, grammar, and vocabulary, learning activities would be less effective. Practice of skills becomes most realistic when learning experiences are integrated in a curriculum unit, in holiday or seasonal preparations, or in special entertainments or programs. The teacher's concern is that the arts of language are not neglected in any aspect of the curriculum.

5. Large blocks of time in the daily program provide for flexibility in the purpose, kind, and continuity of experiences. The small periods of time that were part of outdated curriculum methods (ten or fifteen minutes in an inflexible schedule) are now grouped together for an hour's work in general aspects of language. During this hour, the children may work in groups on common problems, or they may practice dramatization, creative writing, or other language activities. In the primary grades, the reading hour is usually kept intact for developmental activities, and a language period is scheduled in addition. In the intermediate or upper grades the organized reading program may become a part of an even larger block of time devoted to the total language program.

---

[4] David H. Russell, "The Issue in Instructional Improvement," *California Journal for Instructional Improvement* (October 1958), p. 5.

LISTENING

Listening is preliminary to the development of other language skills. For many years teachers did not question the idea that young children came to school with a developed skill in listening. Today we understand more about the complexities of this skill, and some schools plan careful and sequential listening programs; some seem to ignore listening as an instructional area.

Nature of Listening

Listening is an ability that involves hearing—the auditory sensitivity needed to identify and "pick up" sound; auditory discrimination—the ability to recognize and distinguish various sounds; and auditory comprehension—the intellectual ability to enjoy the sound or understand the meaning of what is heard. Thus, listening is more than simple hearing; it is the conscious personal and mental reception of sound. (Some educators and psychologists prefer using another term for listening: *auding*. One finds this usage in recent literature about mass communication of radio and television. It is a term with which teachers should be familiar since some authorities advocate using it in classrooms. It usually refers to careful, attentive listening.)

The first communication skill developed and used by the very young is listening. The child must listen so that he may imitate the spoken sounds. He listens to learn. He continues to listen throughout his life until, as an adult, he listens more than he reads, speaks, or writes. The use to which he puts his listening and the amount of skill he develops in part determine his ability to learn and to live with others. Indeed, most people of our world today are influenced more by what they hear than by what they read. Russell points out:

> Children live in a world of sound. They are bombarded from morning to night not only with the sounds of the physical environment but with the words of peers and adults who want them to do something, or at least want to be heard. As Gerald Green puts it in *The Last Angry Man,* his novel of the television industry: "The most overwhelming fact of the twentieth century is the assault on the public ear and eye, the incessant, relentless avalanche of useless information."[5]

The child's ability to listen in school is important to learning. Listening to instructions, to the ideas of others, to stories, reports, plays, conversations, and discussions becomes a means of gathering ideas and finding meaning in daily activities. Especially is this so in the primary

---

[5] David H. Russell and Elizabeth F. Russell, *Listening Aids through the Grades* (New York: Bureau of Publications, Teachers College, Columbia University, 1959), p. 1.

grades when listening skills are more highly developed than reading skills.

Listening Skills

It has been assumed until recently that because children have so much practice in listening, specific training is unnecessary. Also an emphasis on learning to read is a natural one since society places great importance upon the reading skill, for which the child usually has no ability when he enters school. We cannot assume that children need to be taught only to read, however, and do not need to be taught to listen.

Recently language authorities stress the listening aspects of the total communication program. A continuous program to develop the skills of listening, to practice many kinds of listening, and to evaluate systematically contributes to the development of effective listening habits and attitudes.

Listening and speaking are highly related activities with responsibilities for both listener and speaker. Though the performer makes an attempt to be understood and appreciated, it is not his responsibility alone to make people listen. Good listening demands active participation. Listener reaction is reflected in posture, gesture, facial expression, speech, or other overt behavior. A good listener looks at the speaker, is alert, attentive, and responsive.

Certain mental processes are recognized as part of the listening act: anticipating, or thinking ahead of what the speaker is saying; evaluating, or weighing what is being said; reconsidering or reviewing the ideas expressed; and searching within the listener's mind for meaning beyond the ideas being expressed.

Good listening habits must be consciously practiced to be developed. Difficult listening situations should not be avoided; real attention rather than simulation of an attentive attitude is necessary; outside distractions can usually be ignored. One learns to look for the good in what is being said, not just the manner in which it is presented. Too often when criticizing physical appearance or delivery of the speaker, immature listeners lose the good ideas he offers. The most effective listening involves grasping the meaning of large ideas and related items, rather than temporarily recalling single unrelated facts; retention is improved when relationships are understood. Too often young people "tune out" something because of premature evaluation. Listeners should give full opportunity for complete presentation before judging the content uninteresting or inapplicable.

Factors Influencing Listening

Children demonstrate many individual differences in the kind and quality of their listening. As teachers continuously evaluate the learning process, they must also be conscious of several factors that influence the listening of individuals in a group of children.

Physical conditions. Physical conditions influencing the manner in which an individual listens may be of two kinds. First, the physical conditions of the listener himself may have much to do with his ability to listen. If he is tired, ill, emotionally upset, hungry, or hard of hearing, his listening is affected. Sometimes a hearing loss may not be readily ascertained, and the teacher may think the child inattentive for some other reason. Second, the physical conditions of the environment may influence individual or group listening. Such conditions include temperature, the quality of air in the room, the comfort of the furniture, and distracting noises within or adjacent to the room. The speaker's voice quality, gestures, poise, type of speech, humor, or dramatics in presentation may be influential factors. If the communication source is other than a speaker, factors such as quality of sound, stage arrangement, and acoustics may affect the quality of listening.

Psychological conditions. Psychologically, a very different group of factors may influence listening. Attitudes, experiences, and personality traits will influence the interpretation of what is heard. For example, the Republican listens to a Democrat with a different mind set from that of a Democrat listening to the same speaker. A flute player listens to an instrumental solo with a feeling different from that of the listener who does not play an instrument. Prejudice or lack of sympathy for the speaker or his cause will, of course, influence the ideas received and the interpretation of the words. Egocentricity, ethnocentrism, bigotry, humanitarianism will "tune out or in" certain aspects of verbal material being presented. Boredom, lack of interest in the subject, and the general attitude toward the speaker will make a difference in what is heard.

Conditions of experience. The experiential background of the listener is another cause of the presence or lack of interest and understanding of what is heard. People who are familiar with jazz will enjoy a jazz band more than will the listener who is familiar only with more conservative music. Meager experience with a topic being discussed influences the interest of the listener. An unhappy past experience might arouse antagonistic attitudes. Limitations of vocabulary influence the amount and kind of ideas assimilated. The teacher must know his pupils if he is to help them listen. He must be familiar with their overall health and particularly with their physical limitations. He must be sensitive to unusual evidence of fatigue or other emotional or physical distress. He should understand something of each child's family background so that he may be cognizant of certain values that produce acceptance, prejudice, or other influencing attitudes in listening. Not only should the teacher be familiar with the experience background of his pupils, but he should make an effort to develop common experiences on which learning to listen can more effectively be based.

Developing Skill in Different Kinds of Listening

The first prerequisite for a good listening program is the teacher's clear understanding of the various kinds of listening and how they may be developed in children. He must be able to bring attention to and explain different listening skills to children in specific situations that will bring meaning to the art of listening. Children need to think about various kinds of listening and evaluate their own. Anderson distinguishes between nine levels of listening.[6]

Different levels of listening are really different degrees of involvement. Some activities to be as satisfying call for much less involvement than others that demand a high degree of dedication. The following situations are examples of listening levels in terms of different purposes.

1. Hearing sounds of words but not reacting to the ideas expressed: a mother knows that Joey is speaking.
2. Intermittent listening—turning the speaker on and off: hearing one idea in a sermon but none of the rest of it.
3. Half listening—following the discussion only well enough to find an opportunity to express your own idea: listening to a conversation to find a place to tell how you handled a child.
4. Listening passively with little observable response: the child knows the teacher is telling them once again how to walk in the hall.
5. Narrow listening in which the main significance or emphasis is lost as the listener selects details which are familiar or agreeable to him: a good Republican listening to candidate from another party.
6. Listening and forming associations with related items from one's own experiences: a first-grade child hears the beginning sound of Sally, says and said, and relating it to the letter s.
7. Listening to a report to get main ideas and supporting details or follow directions: listening to the rules and descriptions of a new spelling game.
8. Listening critically: a listener notices the emotional appeal of words in a radio advertisement.
9. Appreciative and creative listening with genuine mental and emotional response: a child listens to the teacher read *Miracle on Maple Hill* and shares the excitement of sugar making.

---

[6] P. S. Anderson, *Language Skills in Elementary Education* (New York: The Macmillan Company, 1964), p. 82.

Other experts in the field of language arts have developed similar classifications of the kinds of listening. Generally, they identify two categories: *marginal* or *casual* and *attentive* or *concentrated* listening. The casual type is exemplified by the very informal listening of a teen-ager as he studies near the playing radio. He is conscious of the music in the background, but listens attentively only when something is of special interest. Other examples of casual listening are to the music at a tea or in participation in social conversations.

Concentrated listening is of several varieties. There is appreciation or entertainment, in which one listens to a concert, drama, or poem. There is the more demanding kind in which one listens to directions, makes plans, or evaluates work or material. Much of this kind of listening may involve personal reaction so that questions may be asked or suggestions made. There is also the kind of concentrated listening that one does when specific points of view are presented, as in campaign speeches. Problem solving also is related to this kind of listening. One listens and reacts according to certain knowledge or experience. One thinks critically to be able to perceive weaknesses, lack of authenticity, or bias. This kind of listening requires the greatest effort.

In every phase of the child's life, demands are made upon him that involve listening. Such a demand may be the warning blast of an automobile horn on the street. It may be the frightened cry of a younger sibling. It may be the careful directions on how to prepare a booklet or solve an arithmetic problem. It may be the fun of listening to a joke, or the challenge of helping a fellow student solve a difficult situation. Children need help in deciding what amount of attention is needed and what kind of personal reaction is demanded by different situations. The environmental, psychological, and experiential factors determine the kinds of listening needed.

Nichols[7] has identified the ten worst listening habits in America today. Teachers might take a clue from these as they plan their listening program:

1. Calling the subject dull.
2. Criticizing the speaker.
3. Getting overstimulated (becoming so excited that persons miss what is being said).
4. Listening only for facts.
5. Trying to outline everything.
6. Faking attention.
7. Tolerating distraction.

[7] Ralph G. Nichols, *The Supervisor's Notebook,* Vol. 22, No. 1 (Glenview, Ill.: Scott, Foresman and Company, 1960).

8. Choosing only what's easy.
9. Letting emotion-laden words get in the way.
10. Wasting (or misusing) the differential between speech and thought speed.

Creating Environment for Good Listening

Developing skill in listening depends on the way the teacher organizes study habits and sets the physical and psychological environment for listening in all areas of the curriculum.

Teacher's voice and speech. The first consideration is the teacher's voice and speech. He must be sure that he is heard. His voice must reach the children at the back and outer edges of the group, without being too loud. Most effective teachers use a soft, warm voice tone that can be heard by all, but does not have so much volume that the children have to tune out part of it. The teacher's voice should have life, warmth, energy, and enthusiasm.

The teacher's voice is used in a variety of ways. He does not put the children to sleep by using a monotonous drone, but he varies the tone and pitch of his voice as the situation demands. He is sure also that only the child who needs to hear him will hear; if he is speaking to a small study group he talks loud enough for that group only. He is not the one to do most of the talking, but seeks a fair balance of listening and speaking.

Manner in which the teacher gives instructions. A second consideration in setting the listening environment is the manner in which the teacher gives instructions. Frequently the young and inexperienced teacher will give the same directions in the same words and tone two or three times. The children learn quickly that it is not necessary to listen until the third time. The experienced and effective teacher is sure that all youngsters are ready to listen and then gives clear, concise directions only once to a fully listening audience. This kind of "listen once" study habit, developed carefully, will save much time and energy for both teacher and student.

Children's voices and manner of speaking. Another consideration is the children's voices and manner of speaking. Children must also be heard by the group, whether it be the total class or the small reading group. Each child must learn to change the volume or rate of his speaking to suit the situation, and to watch others to see that he is understood, as a matter of courtesy. The listening children must develop the same habit of listening once. Sometimes teachers hinder this development by repeating what each child says to insure that it is heard. Unintentionally the teacher may change the words and the meaning of the child's original idea. Such a risk is entirely unnecessary if the children speak to the whole group, and the group is "tuned in" for listening.

Physical environment. The physical environment is another consideration in the development of good listening habits. A quiet, comfortable classroom with children arranged as closely and compactly as possible is most effective for group listening. Children can converse much more easily within a small area than across a whole classroom, so planning and evaluating sessions should be held in a circle group at the front of the room, away from desks. Quiet discussions should be avoided when other children are playing noisily outside the windows of the classroom. When working with only part of the class, the teacher should arrange small groups so that talking within each group will not disturb the rest of the class.

Providing Listening Experiences

For the most effective listening program, the teacher should provide many kinds of listening experiences. Throughout the day opportunities for listening should be utilized, and children should be helped to sense the specific purposes of each situation. Even background music can be a pleasant and relaxing experience when used judiciously. Children should not be listening to the teacher all day. They must have experiences in which they talk and listen to each other, in which they can learn to react to the ideas and problems of others and solve problems cooperatively. Making comments or asking questions in reaction to what is heard is an important part of the listening activity.

The teacher must also be conscious of the children's readiness for each listening experience. *Readiness* in this use does not mean an abstract attitude related to all listening situations. Rather, listening readiness requires an experience background for each particular situation, the development and clarification of vocabulary necessary to it and guidance in the identification of major ideas. By recalling related understandings or materials, considering new words, and otherwise developing anticipation of the situation, the teacher can prepare the children for the listening experience, usually by speaking only a sentence or two.

READING

The reading program in the modern elementary school is best conceived as a broad program in which everything a school does to promote growth in and through reading is considered an integral part. Reading is taught as a practical, functional skill that extends into every part of the daily program. Reading is not considered a separate subject, for every "subject" demands certain reading skills. The reading program is something more than a specific hour in which the children are grouped for purposes of instruction in reading. There is guidance not only in basic mechanical skills, but also in reading and research in content fields, reading for fuller personal development and recreation, and reading to appreciate good literature. When it is needed, remedial reading instruction is offered. Methods and materials are adjusted to abilities and interests of the individual child. This broad program ties the child's reading to his own experiences, emphasizes reading to supplement experience units and to develop skills of thinking, and gives the child understandings beyond the immediate environment to the outer regions of fact and fiction. Books are sought as teachers and sources of information; they are recognized as forces in shaping attitudes and enriching language and life.

Nature of Reading

Experts do not attempt to explain the reading process in a simple sentence or two, because it is not a simple, single act or skill applicable to any printed material. Reading is a complex of abilities varying in difficulty in different kinds of reading situations. Basically, the act of reading is an individual's interpretation of certain printed symbols and an integration of the meaning within himself. *Reading is more than recognition and pronunciation of words.* It involves the total mental processes through which a person recalls concepts and meanings as a result of the recognition of printed symbols.

Three interpretations of the nature of reading indicate variation among authorities in the meaning of the word. In its broadest sense, *reading* has been defined as the intelligent response to all sensory stimuli. From this point of view it may be said that we read visual, aural, tactile, gustatory, olfactory, thermal, or kinesthetic stimulation. In other words, some sort of meaning is drawn from an experience by "reading" the experience. This definition is recognized as being synonymous with education, with learning, with experiencing.

A second point of view about reading is that which interprets it as the intelligent interpretation of all symbolic representations. This would mean that a person interprets a picture, a graph, a map, as well as the printed symbols of language.

Dictionary definitions of reading emphasize the intelligent interpretation of the printed symbols of language or numbers. This definition, which refers to the process by which one looks at, recognizes, and draws meaning for himself from the printed symbols, is the definition that educators consider the most pertinent.

In describing the complexity of the reading act, Gray identifies four steps, or dimensions, in the total reading process:

1. *Perception,* or the ability of the individual to perceive a word and identify one word from another. This perception involves the understanding of the pronunciation of the word.
2. *Comprehension, or grasp of meaning of the symbol* involving two parts: the literal, or sense meaning that identifies what is there, and the supplementary meanings, or recall gained from the reader's experience and his ability to "read between the lines" and to recognize the thing left unsaid but intended or inferred.
3. Interpretative *reaction,* entailing appreciation of the meaning, and/or a critical reaction to it. The ideas are evaluated in the reader's mind, fundamental assumptions examined and their validity tested.
4. *Integration* or fusion of the identified ideas with all our experience and knowledge. Such integration affects the individual through changed attitudes, different thinking, new insights of experience, changed personality.[8]

These four dimensions of reading demonstrate that what many consider to be a simple skill or act is in reality an involvement of physical and mental processes that may result in some change of the total person.

Approaches to Reading

Language arts and especially reading as a part of the elementary school curriculum have had a number of different emphases as a result of changing social problems in our nation. (See Chapter 3.) Purposes have ranged from the development of religious and patriotic values to the more utilitarian motives of today. The production of new materials and equipment has influenced a greater appreciation of instructional processes. An understanding of individual differences has also influenced change. Educators are well aware that a large portion of our population are poor readers and ineffective listeners and that many speak incorrectly and write illegibly. Much research has been completed; numerous plans, strategies, and programs have been promoted and evaluated in an attempt to improve the quality of literacy in our country.

Existing reading programs can be grouped around two organizational bases. First are those that emphasize a structured, sequential plan dependent upon carefully prepared materials. Among these are the developmental programs using basic textbooks, the programs with lin-

---

[8] William S. Gray, *On Their Own in Reading* (Glenview, Ill.: Scott, Foresman and Company, 1948), pp. 35–37.

guistic emphasis that attempt to follow some of the scholarly analysis of language, and the use of the Initial Teaching Alphabet. Plans utilizing the various types of automated programmed instruction also fall in this category, though many of these stress individual progress. Second are those plans that are based upon more flexible use of materials emphasizing child experience and the unique interests and needs of children. Among these are the language-experience program and individualized instruction.

The approaches discussed on the following pages are an attempt to explain the *basic procedures and philosophy of those educators who have been instrumental in developing them.* Teachers will find that variations of each are in use throughout the country. There are many unique locally developed programs that have not been discussed here. To each approach questions have been raised and both emotional and rational opposition expressed. Commentary on general advantages and disadvantages of these innovations are withheld for a later section. *We must remember that the success of all these programs depends on special materials and specific teaching procedures that cannot be effectively utilized without careful thought and planning.*

Developmental reading program. This program, also known as the basal reader approach, is the most widely used program. In this program, reading is taught to children in carefully planned, sequential lessons that follow a series of readers and the practices recommended in the teachers' manuals and other supplementary materials. The basal readers are characterized by careful and systematically controlled vocabulary. Further content development progresses on a meaning-frequency principle and planned sequential introduction of new reading skills. The program is called "developmental" because ". . . the child makes continuous progress in learning to read by a natural transition from one level to the next. What is learned at any one level becomes a foundation for what is to follow immediately after."[9]

The several levels of progress in reading can be distinctly identified. *Reading readiness* is widely accepted as the first level of development in reading. The readiness period is an actual stage of growth and preparation for the complex task of interpreting printed symbols, and includes all the reading development that precedes actual reading from a book. Readiness for reading involves within a child a combination of certain stages of physical, emotional, social, and mental maturity with certain understandings, skills, purposes, attitudes, and information.

An adequate reading readiness program involves two major developments: First, the development of a wholesome classroom atmosphere and

---

[9] Miles A. Tinker and Constance M. McCullough. *Teaching Elementary Reading* (New York: Appleton-Century-Crofts, Inc., 1962), p. 17.

a secure and friendly rapport between teacher and children. In developing the psychological atmosphere of his class, the teacher does some purposeful thinking, much planning, and constant evaluation of his actions and the type of activities he provides for children. Second is the development of certain skills, mostly physical and mental, that are necessary foundations for reading. These may include (1) seeing well and focusing exactly; (2) hearing distinctly; (3) relating certain sounds to symbols or understandings; (4) speaking correctly and accurately, enunciating clearly, and using language easily to share experiences, to discuss activities, to tell stories, and to plan or to evaluate; (5) playing well in groups, adjusting to the work activity of the whole group, sharing materials, living naturally and confidently with others and demonstrating emotional security in relationships with others; (6) having a good understanding and use of concepts and word meanings and the ability to organize and classify ideas; (7) having an adequate background of experience.

The *primary reading* program can be separated into two levels. The initial level is one developing positive reading interests and attitudes, curiosity, and the desire to read. The emphasis is on "reading for meaning," which requires adequate experience background. Materials contain a predominance of simple pictures so that meaning is extended and children can enjoy the stories in spite of limited sight vocabulary. Gradually the picture material is decreased to rely more on the verbal content for meaning. The goal is the achievement of absorbed attention to the content and ease in interpretation of the printed symbol.

The second level of the primary period is characterized by rapid progress in the children's power to understand and deal effectively with printed words. Reading has more varied purposes, and skill in reading as a thought-inducing process is becoming more effective. The child reads more frequently on his own; a rich variety of fairly simple materials are made available to intrigue him and answer questions for him. At this stage the materials are still related to things and events within the immediate environment or experience of the child. Speed in silent reading develops beyond that of oral reading. The word recognition program is strengthened so that independence is increased and reading experiences may be extended. The teacher diagnoses continuously the strengths and weaknesses of each individual in this critical stage of development and reinforcement of the reading skills. The aim is to avoid failure and to correct bad reading habits.

By the end of the third grade a child should have an active interest in reading and in procuring ideas through reading. He reads a variety of materials, uses a book easily, attains fluency in oral reading and interest in silent reading, and has the ability to work out for himself some of the unfamiliar words he encounters.

In the intermediate years, or grades four, five, and six, the child enters a reading level of *increased power and efficiency.* The materials carry him beyond the immediate environment to events and activities outside his own personal experience. The vocabulary and language of the material may be beyond the reader's own oral usage, but not beyond his level of comprehension.

Because of the different ideas, the unfamiliar words, and the many uses for reading, the child must learn a number of related skills. During these years the child learns to use the dictionary, the encyclopedia, and other reference books in the library. Use of more elaborate tables of contents and very detailed indexes is necessary to the research to be carried on. Ability to understand and use the library card catalog becomes necessary. Ability to find specific parts in a book, to skim materials, and to take notes is developed. Phonetic skills are supplemented as children learn to use diacritical markings, to understand more complex rules of word construction, and to relate them to spelling.

In using reference materials, children need to understand that their thinking is also shifting. Pupils are no longer dealing with familiar things and thinking reproductively. Now that they are reading about unfamiliar things the resultant thinking must be creative, imaginative. This is the time that reading beyond and between the lines becomes most important to the interpretation of the material. One must be able to use all he knows, all of his experience, to throw light on the meaning.

Reading in the content fields is currently receiving more attention because specific instruction is necessary to help children transfer from basic reading materials to those of other curriculum areas. One cannot assume a high degree of carry-over. The trend seems to be in the direction of less direct reading instruction for intermediate grades and more instruction that facilitates reading in subject matter content.

Probably the most important basic concept for children to develop is that reading materials vary not only in content and vocabulary, but in structure and complexity; that different materials require different kinds of reading. To reinforce this concept the teacher who helps children read effectively in such content fields as science, mathematics, and social studies provides experiential background that facilitates interpretation and technical vocabulary development. He helps children to read so that they may understand relationships of time and place, and to organize materials and the information gained from those materials. He facilitates the effective use of a wide variety of current periodicals, references, and other sources of information. He provides the techniques and symbols needed for reading maps, graphs, charts, time schedules, catalogs, and similar material. He helps children to differentiate between critical reading, skimming, and surveying, and to recognize when these kinds of reading are appropriate.

Gates identifies seven basic techniques involved in various combinations for different kinds of reading:

1. *Word analysis:* working out the recognition and pronunciation of words.
2. *Deriving word meanings:* deriving meanings of words in context, and sometimes in isolation, combined with the ability to recognize cases of uncertain meaning, and the habit of stopping and looking in a dictionary, or otherwise finding the meaning when necessary.
3. *Range of speed:* ability to read at speeds ranging from slow rates of one hundred words per minute to very rapid skimming.
4. *Accuracy and fullness of comprehension:* learning to read with different degrees of thoroughness, accuracy, or fullness of comprehension.
5. *Rereading and recalling:* the skill of recalling or trying to remember while reading; making the distinction between reading and rereading, on one hand, and reading and recalling or adopting a policy that one rereads when necessary and recalls when possible, on the other.
6. *Thinking while reading:* distinguishing between reading or recall of the substance as it actually appears—mere reproduction—and the kind of reading in which appraisal, evaluation, selection, judgment, or comparison of the ideas takes place during the process. To think while reading, to evaluate, to judge what is important or unimportant, what is relevant or irrelevant, and what is in harmony with an idea read in another book is a technique that is somewhat difficult to acquire.
7. *Strategy for tackling an assignment:* the development of strategies of attack on assignments as a whole. For example, the ideal method of attack in history would depend somewhat on the length of the assignment. The best procedure for studying a highly compact, short chapter might be different from the best strategy for reading several chapters in each of several books for comparative purposes. In both these cases, the ideal attack would be different from that to adopt if one were reading theorems in geometry, definitions in grammar, compactly stated technical propositions in physics, or directions for operating a complicated machine. Still another approach might be taken if one were to survey several books for the purpose of picking up the information bearing on a particular topic. . . . Too often pupils have no variety in their approach.[10]

The developmental reading program, as presented in basal readers, is improved over the years through research. Publishers constantly work on revisions which incorporate new insights. Most of the readers include more interesting and realistic stories, humor, and pathos. Some have

---

[10] Arthur I. Gates, "Reading Abilities Involved in the Content Subjects," in V. D. Anderson and others, *Readings in the Language Arts* (New York: The Macmillan Company, 1964), pp. 352–359.

inserted interracial and interreligious pictures and stories. Teachers' manuals and tests are constantly being improved. Novels prepared for specific reading levels have been introduced, and skills in reading of fiction are consciously taught. Filmstrips, motion pictures, reading lists, charts, and other materials have been developed to be used along with the basal readers themselves.

Linguistic readers. The development of linguistically based materials for the elementary school was first tried by Leonard Bloomfield, a structural linguist who questioned the teaching of reading with a meaning emphasis. His plan was to substitute first an alphabetical code which, he said would naturally result in meaning. He felt children should first understand the letters, then learn to use the words as a whole. Charles Fries, another linguist, expounded the same approach, and identified three stages in reading: (1) the transfer from the oral to the graphic symbol, (2) productive reading for meaning, (3) vivid imaginative utilization.[11]

The influence of linguistics on reading materials and methods has been felt only recently, since reading authorities have become seriously aware of its contribution and have found ways to interrelate teaching of form and structure with meaning and content. Currently, some beginning reading materials with a linguistics approach tend to control sentence structure, utilizing sentence forms that are natural and similar to those used orally by children. Proponents of these materials claim that from literal reading children learn to read critically and creatively, and differentiation is made between thinking skills and reading comprehension.

The Stratameyer and Smith series focuses on sounding and blending, or the teaching of reading vocabulary with stress on sounding out letters and blending them into words. Lefevre texts focus on the whole-sentence approach, in which the whole sentence, as a unit of thought, is used as a basis for reading exercises. The series by Bill Martin, Jr., pays almost no attention to phonetic patterns but gives strong emphasis to the listening-speaking-writing sequence and its interrelations. In addition, it stresses the subtle meanings conveyed by variations in sentence syntax. Both Bloomfield and Fries have published materials that are all text and no pictures. The Stratameyer and Smith series includes pictures and uses animals as principle characters.

We see, then, that the study of linguistics suggests many ways to vary and perhaps improve instruction in reading. To date, each series that has labeled itself as linguistic has stressed a few methods while ignoring other equally promising suggestions. It will take many years to analyze the long-term effectiveness of these materials. It may even be that

---

[11] Charles C. Fries, *Linguistics and Reading* (New York: Holt, Rinehart and Winston, Inc., 1963).

the greatest contributions from linguistic studies have not yet been incorporated in any of the present reading series. As the total linguistic contributions are better understood, the apparent dichotomy between basal readers and so-called linguistic readers will diminish. The basal readers will correct linguistic oversights while the current linguistic readers will expand their viewpoints to incorporate a more rounded and balanced linguistic view.

The initial teaching alphabet. Another approach to the teaching of reading and related language skills is a special instance of attempts to use a linguistic approach to beginning reading. It comes to us from England where some educators have devised a new, synthetic alphabet to substitute for the traditional Roman alphabet. At first called the *Augmented Roman Alphabet,* it is now referred to as the *Initial Teaching Alphabet* (i/t/a or i.t.a.) and is used to replace traditional orthography (T.O.). I/t/a is claimed to be a phonemically consistent alphabet.

Invented by Sir James Pitman, grandson of the Isaac Pitman who devised a shorthand system, the i/t/a contains 44 characters, or 20 more than our normal alphabet. Each character is intended to represent only one phoneme, and looks very similar to our usual lower-case printing. The system does not completely change conventional teaching methods, it merely substitutes the new alphabet. The beginning reader uses the i/t/a until he reaches the stage of development in which he has achieved skill and confidence in interpreting the meaning of the printed word. Then he transfers to materials using the conventional alphabet. The i/t/a is designed to present a simple, consistent printed code for the English language. The table below shows the characters of the special beginning reading alphabet and their phonemic values:[12]

æ	b	c	d	ꬲ		y	z	ʒ	wh	ꬶh
face	bed	cat	dog	key		yes	zebra	daisy	when	chair

f	g	h	ie	j	k		th	ŧh	ſh	3	ŋ
feet	leg	hat	fly	jug	key		three	the	shop	television	ring

l	m	n	œ	p	ꝛ		a	au	a	e	i	o
letter	man	nest	over	pen	girl		father	ball	cap	egg	milk	box

r	s	t	ue	v	w		u	ꞷ	ꞷ	ou	oi
red	spoon	tree	use	voice	window		up	book	spoon	out	oil

---

[12] By permission of Initial Teaching Alphabet Publications, Inc., New York.

The following is a passage using i/t/a symbols.[13]

"cum on, ¢hip, ſhe carnival haſ
cum tω toun," sed pɛet.
"œ, bɒi!" sed ¢hip. "ɪe wont tω ried
on ſhe merry-gœ-round."
¢hip and pɛet ran doun ſhe strɛet.
ſhæ ran tω ſhe middl ov ſhe toun.
ſhær woſ ſhe carnival,
and ſhær wer aull ſhe riedſ.

Proponents of the i/t/a system point out several ways that the alphabet simplifies the reading of English.

1. In the traditional presentation of the written word, using handwriting, manuscript, and upper and lower case printing, several shapes and sizes of letters are used. The i/t/a uses only one shape and changes only the size to denote capital letters. Thus the configuration of words is kept constant so that sight vocabulary develops more speedily. Preparation for transfer is accomplished because 90 percent of our printing is in lower case.

T.O.	i/t/a
dog	dog
dog	dog
DOG	dog
Dog	dog
Dog	dog

2. The i/t/a uses a separate symbol for each sound. Five different vowel sounds represented by only one symbol in our traditional alphabet have five different symbols in i/t/a, allowing the child to sound out many unknown words.

---

[13] From *Early to Read i/t/a Program*, Book 3, by Harold J. Tanyzer and Albert J. Mazurkiewicz. Copyright © 1963 by Initial Teaching Alphabet Publications, Inc., New York. By permission.

T. O.	i/t/a
on	on
one	wun
go	goe
do	dω
women	wimen

3. Various diphthongs are taught as individual letters:

T. O.	i/t/a
that	ʒhat
thin	ʧhin
hash	haʃh
which	whiʤ

4. With i/t/a spelling the reader does not have to see the final silent "e" in a word to identify the sound of the "i" as in like. I/t/a helps to maintain the traditional left-to-right reading habit and increase reading speed:

T. O.	i/t/a
line	lɪen
mine	mɪen
wine	wɪen
dine	dɪen

Instructional procedures with i/t/a involve the child in much writing as he learns to read and use the alphabet. During this writing, there is no need to emphasize correct spelling, only correct use of the symbols. Also, to help children read, a variety of books with familiar or interesting stories are produced in i/t/a to supplement the basic reader.

The British experiment comparing i/t/a with T.O., which began in 1961, has now been concluded, and the results were published in 1967. In this research report Downing draws three main conclusions:

1. I.t.a. as an example of a transitional writing-system for beginning reading and writing in English generally produces superior results in t.o. reading and in t.o. spelling by the end of the third year of school.
2. The success of i.t.a. in improving t.o. literacy skills occurs in spite of an important setback in the growth of these basic skills at the stage of transition from i.t.a to t.o.

3. The traditional orthography of English is a serious cause of difficulty in the early stages of learning to read and write.[14]

Research in use of i/t/a materials is growing rapidly in the United States. The largest investigation, started in September 1963, is being conducted by Lehigh University and the Bethlehem, Pennsylvania, schools. No longitudinal studies have yet been completed to indicate whether pupils who started with i/t/a are readers in the best sense of the word at junior or senior high school levels. Nor do we know whether i/t/a trained children are superior, over time, to those who learned to read by another approach.

The use of i/t/a has been expanded to include specialized institutions for adult illiterates, emotionally disturbed and culturally deprived children, and the educable retarded. It is also used in remedial reading programs in primary and intermediate grades, and in teaching English to foreigners.

The language-experience reading program. At the other end of the continuum from an approach to language through linguistic materials or the consistent and isolated use of a basal reader series is the program known as the language-experience approach to reading. Probably the most deliberate use of the language-experience idea is now employed in the San Diego, California, schools, developed under the leadership of R. V. Allen. In this instance, a long-established idea has gained popularity recently under new leadership.

Lamereaux and Lee, in 1941, set forth an approach to beginning reading emphasizing enriched experiences that children could talk about, record, and read. Experience charts prepared by the teacher from the oral expression of the children became primary reading material. The charts were large, the print manuscript, the content came from the children's own ideas and words, and illustrations were made by the children. As the children read and became familiar with the charts, duplicate sentences, then phrases, and finally words were matched to the original chart in order to develop sight vocabulary.

The present-day program operates in a similar method with a few modifications. Children begin the program in kindergarten. Certain aspects of linguistic study are incorporated.

The language-experience program is so named because the emphasis is placed on experience as a basis for learning, and materials are based upon the child's own language. A child *thinks* and *learns* as he interacts with others in a rich experience-environment. The approach is one that

---

[14] Downing, J., "Research Report on the British Experiment with i.t.a," in National Foundation for Educational Research, *The i.t.a. Symposium* (Slough, Bucks, England: National Foundation for Educational Research in England and Wales, 1967), pp. 49–51.

attempts to build language skills upon those already established within the child, and it uses the child's own interests and needs to do so. The four processes of listening, speaking, reading, and writing are essentially interrelated in order to develop effective reading.

At the beginning children are provided with activities that motivate expression of creative ideas through speech and graphic media. The ideas of "stories" are verbalized by the children individually or in groups, and recorded by the teacher on pictures or in chart form. During the recording process the children observe the relationships of speaking to writing and reading. Their stories are grouped together in booklets. Discussions about the printed words take place so that eventually the children learn about sound and symbol, the alphabet, repetition of words and symbols, punctuation, sentence sense. At this point the linguist's feature of early acquisition of the code is borrowed. Later, the child writes his own stories, which the teacher edits, and he needs formalized spelling instruction and vocabulary development. Eventually he uses more formalized printed materials.

Proponents of this method feel that one of the most important results of the program is the concepts the child develops about himself and reading. The expected sequence is as follows:

1. What a child thinks about he can talk about.
2. What he can talk about can be expressed in painting, writing, or some other form.
3. Anything he writes can be read.
4. He can read what he writes and what other people write.
5. As he represents his speech sounds with symbols, he uses the same symbols (letters) over and over.
6. Each letter in the alphabet stands for one or more sounds that he makes when he talks.
7. Every word begins with a sound that he can write down.
8. Most words have an ending sound.
9. Many words have something in between.
10. Some words are used over and over in our language and some words are not used very often.
11. What he has to say and write is as important to him as what other people have written for him to read.
12. Most of the words he uses are the same ones which are used by other people who write for him to read.[15]

---

[15] Doris M. Lee and R. V. Allen, *Learning to Read through Experience* (second edition) (New York: Appleton-Century-Crofts, Inc., 1963), pp. 5–8, citing R. V. Allen, "Concept Development of Young Children in Reading Development," *Twenty-Fourth Yearbook,* Claremont College Reading Conference (Claremont, Calif., 1959), pp. 12–21.

The language-experience method emphasizes pupil authorship, the production of reading materials emerging from child experience: the children's own ideas, vocabulary, and phraseology. Thus the content is quite flexible. It provides high motivation and meaningful purposes for reading. During the process of developing reading skills children also develop freedom of expression, skills in thinking and an understanding of the value of curiosity.

Individualized Reading

Individualized instruction is not new. Nor is it limited to the reading program. Tutorial and self-help plans in education date back to the Greeks and have been given increasing emphasis in the twentieth century. Through the years the need to teach individuals at their own level and pace has been a persistent problem that has resulted in several efforts to individualize instruction in reading. One effort is a method of presenting reading; other efforts involve the use of specialized materials that promote individual study.

Established authorities in reading have for years advocated "free reading" as a part of the broad reading program in the elementary school. Recently, however, free reading as a method of instruction, developed around individualized guidance, has evoked discussion, experimentation, and controversy.

Basically, the trend toward individualized reading seems to be caused by dissatisfaction with a formal and rigid use of established methods of teaching that rely upon the basic reading series, the manual of suggestions, and commercially prepared supplementary materials. Doubts and questions have been raised about the kind of reading materials imposed upon children and their apathetic reaction to such materials. Educators are seeking to motivate child interest and taste in reading, and to capitalize upon individual differences more effectively than can be done in ability grouping.

There are differences of opinion about the terminology, the procedures, and the effectiveness of the method. Some teachers call it "free reading," "personal reading," "self-selected reading," "functional reading," "life-purpose reading," or "voluntary reading." Most commonly, the new method is termed "individualized reading," meaning that children individually select and read different materials at their own pace, and that the teacher gives guidance in reading on an individual basis. The movement represents a different attitude toward reading and a different kind of curricular development. Reports indicate reading successes at all age levels, growth in reading interests and attitudes, and pride in personal accomplishments.

Characteristics of the individualized reading program. Some generally accepted characteristics of the individualized method of instruction in reading may be delineated:

1. A large assortment of books appealing to varied interests and selected for a wide range of reading levels is made available to the pupils. Roughly from 175 to over 300 books may be collected for one class. The materials consist of trade books, textbooks, subject matter reference books, magazines, newspapers, and complete sets of basic reading series. The books are strategically placed in various parts of the room on readily accessible racks or shelves.

2. Each child is free to browse among the books and to select the one he wishes to read. He will need some instruction on how to browse most effectively, how to determine whether or not he wishes to read a particular book. If the book seems interesting, the child takes it to his seat for more careful examination and the final decision to read it.

3. When books are read, a record of the books completed is made by the teacher or the child. In the child's record, author, title, and date of publication are noted, with a brief comment on the book. To teach children to comment effectively may require patient instruction.

4. Usually a short story describing the contents of the book is written in the child's own words and filed in a folder made for this purpose. Sometimes the child keeps a list of interesting or difficult words encountered.

5. The focal point of the program is the teacher's individual conference with each child. These conferences occur frequently, according to the child's need for consultation. During the conference teacher and child talk informally about the book. The child reads both silently and orally for the teacher, who asks questions to determine the child's interest, comprehension, and progress in specific reading skills. This conference is also the best opportunity for the teacher to check and give guidance in the correct listing and annotation of the book. After the conference, the teacher notes an evaluation on an accumulative record sheet.

6. When weaknesses in a specific skill are noted among several children, a small group is formed for special instruction. The basis for this selection of a group is not reading achievement, but common instructional need. Such a group might work on beginning consonants, perhaps a phrase drill, or on skills such as outlining or skimming. The group might work together only one day, or for a number of days, as necessary.

7. Each child makes a decision about each book he reads. He decides whether the book is worthy of presentation, what form the presentation will take, and when he can be prepared to give it. Then he makes an appointment for time on one of the regularly scheduled presentation days. At this time, he tells about the book, explains why he

likes it, and tries to interest others in the book. Presentations are not formal "book reports," but creative enterprises designed to give just enough information to challenge the interests of friends. Oral reading, questions and answers, or discussions may facilitate the presentation. Pictures, puppetry, dramatization, realia, dioramas, and many other visual aids may be used in the presentations. Occasionally, two or more children who have read the same book may make a presentation together. The work of preparing the presentation is done during the regular reading period.

Important factors in the program. Supporters of the individualized reading program recognize that certain factors are important to the success of the method. Crosby has presented such a list:

> The teacher must have skill and know-how to enable her to draw upon many methods and resources to meet the reading needs of individual children.
>
> The children must be supported and encourged to learn to read in terms of their own individuality and their own unique pattern and pace of growth.
>
> Motivation, the drive of the learner to achieve in reading, must be recognized by helping him seek for himself and choose those books for himself which will be satisfying to him. Expert guidance of teacher and librarian [is] essential:
>
> A climate must be created in which reading becomes not only necessary but irresistible. Rich collections of books in rooms and central libraries are essential.[16]

Demands that stem from such factors can be listed:

1. The teacher must recognize accurately each child's reading difficulties so that he can provide basic instruction in reading skills and abilities.

2. Instruction cannot be erratic when it deals with a complex process like reading. Some system must be followed so that more complex skills can be built upon the more simple ones. The program is not a laissez-faire situation.

3. The teacher must systematically keep in mind the reading needs of each child to a much greater extent than he does when he works with small ability groups, but the materials used in the individual program are more conducive to constant evaluation and recognition of weaknesses.

4. Real and intense interest is necessary for the child to be motivated to work alone or with a minimum of supervision. The teacher may stimulate interest by careful exhibits, related trips, enriched curriculum units, and opportunities to listen to stories read and told by both teacher and children.

[16] Muriel Crosby, "Organizing for Reading Instruction," *Elementary English* (March 1960), pp. 169–173.

5. Without careful help, children may choose books that will not help them progress in reading. The child who chooses a book at too low a level is as much a problem as the child who chooses a book that is too difficult to read. Also, there is the child who may not want to choose at all.

6. The teacher needs some help in selecting the wide variety of books for his classroom. Lists of new titles in trade books, catalogs of reliable textbooks, and numerous other references and visual aids are needed.

7. This type of reading program can be effectively related to other subject matter areas. To use it in isolation would be to defeat some of its purposes.

8. Children may spend too much time and energy on the preparation of presentations. The teacher must guide child activity so that learning is relative to the time spent, and so that irrelevant material is avoided.

9. Because the children work for the most part by themselves the teacher must ascertain that readiness preparation is adequate.

10. Scheduling of time within the daily program for browsing, reading, pupil-teacher conferences, as well as insuring that each child is busy during these times, takes expert organization.

Advantages of the individualized reading program.   Smith lists the most frequently mentioned advantages of the individualized plan as follows:

1. The child proceeds under his *own* motive and drive.

2. He reads at his own pace.

3. Interest is increased because the child reads material of his own choice.

4. The program permits the reading of larger amounts of material than does the grouping plan.

5. Each child is taught the skills that he needs when he needs them; thus he realizes the usefulness of skills.

6. The individual conferences promote close personal relationships between pupil and teacher.

7. There are increased opportunities to integrate reading with other language arts: vocabulary development, writing, listening, spelling; motives to communicate are strengthened.

8. The psychological effect of the program on the child is desirable. Pressures and tensions to meet grade standards are relieved, frustrations arising from failure to read as much or as well as others in a group are avoided, and the stigma of being "behind in reading" is removed. All of these concomitants pay rewarding dividends in mental health.[17]

---

[17] Nila Banton Smith, *Reading Instruction for Today's Children* (Englewood Cliffs, N.J.: Prentice-Hall, Inc., 1963), p. 137.

Programmed instruction in reading. Another attempt to organize content for individualized instruction lies in the field of programmed materials, presented in books and by specialized machines (see Chapter 18). A number of mechanical devices are used with varying degrees of effectiveness to increase the speed of reading. Most of them are modifications of the tachistoscope, in which words may be flashed on a screen at controlled speeds or in controlled phrase length. They act as a pacer for the reader. Trade names of some of these are Metronoscope, Flashmeter, Reading Rate Controller, Controlled Reader, Perceptoscope, Ratemeter, Reading Accelerator. Reading authorities tend to discredit the general use of such devices in the elementary grades when compared to less expensive and more flexible teacher-prepared materials.

Teaching machines using programmed instruction in reading are most effective when dealing with those facts and skills that need repetition for learning. Matching exercises, phonics exercises, exercises in structural analysis are now in use, but one of the problems in their construction is that most of the material presented is dull and unappealing. In addition to individual pacing and repetition, another gain is that the use of programmed materials allows the teacher more time for creative and effective instructional supervision.

One programmed reading primer has been published[18] for use with children who have not yet mastered the first steps in reading. It may be used with first grade children or with older children who need help with beginning reading. The primer contains 2500 frames in 440 pages that are organized in 12 units which take about 15-35 hours of study time during which the child learns to read 65 words used in 35 sentences.

A basic reading series titled "Programmed Reading"[19] has been widely used since 1962. The series uses a logical, systematic, linguistic approach. The child first learns regular sound values, then phonetically regular and irregular sound-symbol groups in an organized sequence presented in context of words and sentence patterns. Sight words are kept at a minimum. Phonic principles and rules are not memorized. After each 50 frames, a series of test frames is included so that progress may be checked.

The publishers of the programmed reading series claim these advantages: (1) the child learns to read at his own pace; (2) learning is free from competition; (3) of the active responses required in the materials, the learner is likely to have 90 percent of his answers correct, and he knows immediately whether his response is right or wrong; (4) the

---

[18] Teaching Materials Corporation, A Division of Grolier Incorporated of New York.

[19] McGraw-Hill Book Company, Webster Division.

required written responses incorporate natural, inductive learning of spelling, punctuation, and grammar; (5) the record of responses reveals to teacher and pupil a profile of strengths and weaknesses and overall progress.

Spache[20] raises several unanswered questions about programmed materials: Is their use most profitable before, during, or after introduction of a skill? Are they drill oriented or will they promote self-discovery and insightful learning? How long need a program be to make a significant contribution to skill development? Of what value are programs that require only an hour or two of effort? For what types of pupils are they most effective, at what ages, under what degree of teacher supervision, and for what purposes?

One program that presents individualized reading materials without mechanical repetition is the *SRA Program*.[21] Eleven separate "laboratories" advertised as a basic reading program for grades 1–14 emphasize developmental aspects and individualized instruction. Conceived as an instructional program for use in regular classrooms under the guidance of the teacher, the materials are designed to present and reinforce recognized basic reading skills. Unified and sequential comprehension and word-study skills are built into the program.

Each "laboratory" is a colorfully packaged and carefully organized box of materials, color-coded to represent a variety of difficulty levels. Each laboratory includes a multiple range of materials so that the child may begin at his own reading level and progress as fast and as far as his own capacity will allow. The primary program is graded at about three-month levels, the intermediate program at five-month levels. Materials are organized into "listening skill builders," "power builders," and "rate builders." Power builders are booklets containing an article or story and exercises in comprehension and vocabulary development. At the primary level twenty different power builders are available at each reading level. In intermediate materials twelve power builders and rate builders represent one level. A key card is available for each power builder so that each child assumes responsibility for correcting his own work, recording it, and plotting his progress. The listening skill builders are unique, and especially developed for the first grade, then maintained in later levels. A special primary laboratory for word games covers the range of phonic and structural analysis skills. Rate builders are timed devices, usually used at intermediate levels under direct teacher guidance. Student record books and a teacher's handbook are provided with the kit.

---

[20] George D. Spache, "Materials for Reading," *The Instructor*, Special Feature (March 1965), p. 14.

[21] Science Research Associates = SRA. Webster offers a similar "Classroom Reading Clinic."

Word analysis. Recent investigations tend to point up the importance of phonetic skills in reading. Though experts do not completely agree as to what, when, and how to teach phonics, a broad program of word attack has been for many years an integral part of the reading program that provides a basis for independent reading. Today the so-called phonetic approach is in reality one of *word analysis,* based on linguistic studies, rather than of the synthesis of letters. Modern methods involve more than "phonics" in that aspects of sight vocabulary, context clues, word form clues, and structural analysis are related to and supplement phonetic analysis. The six techniques that Gray describes so well are briefly outlined here.[22]

The first of Gray's techniques is the *mastery of sight vocabulary,* or the development of a fund of words the child recognizes easily in the printed form. Sight recognition of words is believed by some to be the most important single factor in good reading. In the beginning, sight vocabulary is built upon speaking vocabulary because sound and meaning are basic to word perception. As the sight vocabulary is developed the teacher insures instantaneous perception by giving the child opportunities to meet a single word in many kinds of situations. He presents controlled vocabularies so that the group of words is gradually and meaningfully developed. After the child has gained a fund of sight words, the words will become inadequate as the reading text grows, and the teacher may not be available to identify the new words for him. Thus other means of word recognition are necessary.

Gray's second technique in word attack is the skill of using *context* clues, or the ability to gain meaning from the text and pictures that will help identify the unknown word. As children read, and use the meaning of the text to help identify words, some limitations in this method are recognized because words that are closely related and look similar also have similar meanings, and the "guess" from context may not be correct.

A third technique in word attack is the use of *word-form clues* received by the child when he is able to distinguish the total form or the significant parts of a word to help him identify it. Basic to this technique is the skill of visual discrimination, or the ability to note likenesses, identify slight differences, and remember visual forms. An easy word for children to remember is $\boxed{\text{automobile}}$ because the general form of the word is unique. There is a less noticeable difference between $\boxed{\text{was}}$ and $\boxed{\text{has}}$ and $\boxed{\text{book}}$ and $\boxed{\text{books}}$; to discriminate between these demands clear vision and real perception. However, word-form clues must be combined with other word attack techniques because the frequency of similarities in word forms, such as in *five* and *live,* may mislead the child.

---

[22] Gray, *On Their Own in Reading,* Chapters 4–9.

The fourth technique of word attack is that of *structural analysis,* or the ability to look for meaningful units in words. Developing skill in word analysis involves ability to identify structural forms of root words, compound words, derived forms of words (adding prefixes and suffixes), and inflectional variants (adding *-s, -ed, -ing,* etc.) of words. Visual analysis must be checked with both sound and meaning, or pronunciation and understanding, of the individual words and the pronounceable units within them. The child must be thoroughly familiar with the spoken word before he can make such an analysis. Structural analysis is not just "finding little words in big words," but looking for parts of words with a meaning or a pronounceable unit.

Phonetic analysis, the fifth of the word attack skills, has recently had much publicity, but, again, it is only one of several ways to identify a new word. Phonetic analysis is the association of proper sounds with the printed word form. Phonetic analysis is one of the most intricate of the word recognition skills, because of the complexity of the English language and the variability of pronunciation within it. Though we have only twenty-six letters in our alphabet, approximately forty-three separate and distinct phonemes, or sound units, have been identified. One consonant or one vowel letter may have several sounds, according to its position and use in the word. To learn when a vowel is "long," or when a consonant is "silent," or how one letter influences the sound of another is generally taught over a period of years. Often a single phonetic clue, when combined with other clues, such as meaning, word form, or context clues, will tell the reader what the word is.

The last important technique in learning to identify new words included among known words is the development of *dictionary skills.* A child needs a dictionary when he can find no speaking-meaning counterpart for understanding the pronunciation and meaning of a word.

Thus we see that word analysis involves the development of a number of interrelated skills that are begun as early as first grade and developed throughout the elementary school. Though each technique has its limitations, every good reading program involves the use of the six skills, and every good teacher understands thoroughly the kinds and quality of skills necessary to the children of his age group.

Supplementary reading materials. Another area within the reading program that today causes much concern is the use of supplementary reading materials. These are the materials collected and prepared by the teacher for his classroom to supplement the regular work. Use of the basic reading series alone does not produce the rich reading program that is desired for children. The teaching manuals themselves suggest many kinds of activities and various kinds of materials to help children make more meaningful progress on the road to reading. The reading program is a necessary part of the whole curriculum, and therefore appropriate materials for various subjects sometimes become a problem.

Every classroom has in it a library table and bookshelves for various kinds of supplementary reference material. In the upper grade levels the reading range of this material becomes more greatly varied in directions both below and above the grade level at which the children work. On hand is a large selection of "trade books," or literature other than text-books, that represents a wide range of interests and reading levels suitable to a group of children. Books today are increasingly interesting, well-organized, and planned with effective format. The school librarian or the district or county librarian makes available the best on the market. Usually placed with the trade books are some of the texts of other series at a level of reading slightly lower than the books in which the children regularly work. Some basic series also have supplementary books designed to enrich the usual texts.

The classroom is usually supplied with a number of reference books. Dictionaries adequate for the age group are on shelves or in desks. Encyclopedias are frequently found in upper-grade classrooms or are available in the school library. Books suitable for science, social studies, and other subject matter areas are also carefully selected in terms of interest and reading level.[23]

Independent seatwork. This should be meaningful, purposeful, and related to learning goals and immediate plans. Materials in reading work-books are frequently used with small groups and related to daily lessons. Workbook pages are not completed indiscriminately by children, for constant teacher supervision is important to effective use. It must be remembered that workbooks or other kinds of seatwork cannot be a substitute for the teacher. The use of many workbooks throughout the day is considered ineffective teaching.

Various activities are valuable for independent work during the reading period. Carefully prepared, semipermanent reading games are preferable to a half-dozen worksheets a day, and quiet activities related to the social studies are considered excellent when other assignments are completed. Reading activities related to scrapbooks, art, drama, and puppetry are useful in the enrichment of the reading program. Variety is essential because no one pattern of seatwork materials will fit the instructional needs of all children. These questions help to evaluate seatwork and other independent activities in the classroom:

1. Is each activity purposeful and educationally sound?
2. Does each activity challenge the child to vigorous effort?

---

[23] Other materials that teachers will be interested in investigating are the Linguistic Blocks (Scott, Foresman), the Dolch game (Garrard Publishers), and the EDL Learning Station.

3. Does each activity provide opportunities for satisfaction in accomplishment?
4. Are the activities sufficiently varied to provide for wide differences in ability, interests, and educational needs?
5. Do the activities strengthen the learnings being emphasized in the total program?
6. Do the activities relate to children's current interests and to other class activities?
7. Do the activities help to develop special interests and abilities?
8. Do the activities aid in the development of desirable work habits, such as independence, self-direction, self-control, coordination, neatness?

The Many Innovations

The variety of innovations related to teaching materials and teaching methods range from seemingly bizarre ideas to sound programs empirically developed. One may read expensive advertisements about new systems for increasing reading speed, teaching beginning reading, or providing for remedial reading. Some cite testimonials by senators, lawyers, and doctors. Some programs are created by knowledgeable teachers, others by teachers who are not cognizant of all the factors needed to develop a valid program, and still others by noneducators who offer untried procedures.

The reaction to many of the new approaches among established reading authorities shows great diversity of opinion. All of the innovators claim good results. For example, all report that the learner develops positive attitudes, high enthusiasm, self-reliance, and confidence. Is this because the program is merely different? Can too much emphasis be placed on new aspects of a reading program? Can children really be hurt educationally by poorly tried and tested materials and procedures?

Since learning to read is a basic task for all children, this curriculum area receives more than its share of innovative approaches. We must keep in mind that constant experimentation and careful evaluation can improve our reading materials and techniques. Innovative programs need not be utilized to the exclusion of other programs. We may take clues from some of them to apply to a general instructional situation. For example, the careful organization of linguistic and programmed materials may have implications for the future. Also, i/t/a use of a variety of related reading materials and careful integration of writing with the reading program might well be transferred to other instructional programs. That innovations are being developed is an encouraging trend, because educators realize that instruction can be improved and curriculum made more effective.

RECOMMENDED READINGS

BLOOMFIELD, LEONARD, and CLARENCE L. BARNHART. *Let's Read—A Linguistic Approach.* Detroit, Mich.: Wayne State University Press, 1961.

BOND, GUY L., and EVA BOND WAGNER. *Teaching the Child to Read* (fourth edition). New York: The Macmillan Company, 1966.

DARROW, HELEN F., and VIRGIL HOWES. *Approaches to Individualized Reading.* New York: Appleton-Century-Crofts, Inc., 1965.

FERNALD, GRACE M. *Remedial Techniques in Basic School Subjects.* New York: McGraw-Hill Book Company, Inc., 1943.

FITZGERALD, JAMES A., and PATRICIA G. FITZGERALD. *Teaching Reading and the Language Arts.* Milwaukee: The Bruce Publishing Co., 1965.

FRIES, CHARLES C. *Linguistics and Reading.* New York: Holt, Rinehart and Winston, Inc., 1963.

HEILMAN, ARTHUR W. *Principles and Practices of Teaching Reading* (second edition). Columbus, Ohio: Charles E. Merrill Books, Inc., 1967.

HERRICK, VIRGIL E., and MARCELLA NERBOVIG. *Using Experience Charts with Children.* Columbus, Ohio: Charles E. Merrill Books, Inc., 1967.

LEFEVRE, CARL A. *Linguistics and the Teaching of Reading.* New York: Mc-Graw-Hill Book Company, Inc., 1964.

MC KEE, PAUL. *Reading.* Boston: Houghton Mifflin Company, 1966.

MILLER, LYLE L. *Accelerating Growth in Reading Efficiency.* Minneapolis: Burgess Publishing Company, 1967.

SMITH, JAMES A. *Creative Teaching of Reading and Literature in the Elementary School.* Boston: Allyn and Bacon, Inc., 1967.

STRANG, RUTH, CONSTANCE M. MC CULLOUGH, and ARTHUR TRAXLER. *The Improvement of Reading* (fourth edition). Columbus, Ohio: Charles E. Merrill Books, Inc., 1964.

TAYLOR, SANFORD E. *Listening.* Washington, D.C.: NEA, Department of Classroom Teachers, 1964.

Communication: Expressive Language Arts

8

The expressive language arts, as identified in Chapter 7, are the means of transmitting personal ideas, the outgoing phase of communication. They hold as important a place in the elementary school curriculum as do the receptive language arts.

ORAL COMMUNICATION IN THE SCHOOL

Speech is that primary phase of communication utilizing symbolic vocal sounds and involving highly complex language structure. Speech is made effective not only by variety in words and phrases but also by manipulation of voice, facial expression, and bodily gestures. Variations and combinations of tone, pitch, inflections, pause, rhythm, and stress distinguish the speech of one person from another or of one language from another. Through speech people express feelings, impart knowledge, solve mutual problems. Man's ability to talk was fundamental to the development of civilization because he could pass along collective learning by word of mouth.

Spoken language developed slowly, beginning with grunts, groans, and pantomime. Initially perhaps man's communication was as limited as that of the dog, which can vary its bark in tone, pace, and urgency. But the development of sophisticated language by use of the larynx and the brain differentiates man from lower animals and their cries. The languages of men are effective tools because of their complex and ordered relationships between the elements of sound and symbol. An intricate language enables man to communicate high level abstractions, concepts, and innuendoes.

Spoken language, or "talk," has been summarized by Brooks:

1. *Requires a minimum of two people.* Of course, talk may be practiced by one person, and often is, both by the very young when they are experimenting with and learning speech sounds and their meanings, and by the adult when, for instance, he reviews his bank statement, or hits his thumb with a hammer.

2. *Utilizes a linguistic code mutually understood.* Even if two languages are used, mutual understanding is no less necessary.

3. *Assumes a common area of reference.* The common area of reference may not always be easily identified, but talk assumes the predisposition to find one.

4. *Is an interchange between participants.* Both participants receive as well as give in talk.

5. *Relates each speaker to the other and to their immediate environment.* The vocal behavior of the speaker is always related to the response, real or anticipated, in the hearer, and vice versa. Thus the relationship is of a reciprocal or dyadic kind.

6. *Is bound to the present moment.* Only with the aid of the graphic-material band can language escape from the present and the immediate; that it has been able to do so is, of course, one of the supreme facts of human culture.

7. *Involves only the vocal and auditory apparatus.* Although activities in the audio-lingual band can dispense with the gestural-visual and the graphic-material, the reverse is not true; except for pantomimes or pictures, there is nothing in the gestural or the graphic that does not stem from and depend upon the audio-lingual. We talk constantly with persons whom we do not see, in our homes, at work, and by telephone; such conversations are typical of talk in its purest form.

8. *Deals indiscriminately with what is real and what is postulated.* The total environment that can be symbolized by talk includes not only the real world that surrounds the speakers but also the infinitely greater ideational world to which they have access simply because they are alive and human; talk as the meeting point of these two realms stands in need of much further study and elucidation.[1]

The young child comes to school with some facility in speaking. He has listened and learned. At an early age he established ability to communicate through "muted language," or the unsaid meanings conveyed by bodily movements, gestures, and facial expressions. He progressed beyond this ability, and developed enough vocabulary to communicate orally with other children and with his teacher. He can ask questions and give simple answers to queries about the things with which

---

[1] Nelson Brooks, *Language and Language Learning* (New York: Harcourt, Brace & World, Inc., 1960), pp. 29–30.

he is familiar. His use of language has helped him to reveal to others his needs and desires: that he is hungry, that he is pleased, that he is angry. His speech enables him to become part of play groups. He can influence others in their actions and in their feelings by the things he says. Most of what he knows about his world has come through his experience and through oral exchange of ideas.

The child brings to school an ability to speak simply and a characteristic manner of speaking. His expressions, idioms, inflections, and mannerisms, which have been learned from his family, may or may not be accepted patterns of speech in other social classes. Variations in diction, grammar, and colloquialisms may present problems in group situations.

KEY QUALITIES OF SPEECH

VOICE	*Volume*	A voice is loud enough to be heard.
	Pitch	The voice is pitched in a natural key. It may be high, medium, or low. The pitch changes and varies with meaning.
	Inflection	The voice glides from one pitch to another.
	Quality	A voice is clear and distinct. It is free from huskiness and nasality. It is free from shrillness and harshness. It has fullness rather than breathiness.
RATE	*Tempo*	Rate varies with the mood or emotions.
RHYTHM	*Flow*	Normal speech is uninterrupted. It is free flowing.
	Smoothness	It is rhythmic. It is free from repetition or prolongation.
ARTICULATION	*Formation of sounds*	Speech sounds are produced accurately.[2]

The emphasis upon oral language is necessarily greater in the primary grades than in the intermediate grades. Until children can read fluently, oral communication is the basic medium of instruction. Much of their knowledge has been gained through the spoken word; they speak to demonstrate knowledge or seek information. Children are encouraged to speak. By saying something, accepting teacher guidance, and developing self-evaluation, the child improves his speech, his vocabulary, and his effectiveness in oral communication. The teacher who "frees the child to talk" encourages informality and spontaneity, and by so doing lays a foundation for effective and creative written language skills.

---

[2] Adapted from V. D. Anderson and others, *Readings in the Language Arts* (New York: The Macmillan Company, 1964), p. 77. (Excerpted from Publication No. 479, 1949, Los Angeles Public Schools.)

For purposes of instruction in school, oral communication experiences may be divided into two groups. First are those that involve face-to-face relationships in which the speaker is actually talking to others, or expressing ideas that result in immediate and personal reactions from the listener. These experiences may include such activities as conversing, reporting, telling stories, and giving directions. The second category includes situations in which the speaker is playing some sort of role, either to an audience or for the benefit of a fellow participant, as in dramatic play. Creative dramatics, puppetry, and verse-speaking choirs fall into this category.

Face-to-Face Speaking Relationships

Though conversation is the most common natural type of oral communication for adults, it is commonly planned for in school programs. Informal and undirected conversation takes place naturally on the playground, but in the classroom conversation must be encouraged during milk or snack times, at the lunch table, before dismissal or at other times during the day when it will not interfere with study. In a free atmosphere the development of conversation is spontaneous.

Small talk and humor are encouraged. One person may express an idea and others may react to develop it; all have the fun of listening and reacting. Topics proposed at random are amplified, or there may be digressions. Children learn to be verbally courteous, to express interesting and appropriate ideas, to take turns speaking.

Discussion. Discussion is a form of conversation wherein impromptu reactions take place among children, but usually some point of study or the solution of some problem is intended. Discussion is more carefully controlled than informal conversation; children develop the trend of thought to reach a specific end. Discussion helps to clarify thinking, gather new ideas, make reasonable judgments, accept various points of view. Children do not make speeches but comment briefly and succinctly. Questions are asked and answered. As children mature, the complexity of ideas and their interrelationships grow to increase the depth of discussion. Teacher guidance is indirect and inconspicuous, for the children need opportunity to make the mental explorations and to give the consideration necessary to reach a conclusion. Discussion is essential to cooperative planning and evaluation periods.

Share-and-tell period. Closely allied to general discussions is the time during the day when children gather together to share their experiences and tell each other about items of news. This time is generally called the "share-and-tell period" in the primary grades and the "current events period" in the intermediate grades. Frequently a child acts as chairman, calling on those who wish to speak. The children bring artifacts, pictures, and other materials to make their presentations interesting. The trend is toward giving children an opportunity for this sort of sharing every day, even if it may be very short at times. The first few minutes of the morning seem most appropriate, since children then get the news off their minds and the materials brought to class can be adequately exhibited for later leisurely examination.

Children are helped to achieve clarity of speech, a simple easy manner, and the ability to select worthwhile bits of information. Listeners are encouraged to respond with comments or questions, to develop discussion with little teacher intervention. The purposes of the share-and-tell period are defeated if child after child says his piece with no reaction from the class or with only an occasional comment or question from the teacher.

Taking part in meetings. Related to discussion, and similar to the presentations of share-and-tell, is the oral exchange during class or club meetings. Here children express opinions, relate experiences, and present ideas relevant to specific problems in a structured situation where each child is individually recognized and comments are directed to a specific person. Such discussions involve records in the form of minutes and require leadership from a chairman and a secretary. Organization for such activities is very informal in the primary grades, but as children grow older they can conform to more formal rules of parliamentary procedure.

Giving directions, explanations, announcements. To give directions or explanations children must have the ability to think through a matter and arrange a sequence of ideas before speaking. The situation demands appearing before a group for a short period, talking clearly and succinctly, making sure that all items have been presented. The manner of the speaker is direct, precise, and positive; the material is well organized and presented with an air of confidence.

Reporting. Reporting usually demands a more involved presentation than does giving directions. Poor reporting by children may easily result in ineffective learning situations and waste of time. A thorough understanding of the topic, based upon adequate research, careful appraisal and selection of facts, and a planned presentation that stimulates the interest of the listeners are essential to good reporting. The report should seldom be read word for word, though well-prepared working notes are most useful. Well-selected vocabulary, simple and direct speech, and use of complete sentences are encouraged. Some kind of audio-visual material to supplement the spoken words will help make the report more effective. Important to the giving of good reports is the period following the presentation in which the group discusses the ideas presented, clarifying and emphasizing the learning involved.

Interviewing. Teachers capitalize on the child's natural tendency to ask questions as a basis for interviewing techniques. A successful interview includes introductory remarks, questions, note-taking, and an expression of appreciation for the interview. For the intermediate grades, many opportunities for interviews can be found, such as interviewing staff members, resource people, and community workers. In the primary grades very simple interviews that involve no written record can be utilized.

Introductions. The rules for introductions should be taught to children as early as possible. Very young children can introduce parents in a simple and satisfactory manner. As the children grow older, more formal rules for introducing people may be practiced.

Telling stories. The activities in oral communication discussed so far have been those involving face-to-face situations in which the speaker says something and is then guided by the response of his listener. Storytelling definitely demands a response, but that response may not be verbal, for the listener may react with facial expressions, laughter, or sighs. Questions, comments, or exclamations come at the end of the story or rather infrequently during the story.

The storyteller learns many techniques that stimulate the interest and natural delight of the listener, such as variations of voice tone and quality, gestures, facial expressions, bodily movements, colorful words, and a modified form of dramatization. As a storyteller, the speaker must be thoroughly familiar with his theme, present it in correct sequence, and use words the listeners can clearly understand. Young children learn the beginnings of storytelling in their first years of school when they participate in share-and-tell activities and take advantage of other opportunities to tell a group something of interest. Riddles, jokes, and anecdotes, as well as original stories, are encouraged. As the child can handle more ideas and more complex relationships, his storytelling becomes more detailed.

Telephoning. Though one does not actually see the person he talks to while telephoning, the situation is virtually that of a face-to-face relationship. Often children learn to speak over the telephone before they come to school, for the child of today accepts it as a normal part of life. In school, however, children can learn the many uses for the telephone, as well as the specific techniques for placing calls, giving and taking messages, and acting courteously.

A second type of oral language activity is dramatization or role-playing. Dramatization is valuable because children learn new words and ideas, improve enunciation, learn that their voices can be changed in tone and volume, and overcome self-consciousness in an audience situation.

Dramatization. *Dramatization* is a general term that covers a number of activities in which children act out the parts of specific characters. Usually the story has rather formal directions or guides followed by the children. Such dramatization is found in the presentation of a formal play, an operetta, the reproduction of a story from a reader, or the dramatization of a funny experience, with rather formal planning and preparation. Variations include shadow plays, puppets, and pantomimes.

Teachers have found that some children can free themselves from their own personalities when playing the roles of others, and in this way learn to speak more freely and with greater clarity. On one hand, mentally retarded children who may have great difficulty expressing themselves in front of a group find comparative freedom in hiding themselves behind a puppet stage and using puppets to tell a story or take a part in a play. On the other hand, dramatic situations develop creativity and talents of more able children and thus supplement their learning.

Creative dramatics. Creative dramatics is a rather special type of dramatization in which children reenact a story or series of sequences with their own interpretations of the roles. The action is impromptu and unrehearsed. For example, the child who demonstrates to the class the manner in which Jack Horner pulled out the plum does it according to his own idea about pulling plums. The first graders who act out the story of "The Three Billy Goats Gruff" also give their own creative twist to a familiar story. Thus the dramatic representation of a story or theme is creative according to the child's own interpretation.

Dramatic play. Dramatic play is different from the usual dramatics in that no set story is followed, and there is no audience situation. The children utilize their natural tendencies to project themselves into the roles of other people, usually people about whom they are studying and whose work-roles they wish to explore. For example, the third grade is studying the community. When children play the roles of the service station man, the policeman, the grocery clerk, they go through the activities of real people, using props they themselves have designed for the play. The situations are reproduced as authentically as possible, the children playing to the limit of their knowledge. Later, the teacher makes sure misconcepts are corrected or that a little more information is available, perhaps through a story, a movie, or a field trip, or through interviewing a resource person. The play grows, develops, and is modified as the children gain insight into the roles of the individuals they are portraying. Dramatic play is frequently associated with the social studies, for it is an effective means of developing insights into the lives and relationships of people. It is being used increasingly as an effective situation for motivating learning and for determining the quality of learning.

A variation of dramatic play is block play, usually provided for very young children in kindergarten and first grade. Here the materials facilitating the play are blocks or manufactured toys, rather than properties constructed by the children for dramatic play.

Verse-speaking choir. Oral communication performed in groups is termed verse-speaking choir or choric speaking. In this, children speak poetry or poetic prose simultaneously in a manner that emphasizes the beauty of the words and ideas. It is performed before an audience only after satisfactory classroom experience. With young children the verses may be altered by spontaneous repetition in which the group chants a phrase or sentence. As the children become familiar with the medium, voices are arranged according to tonal quality, and solo parts are assigned.

Sociodrama. In still another type of dramatization, the children are assigned roles and given some clue about the character so that they may try to behave as they think the character would. This is the sociodrama. The purpose is to explore with the pupils the solution of a social problem situation with which they are familiar. For example, a fight has occurred on the playground. The causes of the fight are reenacted to determine whether a solution other than fighting could have been achieved. Or the pupils may dramatize their actions toward a new foreign student who is expected to enroll in the class. One action is usually not enough. During the evaluation the children consider the effects of the solution, and then other children are assigned similar roles to see if a more effective solution can be worked out.

A variation of this kind of role-playing is the dramatization of the open-ended story. The children reenact a story that the teacher has read them, and supply their own version of how the story ends. Again, this is the kind of activity that necessitates several actions until a satisfactory solution is achieved.

Special Skills in Oral Communication

Authorities in language arts differentiate between *expressional* lessons, which are provided primarily to give children experience and success in expressing themselves through language, and *training* lessons, which are organized to give children explicit guidance in language skills.

The expressional lessons are more informal, concentrate on ideas or procedures, and emphasize fluency and creativity. The oral communication activities described previously would usually fall into the expressional category. From the expressional lessons, the teacher takes clues for the special abilities to be strengthened in the more formalized *training* lesson. The training lesson provides opportunity for careful instruction, practice, and practical evaluation. Both expressional and training lessons are continued and developed in complexity as the children grow older.

Some of the skills in which the teacher observes progress during expressional lessons and provides instruction during training lessons are discussed here.

Speaking and listening. Speaking and listening are so closely related that the teacher and student need to be aware of their interdependence. They must understand the role of the listener and the advantages of careful listening. The teacher helps the speaker learn his responsibilities in the listening process and the means by which he can motivate interested listening. (See Chapter 7.)

Articulation, enunciation, and pronunciation. The use of acceptable language and a simple and direct manner involve something more than correct pronunciation. *Articulation* refers to the use of the vocal organs (the tongue, teeth, lips, and palate) and the breath in producing consonant and vowel sounds. *Enunciation* refers to the general clarity and distinctness of articulation. Both of these contribute to *pronunciation;* a word may be correctly pronounced but not articulated or enunciated distinctly. To learn to speak distinctly requires accurate listening and good speaking examples. It also requires a sensitivity to good enunciation, an interest in good speech patterns, and a willingness to correct errors by speaking slowly and striving for clarity. The teacher can give much practical instruction to guide normal growth, but difficult speech problems may need the help of a specialist.

Voice and quality of expression. Use of the voice is related to volume and tonal quality. One of the first skills learned is achieving the volume appropriate to the size of the group. A large group demands more volume; in a small reading group, the voice must be heard by the group without being loud enough to disturb others. A child can learn to vary the pitch of his voice and the pacing of his speech to lend interest and emphasis to what he is saying. He can learn the difference between a sad tone and a happy one, and how to avoid monotony. Much of the expressional quality reflects the speaker's attitude toward what he is saying.

Poise. Effective speaking is greatly influenced by the speaker's poise. Children must learn to feel at ease when talking to others in either formal or informal situations. Confidence is built with experience, success, and careful guidance. Attention to details such as where to stand for the kind of speaking being done, at whom to look, when and where to move when speaking, and what kinds of gestures are appropriate will help to develop a poised manner and an effective delivery.

Courtesy. Because oral communication involves social situations, the rules of courtesy apply. Children learn the polite forms of speech as well as courteous behavior. Taking turns and not interrupting are common social rules. Use of such phrases as "please" and "excuse me" are also easily learned. More difficult and more abstract courtesies such as regard for the feelings of others during an argument, ways of offering constructive criticism, and showing the patience necessary to reach a long-sought conclusion require a more mature development.

Organization of thought and content. Effective oral communication demonstrates clear thinking and careful, sequential organization. In the first grade children learn sequential development by telling stories or relating experiences, for even in the simplest of situations the telling necessitates the ability to "stick to the point." As children present more complex ideas and a greater accumulation of information, organization involves emphasis, relationship of ideas, balance of information, timing, supporting details, and other indications of preplanning.

Development of vocabulary. The child's speaking vocabulary is increased and enriched when he is helped to understand the meaning of words. Some words represent concrete objects: the word *rose* may bring a mental picture of that flower. Other words are more abstract symbols: the word *truth* does not represent a concrete object and may be modified in meaning according to different values. Vocabulary can be developed through the children's activities and experiences, through consideration of the many meanings of some words, through sensitivity to the slight variation in meaning of similar words. Since words are best learned in context, the purpose is not merely to learn new words, but to learn to choose the words necessary to convey the intended meaning.

Grammatical usage. Frequently teachers feel that children should always use complete sentences and formally correct language. It is true that in some situations such language is necessary, but authorities today also approve the use of colloquial speech in appropriate situations. In discussions or conversations a word or phrase representing lower social form, or even an incomplete sentence, may be a complete and effective reaction. Children need to understand what a complete sentence is, and when the situation necessitates its use. Illiterate styles should be avoided.

Reference was made earlier to linguistics as the study of the technical structure of language. Linguists perceive language as speech. They indicate that speech is older, produces more communication signals, and is used by more people the world over than is written language. Written language, they say, is merely reiteration of speech in another symbolic form. Therefore linguists emphasize the study of the spoken language.

Authorities agree that decoding of language is the first step in a linguistic approach. Structural linguists identify three sequential and interrelated levels of language that contribute to decoding the language. Basically, they deal with phonology, or the sound system; syntax, or the order and arrangement of words; and morphology, or the forms and grammatical inflections of words.

The *phoneme* is the smallest element of the *phone*, or sound. Grouped together, phonemes form words, or parts of words. There are more phonemes than letters in the alphabet, because many letters denote more than one elemental sound. Authorities do not agree to the number of phonemes in the English language; the counts vary from 30 to 45. For example, the letter "a" may represent five phonemes: at, age, car, all, ago; "s" may represent three: see, fuse, measure. Also, some phonemes may be represented by more than one letter, as the "k" sound: k, c, q, x. The *grapheme* is the written symbol for a phoneme, designed by linguists to represent a single sound from various spellings: ε = e, ea, a, ai, ay, eo, ie, ei, ae, in red, says, said, friend, heifer; æ = a, ai, au, i, in hat, plaid, laugh, meringue.

The *morpheme* is the smallest meaning unit. It may be a word (smallest meaning unit standing alone) or a part of a word, as a suffix, and always consists of one or more phonemes. It is possible for a single phoneme to be a morpheme. For example, the "s" morpheme added to a noun means more than one, as in "books." The "s" in "boy's" is a different morpheme meaning possession. In the spoken language, meaning can be changed by rhythm, pitch, or stress in the voice. In the written language, spelling and punctuation help to change meaning.

Syntax is the arrangement of the group of morphemes and words which form phrases or sentences to communicate ideas. Linguists use the term *utterance* to describe these idea units, their largest unit of study. Lefevre[3] points out the characteristics of the four subsystems of syntax:

1. *Intonation:* the systematic rhythms and melodies of English. . . . The three elements of intonation are pitch, loudness (stress or accent), and pause (juncture). . . . Wrong or awkward intonation

---

[3] Carl A. Lefevre, "The Contribution of Linguistics," *The Instructor Magazine: Reading '65, An Overview of Current Practices* (March 1965).

distorts language and its meaning. Good intonation combines rhythm and melody so that phrases, clauses, sentences, make sense. . . . Rising inflection and pauses that occur within sentences often are marked with punctuation. The difference between the rising tone and the falling tone is a structural pattern signifying a different intent. For example, in a conversation about a prospective trip, one person may ask the other "Are you *going* now?" to which the answer may be "Yes." But the person may say "Are your going *now*?" and, because of the difference in implication, the answer may be "No."

2. *Sentence patterns:* the order of words and parts of sentences. An infinite variety of English sentences can be generated from a few basic patterns, often called *kernel sentences*. Linguists derive a letter-symbol formula for basic patterns, as:

Tom played	NV (noun, verb)
Tom played quickly	NVAdv.
The ball went high	NVAdj.
Tom hit the ball	NVN
Tom is a pitcher	NLVN (noun, linking verb, noun)
Tom is smart	NLVAdj

Structural grammar provides descriptions of these patterns and suggests some of their important transformations: manipulations, expansions, inversions, and substitutions within patterns.

3. *Structure words:* (or junction words) are the sentence joints or "glue" that hold sentence parts together. Structure words have the unique function of showing relationships between parts of sentences. They serve as joints between structural parts, binding the structural joints together. The italicized words in the following sentence are all structure words: *If* you can believe *it, that* small boy is *the* best pitcher *on our* team. There are about three hundred structure words in English, and in frequency and use they far surpass all the rest of our words. They include five sets of markers, the conjunctions, and several smaller sets having limited use, such as intensifiers.

   a. Noun markers: *a, an, the, their, this, my, some,* etc.

   b. Verb markers: *am, are, is, was, have, has been, done, did,* etc.

   c. Phrase markers: *up, down, in, out, out of, above, below,* etc.

   d. Clause markers: *if, because, although, even though, that, which,* etc.

   e. Question markers: *who, why, how, when, where, what,* etc.

4. *Word-form changes:* Word-form changes include two sets: grammatical inflections and derivational prefixes and suffixes. Thus they may indicate grammatical relationships such as tense or number within or between sentences, or they may change a word from one part of speech to another, or otherwise alter its meaning.

   a. Number: The boy likes pie. The boys like pie.

   b. Tense: The boy eats pie. The boy ate pie.

c. Structural word analysis:
   The material is workable. (verb [work] plus suffix [able])
   The material is unworkable. (prefix [un] makes negative)
   The work is difficult. ("work" a noun subject)
   Can you work for me today? (inverted order with marker "can")

To utilize this kind of language analysis well, the four language processes must be closely interrelated. Spelling is taught with reading; writing and speaking are analyzed similarly. Phoneme and morpheme study aid phonetic and structural analysis of words in reading; oral phoneme identification is stressed as part of listening acuity; conscious recognition of phonemes facilitates articulation; the study of morphemes helps vocabulary development; recognition of phonemes and morphemes contributes to reasonable analysis of spelling. Intonation study aids oral reading comprehension; intonation perception helps children distinguish between statements, questions, requests, and demands as they listen. Study of sentence sense gives clues to comprehension and increases fluency in reading; study of word order patterns helps to develop more mature and sophisticated sentences in both speaking and writing.

Linguists claim other advantages for linguistic study in teaching receptive and expressive language arts. Linguistic study, they say, helps the student identify what is significant in language and the way these significant parts function together. Through inductive reasoning, thinking rather than memorization is emphasized as children observe and collect data, identify patterns, and then pose hypotheses to explain patterns.

Evaluation in Oral Language

Because much of oral language is spontaneous and must be maintained as such, evaluation needs some consideration. Three means of evaluation may be utilized.

Standards. Children learn to speak in great part by imitation. Thus an important part of the standard held for children is the teacher's own effective speech, his clear and distinct enunciation and appropriate vocabulary.

Children can set up cooperative standards. After some weaknesses in a specific activity are noted, the teacher may provide a separate situation for children to think through their purposes and arrive at a set of standards. Problems in the share-and-tell period, for example, may result in standards such as these:

Speak so that all can hear.
Don't talk too long.
Ask for questions.

To help a sixth grade class give more effective reports, cooperative consideration may result in these standards:

Know the material well.
Use some aids to illustrate.
Be sure all points are presented in logical order.
Make opportunities for listeners to participate.

Standards are reviewed when preparations are made for the activity, or during a more formal evaluation period when their utilization is appropriate.

Teacher guidance.   Teacher guidance, beyond the development of standards and the setting of a good example, is most easily provided through verbal correction, done incidentally and tactfully to avoid personal embarrassment. If possible, the correction is made so that only the speaker can hear the teacher's quiet voice at the moment of the mistake. If the child does not react, no further effort is made at that time. Frequently the teacher can anticipate mistakes and help to avoid them by a suggestion before the individual speaks. Favorable comments are most important. Also, teacher guidance includes kindly control of the aggressive talker and encouragement of the shy or retiring individual.

Group evaluation.   Important to self-evaluation and to the total learning of the class is the use of group evaluation. An analysis after a discussion or dramatization can emphasize the good accomplishments as well as the weaknesses that may need more attention. Children can sense a successful oral communication activity by evaluating their own interest and participation and by determining whether the ideas were well understood. The teacher can improve both group and self-evaluation by using a magnetic recording tape that can be played back immediately or saved to compare with a similar situation.

WRITTEN COMMUNICATION IN THE SCHOOL

The ability to express oneself clearly in writing is almost as necessary as fluency in speaking. Writing effectively is much more difficult than speaking because the writer must anticipate ambiguities, differences of opinion, and questions, in order to produce exactly and clearly what he means. He cannot watch the faces of his listeners for clues that further explanation is needed, nor can he ask for questions. He cannot rely on tone of voice, facial expressions, gestures, or innuendoes to help him in expression. To communicate in writing a person must write legibly, spell correctly, and use acceptable language structure and a writing style that conveys ideas meaningfully.

Before children can learn to write accurately they must have an experiential background in other language arts. As children learn to recognize printed words, they can begin to reconstruct those words with pencil on paper. The ability to write requires a firm understanding of the symbols created to translate the spoken word to the written word.

Usually children begin to write in the first grade, but spelling is not presented formally until the latter part of the second or during the third grade. The study of the alphabet is usually deferred until the third grade, when reading and writing are developed to the point of making dictionary work practicable. Correct grammatical usage is introduced with oral communication; when the child begins to write, the transition is made to written material.

As with reading, the proper maturity of the eye and the large and small muscles of the body and the mental capacity to understand the meaning of words are necessary before children can be taught to write. In early development of the written word, its relationship to oral language development is very close and they are highly interdependent. The spoken word must be thoroughly understood before it can be read or written.

From Manuscript to Cursive

Handwriting is the process of manually putting on paper the written symbols of our language. Recently business and industry have complained bitterly about the poor legibility of the handwriting of American adults. Research supports the fact that the quality of handwriting has declined. Thus there is a trend toward more specialized instruction and more emphasis upon legibility and speed in writing. A real purpose for handwriting is sought. Instruction upon mechanics is presented when the need is demonstrated. Self-diagnosis and self-correction are emphasized. To anticipate and identify individual or group needs is the teacher's real task. The trend away from formalized copying procedures continues. Tidyman and Butterfield list reasons why traditional formalism in handwriting is being discarded:

1. The methods used—postures, copy, and drill exercises—are inappropriate for children.
2. The results are artificial and there is little carry-over into actual writing in school and in life.
3. Some scripts, in spite of pleasing appearance, are difficult to read.
4. Learning to write is unnecessarily complicated.
5. The extreme emphasis on drill takes all the joy out of learning to write.
6. Emphasis on formal drill disregards the natural stages in the neuromuscular development of children.

7. Individuality of style is unnecessarily sacrificed to the fetish of uniformity.
8. In spite of years of training, children fail to acquire a free, easy handwriting movement.[4]

Anderson[5] lists eight changes that have recently become apparent in handwriting programs:

1. Cursive writing is losing its place as a recognized part of the early primary program. The simpler forms of manuscript or print-script writing are preferred. Print script is being accepted as desirable writing in all grades.
2. Children no longer trace letter forms except under critical circumstances. Writing in the air is considered inappropriate and wasteful.
3. Children who show a strong preference for writing with the left hand are no longer required to learn to write with the right hand.
4. The use of the rhythmical aids is discouraged. The size and shape of the various letters are so different that an absolute conformity to set rhythm is unnatural.
5. Accessory drills that presumably contribute rhythm and freedom in muscular movement are minimized. The use of ovals and related exercises are used much less than in the past.
6. There is less emphasis on speed in writing.
7. Fountain pens and ballpoint pens are used in classroom practice.
8. Such incentives as penmanship certificates and pens are not widely used, although still available.

The developmental program in handwriting begins with manuscript writing, or print script, which is that form of writing closely resembling printed letters. The transition to simple forms of cursive writing, or that writing in which letters flow together in a running or connected style, is made later.

A well planned program of instruction in handwriting anticipates the needs for written expression and provides for the gradual development of the skill as the child progresses through school; i.e., as his needs for written expression grow and increase, practice to facilitate these needs is incorporated into the program.[6]

Manuscript writing. The first day of first grade in school, the teacher may write on the chalkboard at the child's eye level a simple sentence, "We are in the first grade." He helps the children "read" this and at the

---

[4] Willard F. Tidyman and Marguerite Butterfield, *Teaching the Language Arts* (New York: McGraw-Hill Book Company, Inc., 1951), p. 361.

[5] V. D. Anderson and others, *Language Skills in Elementary Education* (New York: The Macmillan Company, 1964), p. 99.

[6] Emma Harrison Myers, *The Whys and Hows of Teaching Handwriting* (Columbus, Ohio: The Zaner-Bloser Company, 1963), p. 11.

end of that first day the children proudly go home to tell Mother that they can read! The children have been exposed to some written symbols, meaningful in thought to them. Though they simply memorized the idea and not the form of the symbols, they have, in fact, started on the long road to learning to read. In writing this simple sentence the teacher used manuscript writing, which is very similar to the print in preprimers and other texts. He used the exact letter formation and strokes that the children will use later. He continues to use this type of writing for all classroom work, preparing children for later imitation, and creating a readiness for writing. Children become familiar with the formation and character, as well as with the meaning, of the symbols.

As manuscript writing has come into use, a few arguments against it have been pressed, most of them stemming from the fact that the form is not socially acceptable and that signatures in manuscript have not generally been legal. This argument has lost strength as banks have begun to accept script signatures that are regularly used by individuals.

There are several reasons for the wide acceptance of manuscript as the beginning step in learning to write. The first reason is a physiological fact: the small child's fine muscles of the hand, arm, and wrist joints are not yet developed. Cursive writing requires that a writer put his pencil on the paper and move his arm and hand rhythmically but without pause until the whole word is completed. In manuscript writing, each letter is made with one or more independent strokes; thus a child has an opportunity to pause or rest if necessary within a word or even within a letter. Second, since the letters are similar to the symbols of the printed texts, transition from reading to writing is not so difficult as it would be between cursive and the printed form. Children using manuscript tend to use large vocabularies and write more fluently as beginners. The third reason relates to the legibility of manuscript. The forms of the letters (circles and straight lines) are so simple that children can easily copy them, learn to write them, and evaluate their own mistakes. The slant is always perpendicular; spacing is simple. Extra strokes and flourishes are not necessary. Consequently, most children can achieve legible writing with a minimum of practice, and the manuscript deteriorates less under the pressure of speed. For these reasons, more schools are continuing instruction in manuscript beyond the primary grades.

There are some variations in the forms of manuscript used throughout the nation. Though these variations are few, a teacher determines which system his school is using, and never deviates from it. The primary teacher especially should be most competent in his format of manuscript, for he uses it constantly. Special attention is given to alignment, proportionate height and size of letters, spacing, vertical structure, and the use of circles, straight lines, and parts of circles in forming letters.

Usually children begin writing by learning to manuscript their own names. Then a word or two may be learned as the child needs to label a picture or some other work. The teacher is constantly alert to the situations that call for writing. Labels, cards to parents, stories, and letters provide a real purpose for writing.

As the children grow in their need to write, the teacher may facilitate independent writing by providing each child with a word box containing the words he needs. In this way, spelling is integrated into handwriting and composition instruction. When the child asks for a word, it is written on paper of appropriate size. The child studies that word—several methods, mostly kinesthetic, are utilized—then writes it in his story. After he has used the word properly, he files the word according to its first letter in his box. If he has occasion to use the word again, he looks in his box and thus refreshes his memory. If children become familiar with the alphabet in this way, less formal instruction is needed in third grade.

Transition to cursive. The transition from manuscript writing to cursive writing is usually begun at the end of the second grade or in the third grade. By this time the children have achieved proficiency in manuscript writing, and their muscles have developed. The change is made gradually, more slowly for some than for others. Usually, third graders are instructed to form large letters, and by fourth grade they achieve standard size.

For cursive as for manuscript writing, the school should have a stated form and method used throughout the grades. Of the several writing systems available, each provides excellent manuals and evaluation scales, and gives explicit instructions for developing letter formation, size, spacing, slant, alignment, proportion of letters, and weight of line.

In a research study of current handwriting practice, Herrick and Okada summarized as follows:

1. The three most commonly used resources for teachers are alphabet display cards, a handwriting book for each child, and a teachers' guide accompanying a commercial system.

2. While alphabet display cards are commonly used, other visual aids such as scales for judging quality, body position charts, diagnostic charts, and filmstrips are used infrequently to facilitate instruction.

3. Special handwriting teachers and handwriting supervisors are almost non-existent in schools; handwriting instruction is a responsibility of the classroom teacher.

4. Only one-third of the schools in the nation and in the state of Wisconsin use some scale in evaluating children's handwriting. The Freeman scale is the one most commonly used, followed next by scales developed by local school systems. The scales mentioned above plus the West and Ayres Scales account for 95 percent of the scales used in programs of handwriting instruction. The use of a

scale to evaluate handwriting seems to be tied to the use of a corresponding commercial system.

The examination of these findings supports the conclusion that programs of instruction in handwriting are determined largely by the commercial systems used. Few school systems develop their own handwriting program and if they do, this program is implemented primarily by the purchase of appropriate instructional materials from a number of the commercial systems available. Perhaps most serious of all is the meager effort going into the development of better evaluation procedures in this field. Most of the scales, even though revised, are not particularly suitable for instructional purposes.[7]

Greatest concern about present practice lay in the area of evaluation. Therefore in later studies, Herrick and Erlebacher developed the Wisconsin Scales for Evaluating Quality in Handwriting in which they have made the following claims:

It has been possible:

1. To develop a master set of 600 scaled handwriting samples for grades four, five and six which provides:
   a. A recent definition of a comprehensive continuum of writing legibility for school children of this age.
   b. A cardinal scale of legibility which will permit computation of known differences in legibility between two samples of writing.
   c. A means for identifying scale samples of similar writing style through a reliable procedure for measuring the slant and size of writing.
   d. A research tool which has greater power for dealing with legibility in handwriting than any scale that new exists.

2. To develop master sets of scaled samples which will permit:
   a. The development of handwriting scales for school use for different conditions of grade level, desired levels of legibility, and variation in slant and size. No recent handwriting scale in school use has this potential.
   b. The collection of a set of scaled research samples which will permit the study of (1) the limits within which deviation in the slant and size of writing makes a difference in legibility and (2) the factors in the writing record which differentiate between good and poor writing.
   c. The development of a table which will indicate for a given difference in legibility, the number of judges necessary to place a given handwriting sample on the scale at a determined level of confidence. Reliable placement of a sample on a two-point scale,

---

[7] Virgil E. Herrick (editor), *New Horizons for Research in Handwriting* (Madison: The University of Wisconsin Press, 1963), p. 27. Reprinted with permission of the copyright owners, The Regents of the University of Wisconsin.

for example, representing great differences in legibility obviously does not require fifty judges.

3. To develop a scaling procedure which holds promise for the evaluation of a wide array of complex learning and artistic products such as compositions, paintings, and designs. Any school system could easily develop its own scales in handwriting and composition through the use of this procedure.

Limitations are:

1. The master list of 600 scaled samples is not easily available to all possible users. At present it is limited to research use.

2. There is some question whether the length and substance of our writing sample, "The quick brown fox jumps over the lazy dog," provides an adequate scale referent for lengthier writing samples of different content.

3. The scaled samples are restricted to cursive handwriting done in the main by right-handed writers. Obviously this scale will not deal with manuscript writing, and it is likely that extreme samples of left-handed writing would not be accurately scaled by comparison with the master samples. The same scaling procedure should be used for developing a master list of manuscript samples.[8]

Anderson has listed some appropriate grade expectancies in handwriting which give the teacher an overall point of reference:

By the end of kindergarten, most children may be expected to possess the following knowledge concerning handwriting:
1. Writing is a form of communication. It is language shared through signs. Signs, names, and other written symbols have meaning.
2. In some cases, a child will be able to write his first name.
3. Some familiarity with the forms of print-script writing as the teacher uses it in recording children's stories, labeling pictures, or writing names.

By the end of grade one, most children may be expected to:
1. Write in print-script form all letters—both capitals and lower case.
2. Write his name and address.
3. Write simple original stories.
4. Understand and practice proper spacing between letters of a word and between words of a sentence.

By the end of the second grade, a child should:
1. Be able to do good print-script writing in daily lessons.
2. Know about margins, heading of paper, and spacing.
3. Write a friendly letter.

---

[8] Herrick, pp. 230–231.

4. Know the correct use of the terms: capital letters, period, question mark, comma as used between city and state and in dates.
5. Write print script with apparent ease.

By the end of the third grade, a child should be able to:
1. Use both print script and cursive writing to meet his daily needs.
2. Write his own name, his school, city, and state in cursive style.
3. Analyze and improve his own written work.
4. Write with reasonable speed.

During grade four, the child should be able to:
1. Write correctly, friendly letters (one or two good paragraphs).
2. Write notes to friends and classmates.
3. Write original stories, poems, plays, and programs.
4. Show evidence of retaining manuscript writing as a supplementary tool.
5. Meet the grade standards as indicated on a handwriting scale.
6. Recognize and correct his errors in letter formation.

By the end of grade five, the child should be able to:
1. Write a business letter.
2. Take notes in class.
3. Plan and present written reports.
4. Use pen and ink neatly.
5. Attempt writing on stationery without lines.
6. Meet grade standards with regard to legibility and speed (50–60 words per minute).

By the end of grade six, the child should be able to:
1. Proofread and rewrite many first writing efforts.
2. Take pride in submitting neat, orderly papers in all class work.
3. Meet grade standards of legibility and speed.

In grades seven and eight, the language teacher should devote some time to writing instruction each week. Teachers of *all* subjects should check and grade papers for neatness and legibility in handwriting. Ideas and the willingness to express them are more important than mechanics, but a carelessly written paper should be handed back to a student to be done over and a grade withheld until the second paper is handed to the teacher. The second effort is accepted if it is an improvement.[9]

Teaching children to form letters by writing them in the air or tracing them is no longer considered effective practice, though attention is given to rhythm and speed of the penmanship.

---

[9] Anderson, *Language Skills*, pp. 101–102.

The quality of materials improves with new inventions. Ball-point pens have been adopted by many schools, eliminating some of the problems of the straight pen. The pencils being used are comfortable to the grasp of the small and poorly coordinated hands of young children. Paper of a size that encourages free movement and that has guidelines appropriately fixed is also helpful.

The left-handed writer. Children who tend to use their left hand for writing are encouraged to do so. These sinistrals, however, face several problems as they learn to adjust to the use of the left hand in a right-handed world. First they need to overcome the feeling that they are different or that there is peculiarity or abnormality in their behavior. They need only realize the advantage of the left-handed performer in athletics to influence the self-concept. Secondly, the sinistral must modify the usual right-handed procedures. When a child writes with his left hand, he covers the words that must be written from left to right. The shape of the pen, and the usual grip upon it, the shape of the letters and their slant are designed for right-handed writers. The methods of instruction, geared to right-handed children, are in themselves problems to sinistrals.

The following procedures are suggested for guiding the left-handed writer: (1) The paper is to be slanted from right to left so that the lower edge is at right angles to the child's arm. (2) The pencil or pen is gripped a little higher than usual (from 1 to 1½ inches from the point) so that the writer may see the letters he writes. Especially crucial is that the writing instrument be slanted over the left shoulder so that the wrist will not be abnormally bent. (3) The hand is held well below the base line of the writing so that loops below that line are not smeared. (4) The slant of the writing is adapted to the left, that is, the slant is either vertical or at any angle from vertical to forty-five degrees left. This is probably one of the most important clues to good left-handed writing, and one least suggested by teachers. (5) Sometimes reversed lighting and special seats with armrests on the left are arranged.

Spelling

THOZE SPELING DEEMUNS

Ralph Dornfeld Owen

A man named Mr. John Pough calls on you and hands you his card. To be polite you try to pronounce his name. What will you say?

Mr. Po	*o* as in dough or toe
Mr. Puf	*u* as in rough or cuff
Mr. Pawf	*aw* as in cough or off
Mr. Poo	*oo* as in through or too
Mr. Pou	*ou* as in bough or doubt

If you are wise you will say, "How do you pronounce your name, Sir?"

This illustrates the fact that no one can know with certainty how to pronounce an English word which he has only seen written or how to spell a word which he has only heard but never seen written.[10]

Is it any wonder that so many of our children are poor in spelling, or that many college students are unconscious of their spelling errors? Spelling difficulties cannot be attributed to any one cause because our phonetically nonregular language presents problems in pronunciation and in regular association of sound to symbol. The problem is confounded by lack of instructional emphasis upon legible handwriting, effective visual analysis, careful listening, and reasonable understanding of language structure.

The aim of spelling instruction is not only to produce accurate spellers, but to do so using the most economical learning activities possible, to help children to facilitate their written expression and recognize the relationships of spelling to listening, speaking, writing and reading, to learn progressively from their own level and at their own speed, and to influence a positive attitude about spelling. The trend is to continue spelling instruction beyond the special lesson to its use in all areas of the curriculum.

The learning of spelling is more than an independent, silent study of words. Nor is it memorization of the correct order of the letters. Rather, it is a study of words with increasing independence in terms of visual and auditory discrimination, pronunciation, enunciation, and meaningful use. Both teacher and child work to develop sensitivity to the form and structure of words and to the phonetic and structural principles involved, and to develop *spelling consciousness.*

The spelling "list." To facilitate systematic instruction many schools use a spelling series developed from research and based upon spiral development of ability. Spelling lists are organized by the authors of the series; simple words are presented first, and more complex words with various kinds of spelling problems are listed in logical order. In the more recent series, the logical order has given way to a linguistic organization based on spelling patterns. The usual format is a workbook in which the words are presented in regularly outlined lessons; the learner completes the exercises in the workbook. Newer series are incorporating a multilevel approach that provides for individual achievement differences among children.

Though some experts today think the use of a list is important, many

---

[10] Ralph D. Owen, "Those Speling Deemuns," in V. D. Anderson, *Readings in the Language Arts* (New York: The Macmillan Company, 1964), p. 203.

believe that the list should be supplemented by words growing out of the special activities of the school and neighborhood. Words from the social studies, science, mathematics, art, other subject matter areas, and the child's own writing needs are identified, recorded, defined, and studied as they arise. These words may be added to the basic series list for testing, or they may be evaluated independently. Frequently children keep records of the supplementary words in dictionaries of their own making or in some other kind of word file.

Special aspects of spelling instruction. The most effective spelling program is highly related to reading and word recognition techniques, and is given attention throughout the school day. In spelling, as in other subjects, teachers modify methods to take care of the different ways in which children learn. A kinesthetic method may work well with one child, an oral method better with another.

One emphasis in spelling instruction is the development of spelling readiness. Readiness involves not only the need to write and the desire to spell correctly, but establishment of preliminary skills in oral and written expression, ability to read, and ability to discriminate between forms of written symbols. Factors of readiness increase in complexity at the various levels of the child's development.

Much doubt exists about the effective use of spelling rules. Because the English language is not based on a simple phonetic pattern, the use of many rules is unrealistic. There are too many exceptions. Mere memorization of spelling rules does not increase the child's ability to spell. The newer spellers, however, contain lists organized around spelling principles so that the child can understand the possible categories. For example, Kottmeyer devotes a unit to the silent letters in his *Basic Goals in Spelling* series. Other spelling series give special attention to such principles as the various spellings of the long *o* sound.

A growing trend is the use of various aids to spelling instruction. If a spelling workbook is used, it is considered the basic minimum, and in some cases its use is confined to slower learners. Teachers add variety and interest to spelling instruction with such devices as spelling games, flannel boards, appropriate reference materials, puzzles, films and filmstrips, and mnemonic devices.

The problem of grouping for spelling is a common one. Many teachers teach as though children progress at the same rate in spelling even though they do not expect the same rate of progress in arithmetic or reading. Because of basic differences in children, some children can master many more words than the average. Others may have to work at limited numbers of words in order to relieve the confusion and frustration of repeated failure that may lead to lack of effort.

Most guides for spelling instruction suggest five ways of becoming familiar with words, using all sensory stimulations. (1) The word is observed and studied, so that the child becomes familiar with the visual pattern of the whole word and the context of the letter symbols. Syllables and distinctive letters in the word distinguish the visual image. Analysis discloses parts of the word that may cause trouble in spelling. Differences between *correspondence* and *correspondance* and between *familar* and *familiar* are noted. (2) The word is spoken, pronounced, and enunciated clearly and accurately. The meaning and the visual image of the word are recalled as the vocal organs work to produce the exact sound. (3) The word is heard. The sound is related to enunciation, visual image, and meaning, as one notices accurate and inaccurate pronunciation. Differences are recognized between *athletic* and *athaletic*. Any confusion among letter sounds is clarified, as in *haladay* and *holiday*. (4) The word is written. When it is written legibly in a sentence, its meaning is made clear and the shape of the word is demonstrated. Silent letters are identified; syllables and sounds are recognized in written symbols. (5) The word is carefully thought through. After having looked at, spoken, listened to, and written the word, the child then thinks about the meaning, sound, and written form. He can check inaccurate formation of derivatives, confusion of homonyms, and transposition of letters.

Fowler lists ten teaching procedures suggested by recent research in spelling:

1. Students should be encouraged to concentrate on words or parts of words which the pretest or errors in written work show are trouble spots.
2. Careful pronunciation of words is an important factor in good spelling.
3. Distributed learning is more productive than mass learning: students should focus on fewer words at one time and have opportunity for practicing these at intervals for recall.
4. Words should be *overlearned*—that is, learned beyond the point of one successful recall.
5. Teachers should not overvalue spelling. Emphasis on spelling as a matter of first importance has given poor spellers strong inhibitions about writing. Since many good students are poor spellers, primary emphasis should be on good writing.
6. The presentation of words in context is less effective than presenting them in list form, except as the context is necessary for identification.
7. Pretests corrected and studied provide the most effective learning.
8. Primary emphasis should be visual imagery, but for many students audile and kinesthetic methods increase the effectiveness of learning.

9. The only rules that should be taught are those applying to a large number of words and having few exceptions. The most useful of these is the one for adding suffixes by changing *y* to *i*, dropping the final silent *e*, and doubling the final consonant. Three other rules are that the letter *q* is always followed by *u*, that English words do not end in *v*, and that proper nouns and most adjectives formed from proper nouns begin with a capital letter.

10. Recommended procedures for teaching rules: teach rules inductively and develop them in connection with the words to which they apply; teach one rule at a time; emphasize both positive and negative aspects. When a rule has been taught, it should be systematically reviewed and applied. Emphasis should be on use of the rule rather than on memorization of a verbal statement.

Teachers may also tape sentences using 100 spelling demons, and allow students to take this taped test at intervals, until they can spell all the words. Spellers who have made a good score at the beginning of the year may be required to take it later in the year to check their retention.[11]

One author lists groups of questions asked of pupils to provide for phonetic, structural, and meaning analysis as well as usage practice in independent study of spelling words. Some of them are listed here:

For phonetic analysis:
>   What other words can I write that sound like this word?
>   What other words can I write that begin (end) like this word?
>   What silent letters are contained in this word?
>   Which syllable is accented?

For structural analysis:
>   Is this a root word for formation of other words? If so, write the new words.
>   What is the prefix, if any, in this word? Can other prefixes be added?
>   Can this word be made plural?
>   Can I write the syllables for this word?

For meaning:
>   What is the dictionary definition of this word? Does the word have more than one meaning?
>   What are some good synonyms for this word? Antonyms?
>   Does the word have a homonym?
>   Is this an action word?[12]

---

[11] Mary Elizabeth Fowler, *Teaching Language, Composition and Literature* (New York: McGraw-Hill Book Company, Inc., 1965), p. 204.

[12] Howard E. Blake, "Studying Spelling Independently," *Elementary English* (January 1960), pp. 29–32.

The teaching of spelling can be one of the most challenging demands on a creative teacher. The development of positive attitudes, the encouragement of self-study, and high motivation may be accomplished by any number of methods. Learning to spell is an individual matter. Though the teacher gives guidance, the major responsibility for learning to spell a word or a group of words lies with the individual child.

Spelling instruction has recently been influenced by the several innovations in the teaching of language arts. References to them may be found in Chapter 7.

Research in spelling conducted at Stanford University[13] gives us some clues and predicts drastic changes in spelling programs because of recent application of linguistics to the language program. Hanna[14] points out:

> A modern spelling program is possible today as a result of new research into linguistics and into teaching-learning theories. Such a modern spelling program will (1) start from the child's possession of a large aural-oral vocabulary; (2) teach him how to break these words into component sounds; (3) lead him to discover the correspondences between the phonemes and the alphabetical letters that have come to represent these sounds in standard American-English spelling; (4) help him discover the influence that position, stress, and context have in the choice of a particular grapheme from among the several options; (5) guide him to go beyond the phonological analysis to examine the morphological elements such as compounding, affixation or word families; (6) teach him how to use all his sensori-motor equipment of ear-voice-eye-hand to reinforce each other in fixing the standard spelling in his neural system; and (7) help him to build a spelling power that should make possible a writing vocabulary "unlimited" or limited only by the size of his spoken vocabulary.

Rudorf[15] lists eight spelling skills as goals for a program:

> Specifically, the abilities we would then be trying to develop (and consequently to measure and evaluate) would include:
> 1. The ability to discriminate between the phonemes of the language.
> 2. The ability to identify graphemic options of each of the phonemes.
> 3. The ability to identify syllables in oral speech.
> 4. The ability to recognize stress when present.

[13] A series of five articles have been published in *Elementary English* on Research in Spelling supported by the Cooperative Research Branch of the U.S. Office of Education and under the direction of Paul R. Hanna.

[14] Paul R. Hanna and Jean S. Hanna, "Applications of Linguistics and Psychological Cues to the Spelling Course of Study," *Elementary English*, Vol. 42, No. 7 (November 1965), pp. 753–759.

[15] E. Hugh Rudorf, "Measurement of Spelling Ability," *Elementary English*, Vol. 42, No. 8 (December 1965), pp. 889–894.

5. The ability to relate phonemes to their immediate environment.
6. The ability to recognize morphemes (meaningful units of phoneme combinations) such as roots, affixes, and inflections.
7. The ability to utilize certain principles of morphophonemics (how morphemes change in combination to form words; for example, the processes of assimilation and synthesis).
8. The ability to relate meaning (as determined by syntax) to spelling (the homonym problem).

Linguistic analysis, relating spelling to reading and the spoken word, tends to extend the study of spelling into special lessons for reading, writing, and oral expression. In this way, the formal spelling lesson using the traditional spelling workbook may be supplemented and supported by lessons in other areas of language arts.

Language Usage

The teaching of formal English usage today is not merely instruction in *grammar;* it is not the memorization of isolated formal technical skills, principles, and rules in punctuation, capitalization, and sentence structure. All of these elements are present in modern language instruction, but *language usage* emphasizes the practical study of the way language works, the relationships of words and phrases to each other within the sentence structure. This kind of instruction employs an analytical, thoughtful approach that includes knowledge of correct form and understanding of the functions of words and their interrelationships and patterns in a sentence.

The oral basis of usage. A background of correct spoken language is taught before the teacher begins to guide language structure in written composition. Children learn to speak with complete sentences, use the proper verb or pronoun, and follow rules of grammatical construction. Most of the standards of English accepted in school are those of the upper middle-class society. Thus while children are learning one kind of usage at school, they may be learning a different kind at home. One of the problems of the teacher is to help the child understand why he needs to master a more formal English, and perhaps develop the use of double standards. Children need to understand that Americans use a variety of language forms, acceptable to specific situations.

In the primary grades the child is helped to understand that "I don't have" is more acceptable as standard English than "I ain't got." In the intermediate grades, children begin to learn some simple rules such as those for plurals and commas.

The need for correct usage in real situations. Effective guidance of correct grammatical usage by children is provided when they write for real purposes. "Real purposes" are not teacher-imposed purposes. If the teacher says, "Today we shall write about spring," some children may not want to write about spring, others may not have an impressional concept or a conscious idea about it. Nor should the teacher say, "Now we shall write. Do a composition about anything you wish." There may not be many wishes. The challenge is to create such a stimulating environment that the child has a desire to write about something upon which he has clear information or deep feelings. The aim is not to eliminate language errors, but to develop a desire to write at an acceptable standard and to build writing habits at that standard.

The influence of linguistics. Though approved methods of teaching grammatical construction in grades one through six have seldom, if ever, utilized diagramming, it has been a part of the more formal approach to language usage in grades seven and eight. The influence of linguistics has changed the single, standard formula for diagramming a sentence to several different methods for analyzing the relationships of words within a sentence. The trend is toward a more functional understanding of grammatical structure.

Training as a result of writing. Once writing has been motivated, excessive criticism of form during the writing can spoil interests or creativity. Natalie Cole, in her own creative style, suggests one method of teacher guidance, as related to punctuation:

> I remember when I was a child. With what joy the teacher jumped all over the paper, putting in punctuation marks! In this way she could vindicate herself . . . it was her excuse for being. It kept before our minds constantly the fact that she was superior. No matter what we would write, she could always find something wrong. It kept us in our proper place. How kind that teacher would have been if once she had praised the content rather than correcting the form. . . . When we feel we must give attention to punctuation, why not take a bit from some child's story and put it on the board and stress its strength and beauty? Then say casually, "There are a few things we could do to this that would make it a little easier to read, but they are not the important things. . . ."[16]

Thoughts and ideas are judged first. Nevertheless, the ability to express ideas clearly and accurately is essential to the content of the ideas. A teacher cannot let a paper go home in poor form, or post it on a bulletin board in poor condition. Common errors, identified, may point to

---

[16] Natalie R. Cole, *The Arts in the Classroom* (New York: The John Day Company, 1940), pp. 107–108.

the need for positive teaching; training lessons are organized to clarify difficulties and give practice in correct application.

Determining content in language usage. What to teach in the area of language usage may be something of a problem if a teacher tries to provide experiences around the needs of children. The training experiences provided are determined by the varied means the teacher utilizes to identify the need: observation, demonstrated written errors, inventories. Instructional emphasis is guided by the errors made by the majority of pupils, or at least by a group that can study one use together.

Language textbooks are available that offer basic understandings preliminary to grammar and a minimum of rules and definitions. Most authorities suggest that these be used judiciously, particularly in the lower grades, and that their best use might be for supplementary and enrichment activities of the program.

Records and Reports

As children learn to write their thoughts clearly and interestingly, they study several different kinds of writing. Letters and simple stories are probably most frequently used in the primary grades, whereas records and reports assume more importance in intermediate grades.

Younger children receive background for records and reports from the construction of experience charts and development of cooperative rules, plans, and standards. The ability to think the whole situation through, organize logically on paper, and illustrate in proper and interesting fashion is developed through practice in constructing the simple primary charts or oral reports.

As children write individual reports, they need the ability to synthesize ideas from different sources and write them in logical and effective style. The use of humor, illustrative stories, and interesting words and phrases is part of the skill inherent in writing an effective report. Ability to quote from references and other people's ideas can also be taught in a simple manner. Most of all, teachers need to encourage creativity in assembling material and presentation.

Creative Writing

Creative writing, as a vehicle for the expression of ideas and feelings, is similar to all other means of creative expression. From the wells of experience and original thought comes creative expression, using words as a medium rather than sound, movement, or the materials of art. Development of ability in the writing of creative stories, plays, poems, and other types of original composition is now frequently integrated into subject areas other than language arts.

In its initial stages, the basis for creative writing is oral, but foundations for ability in creative writing are developed through listening and reading as well as speaking. In the kindergarten and first grade, children may compose delightful oral prose or poetry by dictating to the teacher. As children listen to well-phrased poetry and well-written stories or read children's books, they learn to express themselves orally with greater originality, clarity, and precision. The child who speaks with colorful words, apt phrases, a dash of humor or pathos, does so to a great extent because he has been exposed to such language, understands the subtleties of words, and is encouraged to experiment with literary expression. Creative oral expression later becomes written expression.

Creative writing is usually the result of wide and varied experience. Time and opportunity should be provided for the preliminary experiences as well as for the actual creative act. Creative writing is not produced from a vacuum. Experiences about a circus might include viewing films, posters and other pictures of a circus, visiting a zoo, imitating the movements of circus animals, hearing stories and poems and singing songs about the circus, and discussing activities within a circus. Rich personal experiences such as these are both practical and literary, and constitute a basis for thought.

Free and original thinking precedes the adequate expression of ideas in both oral and written form. Children need time to think, sometimes in silent, introspective meditation. Children also need to develop sensitivity, receptiveness to new ideas, and the habit of thinking independently. In order to encourage original thought the teacher sometimes withholds judgments, and he frequently needs to help children think through nebulous ideas or clarify vague impressions. A permissive, friendly atmosphere in a classroom stimulates the expression of spontaneous, inventive ideas, for children then do not fear criticism, rebuke, or ridicule from the teacher or their classmates. The sharing of ideas stimulates the development of more fluent oral expression upon which written compositions depend. As children talk together, the teacher encourages the use of new words, the study of word meanings, and the choice of unusual, colorful, and dramatic words, neatly turned phrases and pleasing word illustrations. Oral communication among children, guided but not dominated by the teacher, helps to provide the background needed for effective writing.

With greater maturity, skillful guidance, and many opportunities to write creatively, children become increasingly proficient in writing. They become conscious of the differences among words and the variance in meaning between two very similar words. They appreciate the pleasant sounds of certain words used in combination and the ease with which some sentences or phrases can be understood, consciously appreciated, and evaluated. Children enjoy trying to express an old idea in an entirely new manner, in trying to be completely original in style and phraseology. The written expression of fantasy or ideas in relation to very practical situations is easily encouraged.

The teacher's sensitivity to individual differences influences his guidance of the writing situation. Inner motivation and feelings, special interests, and individual mannerisms in writing are to be encouraged. Burrows points out variation rather dramatically:

> The infinite variety of human nature is nowhere more apparent than in the strange and sometimes devious ways that children follow in putting thoughts on paper. Some can write in the midst of swirling activity while others find the presence of even one other person a deterrent. Some love notebooks and the smugness of pages between covers; others choose the freeness of single sheets. Some think out all of a story in advance; others work from the most trivial starting point and know only what is going to happen next. Some write best in solitude; others like to write occasionally with a partner.[17]

Skilled written expression requires a knowledge of correct grammatical usage, accurate spelling, and legible penmanship. Creative writing is both a craft and an art. It is sometimes said that any person of average intelligence can be taught the craft, the mechanics of writing. Certainly teaching the art of writing, the development of an individualistic style and original expression, is a more complex task. Mastering the craft is a prerequisite to achieving the art. Nevertheless, much creativeness has undoubtedly been stifled by teachers who interrupt the flow of ideas by insisting upon mechanical perfection. The better course of action is to defer instruction in these areas until later when carefully planned lessons emerge from demonstrated weaknesses.

The Challenge

As with other areas of the curriculum, forces are at work to revolutionize the teaching of the English language arts. Because of established conservatism, the change takes place slowly. We are in a transitional period. New knowledge, new ideas, new tools of instruction, and new methods are not completely accepted nor their results ascertained. One will see a variety of programs among schools. In the elementary schools, despite the diversity, the study of language holds the greatest emphasis

---

[17] Alvina T. Burrows and others, *They All Want to Write* (Englewood Cliffs, N.J.: Prentice-Hall, Inc., 1952), pp. 109–110.

in the curriculum. This is a real challenge to teachers to determine the way they can best help children understand and use the mother tongue.

It is evident that change in content and method in the language arts is stemming from the application of linguistic study to the language experiences of children. Because the influence is so recent, no single approach has been universally accepted. Educators are busy interpreting the findings of linguistic research, preparing materials, and experimenting with procedure. Probably the one idea we are learning from the milieu of change in teaching language is that no one kind of material nor any single method is superior for all teachers and all children.

RECOMMENDED READINGS

APPLEGATE, MAUREE. *Easy in English*. New York: Harper & Row, Publishers, Inc., 1960.

——— *Winged Writing*. New York: Harper & Row, Publishers, Inc., 1961.

BRUNER, JEROME S., JACQUELINE J. GOODNOW, and GEORGE A. AUSTIN. *A Study of Thinking*. New York: Science Editions, Inc., 1966.

BURROWS, ALVINA T., DORIS C. JACKSON, and DOROTHY C. SAUNDERS. *They all Want to Write*. New York: Holt, Rinehart and Winston, Inc., 1964.

DAWSON, MILDRED A., and FRIEDA A. DINGEE. *Children Learn the Language Arts*. Minneapolis: Burgess Publishing Company, 1966.

FRAZIER, ALEXANDER (editor). *New Directions in Elementary English*. Champaign, Ill.: National Council of the Teachers of English, 1967.

GLEASON, H. A. *Linguistics and English Grammar*. New York: Holt, Rinehart and Winston, Inc., 1965.

GREENE, HARRY A., and WALTER T. PETTY. *Developing Language Skills in the Elementary School*. Boston: Allyn and Bacon, Inc., 1967.

MARCKWARDT, ALBERT H. *Linguistics and the Teaching of English*. Bloomington, Ind.: Indiana University Press, 1966.

PETTY, WALTER T., and MARY E. BOWEN. *Slithery Snakes and Other Aids to Children's Writing*. New York: Appleton-Century-Crofts, Inc., 1967.

PRONOVOST, WILBERT L. *The Teaching of Speaking and Listening in the Elementary School*. New York: David McKay Company, Inc., 1959.

SIKS, GERALDINE B. *Creative Dramatics: An Art for Children*. New York: Harper & Row, Publishers, Inc., 1958.

SMITH, JAMES A. *Creative Teaching of Language Arts in the Elementary School*. Boston: Allyn and Bacon, Inc., 1967.

Expanding Understanding: Foreign Language

9

Teaching of foreign language in the elementary school is rapidly expanding. FLES, the alphabetical code for "foreign language in the elementary school" is becoming increasingly familiar among teachers and administrators.

It is estimated that nearly two million elementary school children are now enrolled in foreign language classes. Pressure for this kind of instruction comes from legislatures, parent groups, high schools and universities, and the Modern Language Association of America. Another incentive is financial aid from federal programs. In recent years more FLES classes have been established, offered to other than gifted children, and continued sequentially through the grades than ever before.

Though increased teaching of foreign language is the trend, there are still a number of questions about its role in the curriculum that have not been answered. Questions such as the optimum age for children to begin the study, the relationship of foreign language to other subjects, particularly the social studies, and whether children can sample a variety of languages are not completely answered. These will be discussed in this chapter. As with all new emphases in elementary school curriculum, there are committed advocates and thoughtful critics of the program.

THE TREND IN FOREIGN LANGUAGE INSTRUCTION

A Changing Attitude

In spite of some controversy over the appropriateness of teaching foreign language to young children, new positive attitudes about it emerging since World War II have been reinforced during the last five years.

There are several major reasons for the growing popularity of foreign language instruction. Probably the most valid and important reason for teaching American children a foreign language is that such study will give depth to the understanding of communication. It is a contribution to the general education of a child. Through study of a foreign language a child learns more about his mother tongue. He learns about the symbolism of language and how this symbolism relates to the life of other groups of people, to other cultures. He finds out about man's great dependency on communication and his need for oral language.

Another reason is cultural. The ease of travel to foreign countries has increased the average American's desire to know something of other languages. He wants to learn a second language not so much for personal gain as for more effective intergroup relationships. An American who can use a second language can identify with another group of people and therefore is better prepared for world understanding. The Modern Language Association of America says: "A language is not only a *means of communication;* it is a *vehicle of culture.* Young children are by nature eager to know how other people live, to learn their songs, their dances, their legends and stories, and their art. Moreover, the child who learns by heart jingles, songs, and verse in a foreign language is cultivating taste for and a love of literature."[1] Properly taught, foreign language helps a child recognize and understand similarities between his own culture and that of another group of people. Brooks contends that the study of a foreign language is the thread that draws together the philosophy, culture, economics, and academic aspects of man.[2]

A third reason for FLES is the generally accepted belief that young children learn a foreign language more easily and with greater enthusiasm than do older children or adolescents. They are imitative by nature and so mimic the facial movements of the teacher, articulate strange sounds fluently, and speak with little self-consciousness. They learn through hearing, speaking, seeing, feeling, and pantomime. They make no conscious analogy to their mother tongue. A young child seems to grasp the "feel" of the language. Eventually, through sequential and continued study, a feeling for sentence structure and the ability to think in the second language are developed. Children at about fourth or fifth grade seem to be intrigued by learning a different language because it is similar to developing a code of their own. Research by educators,

---

[1] P. S. Anderson and others, *Readings in the Language Arts* (New York: The Macmillan Company, 1964), p. 431.

[2] Nelson Brooks, *Language and Language Learning* (New York: Harcourt, Brace & World, Inc., 1960), p. xiii.

psychiatrists, language specialists, and neurologists give us evidence that children can learn to speak and understand a foreign language as early as five years, and that the ages from five to ten are optimal to begin foreign language instruction.

As a result of changing attitudes, more languages are now being taught at more school levels than before. There are more course offerings and higher enrollments. Schools are increasing foreign language services by including classes in summer sessions, providing workshops for teachers, making available instructional guides, and hiring specialists in the field. Commercial producers have modified electronic equipment to make it suitable to classroom use, and school districts are making an effort to put modern equipment and appropriate materials into the classroom. Elementary schools are organizing new programs in spite of already heavy teacher loads and crowded curriculums.

Thus the teaching of foreign language does exist in many elementary schools, and many teachers will be asked to deal with it either in the actual instructional situation or in related supplementary and reinforcement activities.

Existing Elementary School Programs

Foreign language is such a recent addition to the elementary school curriculum that the program is not yet permanently established, nor is there uniformity in its organization.

Though some classroom instruction may begin as early as kindergarten or first grade, the general trend is to begin elementary school foreign language instruction in the third or fourth grade. At this time the average child has attained some facility in his mother tongue, is familiar with the school situation, and has developed some general study skills. He is still flexible enough to respond to the usual procedures for teaching a foreign language to children.

Lessons usually are organized into fifteen-minute periods for primary grades, and twenty-minute periods for intermediate grades. A lesson every day is most effective but good results are gained with lessons three times a week. Once lessons have started, continuity over the subsequent years in school is preferred. Generally, three types of programs are identifiable.

Instruction by a special teacher. The teacher may or may not be a native speaker of the language, but he is fluent and skilled in it. Frequently this teacher comes to the regular classroom and instructs all students. Sometimes selected students go to a room used by the FLES teacher where he can more easily use his specialized materials. Though the special teacher may not see each child every day, he can provide continuity from year to year as the students grow more adept in the language.

Televised instruction. Through scheduled lessons on television, a fluent specialist teaches students in their own classrooms. The regular teacher is responsible for pre-lesson preparation and post-lesson follow-up. He frequently uses a guide that offers procedural plans, reviews, follow-up suggestions, and the means by which children can understand the cultural setting of the language. Advantages of televised teaching lie in the number of students that can be reached, in the use of a skilled teacher with a native accent, in the possibility of taped lessons for special scheduling and repeating to new classes, in the pictured lesson that reproduces a cultural environment, and in the variety of specialized teaching materials that may be utilized. Disadvantages are recognized as the lack of direct pupil-teacher contact, the possible weakness or distortion related to the warm-up or review, and the time lapse between lessons.

Instruction by the regular classroom teacher. Instruction by the classroom teacher takes several forms, depending on the teacher's skill and enthusiasm. Inservice education in the form of workshops conducted by a language specialist can assist the teacher. Frequently auxiliary materials, such as tapes, televised lessons, and workbooks, are provided as supplements. Disadvantages are related to the teacher's lack of a native accent and the possible lack of continuity in instruction from year to year. Advantages are the opportunity to relate the foreign language instruction to instruction in other subject areas, and the regular teacher's greater knowledge of the children being taught.

No matter what type of organization is planned, the classroom teacher becomes involved. If a special FLES teacher provides the instruction in the classroom, the regular teacher ideally remains for the lesson so that he may know what is being taught and be able to follow through at other times during the day or week. If children leave regular classrooms to go to a special room, the teacher needs to know what is being done there and how the children are responding if he is to provide any reinforcing experiences. Special conferences to establish understanding and to develop plans for cooperation and assistance are needed between the two teachers in either case.

TEACHING FOREIGN LANGUAGES

Methodological Approaches

During the last ten years elementary school teachers of foreign language have learned much about teaching a second language from the studies and suggestions of linguists, foreign language scholars, and educators. Some progress has recently been made in developing programs that are less influenced by the unique skills and interests of particular local teachers; continuity in programming is increasing; the great disparity in programs between districts is lessening. Certain common characteristics and procedures are emerging, and teachers are increasingly distinguishing between what might be called the "old method" and the "new method."

The "old" method. The traditional approach to the teaching of foreign languages on the secondary and collegiate levels has been a kind of decoding, deductive, analytical system. Textbooks usually supplied the framework of study, lesson by lesson. The emphasis was upon translation. Students learned vocabulary lists in which words in the new language were equated with words in the mother tongue. Exercises in grammar analysis were introduced early and became a dominant part of the instruction. Rules were learned, and illustrations of the rules were presented. Related English was translated to the foreign language, or vice versa. The learner paired the foreign language to the English equivalent and so thought in English. This approach has not been characteristic of FLES.

The "new" method. The most widely accepted present-day procedure for teaching foreign language has several names: direct, natural, co-ordinate, bilingual, oral-aural, or audio-lingual. As these terms imply, the method stresses the use of foreign language as normal speech, with complete control of the sound system achieved through learning with the ear and the tongue as well as the eye and the other physical senses. It is a direct, natural approach based on active oral participation.

In the beginning the child hears more than he speaks; he hears only the foreign language; English is either minimized or avoided entirely. Meaning is achieved through facial expression, gesture, pantomime, pictorial illustration, or context. As he hears only the authentic pattern of speech, he acquires a set of verbal habits. He listens with a purpose, to recognize and discriminate between the words of the new language. He learns structural patterns rather than isolated words.

The child becomes familiar with the sounds, and then as he listens he imitates the speech of the teacher. He speaks only what he has heard. Use of the tongue, lips, teeth, and other organs of speech may be exaggerated to achieve proper pronunciation and auditory discrimination. Accuracy of pronunciation is emphasized before fluency. Enough repetition is experienced so that memorization of sentence structure occurs as well as of vocabulary. Usually vocabulary is minimized until structure patterns are familiar. Practice is always accomplished in the hearing-speaking situation so that the teacher may give immediate and constant guidance to correct pronunciation.

Only after the child has much familiarity with the spoken word is the graphic symbol introduced, usually in the sixth or seventh grade. By the end of the sixth grade the learner may associate spelling with sounds.

The learner reads only what he has learned to speak. The first reading materials are intensive; that is they are planned so that they easily follow and repeat familiar oral dialogue. Duplicated copies of oral dialogues or experience charts may be used. Later, extensive reading materials within the child's ability are offered for reading pleasure. Supplementary reading that presents cultural information may also be used at more advanced levels.

The child writes only what he has learned to read. First writing may be controlled by the copying of sentences from dialogues, or writing from dictation. Such writing is used to reinforce memory, or to gain facility in changing time or person in sentence structure. Later, directed writing follows the teacher's directions. After the child has mastered a large vocabulary, has become familiar with structure patterns, and has learned to organize ideas orally, he may attempt free composition.

Principles of structure, if analyzed at all in elementary school, are presented only after the learner has heard, spoken, read, and written material in the second language. Translation occurs only at advanced levels.

Other methods. As with any other area of the curriculum, the teaching methods used for foreign languages are not restricted to one or two types. One may see in operation variations of the old method and the new method in a continuum ranging from the most traditional to the very progressive. Several methods other than those already discussed are worth a brief survey.

The reading method emerged as a modification of the traditional system. The following characteristics have been identified:

1. Pronunciation was stressed at first, because even in silent reading a person's mind might tend to suggest sounds for the words in the text.
2. Grammar was taught for recognition only.
3. Oral use of the foreign language in the classroom was restricted usually to pronunciation drills and a few questions in the foreign language to test comprehension of materials read.
4. Translation from English to the foreign language was usually omitted.
5. Reading materials introduced words and idioms at a predetermined rate, and were based on the scientifically prepared word and idiom lists.

6. Materials written by foreign authors were rewritten, where necessary, to restrict the selections to the graded vocabulary level desired.[3]

The eclectic method was developed because of the great amount of time required by the new method. It operated as follows:

1. Oral practice of sounds, phonetic drills, speaking of language phrases, and reading aloud were put into the beginning stages of the language course.
2. Questions in the language and answers in the same were used to test comprehension of the spoken language.
3. Audio-visual materials were used to aid vocabulary learning and to give information on the culture of the foreign people.
4. Grammar was explained deductively in order to save time in the classroom.
5. Compositions or sentences were assigned to test the learning of grammar.
6. Translation was still used as the acid test to determine if the student really understood what he had read.[4]

The Army method, developed for adults during World War II, was unique, and has given present day educators a number of clues for effective teaching of foreign language to children. An analysis of the Army's method of teaching languages reveals the following distinctive educational features:

1. *Maximum course content in minimum time.* The 17 hours of contact with a language each week over a period of 36 weeks gave the trainees 612 hours of instruction and drill, or approximately five times as much as they would have had in the usual college language class during an academic year.
2. *High standards of student selection and performance.* Students were carefully screened for the language work, and high standards of achievement were demanded. Only 29 per cent of the trainees who went to the end of their term were graduated.
3. *Superb motivation.* A trainee in the ASTP tried to succeed in order to remain in an interesting, self-improving situation. Furthermore, he was motivated by patriotism. He could help his country's war effort better by preparing himself to serve in foreign lands.
4. *Integration of area studies with language.* In addition to the 17 contact hours in language per week, the trainees might have up to 10 hours of work in the history, politics, geography, or economics of the area. This extra work brought several other disciplines to bear upon their training in an interdepartmental cooperative organization.

---

[3] J. Wesley Childers, *Foreign Language Teaching* (New York: The Center for Applied Research in Education, Inc., 1964), p. 38.
[4] Childers, p. 34.

5. *Objectives were clearly defined.* The Army wanted its trainees to have a command of the colloquial spoken form of the language to the point of speaking fluently, accurately, and with an acceptable approximation to a native pronunciation; and almost perfect auditory comprehension of the language as spoken by a native.

6. *Classes were small.* Army language classes were limited to 10 students to each instructor.[5]

The teaching of foreign languages has been greatly influenced recently by linguistic analysis. What we have learned from the linguists has been easily adapted within the audio-lingual method. Through the listening-speaking approach, the sequential development of phonology and grammatical pattern, from the most common phonemes to the morpheme and finally to syntax, is presented. The difference lies in the oral approach, with conscious analysis delayed until the oral vocabulary is firmly established.

Audio-Lingual Procedures

The teaching of a foreign language by the audio-lingual method includes some rather specialized procedures because of its emphasis upon oral instruction.

Pronunciation. Learning through listening and speaking places basic importance upon pronunciation. The teacher's own pronunciation is of first concern because the child listens to him and imitates him. His accent should be acceptable in the foreign culture. Enunciation is distinct and exact. He may speak to beginners at a pace a little slower than normal, with the usual inflection and rhythm, and with transition to normal pace coming quickly.

To guide effective pronunciation of the children, four facets of pronunciation are taught. First, the child learns *discrimination* between sounds. He recognizes distinctive phonemic elements that are not used in his mother tongue. He learns the subtle variations in sound that result from different use of the speech organs. Second, the child learns exact *articulation* of the phonemes he has recognized. He watches the teacher speak; then he mimics the teacher's face and mouth movements so that he may manipulate his own speech organs to produce the correct sound. Third, the child achieves *integration* of the articulated phonemes and uses the inflection and rhythm of proper sound variation. And finally, the child achieves *automaticity*, or habitual production of correct pronunciation.

The child who is learning correct pronunciation of a second language develops not only discriminating listening habits, but a means of self-

---

[5] Childers, pp. 45–46.

evaluation. He listens to his own pronunciation so that he may compare it to a standard. He identifies correct and incorrect sounds in his own speech and that of other learners. He hears the difference between his own utterance and that of the model, when corrections are made.

Pattern practice. Pattern practice is the means by which children over-learn the sentence patterns of the new language. The purpose is to present unique language patterns in various repeated forms so that the learner unconsciously and automatically understands them as he hears and speaks them. Pattern practice is gained through dialogue, choral response, question-and-answer periods, and games. In every case the structure should be concretely based, that is, expressing action in a real situation or some other tangible reality. Context provides definite meaning; material is simple so that no guesswork is demanded. Familiar structure may be gradually changed to express variety in person, time, thing, or action by transformation, substitution, expansion, or contraction.

Vocabulary. We have said that long lists of words equated with the mother tongue are not used in present-day instruction. There are two reasons for this. One is that in most languages it is difficult to set up the exact equivalent in English words. The other is that when children gain understanding by means other than translation they learn to think in the new language.

Words selected for use, then, are words that can be easily illustrated by action, pantomime, or picture. Usually concrete words are selected— the names of things or of simple action that can be presented through context clues.

Also we have noted that development of a large vocabulary is delayed until sentence patterns are quite familiar. The question of vocabulary control is a problem related to the audio-lingual method of teaching. Which words, how many, and when they should be introduced are important considerations. When vocabulary is being expanded, children sometimes help select the words. At this point cooperative planning between the FLES and the regular classroom teacher may determine which words can be reinforced elsewhere in the curriculum.

Methods of oral response. Three procedures and their variations are commonly used to emphasize the oral approach in the teaching of foreign language.

1. Choral response, frequently a poor technique when teaching in English, has been found effective in foreign language instruction. It is usually used for pronunciation practice of new words. When the total group responds together they gain confidence in uttering strange sounds. A shy child who otherwise might not try, finds support within the group. The teacher can correct poor pronunciation without embarrassing an

individual. Use of choral response demands exceptional aural discrimination on the part of the teacher but gradually the size of the group can be diminished so that individual response can be more easily identified.

2. Dialogue is used frequently and is particularly appropriate for presentation of new materials because it provides meaningful content. Two or more persons, usually including the teacher, utilize dialogue in varying degrees of dramatization. Built gradually, dialogue reveals meaning without translation, helps children associate phrases and sentences with real-life activities and communication. Language pronunciation and structure, new vocabulary and idioms are memorized without conscious analysis of component parts. Parallel expressions are easily determined.

3. Question-and-answer experiences are another approach to oral use of foreign language. Usually known material is the basis for questioning. Variety can be achieved by the use of visual materials and by pantomime or dramatization as the question is asked or answered.

Throughout all instructional procedures in foreign language, the teacher plans not only the learning of normal speech, but some insight into the cultural setting of the language. Each language experience provides a cultural impact. The arranged classroom environment, realia, films, pictures, records, tapes, and explanations of idioms, words, and situations help children understand something of the culture behind the language. Continuously the teacher compares ways of life, holidays, the people and their activities with those of the children.

Brooks[6] lists the following as skills needed by the teacher to obtain maximum results from the audio-lingual method:

> The teacher should know how to:
> Arrange the schedule of assignments for a semester's work.
> Prepare a unit.
> Prepare a dialogue.
> Prepare pattern practices based upon a dialogue or a literary text.
> Select words and expressions for vocabulary study.
> Seize upon the word or utterance that is of special cultural significance and make its meaning clear.
> Prepare scripts for tapes.
> Voice a tape.
> Make and evaluate tests that involve all the language skills.

Materials and Equipment

With growing popularity of foreign language programs and the financial support of NDEA and ESEA, publishers are making available

---

[6] Brooks, *Language and Language Learning*, p. 146.

more and more materials and equipment that are appropriate to the new method.

The language laboratory.   Growing in availability and usefulness is the combination of equipment and materials making up the language laboratory. The laboratory varies from a portable cart to a built-in feature of the classroom, library, or special language studio. Its components are different combinations of tape recorders and record players with undistorted sound and good fidelity, quality earphones, microphones, and sound-absorbent working spaces containing volume control, selector switches, and places for books and papers. The equipment provides the learner with opportunities to listen to a master voice, then repeat and record or respond to what is heard so that the response can be reviewed and corrected.

The language laboratory offers some advantages of the machine over personal instruction. The isolated work space with earphones tends to minimize outside distractions. There is opportunity for much repetition and overlearning that may be tedious, fatiguing, or irritating to a teacher. Repetition is identical. The voice can be carefully selected for tone and accent, and several voices and accents can be heard. The student proceeds at his own individual pace and becomes involved in self-evaluation as he compares his own response to the model. In some laboratories, the teacher or supervisor can listen in and give immediate help.

Because availability of equipment in itself is no guarantee for learning, best utilization of the language laboratory is its integration with classroom work. It provides repetition, extension, supplementation, and variety to the teacher's instruction. Authorities indicate that a learner should have a laboratory period at least twice a week. Supervision is needed, and this is one reason why some laboratories are situated in a library where a full-time librarian is available. Other problems are related to selection and maintenance of equipment, preparation of materials, integration of the laboratory with classroom instruction, and scheduling the use of the laboratory for all students.

Tapes.   Tapes may be either prepared commercially or made by the teacher. They are most helpful in providing listening or repetition and practice experiences with material previously presented in classroom or laboratory. No English is used. The voice is that of an authentic model, carefully timed and with appropriate tonal emphasis. The content should be interesting and should be presented in carefully planned sequence. Dialogue may be presented with two different voices. Sentences may be transferred to several spoken patterns. Some tapes provide opportunities for the learner to repeat utterances after the model, then to hear a correct response immediately after. Fifteen minutes is the best length for older elementary students.

Other materials. Because of the emphasis on cultural understanding as well as facility with the foreign language, care is taken in the selection of teaching aids that will increase cultural understanding as well as vocabulary meaning. *Realia* include authentic objects, toys, properties that children can see, handle, use. When adapted to teaching purposes, realia can create interest, provide topics for discussion, give means for using vocabulary in context, illustrate human activities, and lead to further research in science or social studies. *Filmstrips, motion pictures, and slides* are used to help children understand more about the way people live in the country. They present dramatic action of the authentic culture. They must be more than a travelogue as utilized by the teacher, hence previous preparation in vocabulary and discussion after the showing are important. (See Chapter 16 for more detailed discussion of materials.)

Organized groups of materials have been prepared as complete teaching kits. One publisher, for example, offers recordings in native-speaker voices; correlated pictures and vocabulary cards; illustrated textbooks; instructional guides; teacher manuals with procedures, lesson plans, and dictionary; and a resource manual that suggests plans, activities, evaluation devices, translations, records, and pronunciation aids. Another program involves six favorite fairy tales in picture, sound, and text. The stories are in graded sequence; vocabulary and sentence structure are controlled. New language forms as well as common conversational expressions are provided in the familiar context of the stories. Publishers of textbooks commonly provide in addition to students' books the workbooks, teacher's edition, tests, flashcards, grading charts, tape recordings, and practice records.

Related problems

The teaching of foreign language in the elementary school is not yet firmly and consistently established. Educators have learned much about appropriate and effective methods and materials, but several questions are still to be answered before the teaching of foreign language can reach its maximum effectiveness.

Language selection. What language or languages should be taught? Should the language be one of worldwide importance such as Spanish or French? If so, what of Russian, Chinese, and other non-European languages? Should the language be that of a large minority group in the community? Frequently this was the answer prior to World War II, as the teaching of German in Pennsylvania Dutch communities, Spanish in the southwestern states adjacent to Mexico, and French in schools near Quebec or New Orleans. Spanish is the most frequently taught foreign language because of the proximity of Spanish-speaking countries. Should the language be whatever the teacher happens to know? Less of this kind of selection is used today than a very few years past. Should children and parents have a selection? To assure continuity of instruction, too many languages cannot be offered.

Geographical isolation is the major factor limiting the widespread use of foreign languages among Americans. Even immigrants soon lose speaking facility in their own languages because they have little use for them here. Americans, finding English increasingly understood abroad, have not needed other languages for business or travel. Consequently, acquiring language proficiency in this country is especially difficult.

Selection of languages is a difficult curriculum decision. Forward-thinking educators recognize the need to teach the languages of some less politically important countries that are not offered in secondary schools and infrequently at the college level. Tagalog of the Philippines and Hindi of India are two examples. That the teaching of foreign languages has recently received increasing curricular consideration is an encouraging trend. When more Americans are familiar with some of the common European languages perhaps further effort can be made to help them understand the languages of emerging nations.

Age. When should instruction begin? The major problems and the greatest controversy seem to evolve around the best age at which to begin the teaching of foreign language. The advantage of teaching a foreign language in high school and college is that pupils have more sophisticated study habits and a knowledge of basic language structure in English. However, in the elementary schools, foreign language is being provided for some children as early as kindergarten and first grade. Many schools begin their program with the fifth and sixth grades. A University of Chicago study in French instruction showed that one semester of instruction at the junior high school level resulted in progress equal to five years of instruction started in the third grade. At any age about one-fifth of all children have real difficulty learning a foreign language. Since motivation is an important factor in the ability to learn, children are less likely to see real meaning, outside of the novelty, in learning a language different from their own. We do not yet have enough evidence to determine when young children should begin study of a foreign language.

Students. Who will be the pupils? Related to the age of beginning is the problem of what children to teach. Should all children have such instruction? Some authorities do not recommend foreign language for *all* children, yet many schools teach it to whole classes. When and how are the less able eliminated? In some schools only the very bright children are taught foreign languages.

Teachers. Who teaches? One of the greatest problems relates to the competence of personnel. The general classroom teacher has little facility with foreign languages unless he happens to have a foreign background. For this kind of instruction, thorough training seems to be necessary. Some teachers trying to provide foreign language experiences unknowingly speak with a poor accent. We do not have enough specialists with elementary school experience to meet the demand for special teachers of foreign language.

How is the addition of another subject to the already crowded curriculum equated to teacher load? When, during a busy school schedule, can the FLES teacher and the regular classroom teacher find planning time to establish rapport and to achieve correlation? How can the FLES teacher contribute to the teaching of social studies units?

How can poor competence in language be improved? Many elementary teachers know very little of the technical structure of the English language, and even less of a foreign language. Because of the method by which they have learned, they translate rather than think in the second language. Few have had instruction in the psychology of learning a foreign language. Often a rich knowledge about and feeling for the culture of the foreign country is lacking. Deficiency in these aspects of teaching a foreign language means retraining for the teacher, either through graduate study in college or university, or in concentrated inservice education within the school district.

Continuity. How long should students continue studying a foreign language? How can children be assured of continuous, sequential instruction through the years? The trend toward the use of special FLES teachers is lessening the problem of continuity but when regular classroom teachers are responsible for instruction it is a very real problem. Even in well established programs with strong inservice training, continuity tends to be irregular. The problem of articulation with the secondary schools also needs consideration.

Parental cooperation. One final problem deals with parental cooperation with the FLES program. Parents can help children develop curiosity about other peoples, thus strengthening motivation. They can encourage children to *use* their limited knowledge. Unless children are encouraged to study and use the new skills, the foreign language instruction in schools can only be minimally effective. Parents' own interest and support of FLES will encourage learning among the children.

The growing trend of teaching foreign language has not developed without criticism and doubt as to the appropriateness of this kind of instruction at an early age. The very advantages advocated by the proponents are seriously questioned by the critics. Some believe that very little intercultural understanding results. They say that young children become enthusiastic about anything taught by a skilled and enthusiastic teacher. It is felt that though younger children indicate greater flexibility in learning the strange sounds of foreign language, older pupils can learn the language more rapidly and with positive scholastic attitudes. Also, there will be less time lag between instruction and use.

Childers reports six diverse reactions to the audio-lingual approach:

1. *Bilingualism.* Claims that the audio-lingual method would produce bilingual students in a short period of time did not materialize; and many teachers became disillusioned as they realized that more time, not less, would be required if the reading and writing skills were to be developed on a par with those of listening and speaking.

2. *Prereading period.* The prereading period, during which the students heard and repeated foreign phrases but never saw them in print, was too long. In some extreme cases books were kept away from the students for a whole semester. Many students learn faster through the eye than through the ear, and these were held back by the long audio-lingual period.

3. *Use of English.* The student's mother tongue was to be eliminated, but teachers found that such an extreme practice was not desirable. English was needed at times to clarify vocabulary items and to explain certain grammatical structures.

4. *Teaching of grammar.* Grammar was not to be taught to the students until a much later period, after the structures had been "overlearned." The brighter students, however, became curious about the structural drills which they were repeating, and wanted explanations. Many teachers began to teach grammar again as a short cut to faster comprehension.

5. *Concept of culture.* Culture was presented as "everyday living" rather than *belles-lettres* or fine arts. The reading of newspapers and magazines did not present the genius of a people as well as did its masterpieces of art, music, and literature, and teachers became critical of the omissions.

6. *Repetitive drills.* Memorization of drills became a monotonous procedure in many classes, unless the teachers varied them and made them interesting. Moreover, the constant participation of the teacher in these pattern drills through supplying basic and supplementary materials placed a greater strain on him than ever before.[7]

---

[7] Childers, *Foreign Language Teaching*, pp. 60–61.

Some educators believe that the extreme audio-lingual approach becomes "training" without the rational approach of "education." For this reason modifications in the extreme aural-oral approach are being made. The pendulum is swinging back from the extreme methods of teaching foreign language by constant repetition in listening and speaking, but it will never return to the extreme traditional grammar-translation method. The degree of rational learning is influenced by two factors, the language being studied, and the age of the learner. Some languages, as German, are completely logical and consistent. Understanding reasons for pronunciation and sentence patterns in such a language would be helpful to the learner. Very young children would have difficulty understanding rules and their ability to think through reasons for patterns or pronunciation is limited. Therefore learning through imitation and repetition would be more acceptable for young children. As the maturation level of the learner increases, so his ability to handle a rational approach to foreign languages increases.

There are some authorities who feel that elementary school children should be provided with a variety of meaningful experiences in several different languages rather than formal instruction in one. Since "sampling," because of the knowledge explosion, is an important trend in other curriculum fields, why not sample among languages? In this way, children would become familiar with a few words and phrases of a language in relation to the geographic, political, and cultural study of the country. The social studies would be strengthened. Children would begin to understand pronunciation of words quite different from their mother tongue. The concept of communication relating to the various people of the world would be extended.

Those problems of FLES relating to teacher capabilities, availability of materials, continuity, and the age at which formal, sequential instruction should begin might well be minimized if children could sample several foreign languages rather than study one in depth. This idea of general familiarization with a number of languages could then include the regional variations and specialized vocabulary of our own American groups.

RECOMMENDED READINGS

ERIKSSON, MARGUERITE, ILSE FOREST, and RUTH MULHAUSER. *Foreign Languages in the Elementary School.* Englewood Cliffs, N.J.: Prentice-Hall, Inc., 1964.

FINOCCHIARO, MARY. *Teaching Children Foreign Languages.* New York: McGraw-Hill Book Company, Inc., 1964.

MASSACHUSETTS COUNCIL FOR PUBLIC SCHOOLS. *FLES, Foreign Language, Elementary Schools: A Study of Teaching Foreign Language to Young Children by the Oral Method.* Boston: The Council, 1957.

POLITZER, R. L. *Foreign Language Learning: A Linguistic Introduction.* Englewood Cliffs, N.J.: Prentice-Hall, Inc., 1965.

THOMPSON, ELIZABETH E. *Foreign Language Teaching in Elementary Schools.* Washington, D.C.: Association for Supervision and Curriculum Development, NEA, 1965.

Quantitative Thinking: Mathematics

10

Arithmetic has, for many years, been an important area of study in the elementary school curriculum. The necessity to be able to use the number system was clear even in Colonial times in the face of demands from fields such as trade, commerce, land surveying, and navigation. Arithmetic was an expected subject for study in the elementary school by the latter half of the eighteenth century, and has from that time on been one of the R's in the so-called three R's portion of the curriculum.

There is every indication that the future will demand even more in the way of ability to "think and do" quantitatively than has the past. Our science and technology demand many people with a high level of quantitative skill. The utilization of high-speed computers for data processing, the precision planning of explorations into outer space, interpretations of time and distance in the wake of worldwide instantaneous communication and jet-powered transportation, master planning for population needs and land use in our burgeoning metropolitan areas all include the need for mathematical manpower. The citizen, too, finds a growing need to be able to utilize mathematics in the face of an increasingly complex set of demands placed on him in his daily life. Understanding and coping with such matters as price indexes, cost-of-living data, taxation formulas, stocks and bonds, and credit and installment buying; managing personal affairs efficiently; and making decisions on public matters—all these place mathematical demands on the general intellectual competence of each citizen. Such realities as these would seem to insure the continuance of mathematics as a vital area for study in the elementary school curriculum.

CHANGE AND THE MATHEMATICS
PROGRAM

The mathematics program in the elementary school has changed over the years in numerous ways. Its purposes have shifted in direction and emphasis, its subject matter has been reviewed and revised, and its teaching methodology has felt the impact of the work of the educational psychologist and the child development specialist. Great changes came about in all of these matters in the period from about 1900 to 1950. Since the middle 1950's the rate of change in the mathematical program of the elementary school has been dramatically accelerated. One could easily argue that general curriculum reform in the elementary school since 1955 has been dominated by mathematics curriculum reform. This was the first area of the elementary school program to undergo serious scrutiny in the wake of demands for a more efficient and effective educational effort. This is the area of the elementary school curriculum that has been most touched by change today. Any elementary school that has adopted a contemporary program of mathematics is asking its teachers to provide and its pupils to undergo an experience with mathematics considerably different from that which would have been found in the school as recently as 1960. Clearly, it is this contemporary program that must be dealt with in the main in this chapter. That which makes it contemporary will be more completely understood if we turn briefly to a characterization of the arithmetic curriculum in the elementary schools in the period 1900 to 1950.

Earlier Arithmetic Curricula

A quotation from the inaugural issue of *The Arithmetic Teacher*, a professional journal focused on elementary school arithmetic, is most revealing with respect to the curriculum at the turn of the century. Brownell had this to say:

> The arithmetic of 1900 differed materially from the arithmetic we now include in the elementary curriculum. . . . Two of its characteristics stand out prominently: (a) it was hard, and (b) it was little related to practical living. . . . Children began the serious business of learning arithmetic as soon as they entered school. In the first two grades they memorized all the simple number facts. By the time they had finished grade three they were well embarked into computation with whole numbers. In grade four they performed operations with common fractions, many of which are now generally deferred to grade five or six, and others of which have been eliminated from school arithmetic. In the higher grades they studied square root and even cube root, worked long and difficult examples with decimal fractions,

percentage, and ratio and proportion, and solved intricate "problems" involving many steps. Learning consisted largely in memorization. Teachers, relying pretty much upon what was in the textbook, showed pupils what to do and then relied upon abundant bodies of practice to produce mastery. Homework assignments were heavy, and many parents were called upon to revive, temporarily at least, skills that they had forgotten. The children who survived this demanding regimen, aided often by two one-hour periods for arithmetic a day, were capable of arithmetical feats far beyond the capabilities of eighth-graders today, whether or not they ever later put them to effective use.[1]

Thus, as the twentieth century opened, the arithmetic curriculum of the elementary school was crowded with difficult content. To whatever legitimate demands business and commerce put on the program had been added a mental discipline theory of intellectual development. Much that was exacted from pupils was to the end of "training" the mind and improving the faculties of reasoning and memory.

There were elementary school educators in the early 1900's who began to raise questions about both the amount and kind of subject matter that was being selected from the field of mathematics to be taught in the elementary school arithmetic program. On the one hand it seemed that too much was being attempted in these first six or eight years of school. On the other hand, it seemed that what was being taught was often unrealistic and not necessary at all. A paper read by McMurry in 1904 before the Department of Superintendence of the National Education Association typifies this concern. McMurry's paper was entitled "What Omissions Are Desirable in the Present Course of Study?"[2] He rooted his discussion in the proposition that the subject matter selected for the arithmetic program should be that which can "be shown to have a plain relation to some real need of life," and he presented a list of topics that he felt could be dropped from the arithmetic program at that time.

This sort of attention to the problem of curriculum planning in arithmetic gave rise to considerable discussion and argument and eventually provided motivation for the undertaking of particular kinds of research. Study was directed in the main along two lines, (1) social usage and (2) the science of numbers. Let us consider each approach briefly, bearing in mind that the major concern in these endeavors was to ascertain which arithmetic subject matter was valuable enough to be taught in the elementary school and when it should be taught. Both of

---

[1] William A. Brownell, "The Revolution in Arithmetic," *The Arithmetic Teacher* (February 1954), pp. 1–5.

[2] F. M. McMurry, "What Omissions Are Desirable in the Present Course of Study?" *Yearbook* (Washington, D.C.: National Department of Superintendence, NEA, 1904), p. 104.

these questions linger on today as important and central to curriculum planning and teaching in this area.

The social usage basis. Social usage, as a basis for selecting the proper subject matter for study in arithmetic, is oriented to the quantitative situations met by the so-called average man in his day-to-day life activities. The attempt is to identify that arithmetic which he actually needs and uses. Prodded by statements like McMurry's, elementary school educators found themselves considering the relationship between the number system and effective living.

A number of studies in the first two decades of the twentieth century agreed that the adult society was called upon to use only a small proportion of the arithmetic that was being taught in the schools.[3] The results of these studies were a direct challenge to the content of arithmetic that custom and tradition had tended to sustain. Later studies attempted to ascertain scientifically what, and how much, arithmetic should be taught. For example, one study concluded that halves, thirds, and fourths were the fractions in common use to the extent that they accounted for ninety percent of adult usage. Beyond these, and in special cases, eighths and twelfths were needed and used by some.[4] Other studies considered such matters as teaching decimals, memorizing tables, and using the fundamental processes with compound numbers.[5] Wilson wrote as follows in 1950:

> In summary, the various studies of usage indicate that the drill program in arithmetic should be restricted to the mastery of the four fundamental processes; fractions in halves, thirds, fourths; eighths in special situations and twelfths in other special situations; and reading of decimals. To date, the usage of percentages and interest has not been adequately investigated. Probably much of the work in percentage should be on a nondrill basis.[6]

This concern over social usage as a basis for the selection of appropriate subject matter for arithmetic undoubtedly reached its peak in the 1930's,

---

[3] Sarah E. Chase, "Waste in Arithmetic," *Teachers College Record*, Vol. 18 (1917), pp. 36–70; G. M. Wilson, *Survey of the Social and Business Usage of Arithmetic,* Contributions to Education No. 100 (New York: Bureau of Publications, Teachers College, Columbia University, 1919); C. T. Wise, "A Survey of Arithmetic Problems Arising in Various Occupations," *Elementary School Journal*, Vol. 20 (1919), pp. 118–136.

[4] G. M. Wilson and C. O. Dalrymple, "Useful Fractions," *Journal of Educational Research*, Vol. 30 (1937), pp. 341–347.

[5] J. E. Buckley, *The Uses of Decimals in Business,* master's thesis, Boston University, 1935; Marion Dalrymple, *Decimals in Industries, Periodicals, and Textbooks,* master's thesis, Boston University, 1933; Dorothy W. Wilson, "Teaching Denominate Numbers and Measures," *Educational Method*, Vol. 16 (1937), pp. 177–181.

[6] Guy Wilson, "Arithmetic," *Encyclopedia of Educational Research* (revised edition) (New York: The Macmillan Company, 1950), p. 46.

though it continues to be of concern to educators at the present time. That the cumulative effect of such studies on the arithmetic program was positive is generally accepted. Singly, social usage is not a sufficient base upon which to plan the curriculum but along with other bases it seems quite usable. The purposes for which arithmetic is taught in the elementary school are rooted in great part in the contribution that understanding and skill in arithmetic can make to more effective living. These early studies had a great deal to do with introducing a kind of reasonableness into the question of content selection in arithmetic for the elementary school. The now oft-quoted idea of arithmetic having a "social aim" is a contribution growing out of such concerns as these.

The science of numbers basis. Attention has been focused also over the years on the number system itself—its various facts, processes, and procedures—as the question of most appropriate subject matter for arithmetic has been pondered. Arithmetic experts who favored this basis for selection were likely to emphasize an analysis of the number system more than of social usage. From this point of view all possible types of number situations are identified, analyzed, and accounted for in arithmetic instruction.

This set of ideas found ready application in the arithmetic of the 1920's and the early 1930's. This was a time when associationist points of view, variously known as connectionism, or the S-R bond theory, were the predominant psychology of learning; they held that each arithmetic situation had to be faced and learned in and of itself if it was to become the "habit" that was sought.[7] Thus, much time was expended in determining the least, but nonetheless comprehensive, number of unit skills, or types of processes, that were part and parcel of the various problems in arithmetic. For instance, in one such study Breuckner called attention to 178 unit skills for fractions—forty for addition, fifty-three for subtraction, forty-five for multiplication, and forty for division—as a basis for curriculum planning.[8] Other such studies can be found in the literature.[9]

Studies focused on the number system as the key to curriculum planning in arithmetic continued to be made through the 1930's and into

---

[7] Edward S. Thorndike, *The Psychology of Arithmetic* (New York: The Macmillan Company, 1922). Note this statement from the Preface (page v) of that book: "We now understand that learning is essentially the formation of connections or bonds between situations and responses, that the satisfyingness of the result is the chief force that forms them, and that habit rules in the realm of thought as truly and as fully as in the realm of action."

[8] L. J. Breuckner and Fred Kelly, "A Critical Evaluation of Methods of Analyzing Practice in Fractions," *Twenty-Ninth Yearbook*, National Society for the Study of Education, Part II, 1930, pp. 525–534.

[9] F. B. Knight and others, *Problems in the Teaching of Arithmetic* (Iowa City, Iowa: Iowa Supply Company, 1924); G. M. Ruch and others, *Schemata for the Analysis of Drill in Fractions*, University of Iowa Studies in Education, Vol. 10, No. 2, Educational Psychology Series, No. 3, 1936.

the 1940's. However, with the increasing use of field theories of learning, growing out of Gestalt or organismic psychology, the general orientation of these studies changed. In keeping with these field theories, the long lists of separate units and combinations to be taught gave way to studies that tried to indicate the overall unity, organization, and relationships within the number system. No longer was each combination seen as a learning task unto itself; rather, every effort was made to help children to generalize their number learnings to wider settings. A "family" approach to learning addition and subtraction, for instance, attempted to help the learner to see the relationships between $3 + 4$ and $4 + 3$ as approaches to the sum of 7, as well as the relatedness of the subtraction facts of $7 - 4$ and $7 - 3$ to these addition facts. Such a use of organization within the number system lent a great deal of security and support to the child faced with this large learning task.

The number system basis is largely responsible for the reference to a mathematical aim in arithmetic instruction that has been used alongside a so-called social aim. The discrepancy that some teachers saw in these aims has largely disappeared. It has been accepted that both aims are important, that there is a good deal of interaction between them, and that each relies heavily on the other for its realization.

The Grade Placement of Arithmetic

Speculation about the specifics in arithmetic that children were to be asked to learn extended also to the grade placement of subject matter. Although really definitive studies are even now not available, the matter has received a good deal of attention and much careful thought. The results in the 1930's of these efforts led to the placement of arithmetic subject matter by age and grade level that most educators were ready to defend as superior to that found in the early 1900's.

Undoubtedly the most extensive attempt to investigate the question of the grade placement of arithmetic topics was done by Washburne and his Committee of Seven.[10] The purpose of their study was to determine the mental age at which the various topics in arithmetic might be most profitably taught to children. Many thousands of pupils were included in the study, which culminated in a "table of placement" that was made available to curriculum workers. This table called attention to the minimum and the optimum mental age at which each arithmetic process, or a large part of a process, could be taught to completion, that is, mastered by children. For example, the following data are taken from the study:

---

[10] C. W. Washburne, "Mental Age and the Arithmetic Curriculum," *Journal of Educational Research,* Vol. 23 (1931), pp. 210–231.

Topic	Minimum Mental Age	Optimum Mental Age
Addition facts—sums over ten	7 yrs. 4 mos.	7 yrs. 11 mos.
Like fractions (no borrowing) addition and subtraction	9 yrs. 10 mos.	11 yrs. 1 mo.
Long division (all types, complete)	12 yrs. 7 mos.	12 yrs. 7 mos.

Using this information educators made decisions as to the grade level at which certain items should be taught. In the case of the material quoted above, a child would be in the second grade before he learned to add sums over ten; he would be in the sixth grade before he learned to add and subtract like fractions; and he would be in the seventh grade before he learned to use long division.

The work of Washburne's committee seemed to spur people into action. The idea that it was unwise to attempt systematic instruction in a given arithmetic process until a child had reached the mental age to profit from it was persuasive. More people than ever before were willing to devote some thought to this question of optimum grade placement. Specialists studied the work of the Washburne committee carefully and published their critiques of it in professional journals.[11] It became evident to most that, although mental age was an important factor in determining the grade placement of arithmetic content, it was only one of several factors to be considered. Along with the mental age factor, so they argued, must be weighed such factors as the general structural difficulty and complexity of particular arithmetic examples, the general social significance of the topic for children at various age and grade levels, and the methodology to be employed in teaching the particular arithmetic under consideration. Investigations of grade placement have not dealt adequately with this complex of factors even yet.

What was done, however, did affect placement of arithmetic experiences in the arithmetic curriculum in the 1940's and into the 1950's. To a much greater extent than in earlier years, a presumed readiness determined grade placement.

Formal versus Incidental Teaching

Considerable attention has been given over the years to the most efficient way to deal with arithmetic in the total elementary school curriculum. Historically, of course, arithmetic has had a time and a place

---

[11] W. A. Brownell, "Critique of the Committee of Seven's Investigations on the Grade Placement of Arithmetic Topics," *Elementary School Journal* (February 1938), pp. 495–507; C. W. Washburne, "Reply to Brownell's Critique of the Committee of Seven Experiments," *Elementary School Journal* (February 1939), pp. 417–430.

of its own in the instructional program. That this arrangement was fitting and proper was not questioned. However, in the 1930's considerable effort was exerted and a number of studies were reported that challenged this historical approach to handling the arithmetic curriculum.

A number of people reported research to show the high incidence of arithmetic content in fields other than arithmetic in the elementary school curriculum.[12] Others published material calling attention to the difficulties that pupils had in managing the mathematical concepts they were meeting in various areas of study.[13] Coming at this particular time, with interest running high in the activity or experience curriculum, such studies were used to support the position that the placing of arithmetic as a separate subject for study in the elementary school was neither wise nor efficient. Evidence of the difficulties that pupils had in handling mathematical concepts and ideas in other subject-matter settings was used against the usual practice of learning arithmetic in one place and applying it in another.

Another argument stemmed from the dissatisfaction and doubts that many elementary school educators had developed over the then prevailing formal, or drill, approach to arithmetic teaching. They believed that this approach was not accomplishing the stated outcomes for arithmetic learning, and they challenged this type of instruction. In the main, the intent of these educators was to show that formal arithmetic was being started too soon in the elementary school, and that a more informal, incidental approach, especially in the early years, would yield better results. To this end various experiments were carried out and provocative results were made available for others to study and analyze.[14]

There soon came efforts to test the effectiveness of arithmetic teaching in the activity curriculum in the 1930's and 1940's. Such efforts were motivated by a combination of the information from studies that showed the high incidence of arithmetic content in other curriculum areas and the growing dissatisfaction with the drill approach to arithmetic.

The arithmetic achievement of pupils in most of the investigations

---

[12] Agnes Gunderson, "Nature and Amount of Arithmetic in Readers for Grades I and II," *Elementary School Journal* (March 1963) pp. 527–540; Clifford Woody, *Nature and Amount of Arithmetic in Types of Reading Material for the Elementary Schools,* Bureau of Educational Reference and Research, Bulletin No. 145 (Ann Arbor, Mich.: University of Michigan, 1932).

[13] Ernest Horn, *Methods of Instruction in the Social Studies* (New York: Charles Scribner's Sons, 1937), pp. 143, 189–193; Lucy Scott, "A Study of Children's Understanding of Certain Statistical Concepts in Social Studies," unpublished doctoral dissertation, State University of Iowa, 1942.

[14] L. P. Benezet, "Story of an Experiment," *National Education Association Journal* (November 1935), pp. 241–244; January 1936, pp. 7–8; Etta Berman, *The Result of Deferring Systematic Teaching of Arithmetic to Grade Six,* master's thesis, Boston University, 1935.

compared quite favorably with achievement under the more traditional forms of teaching.[15] However, some educators took the position that, while much arithmetic learning took place when the activity curriculum approach was used, it was not adequate in and of itself to furnish the base for all of the arithmetic skill that children need to develop.[16] Others questioned the evidence on different grounds. They felt that the units used for experimentation had been purposely selected because of the high incidence of need for arithmetic in them. Still others felt that the record of some of these experiments indicated that work of a more formal and systematic sort had gone on in the classroom along with the instruction that had taken place in relation to the unit.

In 1951 the Committee on the Teaching of Arithmetic of the National Society for the Study of Education took the following position:

> It is the unanimous opinion of the present committee, however, that, after a careful appraisal of such evidence as does exist, and after giving full credit to what has been or is likely to be accomplished under integrated plans, such plans by themselves cannot be depended upon to develop arithmetical concepts and abilities to the level and scope required in life. An especially designed program should include not only provision for systematic and meaningful learning in the arithmetic class but also careful attention to the mathematical needs and contributions of other areas. . . .
>
> Moreover, the acceptance of the proposal that arithmetic be taught systematically, with an important place in the weekly program, in no way implies a denial of the great potential contribution of other areas to arithmetic or a belittling of the importance and difficulty of the mathematical aspects of those areas. Nor does it underestimate the need of a careful plan for co-ordinating the meaningful development of arithmetical abilities in the arithmetic period with their motivation, development, and maintenance in the study of units in other fields. Maximum achievement cannot be obtained either in the arithmetic period alone or in integrated units alone. Both types of instruction are needed.[17]

The position taken by this committee is essentially sound today. At the same time, a way of effectively relating arithmetic to other areas of the elementary school curriculum continues to capture the attention of many elementary school mathematics educators. The evidence strongly

[15] Henry Harap and Charlotte E. Mapes, "The Learning of Fundamentals in an Arithmetic Activity Program," *Elementary School Journal*, Vol. 34 (1934), pp. 515–525; Harap and Mapes, "The Learning of Decimals in an Arithmetic Activity Program," *Journal of Educational Research*, Vol. 29 (1936), pp. 686–693.

[16] Paul R. Hanna and others, "Opportunities for the Use of Arithmetic in an Activity Program," *Tenth Yearbook* (Washington, D.C.: National Council of Teachers of Mathematics, 1935), Chapter 5.

[17] National Society for the Study of Education, Fiftieth Yearbook, Part II, *The Teaching of Arithmetic* (Chicago: University of Chicago Press, 1951), pp. 18, 21.

suggests that it is possible to utilize both the arithmetic situations that develop in ongoing studies in other areas of the curriculum and a special time in which direct and systematic attention may be given to the study of arithmetic itself. At the moment not a great deal is being done about this for reasons that will be evident in this chapter.

Teaching Methodology in Arithmetic

Great strides had been taken by 1950 in dealing more effectively with the instructional or teaching task in arithmetic. The way in which arithmetic is learned is understood better now than ever before, and this understanding is reflected in the procedures and the materials used in the classroom.[18] The older commitment to the S-R bond theory or connectionist theory of learning, on the basis of which was developed a highly formal, drill-centered set of procedures for teaching arithmetic, has been tempered significantly. In fact, this change has been great enough for the aforementioned Committee on the Teaching of Arithmetic to make the following statement in 1951:

> These arguments for the systematic teaching of arithmetic should not be taken as a defense for types of instruction, fairly prevalent, which consist mainly of formal, repetitive drill. As someone has said, "Systematic teaching is not synonymous with formal teaching." The members of this committee are as opposed to such methods as are the proponents of the experience curriculum. They favor the meaning theory, involving the active processes on the part of the pupils of discovering relationships, of utilizing concrete experiences, and of generalization. Indeed the meaning-and-discovery approach has been consistently shown to result in superior achievements as well as in greater interest on the part of both teachers and pupils.[19]

The preferred approach to teaching arithmetic in the early 1950's on the basis of this so-called meaning theory can be described as follows:

1. Children were to be helped to understand the subject matter of arithmetic. A great reliance was put on teaching the relationships within the number system and between the various arithmetic processes.
2. The element of purpose was to be introduced into the work children were asked to do in arithmetic. It was clearly recognized that in-

---

[18] Esther J. Swenson, "Organization and Generalization as Factors in Learning, Transfer, and Retroactive Inhibition," and Lester G. Anderson, "Quantitative Thinking as Developed under Connectionist and Field Theories of Learning," in *Learning Theory in School Situations*, University of Minnesota Studies in Education No. 2 (Minneapolis: University of Minnesota Press, 1949), pp. 9–39, 40–73; Carl L. Thiele, *The Contribution of Generalization to the Learning of Addition Facts*, Teachers College Contributions to Education No. 763 (New York: Teachers College, Columbia University, 1938).

[19] National Society for the Study of Education, Fiftieth Yearbook, Part II, p. 21.

struction in this area must include more than the ability to compute, and that number must become increasingly significant in the minds of pupils.

3. Willingness and desire to learn must start at the level of the child. This approach required the selection of quantitative situations that may be significant and interesting to children, and the acceptance of childlike approaches to the solution of arithmetic problems at the outset.

4. Teaching was to rely less on telling and showing and demonstrating arithmetic for children and more on providing opportunities for children to try to figure things out for themselves as they met situations that demanded either the development of new arithmetic skills or workable proof of some already known.

5. A wide variety of instructional materials were to be utilized, including such things as counters and flannel boards, in an attempt to provide equipment necessary to support the goals of discovery and meaning in arithmetic learning.

6. The need for repetition and review of arithmetic experiences in the curriculum was recognized and provided for. Material once learned was met again in a planned way to help to counter forgetting.

1900–1950 in Summary

One can say then that the years from 1900 to 1950 were active years insofar as curriculum change in arithmetic was concerned. Curriculum and instruction in arithmetic in 1950 can be described as follows:

1. It was accepted that aims and objectives for arithmetic instruction embraced both a mathematical set of purposes that had to do with the science of number itself, and a social set of purposes that had to do with the utilization of arithmetic skill in living.

2. The conclusion had been arrived at that arithmetic was to have a time and place of its own in the curriculum.

3. The content of the arithmetic program had been simplified for the elementary school, with both of the above sets of purposes in mind.

4. The attempt had been made to make available research evidence for the grade placement of arithmetic learnings which, in spite of certain shortcomings, had been applied helpfully to the curriculum in large part.

5. The commitment was to a methodology for arithmetic teaching that stressed meaning and understanding.

RECENT DEVELOPMENTS IN ELEMENTARY SCHOOL MATHEMATICS

By the beginning of the 1950's it was clear that competence with mathematics was assuming an even higher priority in response to the question of what it means to be educated than it had enjoyed in the first half of the century. Any attempt to anticipate the future to the year 2000 and beyond seemed only to underscore this priority even more. The cruciality of it all was such as to capture the attention of some of the outstanding mathematicians in the United States to the problem of curriculum planning and instruction in mathematics at the precollegiate levels of the school system. In the first instances this attention was focused on the curriculum of the secondary school, but it was quickly evident that it would be necessary to deal with the curriculum of the elementary school as well. Thus by the middle of the 1950's and continuing to the present there was and is a widespread experimental and developmental effort under way to bring about a truly contemporary program of mathematics in the elementary school. The way in which this work is going forward is quite consistent with material presented in Chapters 3–5 in this book. The major participants in the reform projects have been mathematicians, learning psychologists, and classroom teachers. Large sums of money have been made available by private foundations and by government agencies (notably the National Science Foundation and the United States Office of Education) to underwrite the cost of this undertaking. The attempt has been to develop a new and contemporary conceptualization for the mathematics curriculum and for instruction in mathematics, and to move from this conceptualization to the production and trial of materials for getting the job done in the classroom. The ultimate goal is to make easily and readily available to the elementary school a truly contemporary mathematics program.

Current Curriculum Improvement Projects

There are several major projects in operation in a number of different places in the country, each to a degree with its own unique characteristics, but all committed in general to the same overall goal.

There is the School Mathematics Study Group (SMSG) project, the purpose of which is to foster research and development in the teaching of school mathematics, including the elementary school.[20] This was one of the first projects, initiated in 1958, and it has been one of the most productive. Courses have been developed, teaching materials and teaching methods have been devised for the elementary school and for the secondary school. Materials from this project are being used in a great many classrooms across the country.

There is, too, the Greater Cleveland Mathematics Program of the

---

[20] School Mathematics Study Group, Cedar Hall, Stanford University, Stanford, Calif. (Director: E. G. Begle).

Educational Research Council of Greater Cleveland (GCMP).[21] This group has also attempted the development of an articulated and sequential program in mathematics for kindergarten through grade twelve. The goal has been, especially, to provide materials that will enable pupils to think their way through mathematics and to see it as the structured subject matter that it is and not just as isolated elements of information to be memorized.

The Madison Project of Syracuse University and Webster College is of a somewhat different kind.[22] Started as an effort to revitalize the preparation of teachers in mathematics, it has gone on to develop and disseminate a supplementary program in mathematics with materials for use starting with the nursery school. There has been a special effort to deal with the kind of creative learning experience in mathematics which children can have in school and outside of school. Some of the mathematics included is relatively novel for use at the grade levels suggested, such as coordinate geometry, an axiomatic approach to algebra, and mathematical logic. A second part of the content deals with topics which are usual at the grade levels in question, but an attempt is made to provide materials that will improve the child's opportunities to understand the topics.

In a similar vein the University of Illinois Arithmetic Project (UIAP) is not attempting to develop a systematic curriculum at any grade level but is instead providing materials which, in their words, "provide day-to-day, here-is-something-to-try" ideas for the classroom.[23] The central theme of the project is that the study of mathematics should be an adventure, requiring and deserving hard work. There is a direct attempt to provide materials that will appeal to children and still be quite correct mathematics.

Several others projects could be cited that are very much like these four in scope and intent, but these will serve to illustrate what the total group of projects is like. Since these projects have been under way there has been much reference to the "new mathematics" for the elementary school. This has been misunderstood to some extent. The "new" must be seen in relation only to that curriculum which was common in the elementary school prior to 1950; the reference is not to new mathematics as such. Children are still taught to do just about everything that they were taught to do before the advent of what is better referred to as a con-

21 The Greater Cleveland Mathematics Program, Educational Research Council of Greater Cleveland, 446 Rockefeller Building, 614 West Superior Ave., Cleveland, Ohio (Director: George S. Cunningham).

22 The Madison Project of Syracuse University and Webster College, 8356 Big Bend Blvd., St. Louis, Mo. (Director: Robert E. Davis).

23 University of Illinois Arithmetic Project (UIAP), 887 Commonwealth Ave., Newton, Mass. (Director: David A. Page).

temporary mathematics program. They still count, add, subtract, multiply, divide; they work with whole numbers and with fractions; they solve word problems. Nevertheless there are some important departures or differences evident:

1. Children are being introduced to some aspects of mathematics at an earlier age than had come to be customary. Mathematical ideas are "planted" earlier, and then returned to recurrently through the elementary school years.
2. The curriculum is coming to be a mathematics program and not just an arithmetic program. This is evident in the utilization of geometry and algebra in the elementary school years.
3. There is careful attention to the use of a more mathematically appropriate language in the contemporary program, and this is different in many instances from what has been the case.
4. There is a great concern for the development of concepts that underlie the mathematics system. What is sought is the best balance between concept development, computational skill development, and application in a variety of settings.

The general plan of organization for the curriculum is a spiral one, with some elements from all of the major mathematical areas that are included in the curriculum found at each grade level. Concepts and skills thus are extended in meaning and efficiency as pupils move through the years of the elementary school.

Scope and Sequence of Topics

While there are some differences between various current mathematics programs, there are certain themes or strands which are found in all of them and to which different projects give various degrees of attention. For instance, all of the contemporary programs would be found to include work dealing with these topics:

1. The system of whole numbers and the rational number system.
2. Geometry.
3. Measurement.
4. Concern for application, for problem solving.

To varying degrees the programs would include:

5. Algebra, especially the mathematical sentence.
6. The concept of set.
7. Logic.
8. Function.

Let us comment briefly on this coverage and call attention to a typical scope and sequence of topics for some of these areas.

Number systems. The emerging mathematics program in the elementary school continues to be concerned primarily with the system of whole numbers and the system of rational numbers. The system of whole numbers refers to the naming of numbers, or numeration, to counting, and to operations on numbers—that is, addition, multiplication, subtraction, and division. The system of rational numbers includes fractional numbers, fractional numbers expressed as decimals, and percent. Counting continues to be central to the work with whole numbers, and the concept of set (discussed later here) is utilized effectively in relation to it, as the counting of members of a set. Following from this, addition is seen as a matter of counting the members of two sets and thus obtaining a new third set. Subtraction can be approached via the set concept, too, and as the inverse of addition. One starts with a set of objects, reorganizes it into two subsets, removes one subset, and counts the members in the remaining subset. Eventually addition and subtraction are handled in more usual or standard ways: addition is spoken of as adding two addends to find a sum, and subtraction is spoken of as subtracting a known addend from a known sum to find the other addend.

Multiplication involves putting sets together, as does addition, and is sometimes viewed as the repeated addition of equal sets. Division involves separating sets, as does subtraction, and is sometimes viewed as the repeated subtraction of equal sets. Thus multiplication and division are seen as inverse operations, as are addition and subtraction. Eventually multiplication is seen as an algorithm which multiplies two known factors to find a product. Division is viewed as an algorithm in which a known product is divided by one known factor to find the other factor.

Developing an understanding of these operations with whole numbers includes finding out the ways in which these operations are alike and the ways in which they are different. Concern for these relationships has brought attention to certain properties of the number system, or laws or principles which can be derived from it. Thus, an attempt is made in many contemporary programs to deal with propositions such as these:

1. The commutative property for addition: the order of two addends may be changed without changing the results, or the sum.
2. The commutative property for multiplication: the order of two factors may be changed without changing the results, or the product.
3. The associative property for addition: in addition with three or more addends, the addends may be grouped in different ways without changing the result, or the sum.

4. The associative property for multiplication: in multiplication with three or more factors, the factors may be grouped in different ways without changing the results, or the product.

5. The distributive property for multiplication with respect to addition: when two or more addends are to be multiplied by the same number, the sums of the addends may be multiplied by the number, or the products of the factors may be added.

6. The distributive property for division with respect to addition: when two or more addends are to be divided by the same number, the sum of the addends may be divided by the number, or the quotients may be added.

The assumption is that an understanding of such properties of the number system as these gives augmented power to the pupil to be independent in and have control over quantitative thought.

The concept of set. This factor has come to be a central one in the communication of ideas in mathematics. It is only natural that efforts to introduce a contemporary program of mathematics into the elementary school would include attention to and use of it. Set refers, mathematically, to more than just a collection of objects (though such a collection can be seen as a set). It carries with it the idea of "the well-defined property"; once a particular set has been described one can determine whether or not other objects are members of the set. (If set X is defined as the set of even numbers between 1 and 9, we know, then, precisely the members or elements of set X.) Thus, set carries with it the idea of a collection of carefully described or defined objects. Modern mathematics programs use the concept of set, and they use considerable set notation. For example, set can be marked off by brackets; elements in the set are separated from each other by commas; n is placed in front of the set of brackets to indicate that the number property of the set (and not the set itself) is under attention. In set notation this would appear as

$$A = \{x,y,z\}; n \{x,y,z\} = 3 \text{ or } n (A) = 3.$$

Fractional numbers are introduced early in the elementary school in contemporary programs, and again the concept of set is utilized. Children are helped to see commonly met fractions as subsets of a given set of objects by comparing the number of members in two sets. Thus, if there are two members in one set and one in another, they find that two thirds of the members in the two sets are in the first set. Denominator, as a part of the language of mathematics, is seen as naming the number of parts into which a physical object is separated, and numerator as naming the number of parts being considered. Of course, children also learn to perform all operations on fractional numbers.

Decimals are seen as symbols for fractional numbers when the second (or third, etc.) number, expressed as a fraction, is a power of ten. Here an understanding of place value in the number system is used, and pupils are helped to see that places to the left of a decimal point are referred to as ones, tens, hundreds, and thousands, while places to the right of the decimal point are read as tenths, hundredths, and thousandths. Pupils are taught, in turn, to perform all of the basic operations with decimals.

The teacher approaches percent by helping pupils to see that a given ratio can be expressed (1) as a fraction, (2) as a decimal, or (3) as a percent. The goal is to develop the meaning of percent and computational skill with percent. The culmination is to be found in the ability to use percent appropriately in problem solving.

An example of a scope and sequence pattern for this aspect of the elementary school mathematics program is as follows:[24]

1. NUMBER AND NUMERATION

Primary grades

Understanding 1–10 (order; one-to-one correspondence; comparing sets; cardinal and ordinal concepts);
Writing basic numerals, 0–9;
Understanding and counting the teens, 11–19;
Understanding counting by 10's, 5's, 2's, 3's, 4's;
Understanding order of counting to 100, to 1000;
Understanding base 10, place value, and additive principle to 10,000's;
Understanding meanings of 0 as no frequency in a place, not any, and a reference point;
Rounding numbers to nearest ten, hundred, thousand;
Learning Roman numerals through L (50).

Intermediate grades

Extending understanding of place value to hundred thousands, millions, and billions;
Understanding the expression of 100,000 as $(10 \times 10 \times 10 \times 10 \times 10)$, 1,000,000 as $(10 \times 10 \times 10 \times 10 \times 10 \times 10)$, 10,000,000 as $(10 \times 10 \times 10 \times 10 \times 10 \times 10 \times 10)$, and so on;
Introduction to exponential notation, for example, 100 as 10^2, 1000 as 10^3, 10,000 as 10^4, and so on;
Rounding numbers to the nearest ten thousand, hundred thousand, million;
Learning Roman numerals to M (1000).

2. NUMBER OPERATIONS AND COMPUTATIONAL PROCEDURES WITH WHOLE NUMBERS

Primary grades

Understanding addition and subtraction as combining and separating operations having an inverse relationship; subtraction as comparing;

---

[24] Frances Flournoy, *Elementary School Mathematics* (Washington, D.C.: The Center for Applied Research in Education, Inc., 1964), pp. 9–12.

Learning the order and grouping properties or principles for addition;

Understanding addition facts to sums of 10 and to sums of 18; related subtraction facts;

Solving simple equations applying addition and subtraction relationships;

Understanding addition and subtraction with two-, three-, and four-digit numerals, with and without regrouping;

Learning column addition to six one-digit addends and four ·three-digit and four four-digit addends;

Understanding multiplication and division as operations in combining equal sets and separating a set into smaller equal sets, and as having an inverse relationship; division as comparing;

Learning the order, grouping, and distributive properties for multiplication, and the distributive property for division;

Learning multiplication facts through sets of five or more and their reverses; related division facts;

Learning multiplication and division with two-, three-, and four-digit numerals by a one-digit multiplier and a one-digit divisor;

Solving simple equations applying multiplication and division relationships;

Understanding uneven division;

Applying skills in problem-solving.

Intermediate grades

Extending addition and subtraction experiences with properties, facts, and computational exercises;

Learning the remainder of the basic facts of multiplication to multipliers of 9 and reverses; related division facts;

Extending multiplication and division experiences with properties and computational exercises, including two- and three-digit multipliers and divisors;

Extending experience in solving equations applying operational relationships;

Applying skills in problem-solving;

Understanding primes, composites, factors, and multiples.

3. COMMON FRACTIONS

Primary grades

Understanding halves, thirds, fourths, sixths, and eighths of one whole;

Understanding and finding fractional parts of a group (using partition division);

Understanding simple multiple part fractions as ⅔, ¾;

Comparing simple fractions and understanding simple equivalent fractions;

Understanding 2/2, 3/3, 4/4, and so on, as names for 1.

Intermediate grades

Extending understanding of fractional parts of a whole, as tenths, twelfths, sixteenths, and so on; finding fractional part of a group; comparing fractions and expressing equivalent fractions;

Using the terms *numerator* and *denominator;*

Understanding the concept of ratio;

Understanding and skill in adding and subtracting fractions with and without like denominators;

Understanding and skill in multiplying and dividing fractions;

Applying skills in problem-solving.

5. DECIMAL FRACTIONS AND PERCENT

Primary grades

Recognizing various coins in our system of money;

Understanding relationship of each coin to cent; of $1 to 100 cents;

Counting money to 50 cents, to $1, to $5, to $10;

Understanding equivalent amounts of money (as a dime is equivalent to two nickels, a half-dollar is equivalent to two quarters);

Making change for various amounts to $10;

Writing cents (such as 25¢); reading and writing dollars and cents (such as $1.55); reading and writing cents with dollar sign and decimal point (such as $.58);

Adding and subtracting simple amounts of money, using dollar sign and decimal point;

Multiplying and dividing simple amounts of money, using dollar sign and decimal point.

Intermediate grades

Understanding meaning of tenths, hundredths, thousandths, ten-thousandths, hundred-thousandths;

Understanding idea of extending place to right of the ones place with each place $\frac{1}{10}$ the value of previous places;

Expressing value of each place; $\frac{1}{10}$ as ($\frac{1}{10} \times 1$), $\frac{1}{100}$ as ($\frac{1}{10} \times \frac{1}{10}$), $\frac{1}{1000}$ as ($\frac{1}{10} \times \frac{1}{10} \times \frac{1}{10}$), $\frac{1}{10,000}$ as ($\frac{1}{10} \times \frac{1}{10} \times \frac{1}{10} \times \frac{1}{10}$);

Reading and writing decimal numerals;

Expressing decimal fractions in equivalent common fraction form, and common fractions in equivalent decimal fraction form;

Rounding decimals to nearest tenth, hundredth, thousandth;

Adding, subtracting, multiplying, and dividing decimal fractions;

Understanding concept of percent as per hundred;

Changing percent to decimal and common fraction forms;

Finding percent of a number, what percent one number is of another, and finding a number when it is expressed as a percent of another;

Applying decimals and percent in problems.

Geometry. Most of the contemporary elementary school mathematics programs make use of geometry. The focus is on the development of some simple but basic geometric concepts. Included is attention to such basic concepts as point, line, line segment, space, plane, curve, circle, ray, angle, triangle, and quadrilaterals. It is held that representations of such simple geometric ideas can be identified readily in the world around the pupil. The approach to the development of such concepts and ideas is generally an intuitive one, as pupils are urged and helped to think about, to use language to describe, and to derive generalizations concerning the sizes, the shapes, and the relationships between objects in the physical world. Notions of similarity, symmetry, parallelism, congruence, and others can be developed in this setting, too. The attempt is to encourage freedom of thought and intuitive perception, with just enough formal vocabulary used to enable pupils to express their ideas clearly and precisely. There is little concern for complex terminology or for formal proofs in the elementary school. The geometry included in the curriculum is used, then, to help with the arithmetic part of the program. It is also used in its own right, so to speak, as a basis for more formal and extended work in the secondary school. A scope and sequence for geometry might be as follows:[25]

7. GEOMETRIC CONCEPTS

Primary grades

Drawing line segments of given length with rulers;
Learning to recognize pictures of line segment, circle, square, rectangle, triangle;
Associating plane shapes with forms in the environment;
Learning characteristics of rectangles; square as a special rectangle;
Measuring length and width and writing dimensions of plane shapes in inches.

Intermediate grades

Learning the idea of an angle; learning to recognize right angles and right triangles;
Understanding right triangle as half a rectangle with same dimensions;
Recognizing triangles that are not right triangles; learning characteristics of equilateral triangle;
Understanding concept of parallel lines;
Recognizing parallelogram;
Using term *quadrilateral* for square, rectangle, and parallelogram;
Understanding concept of perpendicular lines;
Learning that the distance from any point on circle to center is same, measuring radius and diameter of circles;
Learning concept of three-dimensional figures as rectangular and triangular prisms.

Measurement. Measuring, as a process of comparing, has an important place in the modern mathematics curriculum. As a process it is concerned with selecting a unit of measure and comparing it appropriately with whatever is to be measured to see how many of the units are contained in it. Pupils are helped to see measurement as *direct* when a direct comparison of the unit of measure with an object measured can be made (as with length or weight), and as *indirect* when the association of the unit of measure with that which is measured is indirect (as with time, velocity,

---

[25] Flournoy, p. 13.

or temperature). They are helped, too, to see the way in which measurement has basically a *magnitude,* not a *multiplicity,* referent.

There is concern that pupils gain some real sensitivity to the reasoning behind the importance that has been attached over the years to greater uniformity in measurement units and to greater precision in measurement with units. The realities of lack of uniformity in measurement units, in the sense of possible consequences in life situations, is rather readily grasped when pupils are introduced to the bases for many early measures, such as (a) girth: distance around the body, (b) span: from end of thumb to tip of little finger, (c) palm: breadth of four fingers side by side, and (d) acre: amount of land that could be plowed in one morning. Children are quick to grasp the significance of such bases for units in terms of differences in human size and skill. The development of the metric system in France in the eighteenth century, with its high level of precision for units of measure takes on new meaning. Its adoption and use internationally in science is impressive and the fact that even the inch, foot, yard, and mile units which we commonly use in this country are officially defined in terms of the meter adds to their understanding.

The reality of measurement as always being approximate is likewise learned. In spite of improvement in instrumentation and application some degree of error is present in measurement, and pupils are helped to comprehend this fact. They are helped to grasp the situational dimension of concern over precision. For instance, they are helped to evaluate the consequences to the butcher and to his customer of more or less precision in the weighing out of meat for sale in comparison to the consequences of error in measurement when a pharmacist goes about filling a medical prescription for a customer.

A scope and sequence for measurement would be as follows:[26]

4. MEASUREMENT

Primary grades
Understanding the concept of measurement as comparison and the meaning of standard measures;
Telling clock time and learning time relationships; understanding hour, day, week, month, year, decade, and century relationships;
Learning the common linear, liquid, dry, weight, and quantity measures and relationships;
Understanding how to read a thermometer, above and below 0°;
Learning to change from one measure to another.

Intermediate grades
Understanding measurement as approximation;
Extending experiences with common measures and relationships and changing from one measure to another;
Using denominate numbers;

---

[26] Flournoy, p. 11.

Understanding concept of time zones in the United States and throughout the world;

Interpreting latitude and longitude;

Learning metric measures;

Understanding and finding perimeter and area of rectangular and triangular plane figures;

Understanding and finding volume of three-dimensional rectangular shapes.

Algebra. It may be somewhat misleading to call attention to algebra as a mathematical element in the newer elementary school programs. At the same time the attention afforded to the *mathematical sentence* in most of these contemporary programs is most correctly identified as being related to algebra. A mathematical sentence is a statement about numbers, sets, points, lines, and so on. The attention given to the mathematical sentence in the elementary school program is not a simple transposition of algebra normally taught in the secondary school to the elementary school. It does signify the movement downward of the beginnings of algebraic thinking in that attention to even the mathematical sentence has normally been reserved for the first year of algebra in the secondary school.

It is possible that algebra may turn out to be one of the major elements that was missing in the arithmetic programs of the 1930's and 40's. There was always a great deal of attention to real-life problems that included quantity in those earlier curricula. The pupil was urged to think about and to identify the arithmetic problem that was inherent in the situation. Usually this was a matter of deciding whether to add, subtract, multiply or divide. There was a great deal of time spent on developing computational skill for command over the various operations that can be performed on the number systems. But there was little or no time spent on restating the quantitative aspects of the real-life situation mathematically—that is to compose and express in one or more mathematical sentences that which was put before the pupil initially in simple narrative style. For this reason, it may well be that attempts to introduce pupils to mathematical sentences, and to help them to develop skill in both reading them and writing them will contribute much to the independence in problem solving which is sought. In the process pupils will be helped to realize that mathematical sentences can be either true or false. They learn to identify sentences in which truth or falsity can be established as *closed* sentences. Inversely, they identify sentences that are neither true nor false as *open* sentences. Open sentences in mathematics are viewed as being like incomplete sentences in general language. Pupils are helped to become proficient in completing them—usually making them true—and in the process making them closed. They begin to think and discuss in terms of the *solution set*—that is the set of all numbers that may make a given open sentence true and closed. This supports the idea of several and not single correct answers to mathematical problems. Students are also helped to gain greater understanding of the "equality-inequality" phenomenon through the use of mathematical sentences. The relationship expressed in some sentences is understood to be such as to call for the equal sign to symbolize the "equation" characteristic of the sentence. Other sentences are seen as making it necessary to employ any of several other symbols (not equal to $\neq$; greater than $>$; less than $<$; etc.) to indicate inequality in the relationship expressed in the sentence. By devoting time and attention to this rather straightforward algebraic element of the mathematical sentence, the teacher opens a considerable new learning opportunity for pupils. It may well prove to be one of the most advantageous additions to the elementary school mathematics program that has come along in the reform effort.

Problem solving. In a sense problem solving is the *sine qua non* of mathematics. Thus, attention to problem solving in the curriculum of the elementary school is imperative. For a long time the effort has been made to set the arithmetic curriculum in an overall problem-solving context. To some extent this had been attained by the early 1950's. Still, it was most common to hear elementary educators speak of the dilemma they faced in helping pupils to work successfully with what are usually called thought, or word, or story problems. These are descriptions of situations which contain a quantitative element, along with one or more questions which are answerable only by using arithmetic understanding and skill. To develop competent problem solvers continues to be a major concern in contemporary mathematics programs as it has been in the past.

There are two kinds of problems that can be identified as appropriate for the mathematics program. The first, and the one that has been attended to more over the past thirty years, is the problem that focuses on everyday situations that are quantitative in nature. The second is the more straightforward mathematical problem itself. The first calls for the efficient application of mathematical skill to problems of living. The second calls for the efficient application of mathematical skill to further and more complex mathematical problems. While the contemporary programs are concerned with both, they have done much more with the second of the above two situations. It is not that they wish to overlook the first; it is simply that these new programs have not yet had time to develop the application dimension as completely as they eventually must. At the present time there is at least one project that is attempting a more direct application relationship with the science curriculum of the elementary school.[27] This project indicates the desirability of doing

---

[27] Minnesota Mathematics and Science Teaching Project (Minnemast), 720 Washington Ave. S.E., Minneapolis, Minn. (Director: James Werntz, Jr.).

something about the "application outside of mathematics" part of the included problem-solving goals. While this application dimension is being developed, the sensitive teacher will have to exploit as often and as thoroughly as possible the naturally recurring situations in the classroom and around the school which include quantitative problem-solving opportunities. These situations must be seen not as substitutes for mathematical problem solving itself, but as opportunities to sensitize children to the more everyday uses to which much of their growing mathematical power may be applied.

Logic. It is in relationship to skill in problem solving that attention has been devoted to logic in most of the contemporary curricula. To be competent mathematically is to be able to use the basic tools of logic. There is a great deal of logical reasoning—of careful, step-by-step approaches to conclusions in mathematics—or more accurately to answers, or solutions, or truth sets. The whole process of arriving at such conclusions takes place in a sequence guided and controlled by laws specific to the branch of mathematics being used. Logic looms as the basic language of mathematics, and students must be helped to become competent with it. It is useful to students as they organize their ideas, and it is of help as they attempt to ascribe meaning to them. Some attention to logic also makes its contribution to the overall necessity for precision in the use of terms in mathematical thinking. The way meaning changes as quantifiers change (all − some), the way just one counter-example can disprove a generalization, the nature of an inference and the rules of inferential thinking, the nature of proof—attention to topics such as these can sensitize the pupil to the vital role of precise terms in logical reasoning. Direct concern is wisely devoted to the great amount of if-then thinking and if-then statements that are so much a part of mathematics. All of the contemporary mathematics programs for the elementary school pay some attention to logic, and a few of them make it a central part of the overall conceptualization of the curriculum.

Procedures for problem solving. Since children do tend to attack arithmetic problems in a somewhat random manner, they need help in the development of more systematic procedures for problem solving. Thus, the methodology in arithmetic calls for direct attention to procedures. Much effort is directed toward helping children see the relationship between the question or questions to be answered and the known facts in the problem situation, toward helping them to develop ways of interpreting problem situations and ways of visualizing the arithmetic that must be done. Such efforts usually include a number of sequential steps:

1. Reading the description.
2. Recognizing the problem situation.

3. Identifying the facts; noting relationships involved.
4. Determining the process or processes to be used.
5. Estimating the answer.
6. Performing the computation.
7. Checking the answer for reasonableness and accuracy.

The results that accrue from direct attention to problem solving show gains for the learners. While pupils may not use the step-by-step procedure provided as a model, they do develop a somewhat more systematic approach to problem solving that they can use. It appears that the school is better off to utilize fewer problems, focusing carefully on interpretation, meaning, and procedure in problem solving, than it is to try to cover a problem load that is heavy and causes the teacher to pass lightly over the important aspects of problem solving.

There is also a growing tendency to spend time in class with mental problem-solving experiences. The situation is discussed, important elements in the situation are noted, and the computation called for is handled without pencil and paper. Mental problem solving is a very profitable use of time as many of the quantitative situations met in living must be solved in this way.

Problem solving and reading skill. Authorities also suggest that certain special reading skills are involved in the solution of descriptive, situational problems. The overall reading skill of a child, the extent to which his arithmetic vocabulary has been developed, and the ease with which he can read and interpret the style of expression used in word problems are related to problem-solving ability. These skills must be considered as curricula are developed and as teachers work with classes. Reading instruction can, at times, utilize arithmetic content, and the teacher can become sensitive to the fact that he is extending a child's overall facility with reading when he spends time helping him to "read" situational problems in arithmetic.

TEACHING METHODOLOGY IN
CONTEMPORARY MATHEMATICS

The matter of teaching methodology has been of central concern in the projects already identified here almost as much as has the matter of content selection and arrangement itself. One recent publication puts it this way:

> Those who view mathematics for young children in these terms have missed the spirit and intent of the new programs. They view content and terminology as being synonymous with modern mathematics programs when in actuality these are but vehicles enabling

young children to enter into experimentation, discovery and creativity.[28]

Implicit in a statement such as this is the necessity to strike a particular stance toward methodology for teaching if the goals of these new programs are to be achieved. In the main the attention to method has embraced three matters:

1. Application of the structure idea to pupil readiness for mathematics learning.
2. Concept development in children as regards mathematical concepts specifically.
3. Discovery as an element in learning and the implications of discovery for teaching procedures.

Let us consider each of these briefly here. It may also be useful to refer back to Chapters 3–5 in relation to this discussion.

Structure in Mathematics and Teaching Method

Earlier chapters here, notably Chapter 5, have dealt in general with the growing value which curriculum planners have put on the idea of structures in knowledge in relation to curriculum design and to teaching. These ideas have been applied as directly and as completely in mathematics as in any other area of the curriculum. The commitment is clear in contemporary programs to a methodology which utilizes the structure of mathematics to assist pupils in learning and in retaining mathematical knowledge, and in helping to meet the "readiness" problem in teaching on grounds more complete than has been the case to date. An illustration of the importance attached to structure in mathematics is found in the following statement:

> It is easier to memorize words than nonsense syllables. It is easier to memorize numbers expressed with digits in a systematic pattern than in a random sequence. In like manner, learning in mathematics is accomplished most economically and effectively when the emphasis is on structure and on relationship and organization in what is learned.[29]

Learning theorists have also called attention to the utilization of structure in helping teachers decide when to teach what to a given group of pupils. For instance, note Gagne's statement:

---

[28] Ronald C. Welch, "New Mathematics in the Primary Grades," in *Primary Education: Changing Dimensions* (Washington, D.C.: Association for Childhood Education International, 1965), p. 44.

[29] John L. Marks, C. Richard Purdy, and Lucien B. Kinney, *Teaching Elementary School Mathematics for Understanding* (second edition) (New York: McGraw-Hill Book Company, Inc., 1965), p. 11.

The planning that precedes effective design for learning is a matter of specifying with some care what may be called the learning structure of any subject to be acquired. In order to determine what comes before what, the subject must be analyzed in terms of the types of learning involved in it.[30]

This statement builds a linkage between curriculum planning that attends to structure and instructional planning that attends to the same characteristics of a field of knowledge.

Thus, structure of mathematics is looked to for help in making decisions that have to do with the methodology and the timing of instruction in the mathematics program.

Concept Development and Teaching Method

Contemporary mathematics programs for the elementary school have placed a high priority on concept development as being an essential if many of the goals set for such programs are to be realized. At the close of the 1950's the National Council of Teachers of Mathematics attempted an identification of basic mathematical concepts which pupils should learn as they move through the school system. There was an accompanying illustration of the ways in which children at various levels of the school system might be taught to deal with these concepts. Indentifiable in these illustrations were levels or stages of concept development which might be termed (1) presymbolic, (2) modified or semisymbolic, and (3) complete symbolic or abstract.[31] Shortly after the mathematics curriculum reform movement was under way in the late 1950's and the early 1960's, participants in it were much influenced by the work mentioned earlier which Jean Piaget had been doing for a number of years in Switzerland in an attempt to understand better children's thinking and the way in which they learned concepts and generalizations. Especially were they attracted to an attempt to relate what Piaget had to say to teaching procedures and to instructional materials. Noteworthy was the effort made to understand what the sequential development in concept formation which seemed to be evident in children demanded from mathematics teaching. In this country, Jerome Bruner wrote of concept formation and of children's thinking catching the attention of the people involved with mathematics reform.

---

[30] Robert M. Gagne, *The Conditions of Learning* (New York: Holt, Rinehart and Winston, Inc., 1965), p. 25.

[31] Kenneth E. Brown and others, "Promoting the Continuous Growth of Mathematical Concepts," in *The Growth of Mathematical Ideas: Grades K–12,* Twenty-Fourth Yearbook (Washington, D.C.: National Council of Teachers of Mathematics, 1959).

What is most important for teaching basic concepts is that the child is helped to pass progressively from concrete thinking to utilization of more conceptually adequate modes of thought.[32]

Bruner has subsequently identified three stages in the sequence of concept development in children. He sees the first stage (ending at age five or six) as one in which the child manipulates objects on an intuitive level, by trial and error rather than by thought. The second stage, which comes after the child has entered the elementary school, he refers to as the stage of concrete operations—of getting data about the real world and organizing them for selective use in the solving of problems. The third stage (ages 10–14) he calls the formal operations stage. At this level the child acquires the ability to operate on hypothetical propositions and is not limited to what he has experienced or what he is now experiencing. Much of the attempt to relate pedagogy to concept learning is an attempt to understand and take cues for teaching from these presumed levels in children's thinking. What follows is an attempt in the early elementary years to exploit concrete experiences to the end of sensitizing children to quantity and to quantitative concepts. A little later there is work with manipulative materials, such as counters, discs, and tallies. These are used to help children to depict and to reconstruct quantitative situations. They no longer deal with the real objects themselves, but with something that represents the objects—but still something that can be handled, grouped, regrouped, and so on.[33]

Finally, efforts are made to move children to an awareness and use of the abstract symbols of the number system itself. Five counters become 5; three tallies become 3. It is clearly recognized that understanding and skill at this abstract level is most necessary and desirable. It is also recognized that it takes time to arrive at this stage of development, with different children reaching this level at different times. And it is accepted that some children will be capable of much better thinking and working in the abstract than will others. However, the awareness and use of abstract number symbols in dealing with quantitative situations is a goal that the school helps each child to realize within the limits of his potential.

From this insight into concept development comes a sequence of experience in arithmetic learning, especially with young children, that starts with the real and the concrete, moves to a form of modified reality, and culminates in work with abstract number symbols. Depending on the

---

[32] Jerome Bruner, *The Process of Education* (Cambridge, Mass.: Harvard University Press, 1961), p. 38.

[33] See Foster E. Grossnickle, "The Use of Multi-Sensory Aids in Developing Arithmetical Meanings," *Arithmetic*, Supplementary Educational Monographs No. 66 (Chicago: University of Chicago Press, 1948), pp. 1–14.

specific situation, this sequence may be utilized in one period of instruction or over several days of instruction. For purposes of "proof" and testing for adequacy in learning, this sequence may be traveled in reverse, the children proving with counters what they have done with symbols.

Discovery in Learning and Teaching Method

Closely related to interest in concept development is the current commitment to the necessary role of discovery, if children are to learn mathematics meaningfully. It is held that children must have an opportunity to discover facts and principles of mathematics for themselves. To some educators this course of action may appear to be unwise. They would still replace time and attention to discovery with repetition and rote learning. The great majority of elementary educators realize that this seemingly efficient method holds false promise only; therefore they are committed to an approach to teaching and learning that embraces the role of discovery. Swenson wrote as follows a few years ago on arithmetic in the primary grades:

> Enough research studies have been done on the comparative results of different methods of arithmetic instruction in the primary grades to support the statement that methods which lead the children themselves to discover relationships and note generalizations yield superior learning results.[34]

In a similar vein Thiele worked from the following assumption, among others, in a statement in the same publication with respect to arithmetic in the middle grades:

> Psychologically, teachers cannot give children meanings. They must be discovered by children themselves. Teachers can do no more than guide, stimulate, create situations, bring about conditions, and generally speaking, help children gain meaning.[35]

A statement from a recent publication furnishes evidence as to the extent to which this general feeling still prevails in the matter of method in teaching in mathematics:

> For whether one speaks to mathematicians or physicists or historians, one encounters repeatedly an expression of faith in the powerful effects that come from permitting the student to put things together for himself, to be his own discoverer.[36]

---

[34] National Society for the Study of Education, Fiftieth Yearbook, Part II, p. 74.
[35] National Society for the Study of Education, p. 80.
[36] Jerome S. Bruner, "The Act of Discovery," in Richard C. Anderson and David Ausubel, *Readings in the Psychology of Cognition* (New York: Holt, Rinehart, and Winston, Inc., 1965), p. 607.

There is no question that a methodology that is discovery oriented is appropriate and vital to the contemporary mathematics programs. There is a question, however, as to just how much of a pupil's mathematics he should be expected and helped to discover for himself. Each teacher must be sensitive to the balance that is useful between learning from discovery and learning that emanates from a more guided experience in which the teacher resorts to deductive methodologies and expository or "telling" teaching styles.

Certainly the teacher wants the children to discover facts and principles for themselves, but he actively participates in the process, and the children's success is in great part related to the teacher's skill. He does hold his telling and his explaining to a minimum, and he illustrates and demonstrates sparingly. The teacher does try continuously to *lead* pupils to discovery. This he does for the most part by proper selection of problem situations and by careful and insightful questioning during the arithmetic experience that follows. He draws the discovery out of the children, moving from the known to the unknown. He provides, also, a wide range of materials for children to use which are well suited to exploration in quantitative situations. That is, he will have counters, abacus, flannel board, measuring instruments, and the like readily available in the environment so that children may meet the problem situation at the level of abstraction at which they are ready to work. It is known that the ability to discover in arithmetic differs widely among children, and the teacher reflects this difference in the manipulative materials used.

Also, the teacher knows that children cannot discover everything for themselves about an arithmetic process or principle. For example, children cannot discover the standard way of recording a given type of problem without direct help from the teacher. Similarly, much of the vocabulary of arithmetic will have to be supplied to students as they move along.

DRILL AND PRACTICE IN MATHEMATICS

There has been some confusion as to whether users of the newer approaches to learning in arithmetic have found it necessary to make a place for drill and repetitive practice. This sort of activity is still essential in the arithmetic curriculum, but considerable change has come about in how teachers provide for it. The fact that some educators are reluctant to discuss the question of drill experiences is indicative of their negative reaction to the time when the whole arithmetic program was built on a drill theory of learning. In that earlier period drill and rote memorization were the very heart of the curriculum. Many "connections" needed to be developed between given stimuli and appropriate responses if the mind was to develop its arithmetic power and potential. Drill on arithmetic facts and processes was deemed the most appropriate methodology for this development. Thus, instruction started and ended with drill experiences.

Repetitive practice. When association psychology was questioned, persons interested in arithmetic began to provide information on drill, perhaps better referred to as repetitive practice. This information began to throw some real light on the contribution of such experiences to arithmetic learning. It is now known that drill can come too soon, can be pursued too vigorously, and may work as an obstacle to the very things it is supposed to achieve unless it is carefully considered.[37]

It is equally well known that repetitive practice is a necessary aspect of the total curriculum in arithmetic. While pupils need to achieve learning in arithmetic that embodies understanding and meaning, they need, too, the ability for immediate and automatic recall. Children need to be able to see and respond at once with a sum, or a difference, if they are to be as proficient with arithmetic facts and processes as many situations will demand. Thus, the challenge is for the teacher to provide the proper amount of repetitive practice and provide it at the proper time to insure such learning. Attention should be directed to a number of things that help a teacher make this decision.[38]

First of all, repetitive practice must follow the development of understanding of a given arithmetic fact or computational process. It must come after discovery. The beginning of such meaningful practice may follow very closely the discovery act itself, serving as a check on the insight developed by the children as well as providing them with some immediate practice with the type of example involved.

Practice should always, of course, be geared to the level of understanding evident in the pupils. Drill can increase the speed and accuracy of recall, but it cannot furnish a better or more efficient way of doing a given thing. Formal drill is of little value until meaning has been well established; then practice is quite necessary to move the handling of computational processes to the level of automatic response.

One of the most exciting applications of computer-based instruction focuses on drill and practice in elementary school mathematics.[39] Children work at either teletype terminals in their classroom or at

---

[37] W. A. Brownell and C. B. Chazal, "The Effects of Premature Drill in Third Grade Arithmetic," *Journal of Educational Research,* Vol. 29 (September 1935) pp. 17–28.

[38] B. R. Buckingham, "What Becomes of Drill?" in *The Growth of Mathematical Ideas,* pp. 196–224.

[39] Computer-Based Mathematics Instruction, Stanford Computer-Based Laboratory for Learning and Teaching, Stanford University (Director: Patrick Suppes).

individual consoles in an especially equipped classroom annex. By harnessing the potential of the high-speed computer to programmed instructional materials, the teacher is able to individualize arithmetic drill for each pupil each day in light of his right-and-wrong responses in the preceding practice session.

Mastery and drill in arithmetic. The matter of mastery, as a goal in a skill area, is always a source of concern to the elementary educator. While the term is easy to use, it is difficult to define, especially in operational terms. That is, it is difficult to say when a student has or has not achieved mastery of an arithmetic process or procedure. Some teachers would relate mastery to the scores made on practice or drill lessons. This enables one to speak of "100 percent mastery," citing as evidence a perfect score in such a lesson. If drill is to come after understanding, as has been suggested here, there is something to think about in this proposition. It would thus follow that less than perfect scores are accepted as less than complete understanding, and therefore less than mastery. However, this simple sort of logic is quickly clouded by some other considerations. Perhaps the practice lesson was not designed in such a way as to make a perfect score a reasonable expectation. The lesson may have been too long, introducing elements of boredom and fatigue; or the time allotted for completion may have been too short, introducing elements of tension and strain. Thus, the definition of mastery is pushed back to some judgment' as to the number of examples children at various ages or stages should be expected to complete correctly in a given period of time.

One other factor must be considered: the individual learner himself. He may well be establishing his own definition of mastery in terms of either (1) the degree to which the skill he has developed enables him to meet successfully whatever quantitative situations he encounters in the natural course of events, or (2) the relationship that he identifies between the level of skill he has reached and the level of skill of those around him. Either of these definitions, separately or in combination, can lead a given child to the conclusion, often mistaken, that he has or has not achieved mastery in arithmetic.

Thus, an acceptable definition of mastery must of necessity be somewhat complex. It seems profitable to conceive of mastery in arithmetic as being that level of control and response reached by students that enables them to meet quantitative situations with security and accuracy, within whatever time limit particular situations typically demand.

Clearly, the mathematics curriculum is most advanced at the present time in terms of the changing curriculum that is dealt with in this book. It would seem to be fair to speculate that, in a way, the mathematics program will be undergoing its second round of reform and change before many of the other areas have completed the first. The future would appear to be exciting. Efforts will almost certainly be expended in the direction of understanding more completely the way in which particular populations of pupils are able to learn mathematics. The demands on teaching of the goals to which contemporary programs aspire will be explored more thoroughly. The application question will have to be resolved more efficiently. But, all in all, the promise of progress in the next decade is most satisfying.

RECOMMENDED READINGS

DEANS, E. *Elementary School Mathematics: New Directions*. Washington, D.C.: U.S. Government Printing Office, 1963.

The Growth of Mathematical Ideas: Grades K–12, Twenty-Fourth Yearbook. Washington, D.C.: National Council of Teachers of Mathematics, 1959.

HEDDEN, JAMES W. *Today's Mathematics: A Guide to Concepts and Methods in Elementary School Mathematics*. Chicago: Science Research Associates, Inc., 1964.

MARKS, JOHN L., C. RICHARD PURDY, and LUCIEN B. KINNEY. *Teaching Elementary School Mathematics for Understanding* (revised edition). New York: McGraw-Hill Book Company, Inc., 1965.

POLYA, GEORGE. *How to Solve It: A New Aspect of Mathematical Method* (second edition). New York: Doubleday & Company, Inc., 1957.

REPORT OF THE CAMBRIDGE CONFERENCE ON SCHOOL MATHEMATICS. *Goals for School Mathematics*. Boston: Houghton Mifflin Company, 1963.

The Revolution in School Mathematics. Washington, D.C.: National Council of Teachers of Mathematics, 1961.

SWAIN, ROBERT L., and EUGENE D. NICHOLS. *Understanding Arithmetic* (revised edition). New York: Holt, Rinehart and Winston, Inc., 1965.

WARD, MORGAN, and CLARENCE E. HARDGROVE. *Modern Elementary Mathematics*. Cambridge, Mass.: Addison-Wesley Publishing Company, Inc., 1963.

WOOTON, WILLIAM. *SMSG: The Making of a Curriculum*. New Haven, Conn.: Yale University Press, 1965.

Natural Environment: Science

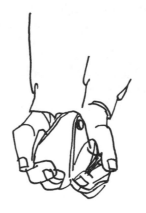

11

The improvement of science programs in elementary schools is a matter receiving priority attention at the present time. Science is increasingly accepted as a basic and fundamental force in the lives of people. The research laboratory is coming to be recognized as the twentieth century "frontier." The application of the discoveries of science to the day-by-day affairs of men continues to improve and expand an already amazing technology. Atomic energy as a power source, automation and the development of the automatic factory, antibiotics for the control and treatment of disease, jet propulsion applied to aircraft, rockets for the exploration of outer space, increased understanding of mental illness—all of these are but a few of the contributions of science that make life both more pleasant and more complex in our time. Few would question the importance of science for the continuing improvement of living. In fact, in a troubled and tense world, our very survival depends on the quality of our science. Any attempt to provide an answer to the question of what it means to be educated in our time must inevitably concern itself with science.

Children have a great deal of understanding to develop as they try to understand science as a process and to build meanings about their natural environment. The child develops a feeling of security in having some understanding of such natural phenomena as the day-and-night cycle, the causes of the seasons, the growth of plants, electricity and magnetism, and the origins of and differences in rocks. Added to these are such technological things as why a jet airplane flies, where the television picture comes from, or what the surface of the moon really looks like.

At the present time science seems to be assured of an important place in the elementary school curriculum. The nature of the program is only now emerging. But there is little doubt that there will be one. For instance, consider the following statement in a teaching guide:

> The need for science as a definite part of the elementary program is no longer a matter of debate. Its need is predicated upon a world requiring an abundance of scientific knowledge.[1]

Another guide states:

> Science is a regular part of the school curriculum. A planned science program is the only way our elementary school pupils can be assured the understandings necessary to intelligent living in a modern democracy.[2]

Further evidence to support this contention is found in the listing of some fifteen major curriculum projects for elementary school science in the 1967 Report of the International Clearinghouse on Science and Mathematics Curricular Developments.[3]

EARLY SCIENCE PROGRAMS

It should not be concluded from these opening paragraphs that there has been no science in elementary schools over the years. There is, in fact, evidence of science programs in our elementary schools for the past one hundred years. Some teachers have characterized the earliest programs as "walks and talks with nature." Children would be helped to identify things in the natural environment; that is, they would make up lists of names of trees, flowers, and other things. Instruction would pretty much start and end with the making of such lists. Sometimes objects in the environment—rocks, or nests, or insects—might be carefully scrutinized, but again, the learning would stop with this careful look. That which was accepted as the "end" of science learnings in these early programs would now be seen as a most vital link to more worthwhile ends. Present thinking would indicate that the learning in these early programs simply stopped too soon.

Most of the early science programs restricted themselves, also, to plant and animal life. Little was done with the physical sciences. While

---

[1] Lakewood Public Schools, *Science in the Elementary Schools—Upper Grades* (Lakewood, Ohio: Lakewood Public Schools, 1956–57).

[2] San Bernardino City Schools, *Science Guides—Elementary Grades* (San Bernardino, Calif.: San Bernardino City Schools, n.d.).

[3] J. David Lockard (compiler), *Report of the International Clearinghouse on Science and Mathematics Curricular Developments,* American Association for the Advancement of Science and the Science Teaching Center, University of Maryland, 1967.

this imbalance persists still to a degree in elementary school programs, it is recognized, and efforts are being made to correct it. The present state of development of science makes it imperative that the physical sciences be included.

One characteristic of much of the early elementary school science should be noted. Almost all of the science that was taught, limited though it may have been, utilized firsthand experiences with the natural environment. Children actually looked at trees growing or at wild flowers in the woods and fields. They searched out nests in trees and rocks along the banks of streams. The importance of this firsthand contact with the natural environment is readily recognized. In fact, the boost that modern science textbooks gave to science instruction has fallen short of expectations to the degree that children have been held to a "reading about" experience in the classroom.

SLOW DEVELOPMENT OF SCIENCE PROGRAMS

Concern for science in the elementary school has fluctuated over the years. Reflect on this statement in an elementary school science course of study, published in 1948, as it tells this story in the history of a particular school system:

> No subject in our school program has undergone such mutations as elementary school science. This subject in the form of natural history was taught in upper grades of certain of our public schools from their organization, and in all by 1850, but was dropped from the course in 1853. Elementary school science was reintroduced in 1857 in the form of object lessons for the lower grades. The science work was broadened in 1870 and physics was added for the sixth and seventh grades. This was, however, omitted from the new course of study of 1880. Effort was again put forth in 1895 to give science instruction an important place in the schools. This course was carried forward for ten years, when in 1903 the instruction in the upper grades was eliminated and that for the lower simplified and joined with language . . . with no separate place upon the program. . . . [From] 1903 to 1926, there was little elementary science taught in Cleveland. In 1926, however, a committee prepared a tentative outline in elementary science. With the establishment of the curriculum center for elementary science at Doan School in February, 1928, the subject was given a definite place in the program of the schools.[4]

Assuredly, this "on-again-off-again" approach to the teaching of science in the elementary school has been evident in school systems generally over

---

[4] Cleveland Public Schools, *Science Course of Study: Sixth Grade, Cleveland Public Schools* (Cleveland, Ohio: Cleveland Board of Education, 1948), p. 9.

the years. There are strong signs at the present time, fortunately, that this will not be the situation in the future. Science and technology in our society are accepted as the vital cultural elements which they are, and efforts are being made to develop significant school programs for children that deal with them. These efforts are identifiable to the point that it is possible to speak of a "new movement" in elementary school science programming that dates from about 1960. More will be said about this later. Let us first consider what it is to which this very slow and halting development of science in the elementary school in the past can be attributed.

OBSTACLES TO SCIENCE PROGRAMS

First, there have been doubts about both the necessity and the feasibility of including science in the elementary school program. As for necessity, there has been in past years a feeling that science was something that could be studied and experienced later—meaning sometime after the elementary school years. To many teachers there seemed to be more important and more desirable things to do for and with children in their first years at school. The result has been a kind of apathy about the whole matter, with not enough people really convinced of the value of science in the elementary school. This apathy has combined with some expressed doubts about the readiness of young children for science. The mental picture held by many lay people of the scientist at work in the laboratory, busy with complicated equipment and complex formulae, just did not fit their assumptions about and expectations for children. They doubted that children would be successful with science; they questioned that children would find science appealing.

Fortunately both of these obstacles to improved science curricula in the elementary school are being reduced. The vital role which science is seen as playing in our lives has pretty well eroded the notion that the teaching of science could justifiably wait until after the elementary school years. To know science is seen by most people as an unquestioned dimension insofar as "being educated" is concerned. And there is a great deal more support for the position that any curricular description of "the fundamentals" in our time must include a place for a science program.

Support for a science program in the elementary school has come from studies of the nature of childhood itself. Out of this information many teachers have concluded that children are more naturally scientists than they are anything else. Certainly they are curious; they seek explanations; they want to know why things happen. They enjoy the security of prediction, of being able to say that a given thing will happen under certain conditions. Children tend to be imaginative and creative in much that they do. They are innovators of the first order; they are continuously trying, making, doing—all to the end of satisfying an insatiable curiosity. This picture is certainly suggestive of the "profile" of the scientist.

Research of various kinds has been conducted, too, to try to identify some of the strong interests and concerns of children—the things that capture their attention and that they would like to know more about. In all such studies, there have been many questions raised about science and technology. Children ask many questions in this area, and they indicate strong interests in things scientific. For example, a study a few years ago asked children to indicate the things they would most like to be able to ask somebody about or to look up in a book; first priority was given to science. More children had more concerns that fell into the category of science and technology than anything else.[5] Other studies focused on this matter have come up with similar results. As a group, the studies indicate strong science interests in children, and they tend to show a pattern of wide interests ranging over the various fields of science. Thus, the nature of childhood complements the strategic nature of science in the modern world. Children are reflecting the fact that they are growing up in an age of science. Interests are learned, and children are learning well. Pupils in the elementary school are ready to accept science learnings. It is up to the school to make available a provocative and informative program.

Second, teachers have not always felt secure in handling science study in the classroom. Typically, their own science backgrounds have been meager, and this shortcoming has led to ambivalence about the science they would make available to children in their classroom programs. Too, some teachers who had studied science as a part of their own general education were at a loss to devise ways of bringing science to children. The gap between their adult learnings and the beginning learnings of children was too great for them to bridge procedurally. It must be remembered, too, that as persistent areas of interest develop at the adult level it is rather obvious that science is more often a male interest than a female one. With our elementary schools staffed so heavily with women teachers, there has not been as much professional interest in science within the teaching corps itself.

The problem of teacher readiness persists today and must be dealt with if science is to flourish in the elementary school. Happily, certain changes are being made that may eventually work to the advantage of elementary school science. Most colleges and universities now require considerably more science as a part of the fixed general education experience of all candidates for undergraduate degrees. Over the years, this

---

[5] Herbert C. Rudman, "The Informational Needs and Reading Interests of Children in Grades Four through Eight," *Elementary School Journal,* Vol. 55 (May 1955), pp. 502–512.

requirement will mean that teachers will be better informed and more skillful generally in the area of science. Also, there is some trend toward having prospective elementary school teachers carry the equivalent of either single-field or broad-field subject-matter majors in their preparation for teaching. Some will select science and this will provide the elementary school with personnel who can take a leading role in science instruction. Departments of education are increasingly offering course work in methods for teaching science in the elementary school, and these will help teachers to meet the general problem of timidity and shyness toward science teaching. Research strongly suggests that the methods of teaching used in science in superior classroom programs differ significantly from methods used in programs that have been evaluated as only mediocre.[6]

A strong assist in teacher education has come from the institutes sponsored by the National Science Foundation and by the National Defense Education Act. Usually held in the summer and to some extent during the academic year, these have focused on teachers already in service in school systems and have added to the effort aimed at mid-career development in teacher education. Also almost all of the curriculum improvement projects that are being developed in science include materials aimed specifically at the preparation of teachers to handle the science teaching called for in their proposed curricula. Much remains to be done in insuring subject matter and pedagogical security and adequacy for teachers; the newer science programs are quite demanding in this respect. But progress is being made.

Third is the fact that the development of an acceptable science component in the curriculum of the elementary school has been seen as being too "expensive." One aspect of this "expense" has been related to the fact that the curriculum is already "crowded"; that is, there has been much more to do than time in which to do it. If a new science program is to be introduced, or a minor science program made more significant, it is inevitable that time will have to be found for it. Science has had to compete with certain priorities that have operated in elementary education for many years insofar as time allotments enter into this.

The other way in which "expense" enters into this centers on the amount and kind of equipment and facilities that are called for in an adequate science program. Here, too, there has been considerable ambivalence. On the one hand, limited budgets have tended to discourage new curriculum ventures. On the other hand, there has been much talk to the effect that an ingenious teacher could provide an exciting and stimulating science experience for children with just a few items out of the

---

[6] Max Berryessa, *Factors Contributing to the Competency of Elementary Teachers in Teaching Science,* unpublished doctoral dissertation, Stanford University, 1959.

family kitchen and garage—a little wire, a pie pan, a dry cell, and other things. Schools may not realize that this frugality is more a function of the situation than it is of choice, and so they do not budget the amount of money that further development of the science program demands.

Gradually though, the "expense" arguments, too, are being eroded away. More current practices testify to the fact that a place is being made for science in the elementary school program. Time is being found for it by various types and kinds of rearrangements in the school day and week. The availability of money in the budget to support the program is improving as well. Here the infusion of federal monies is making a difference.

Still, it would have to be said that to some extent all three of these conditions continue to exist and to act as obstacles to the development of the science strand of the curriculum. The situation is improving, but there is still apathy to overcome, teacher competence to develop, and money to be allocated.

THE NEW MOVEMENT IN SCIENCE

Earlier the statement was made that there has been an identifiable "new movement" in elementary school science since about 1960. Perhaps it would be more accurate to say an "increased effort," for surely by 1960 there was in many elementary schools a useful science program being made available to children. But, in the late 1950's and especially in the face of the challenge of Soviet science, there seems to have been a new kind of awakening to the need for an improved science curriculum on all school levels, including the elementary. Noteworthy and of fundamental importance to this development was the fact that a goodly number of outstanding scientists as individuals, and professional associations of scientists as such, became interested in the problem and sought ways of participating in curriculum improvement projects. Following to some extent the model presented to them by the involvement of mathematicians in similar projects in that field, scientists have worked along with classroom teachers, with learning psychologists, with media specialists, and increasingly with science educators since about 1960 in reexamining the problems and the possibilities for science in the elementary school.

Attention will be given here to some of the thinking that has thus far gone into this and to some of the positions and points of view that have been taken by those involved.

What Is Science?

Clearly if one would propose to develop a science curriculum, one would have to be able to say what science is. Let us take three ideas that together give a rather meaningful definition of science and that would be consistent with current curriculum projects in that area.

First, science is a study of the environment, more particularly of the natural environment. It includes both the *physical* (earth, sky, energy, matter) and the *biological* (plants, animals, life, growth) aspects of the natural environment. Science concerns itself with trying to understand this natural environment; with trying to help man to adjust to it in comfortable, efficient, and safe ways; and with trying to control it and use it to the advantage of man. Concepts are developed and generalizations are stated.

Second, science is a method of solving problems. In the problem-solving methods of science, man possesses an intellectual tool of the highest order. The systematic way in which the scientist identifies and defines problems, projects hypotheses or hunches, gathers and interprets data to support or to negate them, and records his findings has provided man with a model for seeking the truth in science and for solving a great many of life's problems generally.

Third, science is an attitude. Science demands objectivity; there is no place for personal bias or prejudice. The explanation for something is in the findings, not in the mind or the desire of the scientist. It is an attitude that calls for open-mindedness and a readiness to change one's mind in light of the evidence. Things are as they are; there is no place for superstition, mysticism, or witchcraft. The truth of the matter is in the phenomenon itself; it is there to be checked and verified by others.

Thus, science is a product in the sense of facts, concepts, and generalizations. It is process in the sense of a problem-solving enterprise. It is predisposition in the sense of the objective posture it demands of those who would become involved with it.

What Is the Job of the Scientist?

The fundamental job of the scientist, then, is to search out facts about the natural environment. His major tool is observation; he may use intricate apparatus and equipment to make his observations more accurate or to observe phenomena otherwise unobservable. Thus, his laboratory will include microscopes, telescopes, cameras, X-ray machines, and the like. In the facts he discovers he may perceive relationships that lead to generalizations, or to laws of science. Just what the worth of any given fact or relationship will be, once discovered, is difficult to say. However, one does not have to look very far to be aware of the major changes that have been wrought in our lives as a result of the searchings of the scientist.

The application of the facts and generalizations discovered by the scientist to the practical affairs of life is more accurately referred to as *engineering* than as *science*. It is engineering that develops the various technological improvements that are part and parcel of present-day living. It is engineering that develops rockets, satellites, and atomic-driven submarines and ships. It is science that makes available the fundamental knowledge upon which such engineering feats are based. Thus, to an understanding of what science is, and in a sense growing directly out of it, can be added an understanding of what the scientist does. And out of such information and insight as this emerge the goals and objectives toward which the science curriculum is oriented in the elementary school.

Purposes of Science in the Elementary
School

The following goals appear to be acceptable and necessary:

1. Children should be helped to know some science facts, and to develop some meaningful concepts and generalizations that they can use in their attempts to understand and manage the natural environment.

2. Children should be helped to use the processes of inquiry which are the *sine qua non* of the sciences; to become aware of and skillful with the scientific method.

3. Children should be helped to develop a scientific attitude, to become objective, open-minded individuals, dedicated to an evidence-based truth.

4. Children should be helped to understand and appreciate the dependence of our society upon scientific and technological achievement, to see science as a basic part of modern life, and to anticipate change as a consequence of technology.

5. Children should be helped to sense the intellectual and personal satisfactions that are derived from the pursuit of science, for either the professional or the layman.

6. Children should be helped to know something of the careers in science that are open to them and of the realities of the life which the scientist leads.

These are goals which the new movement in elementary school science would accept. In fact, these are goals which to a great extent have been accepted by the old movement, too. They make clear the necessity for contact with the subject matter of science; and they make clear the necessity for experience with the methods of science. That is, they make a place for both the product and the process of science. As stated, they are quite broad and general, and only suggestive of the sort of curriculum plan that should be developed. Goal statements such as these still have to be refined toward the behavioral kinds of statements mentioned in

Chapter 4, both to give more useful direction to the work of the teacher and to aid in the evaluation of their accomplishment. The curriculum improvement projects that have been launched in this area have tried to come to grips with this matter of goals. Much that is new in their curriculum proposals stems from a somewhat different interpretation of the meaning of goals such as those cited above, as well as from fresh ideas about suitable and feasible means of accomplishing them. It could be said that this careful attention to goals in the current projects is a rather natural consequence of their efforts to reassess and reestablish a basic rationale for science teaching in the elementary school. Now let us move on to consider some of the newer emphases in arriving at an acceptable curriculum plan.

Continuing a Unified Science Curriculum

The science taught in the elementary school is a unified or general science. It is unified or general in the sense that it contains no specialized courses such as chemistry and physics. Some special interest groups or clubs may be formed in an elementary school with their work organized around a special area of science, such as geology or astronomy. Still the general orientation in science curriculum development at this level has been to science as a whole, and this orientation is one to which the new movement in elementary science is also committed.

Such a unified approach calls for a balanced curriculum. In 1947 a yearbook of the National Society for the Study of Education contained a policy-like statement about programming which stated as follows:

> By the end of each year the children should have experienced some growth in the broader areas of the physical and biological environment, such as the following:
>
> *The Universe.* Here provision is made for the study of the stars, the sun, the moon, the planets, and their interrelationships. Pertinent materials would include those essential to an understanding of the causes of day and night, seasonal changes, tides, eclipses, and (less commonly) the vastness of the Milky Way galaxy and galactic systems beyond our own.
>
> *The Earth.* Among the pertinent topics in this phase of the environment are such problems as the origin of the earth, the formation of mountains, weathering of rock into soil, erosion, volcanism, prehistoric life, and the forces which have changed and are still changing the surface of the earth.
>
> *Conditions Necessary for Life.* What living things need in order to exist, how they are affected by changes in the environment, and the struggle for the conditions necessary to life are suggested materials in the development of this aspect of the environment.
>
> *Living Things.* Suitable materials include the variety of living things,

the social life of animals, adaptations for protection, life cycles of plants and animals, how living things obtain their food, the economic importance of living things, and man's influence upon nature.

Physical and Chemical Phenomena. Such chemical phenomena as rusting are considered in this phase of the environment. Physical phenomena which may be appropriate include light, sound, gravity, magnetism and electricity, changes in the state of matter, and the phenomena associated with radiant energy and atmospheric changes.

Man's Attempt to Control His Environment. In this aspect of science the child may study man's control in gardens, on farms, in orchards; his inventions and discoveries; his use of power, of minerals; his control over living things; his study of places he cannot reach directly; and other topics.

In addition to the areas of the physical and biological environment, the curriculum maker and the teacher should consider the areas growing out of living and social needs, such as health, safety, conservation, economics. It is evident that these areas of living will utilize content described in the areas of the physical and biological environment and will form the basis for the development of desirable knowledge, attitudes, and appreciations.[7]

This statement, and others like it, had considerable effect on curriculum planning. Undoubtedly at the present time the majority of elementary schools are committed to science programs that are much like that suggested by this NSSE statement.

As the current effort to improve the teaching of science in the elementary school got under way, however, there were questions raised as to the adequacy of this sort of framework for curriculum planning. There was some strong concern for a framework that would make possible even more unification in the curriculum than had been achieved thus far. The American Association for the Advancement of Science undertook to study the situation and made a report of their recommendations in 1960–1961. Their statement was arrived at through the joint efforts of science teachers, science educators, scientists, and learning psychologists. The agreement reached was to the effect that the following broad science concept areas would provide an improved framework within which to organize the elementary school science program:

1. Cosmology—character of the universe as an orderly system.
2. Evolution.
3. Ecology—mutual relations between organisms and their environment.
4. Structure and Function.
5. Reproduction and Development.

---

[7] National Society for the Study of Education, *Science Education in American Schools,* Forty-Sixth Yearbook, Part i (Chicago: University of Chicago Press, 1947), pp. 75–76.

6. Structure of Matter.
7. Energy Interrelations and Change of Matter.[8]

One finds attempts to use this AAAS recommended way of ordering the science experience in the school, or one much like it, in the experimental and developmental work of the ongoing curriculum improvement projects. Obviously there is a relationship between the earlier noted NSSE statement and the AAAS framework, but the latter is even more clearly oriented to concept areas and away from disciplines. In fact, what follows from the AAAS framework is a prediscipline or nondiscipline way of viewing science and the science curriculum plan.

UTILIZING THE STRUCTURE OF SCIENCE FOR CURRICULUM PLANNING

You will remember that the first two of the general purposes suggested for science in the elementary school were these:

1. . . . to know some science facts, and to develop some meaningful concepts and generalizations . . .
2. . . . to use the processes of inquiry which are the *sine qua non* of the sciences; to become aware of and skillful with the scientific method.

Certainly the new movement in elementary school science is characterized by attempts to plan the curriculum by utilizing the structure of science, both its conceptual dimension and its methodological dimension.

Concepts and the Structure of Science

Science demonstrates the earlier mentioned accelerated rate at which new knowledge is developing probably more than does any other area of endeavor. Estimates are that scientific knowledge is growing at a rate which doubles it about every ten years. The question as to what knowledge is of most worth in science, and therefore to be included in the school curriculum, is a pressing concern for the curriculum planner. The idea of getting at the basic structure of the disciplines—of isolating those elements of a subject matter that have real "survival" potential for understanding in the future—has directed the attention of the planners to the study of concepts. There is an effort in ongoing curriculum improvement projects to identify the key or fundamental concepts and the main ideas that are derived from them to provide a knowledge base for science

---

[8] John R. Mayor and Dael Wolfle, *Feasibility Study of Major Efforts to Improve Science Courses in Elementary and Junior High Schools* (Washington, D.C.: American Association for the Advancement of Science, 1960–61); John R. Mayor, "Science Teaching in the Elementary and Junior High Schools," *Science*, Vol. 1331, No. 3469 (June 23, 1961), p. 2021.

teaching. At the moment this seems to be the best way of dealing with what is an ever-growing and ever-changing body of knowledge.

In a sense this is not a wholly new approach to the determination of content for the science curriculum. Craig, a pioneer in elementary school science, described in his early work an approach to subject matter selection that was related to this. After dealing with the matter of objectives for science he suggested the following for their realization:

> Examining treatises on science to determine how these objectives can be analyzed into their constituent elements.
>
> Assigning these subordinate concepts as specific objectives to various grade levels on the basis of their logical development.[9]

Thus, it is not a completely new departure to look to the subject matter of science for what children should be taught. It is true, however, that the selections made over the past thirty years have been highly influenced by a "use" or "applications" kind of approach to science. The preference today is to select concepts to be developed with the aim of understanding science as such and only in a very secondary way to be concerned with the uses or applications of these concepts.

The newer curriculum designs for science are utilizing, also, the notion of spiraling conceptual development over the elementary school years. Ideas met in the earliest years and in the most simple of settings are revisited in later years for further refinement and added meaning, and in more complex settings. Spiraling, too, has been an emerging idea in science education for a number of years. To a degree, textbook series have tried to use spiraling within their graded series, and school systems have incorporated this idea into local curriculum guides.

The great difference between the old curriculum and the new lies in the nature of the concepts and generalizations selected for inclusion in the sense of their significance for arriving at an understanding of science and the way in which the scientist perceives nature and natural order at this time. This is a consequence in great part of educators' having been able to capture the attention of scientists themselves to the task of curriculum planning.

Here are excerpts from a recent book that illustrates the quality of thought that is being applied to instructional questions about science in the elementary school.

> One significant difference between modern science education and some former approaches is in the emphasis now given to fundamental understandings. Perhaps nowhere is this attention to fundamentals

---

[9] Gerald S. Craig, *Certain Techniques Used in Developing a Course of Study in Science for the Horace Mann Elementary School,* Contributions to Education No. 276 (New York: Bureau of Publications, Teachers College, Columbia University, 1927).

better seen than in units on energy. In the present one on heat, intended for children of the middle grades, a serious effort is made to acquaint them with molecular theory. Too hard? Not if approached on an intuitive plane that stresses concrete experiences, in contrast with verbal learning. Children will explore such concepts as heat and temperature, expansion-contraction, heat transfer, and changes of state. As is typical at this level, we shall be concerned mostly with physical, rather than chemical changes.

In this particular instance four basic generalizations are set out for development, along with certain so-called contributing ideas that add meaning to them. The knowledge framework thus found is as follows:

Generalization I: Most materials expand when heated and contract when cooled.

    Contributing Idea A. Solids expand when heated and contract when cooled.

    Contributing Idea B. Liquids expand when heated and contract when cooled.

    Contributing Idea C. Gases expand when heated and contract when cooled.

Generalization II: Adding or taking away heat can cause materials to change state; different materials change state at different temperatures.

    Contributing Idea A. Solids melt into liquids when heated; liquids freeze into solids when cooled.

    Contributing Idea B. Liquids evaporate into gases when heated; gases condense into liquids when cooled.

Generalization III: There is a difference between the temperature of a material and the heat it contains.

    Contributing Idea A. Temperature is the measure of how fast molecules are moving.

    Contributing Idea B. The amount of heat a material contains depends on how many molecules it has, as well as how fast they are moving.

Generalization IV: Heat energy may come from many sources; it travels by conduction, convention, and radiation.

    Contributing Idea A. Many sources of energy can be changed to heat energy.

    Contributing Idea B. Sometimes heat travels by conduction.

    Contributing Idea C. Sometimes heat travels by convection.

    Contributing Idea D. Sometimes heat travels by radiation.

    Contributing Idea E. Knowing how heat travels allows us to control it through insulation.[10]

---

[10] Peter C. Gega, *Science in Elementary Education* (New York: John Wiley & Sons, Inc., 1966), pp. 107–129.

To some extent all of the experimental projects in elementary school science are oriented toward feasibility. They are based on a clear recognition of the importance of science in modern life and on confidence that children of elementary school age can profit from a well-conceived science program. There is a need for teachers to determine more exactly just what it is that children can and cannot do; there is a need to determine more exactly the specifications which instructional materials and equipment must meet to be useful to children. Space does not allow us to review all of the projects that might be described here. We will focus on three of the more extensive and interesting ones to illustrate what is going on, with excerpts from the earlier mentioned report on the current status of curriculum development in science and mathematics.[11]

Elementary Science Study

One of the best known projects, the *Elementary Science Study* (ESS), is sponsored by Educational Services Incorporated.[12] The project is not involved in the development of a sequential curriculum for the elementary school, but rather with the development of a wide variety of instructional units that can be used in various combinations and at several grade levels. The units are designed so that children have access to them in an open-ended way. A variety of materials and equipment is made available for pupil use in the units; the materials, instead of being "scientific," look like things normally available to children in their own environment. The units have content goals; they are also intended to increase the problem-solving skills of pupils, to improve pupils' ability to face a new set of materials and to begin an investigation into questions about it, and to improve pupils' ability to predict results under what are essentially experimental conditions. Let us describe briefly here some of the units that this project is making available commercially for the classroom:

> *Growing Seeds* (Grades K–3). In this unit children plant a collection of seeds and non-seeds to see which ones grow. After planting the seeds, they dig up some of them to find out what happened underground. Then each student plants a new corn seed and cuts a strip of paper daily showing the height of his plant.
>
> *Melting Ice Cubes* (Grades 4–5). This provides an informal introduction to heat and temperature. Children are given half-inch cubes of wood and aluminum to put on ice. By putting stacks of blocks (heated blocks and cold blocks) on the ice, the children try to determine

---

[11] Lockard (compiler), *Report*, 1967.

[12] Educational Services Incorporated, *Elementary Science Study* (ESS), 55 Chapel Street, Newton, Mass. (Contact: Randolph Brown).

whether the difference in sinking in is caused by weight or by something else. They also melt away whole ice cubes (in air vs. in water, in lots of water vs. in a little water, and in big cups vs. in little cups). They also use other shapes of ice (flat, round, and crushed) and compare their melting times with cubes of equal weight.

Kitchen Physics (Grades 5–7). This is a first course in science drawn from the child's environment. The student investigates the properties of common liquids—typically water, soapy water, oil, alcohol, and syrup. He considers a number of questions about the behavior of these liquids. The questions direct his attention to such attributes as the way liquids are absorbed, evaporate, drop, steam, and interact with various surfaces.

A variety of kinds of materials are handled by pupils in working through these units; they read, they see filmstrips, they handle things. They are heavily involved with "doing"; the teacher does a minimum of telling. The hope is that this is a sound approach to a more meaningful science experience for children.

Science Curriculum Improvement Study

Another major project, the *Science Curriculum Improvement Study* (SCIS), is sponsored by the University of California (Berkeley) and is directed by Robert Karplus.[13] Karplus is a theoretical physicist who became interested in elementary school science instruction. His conclusions were that science instruction to be effective had to be simplified and that it had to be organized on a very different basis from the usual logical subject-matter presentations to which the scientist was accustomed. To that end this project is attempting to develop a complete and integrated elementary school science curriculum in which the included teaching units are conceptually interdependent. The stress is on concepts and phenomena; process learnings are a by-product of the pupils' experimentation, discussion, and analysis. The approach is centered on materials. The classroom is the laboratory. Children become acquainted with specific examples of objects and organisms, examine natural phenomena, and develop skills in manipulating and recording data. After children complete these preliminary explorations, the teacher introduces the scientific concept that describes or explains what the children have observed. This experience is referred to as the "intention" lesson. Following this lesson, the teacher provides other experiences that present further examples of the concept and are referred to as "discovery" lessons. Through this procedure the child is expected to recognize that the new concept has

---

[13] University of California, Physics Department, *Science Curriculum Improvement Study* (SCIS), Berkeley, Calif. (Director: Robert Karplus).

applications to situations other than the initial example. The discovery experiences reinforce, refine, and enlarge upon the content of the presented concept. Subject matter dealt with is drawn from the physical and life sciences and is to be used in the elementary school grades, though the sequential nature of the program takes precedence over any particular grade level designations for the placement of learning units. A project report describes some of the already produced materials as follows:

> *Material objects.* The main objective of this unit is to teach the child to recognize material objects in his environment and to distinguish their properties. The first chapter introduces the child to concepts of objects and properties, and aims to develop careful habits of observation, the ability to discriminate fine differences and recognize broad similarities, and vocabulary useful in describing objects. The second chapter introduces the concept of material through the comparison and sorting of similarly shaped pieces of aluminum, brass, pine, walnut, and polystyrene. This concept is then applied in additional work with other woods and metals, as well as with rocks, liquids, and gases. In the third chapter, the child compares objects with respect to one property that exhibits quantitative variation; he practices serial ordering. This activity introduces a semiquantitative aspect to the child's comparison of objects. In the fourth chapter, the emphasis is on the child's acting upon objects. The child experiments with various materials (ice, lump sugar, rock candy) in order to change their form while retaining their identity. He tests whether objects float or sink in water, and he uses air to displace water from submerged containers. These experiments give the child opportunities to apply what he has learned about material objects and their properties and, at the same time, provide an informal introduction to the concept of systems, which is part of a later physical science unit in the program.

Science: A Process Approach

Most of the current curriculum improvement projects include attention to modes of inquiry and ways of investigating into natural phenomena. It is judged to be most crucial that children should be given an opportunity to discover, and to learn sound methods of validating knowledge about the natural world as a part of their science experience. All of the current projects stress this process dimension, but one of the most complete of them has committed itself almost exclusively to it. That is the project for which the American Association for the Advancement of Science is responsible, called simply *Science—A Process Appoach.*[14]

To emphasize process is to emphasize the methods of work used by the scientist and to develop child competence with these methods and

---

[14] American Association for the Advancement of Science, *Science: A Process Approach*, The Association, 1515 Massachusetts Ave., N.W., Washington, D.C. (Director: Dr. John Mayor).

processes. The following are typical of some of the process skills attended to:

1. *Classifying* various types and kinds of natural phenomena in ways that help one to handle them (size, shape, color, etc.).
2. *Arranging* phenomena in an ordered series along some dimension that makes sense for them (weight, size, texture, etc.).
3. *Observing and describing* similarities and differences in natural phenomena, and changes in natural phenomena (size, shape, motion, relationship, etc.).
4. *Measuring*, using units and scales appropriate to different types of natural phenomena.
5. *Hunching, guessing, hypothesizing*, engaging in simple 'if-then" thinking including doing, observing, and reporting.
6. *Manipulating objects* to produce simple cause-effect relationships, describing changes; stating rules that apply.
7. *Inferring*, making various plausible explanations for things that happen.

The process approach to science learning calls for a laboratory experience much more extensive than anything typically found in the elementary school years in the past. Much of science over the years has been a reading, not a doing experience. At best there have been some demonstrations in the classroom of known scientific principles and regularities, usually controlled and conducted by the teacher with perhaps one or two children used as holders of equipment or having some similarly minor involvement. With the new commitment to discovery-oriented teaching and learning pupils plan and conduct simple experiments, to some extent in the primary years, and certainly in the intermediate grades. They discuss and clarify problems and questions; they procure necessary equipment and subjects; they observe carefully and regularly; they gather and record data systematically. The conclusions they accept have to be found in the data, readily verifiable by others who would follow a similar pattern of experimentation.

As with the matter of utilizing a basic concepts approach to curriculum content, it is still to be determined just how extensive and successful these encounters with the processes of science can be for children. Just how independent children can be about this kind of approach to science learning, and just what the role of the teacher will need to be, are matters of concern in most of the ongoing curriculum improvement projects. To date the evidence as to feasibility is encouraging. Suchman conducted studies in about 1960 with groups of fifth grade children in an attempt to see if they could be helped to learn something of the tactics of scientific inquiry. His approach, in which he used physics, was to show a short silent film in which something could be observed as happening. Pupils were asked to observe carefully to get data, and they could ask the teacher questions that could be answered with a "yes" or a "no." Any given inquiry session lasted about thirty minutes. It was his conclusion that the inquiry skills of children at this age level could be so improved. The children wanted explanations for what they had seen and were willing to inquire to get them. He felt that this sort of experience would be an excellent supplement to a regular science program that was more focused on the product side of the enterprise.[15] Experience with the process-focused AAAS project has been generally successful, too. A certain amount of demonstration teaching is found to be useful in an otherwise inquiry-oriented program, and there is undoubtedly a place for both types of experiences in the elementary science curriculum. They need to be used with insight into what each can do best for learning. The discovery kind of learning makes demands that some teachers may find difficult to meet. Teachers must be comfortable with both the subject matter under study and with the methods of the subject matter as well, and they need to be able to handle simple laboratory equipment and oversee the work of pupils without dominating or directing it unduly.

The units which these projects and others are devising for the classroom present an ambitious undertaking for teacher and pupil alike. Authors of the projects are making special efforts to include adequate information for the preparation of teachers to handle the experiences, but that adequacy remains to be tested in a thorough way. Children seem to be attracted to the kind of science experience which these projects are trying to make available to them. Results to date are encouraging, but again there is much to be done by way of evaluation before firm conclusions can be drawn. In all of the projects under way there is an attempt to use ingenuity in the development of novel and interesting approaches to what is to be learned. Most of the projects are still involved in the development of specific units of work or lessons, and only the AAAS *Science—A Process Approach* project mentioned earlier has thus far produced a full curriculum for a K–6 elementary school program. The others are either working on the development and the test of units for particular age groups or for particular aspects of science.

Science Learning and Social Significance

It is not sufficient simply to teach science concepts and methodologies. One of the general purposes of the school science program is to

---

[15] J. Richard Suchman, "Inquiry Training in Science," *Science Teacher,* Vol. 27, No. 7 (November 1960), pp. 42–47.

help children to sense the role of science in modern life and to appreciate the contributions made thereto by science. Included is the hope that children can be helped to accept the inevitability of change in the years ahead as a consequence in great part of our science, and can learn to anticipate change as much as is possible. This raises the old question of the extent to which the curricula in science and in social studies should come together to the advantage of both. Many current leaders in science education are reluctant to move too quickly to this question. They say that only in the past few years has science managed to escape almost complete domination by the social studies in the elementary school. Consequently while they recognize the fact that there is great social significance attached to much of what science has done and will do, they are unwilling to think, beyond certain very limited arrangements, about joining science and social science curriculum plans. At the same time some science educators are taking positions on this matter which are a little less hard. Consider this for example:

> In an effort to help children see science in relationship to man and his environment, whenever possible, science should be a part of the total elementary school curriculum. This integration of science with other subject matter, as opposed to the separate subject approach where, for example, the geography of Long Island and the history of Jamestown were presented separately in the same morning, helps strengthen the bonds between science and the concepts and subject matter of other areas of the curriculum. By integrating science with other areas of the curriculum, it is not meant that science as a recognized subject should be lost; instead time is organized and learning experiences are planned in the curriculum so that science enriches and is enriched by other curricular areas. When a science concept such as the transmission of electric (radio) waves through a vacuum (space) is presented in conjunction with a social studies course on the international implications of space and space satellites each subject profits from the other. By understanding the forces and properties of our universe a more meaningful comparison of the early explorers of America and the modern pilgrims or explorers into space is developed. Such common problems of spacemen and pilgrims stressing the closeness of the social studies and science are shown:

>> How did they get from one place to another? How did they steer their crafts?

>> What were their crafts made of? What aspects of our universe helped them? Hindered them? What did they eat and how did they get their food? How did they know where they were? Why did they go?

> Without the loss of any science material, studies can be prepared in order to provide for the integration of science with the other areas of the curriculum. In this way, the child can be helped to see by example and not by preaching that science helps man interpret and understand

his environment from all aspects: health, safety, ways of making a living, ways of transporting, and communicating.[16]

This is a statement endorsing integration and relatedness that would sound familiar to most elementary school educators. Its appearance in a current professional text in science would indicate that such thinking is not a lost point of view. In our judgment the very nature of the work to be done on the science program for the next several years, however, is such as to mitigate against a great deal of attention being given to this matter of relatedness. Still it is seen as being important to the extent that it will continue to capture some of the attention of the curriculum planner and of the classroom teacher as well.

Science Learning and Children's Interests

Present developmental work in science is also characterized by a position for a structured program and against an unstructured one. In the main this is a position that has to do with the extent to which expressed child interests will determine the science curriculum. This is easily placed in the context of the earlier statement (Chapter 2) on the competing ideas that have characterized curriculum planning in elementary education over the years. Children's interests and concerns are not completely lost sight of, but they are not used as a determinant for an emerging framework for the science curriculum. They are attended to in attempts that are being made to design learning experiences which children will find interesting and to which they will be attracted. Thus, the science curriculum is determined neither by current social problems nor by the interests of children.

The idea of a new subject-centeredness and a predesign in curriculum planning is demonstrated by the rationale basic to most of the current curriculum improvement projects in elementary school science. Consider these points that were made in a 1960 yearbook devoted to rethinking science education:

1. A structured program provides a framework of science principles which can help teachers unify their own experiences and give them confidence in meeting difficult classroom situations that arise. The answer suggested a decade ago to children's questions—"I don't know, but let's find out together"—is not sufficient for all of today's needs.

2. A structured program does not have to be a rigid one. Within the broad content areas, there are many choices which permit the

---

[16] Arthur Carin and Robert Sund, *Discovery Teaching in Science* (Columbus, Ohio: Charles E. Merrill Books, Inc., 1966), p. 27.

teacher to adapt the program to the needs of the class. Both the unit approach and the provision of a variety of materials and situations which foster children's creativity and originality are possible within a structured program.

3. The freshness engendered by the use of unanticipated incidents is not lost in a structured program. Indeed, the incident becomes more significant because the teacher sees it as a part of the whole and thus may be able to convey its importance to the pupil. A structured program helps the teacher anticipate, identify, and incorporate into the the program the many incidents which arise during the school year.

4. While it is true that children come to school with many interests, it is also true that interest can be aroused and cultivated by what takes place in school.

5. A structured program makes it easier for children to acquire the science concepts essential for their understanding of the complex world they live in.

6. A structured program is a democratic one: many can share in building it and changing it. It provides a common framework for testing and evaluation by the children as well as by the teacher.[17]

These items were listed in response to a question as to the role of children's interests in the development of an improved science curriculum. Clearly, there is to be considerable predesign for the foreseeable future.

Science and the Image of the Scientist

The last two of the six general purposes to be achieved in the science program that were cited earlier had to do with helping children to

. . . sense the intellectual and personal satisfactions that are derived from the pursuit of science. . . .
. . . know something of the careers in science that are open to them and of the realities of the life which the scientist leads.

Science will need able manpower in the years ahead in order to maintain and improve on its current position of eminence in the world. An important aspect of this need is the image of the scientist and of his work that is held by students, some of whom might conceivably be possessed of considerable scientific talent. A study several years ago concerned with the image of the scientist, and of pupil attitudes toward science as a career showed that few high school students had a favorable image of the scientist.[18] This study was done in 1957, and there is perhaps some

---

[17] National Society for the Study of Education, *Rethinking Science Education,* Fifty-Ninth Yearbook, Part ɪ (Chicago: University of Chicago Press, 1960), p. 128.
[18] Margaret Mead and Rhoda Metraux, "Image of the Scientist among High School Students: A Pilot Study," *Science,* Vol. 124 (August 30, 1957), pp. 387–390.

reason to believe that the image of the scientist may have improved as a result of the publicity given to our achievements in space science since then. But the fact remains that one consequence of the science experience which pupils have at school should be a realistic picture of scientists, and of what they do and how they live. If current efforts insure that children will have a personal kind of experience with science as enterprise in the elementary school years, the image of the scientist may take a more positive turn in the future. This would seem to be important both from the standpoint of support for those young people who might be ready to consider a career in science, and for the great mass of the public who must be supportive of science if science is to have the financial resources placed at its disposal that its continued growth and development demand.

Just what the next decade will lead to in elementary school science is hard to say. While the new movement is young it is also vigorous. The great diversity among projects will probably continue for some time to come. The evidence that is beginning to come in on some of the projects shows encouraging results. The differential impact of much of the programming on rapid and slow learners poses a real challenge. The response of the "disadvantaged" children to many of the experimental units has been encouraging. Teachers show a real determination to keep at the task of developing a more adequate science curriculum in the elementary school. Science is a fundamental for today's children as surely as anything else that the school might aspire to provide for them.

RECOMMENDED READINGS

BLACKWOOD, PAUL E. "Science Teaching in the Elementary School: A Survey of Practices." *Journal of Research in Science Teaching*, Vol. 3 (1965), pp. 177–197.

BLOUGH, GLENN O. *It's Time for Better Elementary School Science.* Washington, D.C.: National Science Teachers Association, NEA, 1958.

BLOUGH, GLENN O., JULIUS SCHWARTZ, and ALBERT J. HUGGETT, *Elementary School Science and How to Teach It* (revised edition). New York: Holt, Rinehart and Winston, Inc., 1958.

DUNFEE, MAXINE, and JULIAN GREENLEE. *Elementary School Science: Research, Theory and Practice.* Washington, D.C.: Association for Supervision and Curriculum Development, NEA, 1957.

FREEMAN, KENNETH, and others. *Helping Children Understand Science* (revised edition). New York: Holt, Rinehart and Winston, Inc., 1959.

GEGA, PETER C. *Science in Elementary Education.* New York: John Wiley & Sons, Inc., 1966.

HANEY, RICHARD E. *The Changing Curriculum: Science.* Washington, D.C.: Association for Supervision and Curriculum Development, NEA, 1966.

HUBLER, CLARK. *Working with Children in Science.* Boston: Houghton Mifflin Company, 1957.

LEWIS, JUNE E., and IRENE POTTER. *The Teaching of Science in the Elementary School.* Englewood Cliffs, N.J.: Prentice-Hall, Inc., 1961.

NATIONAL SOCIETY FOR THE STUDY OF EDUCATION. *Rethinking Science Education,* Fifty-Ninth Yearbook, Part I. Chicago: University of Chicago Press, 1960.

SHECKLES, MARY. *Building Children's Science Concepts* (Practical Suggestions for Teaching No. 15). New York: Bureau of Publications, Teachers College, Columbia University, 1958.

Human Arrangements: Social Studies

12

To assign time to the social studies as a part of the curriculum is to insure the study of man in his interactions with other men and with the natural environment. Such study includes attention to (1) the arrangements that people devise for living and working together, (2) the customs, institutions, and value systems that emerge as aids to persons living together with satisfaction, (3) the ways in which people utilize the natural environment to meet their needs, and (4) the adaptations people make to the natural environment when they can neither use nor control it to their advantage. It is in this network of human relationships and accommodations to nature that man's personal and social needs must find satisfaction.

Our society looks especially to the school to help insure that each succeeding generation will understand, value, and practice democratic ways as these have come to denote the kind of life that most Americans find satisfying. *Citizenship education* has been a central responsibility in public education for many years.

The elementary school has long been expected to contribute to the social education of children, to begin a systematic approach to knowledge and understandings, values and attitudes, and skills and abilities that are associated with the social studies. Elementary educators have themselves tended to place a high priority on the social studies in the elementary school curriculum. It is not uncommon to hear the social studies spoken of as the very "heart" of the elementary school program. Note the tone in this passage from a 1957 yearbook devoted to the elementary school social studies program:

> The subjects of the elementary-school curriculum, consequently, do not stand upon one plane of importance. The social studies in particular occupy a unique position in the school program, since their purpose, as has been pointed out, is fundamentally the major purpose

of the whole school. . . . It is obvious that social studies merit an important place in the curriculum of the elementary school—as important a place as civic literacy, civic responsibility, and civic competence must have in contemporary life if we are to continue a free people.[1]

Similarly, studies of children's interests and questions indicate that they are concerned about things which are associated with what we tend to see as social studies—the origins of early man, the development of nations and governments, the causes and effects of war, the search for peace, and other social matters.[2]

TYPICAL DEFINITIONS OF THE SOCIAL STUDIES

The most typical definitions suggest that the *social studies* are those portions of the social sciences selected for instructional purposes in the school. The definitions state that the selection of subject matter will be made from history, geography, political science, economics, sociology, and anthropology.[3] In the elementary school the usual practice has been to restrict the selection to history, geography, and political science (as civics). Only rarely and indirectly have the other social sciences been used in the social studies program. To some extent there has been a recognition of the need to include *process* in the social sciences as content for study, too, but until of late this has not been a major concern of definitions offered. Over the years there has been a tendency to recognize the possibilities for teaching toward the goals of the social studies in ways that go beyond the formal curriculum, so that two other terms have become common which could be seen as broadening the definition of the social studies suggested above. These two terms are *social education* and *social learnings*.

The Broader Concept of Social Education

Considerable support has developed, born of experience in elementary schools, for the idea that a real contribution can be made to promote

---

[1] Helen Heffernan, "Social Studies in Relation to the Total Elementary-School Program," in *Social Studies in the Elementary School,* Fifty-Sixth Yearbook of the National Society for the Study of Education, Part II (Chicago: University of Chicago Press, 1957), pp. 122–123.

[2] Emily V. Baker, *Children's Questions and Their Implications for Planning the Curriculum* (New York: Bureau of Publications, Teachers College, Columbia University, 1945); Edythe E. Clark, *What Children Want to Know about Their World,* unpublished master's thesis, Boston University, 1952; Herbert C. Rudman, "The Informational Needs and Reading Interests of Children in Grades Four through Eight," *Elementary School Journal,* Vol. 55 (May 1955), pp. 505–512.

[3] Edgar B. Wesley, "The Social Studies," in W. S. Monroe (editor), *Encyclopedia of Educational Research* (New York: The Macmillan Company, 1950), p. 1214.

desired citizenship objectives if certain aspects of the general life of the school are more consciously utilized. Thus, organized service projects such as a lost-and-found service or a school store are seen as fertile activities for exploitation. Also, the operation of appropriate forms of classroom and schoolwide student government groups, the support of periodic social service drives such as the Junior Red Cross program, and participation in school playground and safety patrols are viewed in a new and more instructive light. The term *social education* has now come to be used for all school activities that contribute to and can be utilized for the accomplishment of the goals formerly associated only with the social studies program. As such, the term is broader than *social studies,* and is used by most educators in this broader sense.

The Broadest Concept: Social Learnings

As educators have begun to think more comprehensively of the efforts of the elementary school to educate in the social sphere, there has come an ever-increasing stream of information and arguments addressed to the total social learnings task that the child faces in our culture. These writings have directed attention both to the great amount of social learning that has taken place before the child comes to school, and to the many persons and agencies, both in school and out, who continue to provide social learning experiences to children after they begin to attend school. Such information, coming from cultural anthropologists, sociologists, psychiatrists, psychologists, and pediatricians, as well as from professional educators, has been both provocative and confusing. Although elementary school educators have been attracted to this information, they have not always known how seriously to take it or just what to do about it. Nonetheless, this material is slowly finding its way into general affairs concerning the social development of children, and the efforts of the elementary school in the area of social education are resting on a broader, more inclusive base of information than ever before.[4]

Thus, while this chapter may tend to emphasize the organized social studies curriculum found in the elementary school, the larger setting in which social education takes place and social learnings mature is not to be overlooked. We are aware that, to a considerable degree, every act of teaching and every organized experience at school is an act of cultural transmission with its attendant consequences for personality development and child socialization. But the emphasis selected here would

---

[4] Edna Ambrose and Alice Miel, *Children's Social Learning: Implications of Research and Expert Study* (Washington, D.C.: Association for Supervision and Curriculum Development, 1958); Alice Miel and Peggy Brogan, *More Than Social Studies* (Englewood Cliffs, N.J.: Prentice-Hall, Inc., 1957).

appear to be justified. It is in relation to the organized social studies program that the most complete reexamination is taking place and the greatest change may come about.

The question is not whether a social studies program is needed in the elementary school. Heavy demands to be socially competent and aware have been placed upon all persons. The adequacy of the present curriculum in the social studies is what is being questioned. Well established is the fact that, even though children seem to be interested in social phenomena, the social studies are ranked low by them as a school subject. Surveys of student preferences place the social studies in the bottom quartile. Well known too is the fact that the social studies curriculum today uses only a few of the available social sciences, rather than taking advantage of the full range of these disciplines. That this should continue in the future is difficult for many educators to accept. There is argument, also, over the way in which citizenship education is seen to be the almost complete responsibility of the social studies. Those so concerned believe that the social sciences (and therefore the social studies) can contribute in a major way to citizenship education, but cannot do the total job. More importantly they believe that by not accepting this limitation on the role of the social studies in citizenship education, the very crucial and legitimate contribution that they can make to the task is obscured and weakened. In addition, there remains the long-standing conclusion drawn by many teachers that the usual social studies program in the elementary school deals so little with current social realities as to be almost miseducative for the pupil. These and other matters are developed more completely in later sections of this chapter. The point is that there is restlessness about the state of the social studies in the elementary school and readiness for change.

The sequence to be followed here gives attention (1) to the types of educational goals most commonly associated with the social studies program, (2) to the most common way for the curriculum in the social studies to be organized to accomplish those goals, and (3) to current concerns for the improvement of the social studies including reference to projects and materials only now being developed and field-tested.

GOALS FOR THE SOCIAL STUDIES PROGRAM

We have earlier established the general proposition that school learning is goal-oriented learning. Thus, one would expect to find clearly stated lists of objectives developed and disseminated within school systems to give direction to teachers' efforts in the social studies. And, as suggested above, these would have a great deal to do with citizenship.

What might such a goal statement include? Below are listed twenty-four items on which the National Council for the Social Studies was able to get consensus from a group of some three hundred selected citizens. Working with the Department of Defense following World War II, the Council published the following set of behavioral statements, which defines the good citizen as one who:

1. Believes in equality of opportunity for all people.
2. Values, respects, and defends basic human rights and privileges guaranteed by the United States Constitution.
3. Respects and upholds the law and its agencies.
4. Understands and accepts . . . democratic principles as guides in evaluating his own behavior and the policies and practices of other persons and groups, and judges his own behavior and the behavior of others by them.
5. Understands that, in the long run, people will govern themselves better than any self-appointed group would govern them.
6. Puts the general welfare above his own whenever a choice between them is necessary.
7. Feels that he has inherited an unfinished experiment in self-government which it is his duty and privilege to carry on.
8. Exercises his right to vote.
9. Accepts civic responsibilities and discharges them to the best of his ability.
10. Knows techniques of social action (e.g., how to win support for desirable legislation) and can cooperate with others in achieving such action.
11. Accepts the basic idea that in a democracy the majority has the right to make decisions under the Constitution.
12. Assumes a personal responsibility to contribute toward a well-informed climate of opinion on current social, economic, and political problems or issues.
13. Realizes the necessary connection of education with democracy.
14. Respects property rights, meets his obligations in contracts, and obeys regulations governing the use of property.
15. Supports fair business practices and fair relations between employers and employees.
16. Assumes a personal responsibility for the wise use of natural resources.
17. Accepts responsibility for the maintenance and improvement of a competitive economic system assisted and regulated when necessary by governmental action.
18. Knows in general how other economic systems operate, including their political and social consequences.

19. Knows about, critically evaluates, and supports promising efforts to prevent war, but stands ready to defend his country against tyranny and aggression.
20. Is deeply aware of the interdependence of people and realizes that a good life can be attained only by the organized cooperation of millions of people all over the world.
21. Understands cultures and ways of life other than his own.
22. Cultivates qualities of character and personality that have a high value in his culture.
23. Is a responsible family member and assumes his full responsibilities for maintaining the civic standards of his neighborhood and community.
24. Recognizes taxes as payment for community services and pays these promptly.[5]

This list of items cannot be accepted uncritically as a behavioral description of citizenship in our country. Any citizen might want to revise some of these, and add others before the list would be acceptable to him. This statement does, however, direct attention to what many in our society would accept and expect in the behavior of a person considered to be socially, politically, and economically well educated. And, implicit in these stated behaviors is a demanding and extensive set of educational tasks for the school, including the elementary school.

In further consideration of this, note the relationship between the above twenty-four items and a summary of major social studies purposes reported about five years later by Michaelis. After studying many programs for elementary schools he concluded that their major purposes were to help each child to:

1. Become a democratic person whose behavior is guided by democratic values, who is loyal to the American way of life, and who appreciates the sacrifices and contributions made to promote democratic living here and throughout the world.
2. Develop modes of behavior consistent with democratic values, such as responsibility, concern for others, open-mindedness, creativeness, and cooperation, and to use them in relationships with others.
3. Develop group-action skills and social competency in intergroup relations, recognizing the value of group decision making, showing respect for differences of opinion, and exhibiting high regard for rights of minorities yet abiding by majority decisions.
4. Develop the ability to think critically and creatively and use problem solving skills in situations involving human relationships; use dependable sources of information; locate, evaluate, select, organize,

[5] Ryland W. Crary (editor), *Education for Democratic Citizenship*, Twenty-Second Yearbook of the National Council for the Social Studies (Washington, D.C.: NEA, 1951), pp. 154–160.

and present information effectively; and base action on sound conclusions.

5. Appreciate and respect other persons, cultural similarities and differences among peoples, and the contributions of others to our ways of living, realizing that human dignity and personality are of first importance in human relationships regardless of race, color, or class.

6. Acquire and use functional information, concepts, and understandings of: basic social functions of human living such as production of goods and services, transportation and communication, conservation of resources, aesthetic and religious expression, education, recreation, and government; the impact of scientific advance and education upon ways of living; the effect of moral and spiritual values upon human behavior; ways to improve family life, community living, and national-international welfare; and the increasing interdependence characteristic of modern living.

7. Become responsive to needs and problems of others and act courageously and with integrity to bring about changes consistent with democratic ideals and processes.[6]

Even though this summary was prepared more than a decade ago it would still be accurate for the great majority of elementary school programs today. Curriculum guides in any particular locale might stress some goals over others but almost assuredly they would all be identifiable as accepted objectives for the social studies.

THE PLANNED SOCIAL STUDIES CURRICULUM

An examination of the purposes quoted earlier makes it very clear that there is a place for a planned and systematic social studies program as the major part of the school's total efforts toward social education. Let us turn our attention to the ways in which elementary schools organize for work in the social studies.

Various organizational plans have been put forth and all have had to develop defensible sets of answers to the full range of curriculum questions posed in earlier chapters which dealt in general with patterns of organization for the elementary school curriculum. Such matters as the most appropriate organizing centers for instruction, the proper grade placement of subject matter, a valid plan for determining the sequence of learnings, a commitment to certain methodological principles have all been considered. Undoubtedly in the social studies more than in any other curriculum area have all of the general points of view toward curriculum planning been tried in an attempt to find an improved way

---

[6] John Michaelis, *Social Studies for Children in a Democracy* (second edition) (Englewood Cliffs, N.J.: Prentice-Hall, Inc., 1956), p. 12.

for the social studies to contribute to citizenship education. To some extent all of these general patterns are still evident in today's elementary schools, although certain general tendencies do predominate in both theory and practice.

Two General Approaches to Planning the Social Studies

In general there have been two different approaches used in planning for the social studies, utilizing two different points of departure. One of these approaches takes the subject matter of the various social studies as the principal point of departure for planning the program. The other focuses on the social problems met by man in society and tries to develop a social studies program that would be in harmony with man's continuing efforts to meet and solve social problems effectively. The first approach has been more sympathetic to and influenced by the various tenets of the separate subject and broad fields points of view toward curriculum planning, while the latter approach has found the activity and the core points of view more attractive.

Planning from Subjects

The earliest programs in the social studies were developed around the separate social subjects themselves. History, geography, and civics found their way into the curriculum about the time of the American Revolution and continued to be taught separately well into the twentieth century. During this early period the social studies program reflected rather completely the characteristics of the separate subject curriculum pattern. The program was committed almost exclusively to informational purposes with the evident belief that good citizenship stemmed in the main from knowledge of history, geography, and the organization of government.

Modifications toward a broad field plan. Since about 1920 those committed to a subject matter point of departure for developing the social studies program have modified their planning in the direction of the broad field point of view. There was a growing acceptance of the fact that the relatedness among the various social studies should be made more evident to pupils, and that by developing a social studies broad field this relatedness was more likely to be dealt with in the classroom. Awareness of this relatedness has led, in those schools following such a plan, to the assignment of one larger block of time each day to the social studies; teachers are urged to use subject matter from all of the social studies in carrying out the instructional task. The label *subject matter units of work* in the social studies is a reflection of this broad field development. To a considerable extent this way of organizing the social studies program is still used in the elementary school curriculum, and its influence is obvious in almost all planned programs.

Planning from Problems

The greatest challenges to the idea of planning the social studies program directly from the social subjects have come from the activity and integrative-core points of view in curriculum planning. Both of these positions have sought a more challenging and more dynamic approach to the social studies, a kind of program that would relate more intimately to school and life around the school. Both are committed to the use of organized subject matter as a resource for learning and for solving problems, and both are committed to problem-solving processes as a basis for the teacher's methodology. Finally, both have said that the social studies program is best planned around social problems of importance, but in the implementation of this planning the two points of view differ quite markedly.

Problems in the activity curriculum. Those educators following the activity curriculum base for planning the social studies program are committed to select problems for study that are consistent with the expressed interests and concerns of children. These become the organizing centers for the social studies program; such interests and concerns are seen as emerging over the school year as children continue to live in and to probe their culture. Thus, there is very little predetermination in this approach to the social studies. Problems and questions keep coming to the fore in the classroom during the school year; they are discussed and criticized, and selections for study are made. The planning of the program emerges over the school year. The general impact of this point of view was greatest from about 1920 through the 1930's, and it still influences practice.

The predominance of integrative-core ideas. Most of the general criticisms of the activity curriculum noted earlier have been directed against its use as the base for planning the social studies program. While accepting problem solving as a basis for method, and while supporting the idea of using something other than subjects as the initial point of departure in planning the social studies program, the majority of elementary school educators have not supported the use of children's interests and concerns to the extent that the activity point of view calls for, and they have not accepted the idea of the emergent curriculum. There is some indication that many have felt that process goals are likely to be given undue emphasis at the expense of content goals in the social studies unless the activity point of view is tempered.

This feeling has resulted in a turning away from children's interests, as organizing centers for the social studies, to an acceptance of an identified list of basic human activities as being uniquely fitting for use in the social studies. The use of these basic human activities as the scope of the social studies has seemed to insure that the program will have the necessary breadth of study. Furthermore, it is held that life is lived actually by means of these activities, that social problems and questions take form in terms of these activities, and that their use in curriculum planning should result in a closeness between study in school and life outside of school.

An examination of city, county, and state curriculum guides in the social studies attests to the acceptance and usefulness of this scheme as a curriculum tool. For example, a curriculum bulletin in one of our large cities uses the following list of basic social activities as the centers around which the work is planned:

1. Protecting and conserving life, health, resources and property.
2. Producing, distributing and consuming food, clothing, shelter and services.
3. Creating and producing tools and techniques.
4. Transporting people and goods.
5. Communicating ideas, information, and feelings.
6. Providing an education.
7. Providing for and participating in recreational activities.
8. Organizing and governing groups of people.
9. Expressing aesthetic and spiritual impulses.[7]

The question of curricular sequence in the social studies has come to be answered in different terms, too. The earlier subject-structured programs had found their response to sequence within the subjects themselves. The activity program found its answer to sequence in the continuous teacher-pupil planning procedures that were basic to an emerging sequence of classroom experiences. Influenced heavily by core thinking, a way of handling the sequence matter has developed that is defended on both psychological and sociological grounds. This set of ideas has come to be referred to as the *expanding environment* plan. Following this plan, children first study the very immediate in time and place, and gradually move out into places more removed in distance and

---

[7] St. Paul Public Schools, *Social Studies for Elementary School Children,* Curriculum Bulletin Number 17 (St. Paul, Minn.: St. Paul Public Schools, 1959), p. 4.

more remote in time. Such a program typically focuses on the family and the school in the kindergarten and first grade, moves into the neighborhood, the local community, and the extended local community in the second and third grades, on to the state and the nation in the fourth and fifth grades, and finally to the world for the work of grade six.

This sequence is defended as being sound psychologically because the child focuses first on what he knows and experiences in his day-to-day living, a setting out of which he is more likely to develop accurate beginning awareness and understanding of the operations of the basic human activities in his own life. The more vicarious learning experiences are reserved for the later grades, when children have more chance of handling these learnings successfully on the basis of increased personal development, wider experiences, and a background in careful study of the local situation.

Hanna refines this idea even more and argues the sequence question additionally on the basis of a concept of "communities of men."[8] He calls attention to the many "communities" in which we must all exercise successful citizenship roles in today's world. These run the full gamut from home and family, through school, neighborhood, and local community, to state, region, nation, hemisphere, and on to the world scene itself. He sees in this ever-expanding arena for community participation and citizenship a very persuasive argument for a solution to the problem of sequence in the social studies. This is in great part a sociological analysis that takes its place alongside the psychological rationale mentioned above.

This expanding environment plan for sequence in the social studies has been accepted rather wholeheartedly by elementary school systems. Almost every social studies curriculum today utilizes this principle to a great degree. Hodgson reported on a survey of city school systems in which an "overwhelming preference" for this approach to sequence was found.[9] Fraser, writing in a yearbook devoted to social studies in the elementary school, commented that "Every recent curriculum bulletin or guide for elementary-school social studies examined by the present writer utilizes to some extent this plan [of expanding environments] for establishing sequence. . . ."[10] And in 1962 Ellsworth stated: "The most pre-

---

[8] Paul R. Hanna, "Society—Child—Curriculum," in Clarence W. Hunnicutt (editor), *Education 2000 A.D.* (Syracuse, N.Y.: Syracuse University Press, 1956).

[9] Frank M. Hodgson, "Organization and Content of the Social Studies Curriculum," unpublished doctoral dissertation, University of Southern California, 1953, p. 169.

[10] Dorothy M. Fraser, "The Organization of the Elementary School Social Studies Curriculum," in *Social Studies in the Elementary School*, Fifty-Sixth Yearbook of the National Society for the Study of Education, Part II (Chicago: University of Chicago Press, 1957).

dominant plan for achieving sequence in social studies subject matter in the elementary school continues to be the expanding-environment or expanding-horizons plan for sequential organization."[11]

A RESULTING FRAMEWORK FOR THE
SOCIAL STUDIES

On the basis of these accepted ideas, the tendency now is for the elementary school to plan an overall framework to serve as a guiding structure in the social studies program. Most typically its scope is determined by some use of the list of basic human activities; its sequence is determined by expanding the environments idea. These two dimensions come together at each grade level in a way that focuses the work of that year accordingly.

Michaelis reports the following year-by-year framework for the sequence in social studies as being most frequently found in today's elementary schools.

Kindergarten: Living in the Immediate Environment

Grade I: The Home, The School, The Neighborhood

Grade II: Living in the Community

Grade III: Ways of Living in the Larger Community, and in Other Communities

Grade IV: The History and Geography of Our State, and Living in Other Lands

Grade V: Living in Early and Modern America, and Living in the Americas

Grade VI: The Western Hemisphere, The Eastern Hemisphere, or Global Geography

Grade VII: The Western or the Eastern Hemisphere, Backgrounds of United States History, History of Our State, Our Community, and United States History

Grade VIII: United States History, The Constitution, and The Growth of Democracy[12]

The way in which this sequence follows the expanding environments principle as children move through the several years of the elementary school is quite obvious.

Following from such a year-by-year framework, one then finds topics

---

[11] Ruth Ellsworth, "Trends in Organization of the Social Studies," in John Michaelis (editor), *Social Studies in Elementary Schools*, Thirty-Second Yearbook (Washington, D.C.: National Council for the Social Studies, 1962), pp. 113.

[12] John Michaelis, *Social Studies for Children in a Democracy* (third edition) (Englewood Cliffs, N.J.: Prentice-Hall, Inc., 1963), pp. 143–147.

or problems suggested for development in any particular year that are consistent with the grade-level focus. They also reflect the way in which the "basic human activities" determinant for the scope of the program is used in the selection of particular foci for classroom work. For instance, note this relationship in the following selections made again from the recent Michaelis report (from "Illustrative Topics or Units Included in Recent Courses of Study"):

Grade I: The Home, The School, The Neighborhood
> The family
> Our school
> Workers who come to our house
> etc.

Grade III: Ways of Living in the Larger Community, and in Other Communities
> How clothes are made
> Communication services
> Community living in the early times
> Communities in other lands
> Public services in our community
> etc.

Grade V: Living in Early and Modern America, and Living in the Americas
> Discovery and exploration of America
> Pioneer life
> Our new states
> Our neighbors to the north and south
> etc.[13]

Most social studies specialists believe that the overall planning of a framework such as is suggested here and the advance selection of a number of units of work or study at each grade level help to give a kind of stability and direction to the total program. Since some topics for study are selected in advance, the teacher feels some security in preparation. Still a place is left for some joint teacher-pupil selection of units that are consistent with the framework but that come about as a function of the work of the class.

A Closer Look at Commonest Subject Matter

A closer look at many present-day elementary school social studies programs in action makes possible the following observations with respect to developments in the curriculum.

First of all, it is obvious that there is far greater agreement as to the

---

[13] Michaelis, pp. 143–147.

communities from which units of work are appropriately drawn for the primary grades than for the middle grades. While some schools do treat the local community in the middle grades, the study of living at the local level is most often restricted to the primary grades. The themes of home-school-neighborhood and local community are almost universally used as foci for the social studies in kindergarten and grades one and two. Within this general limitation there is some tendency to spread the study of "community helpers" over all of these years instead of concentrating this study in grade two, and to consider a wider group of "helpers" than was formerly the case. This tendency seems to go along with a change in these studies to focus on the *services*, broadly conceived, that people need, rather than focusing on a small stereotyped group of "helpers." Thus we find various professional people and tradesmen being studied in addition to the mailman and the fireman.

Holidays, studying the flag as a national symbol, learning the pledge of allegiance, and giving attention to the stories and to the birthdays of famous Americans, past and present, all continue to be included as important social studies content over these years.

The study of the local community extends quite regularly into grade three. While the basic human activities of procuring food, clothing, and shelter are the ones most commonly included within these local community studies, there is evidence to suggest that other activities like recreation and education are being given some attention. When "other communities" are studied in grade three, they may be contemporary ones in the United States, or the orientation may be to a community in another time and place. The latter may include an historical study of the local community, or the focus may be on a primitive or "simple" culture in an attempt to see how basic human needs were met in such a setting. The study of Indians may well find its way into the third grade on either of these last two bases.

The difference in meaning between *local community* and *extended community* as used in this grade is increasingly important. Extended communities, such as the Bay Area in and around San Francisco, or the North Shore or the South Side of Chicago, or the Greater New York area, become increasingly important areas to understand as our population concentrates itself in and around large metropolitan centers, extending over county and even state lines.

The state, as a community, is given added attention in the social studies program, to point out the similarity and the relatedness of problems of living at the local and state levels. Typically, the study of the state is undertaken in grade four. This does not mean that the long familiar study of type regions, world around, such as "hot-wet," "hot-dry," and so on, has disappeared from the elementary school. This geographic orientation continues to be the dominant theme in many schools, while in others study of the state is combined in the same year with some study of type regions.

The study of the United States in some manner or form is almost universal as a focus for grade five. If there is any lack of agreement here, it is concerned with deciding whether to take an "historical periods" or "geographic regions" approach to the year's work. Some schools will include attention to our national neighbors—Canada, Mexico, Latin America—as a part of this year's work.

There is probably more variation in content at the sixth grade level than at any other in the elementary school. In great part this variation stems from the trend of the last several years to terminate the elementary school at the sixth grade, and in this light to search for a most appropriate final experience for the elementary school social studies program. Though it is clearly recognized that the social studies program will continue through the remaining years of school there is some tendency to try to "round out" the experience of the first years. Some elementary school educators, influenced by this idea, would center the grade six experience in a kind of world setting, usually a world geography approach with an emphasis on human and economic geography, generally. Such advocates feel that the child born into today's world should not leave elementary school without having been helped to comprehend the world as a community of people. Within such an approach, selected culture units on such countries as India, Japan, and Russia may be developed, pointed toward increased intercultural and international understanding.

More typically one finds either of two content orientations in grade six. One of these extends the study of the Western hemisphere, which would have started with a study of the United States in grade five, into grade six with the focus on Canada, Mexico, and Central and South America. The other focuses on the Eastern hemisphere and deals in the main with Europe, past and present. Still others, searching for a selection of content that would make sense in grades six and seven, would develop the work in grade six around the Atlantic Community, and the work in grade seven around the Pacific community. They reason that life, for many reasons, will be lived in the future around this very natural geographic as well as political division. Such a plan anticipates a return in the eighth grade to a reconsideration of American history in light of considerable world understanding.

Selected socio-technology units on such broad themes as transportation or communication are likely to be interspersed for study. In the development of such units of work, insight is developed into these particular areas of activity in terms of advanced technology; considerable attention is also given to the general social impact of these developments, and to the task man faces in insuring that all such advances are used to make for a better life.

This description is one that will cover the vast majority of social studies programs in elementary schools across the country. But this approach to programming is being challenged, and there are strong arguments advanced for changing it. Many of the forces for change identified in the opening chapters in this book are identifiable in these arguments. Here let us consider what is happening and what is likely to happen in the social studies.

A Look at Change in the Social Studies

A quarrel with the present design. There have been and continue to be questions raised by a number of elementary school educators concerning the principles which underlie the expanding environment approach to programming. These are primarily cast as cautions against a too mechanical use of such principles. Educators who express them question whether children and their experiences really "square" with the principles as much as we might conclude. They argue that children do not move just from home to school to neighborhood and so on as they push out in their social experience. They wonder whether the present expanding environment curriculum may not restrict unnecessarily the social education of children when school experiences are limited accordingly. They support their argument with reference to such things as the increased use of mass media in today's world, especially television and motion pictures, to the greater mobility of the family with respect both to vacation travel and to actual changes in residence, and to our much expanding quantity of children's informational literature. They speculate as to just what the impact of these are on the children coming to the elementary school. They suspect that we are not planning the social studies program to take sufficient advantage of the experiential background of today's children. One researcher, for instance, holds that by means of a series of interviews he was able to demonstrate that children in the primary grades already know most of what the social studies program would have them learn. He felt further that instruction in those grades seldom recognized children's present knowledge and did little to refine children's already partially formed concepts about those aspects of the social environment to be studied.[14]

Strong proponents of the use of the expanding environments principles do not put these arguments down completely. They would still give priority attention to a particular focus or emphasis for a school year. But they contend that a place can be made for explorations into other social matters, too, that loom as appropriate for a given group of children in a particular set of circumstances. Time would be left for a teacher to

[14] John D. McAulay, "Social Studies in the Primary Grades," *Social Education,* Vol. 18 (December 1954), pp. 357–358.

develop studies in his classroom during the year over and above the prearranged ones. They might be derived from current happenings on the state, national, or world scene; they might arise out of events in the local community, or even in the school community itself.

Similarly, they caution against being misled by what might be referred to as the "immature maturity" of young children as we plan the social studies program. That today's child is a better informed one than was yesterday's is accepted. What is held is that children's present knowledge opens up new possibilities for accomplishing significant social learnings with children and a greater responsibility for so doing. But they doubt that the failure of teachers to take advantage of the possibilities is a matter of curriculum design as much as of other things.

A search for a subject matter. One of the difficulties in planning the social studies curriculum has been the identification of a significant subject matter. There has been a long-standing concern over the tendency for too many units in the social studies to center on what is by most standards fairly insignificant subject matter. Something seems to go awry in the translation from purposes to experiences. For instance, units of work on the circus, though interesting to children, are hard to justify for the social significance of their content. Perhaps more to the point, teachers provide legitimate experiences for pupils, but they do not exploit them as they might for social studies learning. The firehouse is visited, Chamber of Commerce officials are interviewed, and so on, but the social, political, or economic learnings that could be developed through such experiences become almost completely subordinated to and obscured by the activities themselves. In our judgment it is this problem of the identification of a subject matter for the social studies that has so often brought confusion to the classroom and disrepute to the social studies program.

One well-known social studies educator has sponsored a number of research studies at Stanford University aimed at the identification of generalizations related to each of the basic human activities around which many social studies programs are built. This effort has provided a structured body of subject matter for the social studies curriculum. Thus, in relation to "organizing and governing," certain generalizations have been identified that children would be helped to begin to develop, and the same has been done for "producing, distributing and consuming" and so on across all of the basic human activities.[15] This is one way of

---

[15] See Paul R. Hanna, "Generalizations and Universal Values: Their Implications for the Social Studies Program," in *Social Studies in the Elementary School,* Fifty-Sixth Yearbook of the National Society for the Study of Education, Part II (Chicago: University of Chicago Press, 1957), Chapter 2.

helping the elementary school educator to arrive at a more substantial content for the social studies program. Planned experiences, in the classroom and out, then have a sense of relationship to a subject matter toward which they are oriented and with which they are identified.

The New Subject-Centeredness and the Social Studies

There has been considerable interest in the most recent past to focus the social studies program more directly on the basic social science disciplines and history. This focus is clearly consistent with the larger curriculum reform movement alluded to in the first part of this book. Proponents of this position believe that it is unrealistic to speak of the social studies as being responsible almost solely and singularly for citizenship education in the usual sense of the idea. They agree that citizenship is an important matter, but they believe that all areas of the curriculum have a vital role to play in it, not just the social studies. Those who take this point of view contend that there are certain unique ways in which the social studies can contribute to this task. They would support a social studies program that was more concerned with social analysis, systematic inquiry into social phenomena, reflective thinking and decision making, social issues and the judgments they entail—all backed up by the use of multidisciplinary sources of data.[16] This they would see as a vital part of citizenship education.

They would prefer to select concepts and generalizations from the social sciences and to deal with them in the curriculum more directly and deliberately than has typically been the case. Such a selection would contribute to citizenship education. As this point of view takes form, the ideas about the structures of knowledge, both conceptual and methodological, mentioned in Chapter 5 come to the fore. In these social science fields, as in others, the bulk of subject matter that could be dealt with is massive, and some selection is mandatory. Teachers have tended to look to each social science in turn to identify the key concepts in the area which children should be helped to understand, and they have tried to find means to involve children with the processes of inquiry used in each subject field. To many social scientists, a careful selection seems to be the only way to derive a manageable content for the social studies curriculum.

As the work of curriculum redevelopment goes forward social sci-

---

[16] Shirley H. Engle, "Decision-Making: The Heart of Social Studies Instruction," *Social Education*, Vol. 24 (November 1960), pp. 301–304, 306; Franklin Patterson, "Social Science and the New Curriculum," *The American Behavioral Scientist*, Vol. 6 (November 1962), pp. 28–31.

ences not heretofore used in the elementary school curriculum are receiving considerable attention. As was mentioned earlier geography, history (and many do not accept this as a social science), and political science have been the disciplines from which the social studies program has been derived. Economics, sociology, anthropology, and social psychology were absent.

The present curriculum improvement effort includes a more direct and systematic attempt to utilize these other social science disciplines in the curriculum and thus broaden the base of the experience which children will have. There are at present a number of national curriculum projects under way that have as their goal the development of feasible ways to bring the subject matter of these otherwise overlooked social sciences into the elementary school program. Senesh, through a project centered at Purdue University and in the Elkhart, Indiana, school system has pioneered the use of economics in the elementary school curriculum. Most of his work to date has centered on the primary grades, and he utilizes the typical arenas of home life and neighborhood life in which to work. He organizes the material in his program around the concepts of economics. The economic concept of "market place" is related to family shopping; "division of labor" as a concept is observable in many ways in community work life. Senesh attempts to demonstrate the way in which the social environment near at hand can be used as the vehicle for beginning the development of the central ideas of a scholarly discipline.[17]

The University of Georgia is headquarters for a project that is attempting to develop a curriculum for use with elementary school children that is built around anthropology. The aim is to develop materials that will introduce the pupil to the structure of anthropology as a discipline, to the ways in which the anthropologist works to gather and process his data, and to the uses of such information and tools of study in one's own social life. Thus far, some of the learning units are deductive in design; others are inductive. There is a careful attempt to utilize the language of anthropology often and correctly. A major goal is to help pupils to understand the way in which an anthropologist thinks about the world. This program is one of the more completely developed ones available to elementary schools at this time.[18]

At the University of Michigan, Fox and Lippitt are attempting to span the fields of psychology, social psychology, microsociology, and the

---

[17] Lawrence Senesh, *Elkhart, Indiana Experiment in Economic Education* (Lafayette, Ind.: Department of Economics, Purdue University).

[18] Wilfred Bailey and Marion Rice, *Development of a Sequential Curriculum in Anthropology for Grades 1–7* (Athens, Ga.: Department of Sociology and Anthropology, University of Georgia).

small-group aspects of social anthropology in curriculum work focused on the intermediate grades of the elementary school. The materials thus far stress inquiry; the pupil must collect data, process them, and form conclusions. He is taught to do these things as he uses the materials provided, working with both stories and with his own social world.[19]

These are samples of what is going on now and of what will probably continue and grow in the future. The way in which a conceptual "map" of the field is developed to guide the design of learning experiences is characteristic of these projects. Attention is given to the intellectual skills that are to be developed by the pupil so that the process-of-inquiry dimension of curriculum planning is not overlooked. There is use of the spiraling idea mentioned earlier to insure that concepts are revisited often enough, and in contrasting and extended settings, during the elementary school years so that adequacy of understanding of both the concepts and the generalizations will follow.

An example of a new social studies program that attends to all of the points just mentioned here and works within an already set framework for the curriculum is the one developed under the direction of Taba in conjunction with the Contra Costa County school system in California.[20] The California state framework within which this program has been conceived suggests the following year-by-year emphases for the elementary school:

Grade One—School Life and Family Living
Grade Two—Local Community Life and Services
Grade Three—Community Life in Other Places
Grade Four—Life in California—Yesterday and Today
Grade Five—A Study of America
Grade Six—The Study of Latin America

Certain basic concepts have been selected by Taba and her staff for development over all of the years of the program. These are cultural change, cooperation, interdependence, causality, and differences. They are recognized as being hierarchical in that they can and do represent different levels of abstractness and complexity in different settings. That is, interdependence between family members or between local community workers is hierarchically different from interdependence between levels of government in a nation or between the governments of nations.

A second level of knowledge used in the Contra Costa County framework is referred to as "main ideas," or generalizations drawn from

---

[19] Robert M. Fox and Ronald Lippitt (directors), Social Science in Elementary Schools, University of Michigan, Ann Arbor, Mich.
[20] Contra Costa County Social Studies Guides, Contra Costa County, Calif.

the several social sciences, and set for study each year in a context fitting for the already given grade level themes. These main ideas serve as the centers around which units of work are developed and represent the most durable sort of knowledge sought in the program.

Specific information and facts are also selected for inclusion as a third level of knowledge. And, of course, their selection is related directly to the main ideas which are to be developed.

The careful and deliberate way in which the program at each grade level has been styled to fit into the overall curriculum and to be worth while in its own right is quite obvious. For instance, consider this statement about the work of the third grade:

A YEAR'S PROGRAM FOR GRADE THREE

The eight-year-old stands firmly within the period of middle-childhood when his basic social attitudes are being formed. Though the scope of his life has been broadened through television and other means of modern communication, he needs help in relating the myriad facts his inquisitive mind absorbs, and guidance in interpreting what he learns.

In keeping with the state framework for social studies this unit is designed to extend what children have learned about community life in the second grade by comparing and contrasting different kinds of communities. The four communities studied are sampled to represent both primitive and modern communities and a variety of geographic conditions. Each community is studied in a separate section, but all are compared with one another and with the community the children already know. This unit is NOT A STUDY OF WORLD GEOGRAPHY. The intent of the unit is that the child will be introduced to some basic relationships between a way of life, environment, and tradition.

The study of each community follows the same pattern of questions:

How do these people provide their basic needs?
What rules govern the family?
How do the people educate their children?
What traditions do they pass on to their children?
What evidences of change are there?

This repeated line of questioning not only allows the students to make comparisons but also suggests that all communities, no matter what their character, serve the same functions. They all provide the essential needs of people, only in a different manner. A few additional ideas are stressed in all units and those are the idea of how change occurs, and how the variations in conditions of life develop a special culture. The information is organized to support major ideas about each culture:

Primitives of Africa

I. People of a primitive culture are extremely dependent upon their immediate environment and their own skills; people of a modern culture use the skills of others and are much less dependent on their environment.

II. Many activities of primitive people are carried on through the family and/or tribe; a more modern community provides for these activities through organized institutions.

III. Changes are taking place in primitive communities.

People of the Hot, Dry Lands

I. Environment influences many aspects of the desert people's life.

II. Some aspects of the desert nomads' way of life are greatly influenced by tradition.

The Boat People of Hong Kong

I. Some people live a very simple life even though they are part of an ancient civilization from which came many things we use today.

II. People develop institutions that support their way of life.

The People of Switzerland

I. Some people across the world have a society that is much like our own.

II. Even a very modern society may wish to preserve some of its customs from the past.

SELECTION OF COMMUNITIES

The following considerations determined the selection of communities to be studied in this unit.

Primitives of Africa

Provides an opportunity for children to contrast a culture that is very different from their own, and to learn the part climate plays in a way of life.

Provides an opportunity for children to see that people have the same basic needs—they meet them in different ways.

Provides an opportunity for the children to become aware of Africa —a continent that will be prominently in the news during their school life.

People of the Hot, Dry Lands

Provides an opportunity to study a people whose way of life is strongly influenced by natural forces—even though they have come historically from a highly developed civilization.

Provides contrast within the same continent, Africa.

Boat People of Hong Kong

Provides an opportunity for the children to study a culture vastly different from ours, but one that is an old and rich civilization.

Provides an opportunity to see how poverty affects a way of life.

Provides an opportunity to become aware of how the great rivers of the world have affected man.

People of Switzerland

> Provides an opportunity to make the children aware that modern living, not too unlike their own, exists on the other side of the world.
>
> Provides an opportunity to become aware of the effect of great mountains on a people.[21]

The orientation each year is toward the development of a few main ideas, as illustrated above. The thinking skills to be developed are as carefully laid out as is the content. Additionally, and perhaps most importantly, the teaching plans for implementing the program in the classroom are most complete. Included are carefully devised strategies and sequences for teaching so that teachers will be helped to know what to do and when, in order that what goes on in their classroom is consistent with the potential built into the overall framework.

The Whole and the Parts

Generally speaking, we support these efforts to broaden the subject matter base for the social studies curriculum. A social education in our time would seem to be satisfied by no less. There is one grave question at the very heart of this activity, however. This has to do with the "whole" that is to eventually come from the "summing of the parts." Clearly, each of these disciplines cannot have a time and place of its own in the elementary curriculum. The result would be fragmentation of the worst order. It would appear that more elementary educators are becoming sensitive to this problem. Discussions are heard about the selection of a "lead" discipline to which learnings from other areas would be related in some fashion. The question here centers on which of the social science disciplines is best suited to this role. Some educators see the answer in a "prediscipline" approach to the curriculum that would deal with whatever concepts and generalizations are selected as important, letting their discipline identification come later in the final years of the elementary school or even on into the secondary school. Often this takes the form of a theme selected for each grade of the elementary school, with work in the social studies for any given year aimed at the fullest possible development of the theme without concern for explicit subject field identifications. An example of such a theme to be developed in a primary grade might be as follows:

1. Man has adapted to a variety of natural habitats; or
2. Man finds new ways to control his relationship to his environment.

---

[21] From *Teacher Handbook for Contra Costa County Social Studies*, Grades 1–6, 1965 (Appendix, pp. 4, 5, 6), developed by Hilda Taba and James Hills.

In an intermediate grade it might be as follows:

1. Technology has changed the production and distribution of goods and services and has created new opportunities and problems for human society; or
2. There is a variety of patterns of development and interdependence within and among nations.

Obviously, any comprehensive attempt to get at any one of these themes would take the class into several areas of social science subject matter. Yet the focus for the pupil would be on the developing theme and not on the discrete bodies of content that are contributing to it. This identification would be sought later. It may be that the basic human activities as organizing centers will be reconsidered in this way; "organizing and governing" is only a step away from political science, and "producing, distributing, and consuming" is only a step away from economics. Whatever the answer, it is imperative that this unified approach be seriously considered as a part of the current improvement effort.

Social reality and the social studies. It would appear, too, that social studies instruction in the elementary school is going to suffer in effectiveness so long as the larger society insists that something less than social reality be dealt with in the school program. If concepts and generalizations are to be built that will hold valid and maximal meaning for children in our time they will need to be built on the basis of current reality and not mythology. Many parents and some educators wonder whether the basic social realities of our time should be taught to children of elementary school age. The truth of the matter is that these children are forming ideas about real social situations and real human behavior in spite of the school. Stendler called attention a number of years ago to the way in which an awareness of symbols of social class developed in the elementary school age group; she found first graders with little or no awareness, fourth graders with some, and sixth graders with sufficient awareness to be rating their classmates on the basis of home and family, occupation of father, clothes, and manners.[22] In the Easton and Hess studies of political socialization, it was reported that children begin to learn about government and politics even before they enter school, and the formative years in political understanding appear to be the years between three and thirteen. By the time pupils leave the eighth grade their studies suggest that political attitudes and values are fairly well established.[23] It would seem to be inevitable with powerful mass com-

---

[22] Celia Stendler, *Children of Brasstown* (Urbana, Ill.: Bureau of Research and Service of the College of Education, University of Illinois, 1949).
[23] David Easton and Robert Hess, "The Child's Political World," *Modern Journal of Political Science,* Vol. 6, No. 3 (August 1963), pp. 229–246.

munication media available, especially television, that children will be exposed to a great many social realities whether or not the school program itself includes them. It may be more profitable for the school to help children toward a more rational understanding of much that they see and hear, rather than to remain aloof from it. Clearly, one would not expect children to study complex and intricate national and international problems that challenge the best of adult minds, but there are many realities that are less complex which, if studied, might well contribute helpfully to the social behaviors cited at the beginning of this chapter that stand as the goals of instruction in the social studies.

Desires for an early effort toward intercultural and international understanding. Some elementary school educators are concerned because the application of the expanding environments principle to the development of the social studies program tends to restrict the study of any culture other than our own until the sixth grade. As they view today's world with its great need for improved intercultural and international understanding they question the advisability of waiting so many years to help children in some systematic way to begin to comprehend and accept the differences among groups of people. In this connection, they sense a real limitation in the type region studies of faraway places that are still often the focus of work in the fourth grade. They believe that too often such studies dwell on physical geography alone, rather than taking a human geography approach that might contribute greatly to intercultural understanding.

The use of culture units in the elementary school program is an issue of long standing in and of itself. The worth of such units has been seriously questioned by some.[24] Those who have observed the development of such studies in years past cannot support the stereotyped treatment of other peoples and their way of life or the general sentimental and "tolerant" way in which these studies have usually been carried out. They question whether such efforts lead to increased intercultural understanding or detract from it.

We tend to support those who believe that today's world makes experimentation concerning ways of increasing this sort of study in the elementary school vitally necessary, and that the impact of modern mass media on children, along with improved instructional tools and procedures, may make it possible for children to study other cultures and peoples at an earlier age than has heretofore been thought possible. It seems imperative that children be given opportunities early and often to

---

[24] Wanda Robertson, *An Evaluation of the Culture Unit Method for Social Education* (New York: Bureau of Publications, Teachers College, Columbia University, 1950).

develop understandings and insights into the lives of people other than themselves. There is evidence to suggest that the failures of earlier years were caused by the poor quality of the learning enterprise in the classroom, and that teachers armed with improved procedures and with proper instructional materials have demonstrated the possibilities of culture studies for children.

A preference for the unit of work. A sound effort in the social studies demands a sound methodology. An effective way must be used to organize for learning in the classroom the social understandings, the values and attitudes, and the skills that are sought. Concept formation and the development of generalizations in the social sphere must be approached with an acceptable scheme for learning. To date, the most effective way of organizing for learning in the social studies is the pedagogical scheme referred to as the unit of work. This way of working relates process and content in a mutually supporting way in the classroom. A variety of instructional materials, resources, and procedures can be utilized in unit teaching. This scheme also makes a place for total-group, small-group, and individual learning experiences—important in their own right as social learnings. There is not sufficient space here to discuss the unit of work in detail, nor is this scheme used only in the social studies. A much more complete discussion follows in the chapter dealing with the teacher's use of time in the classroom. (See Chapter 15.) At this point let us conclude that in the best of unit teaching one finds the dynamic kind of learning experience that is demanded for proper learning in the social studies. Additionally, within the unit approach there is more likelihood that activities such as (a) viewing films and filmstrips, (b) taking trips into the community, (c) acting out plays, (d) keeping records and listening to reports, (e) drawing pictures and murals related to the unit, (f) working in committees on projects and study assignments, (g) preparing exhibits, and the like—all activities that studies have shown to be valued by children—will be utilized by the teacher.[25]

The present learning load in the social studies. A brief discussion is called for here with respect to the learning load of the "typical" social studies program. Teachers find it very difficult to find time for all of the things that they are supposed to teach, especially in the middle grades. The insights we have into the ways children develop meaningful social concepts and generalizations indicate that any attempt to hurry such learning in the interests of getting over the course of study is unwise.

---

25 Linnwood W. Chase, "Individual Differences in Classroom Learning," in *Social Studies in the Elementary School*, Fifty-Sixth Yearbook of the National Society for the Study of Education, Part II (Chicago: University of Chicago Press, 1957), pp. 168–170.

It would seem that a great deal more careful attention to this problem of load in elementary school social studies would be worth while. The ease with which the curriculum may call for the study of a complete continent, or of the vast Pacific Basin area, must be viewed in light of the sort of classroom experience that is necessary if such efforts are not to be wasted. Selecting representative countries, for instance, rather than attempting to cover a whole continent, may be called for.

We are of the opinion that to allow time for a more comprehensive, even leisurely, learning experience with a more restricted range of subject matter to be dealt with is wiser than to attempt too much in the classroom. The "structure" approach to the selection of content for inclusion is taken with this in mind. It is held that children can then transfer their acquired learnings, both content and process, to further new learning tasks in the social studies both within and outside of school.

BEYOND THE SOCIAL STUDIES

It was stated earlier that there is a great opportunity for the elementary school to be effective in the social education of children in ways that are beyond the social studies. This opportunity lies in the fact that the classroom and the school provide, actually, a society of their own in which the very stuff of day-to-day living together provides a reality setting in which social education takes place. Here is firsthand contact with people and with things. Here space, time, and materials are used jointly by many children and adults. Social education is bound to take place in such a setting. The responsibility of the elementary school educator is to be able to exploit this setting fully in the interests of improved social learnings. Children should undergo, in their relationships to each other and to adults at school, a living experience grounded in the basic tenets of democracy.

A Strategic Role for the Teacher

While teachers cannot control the nature of the relationships that will operate between children, they can have a very great deal to do with making one kind of relationship more likely to develop than another. They can determine with considerable certainty the nature of the relationship that will exist between teacher and pupil. Teachers, in their work with children, must attempt to show the face of democracy in a consistent and persuasive way. Providing a proper model for children as they live close to and interact with adults in the school situation is very important.

According to Miel and Ambrose:

Of all the environing conditions, the *human environment* comprises the most pervasive and most decisive factors. It is through people—what they do to, for, and with him—that a child learns who and what he is, what he can do, what he should strive for. It is through people and their responses to his strivings that the child gains his basic orientation to life.[26]

Rasey and Menge comment directly on this point, too. In discussing the cruciality of the human environment they contend that "the philosophies [people] operate upon, the constellation of values that trigger their actions" are most important. And they go on to say that "The teacher's role is influential because his choices and preferences are themselves contagious, and ways of life of young humans have a considerable admixture of the choices and preferences of those in their environment."[27] The findings of other studies that have dealt with this matter are in agreement with the statements quoted here.[28] The impact of human environment, and of the teacher especially, on the social learnings of pupils puts a considerable responsibility on the teacher.

Utilizing Classroom Living for Social Education

There are many social decisions to be made in the operation of any elementary school classroom and they can be approached in such a way as to take advantage of many of the insights noted in the preceding discussion.

Standards for behavior, for instance, must be arrived at, understood, and enforced in every classroom. They can be determined with a great deal of child participation if the teacher chooses. Naturally, the extent and kind of participation will depend on the age of the children, and also on their past experiences both at home and at school. The teacher who is willing to utilize this opportunity has a good chance to approach some significant social learnings concerning authority and social control. Children can be allowed to feel the consequence of living up to or not living up to group-derived decisions that are important to the well-being of the group.

Also, there are many tasks to be done in a classroom to insure that the life of the group will run smoothly. To the degree that these tasks can be shared, they can be used to sensitize children to the necessity of

---

[26] Ambrose and Miel, *Children's Social Learning*, p. 28.

[27] Marie I. Rasey and J. W. Menge, *What We Learn from Children* (New York: Harper & Row, Publishers, Inc., 1956), pp. 23, 39.

[28] Helen Trager and Marie Radke-Yarrow, *They Learn What They Live* (New York: Harper & Row, Publishers, Inc., 1952); Kenneth Wann and Arthur W. Foshay, *Children's Social Values* (New York: Bureau of Publications, Teachers College, Columbia University, 1954).

allocating responsibility and authority to some in the group in the best interests of all. Children can become more aware of the way responsibility and authority in society are delegated to and shifted from one person to another from time to time. Thus, being classroom librarian or ball monitor, or being in charge of the classroom pet, or being the room representative to the school student council give the delegated and the delegators opportunities for democratic learnings.

It is obvious, too, that the opportunities a teacher gives children to participate in planning for the use of class time, or space, or materials, and the criticizing together of the adequacy of such planning, helps in the development of skills and attitudes demanded by democratic living. Such shared decision making will involve conflicting ideas about the way things should be done; in fact, disagreement will be evident over the value of the activities themselves from time to time. Such situations provide a dynamic setting in which the participants, in this case the teacher and his class, are called upon to solve common group problems and to make sound group decisions.

A concomitant of this experience in shared living should, in light of the research reviewed earlier, be the development of stronger individual personalities along the lines of democracy.

Utilizing School Living for Social Education

Everything that has been said about the possibilities for utilizing the classroom living experience for social education purposes is present at the school level in a different way. A schoolwide activity or an all-school experience in decision making involves more people, with more likelihood of varied interests and concerns, and a greater chance for conflicting opinions concerning a most sound course of action. Contacts between children, and between children and adults in the corridors, on the playground, in the lunchroom, or in the gymnasium all carry some potential for social education.

In this larger social setting there is again the necessity for understood and accepted standards for personal and group conduct, and an opportunity for child participation in this "social control" decision. Similarly, there are schoolwide opportunities and demands for social service if the living experience at school is to be as safe and as happy as it should be. A school safety patrol will usually be stationed at busy intersections near the school as a safeguard to the children coming and going to school. Boys and girls in the upper elementary grades can often be found assisting young children on the playground. Selected children can be operating a schoolwide lost-and-found service for the convenience of all. There can be participation by a delegated group of children in many schoolwide decisions that relate to the use of time, or space, or materials. While the final responsibility for many such decisions rests with the adults in the situation, children can participate in an advisory capacity to the benefit of all.

Here again, conflicting ideas, alternative choices, and varied possible courses of action will become evident. The necessity for choice, and the process by which choices are made in a democracy can be learned as situations are faced. Especially, children should not be denied the opportunity to assist in the solution of a social problem at school when the "social machinery" breaks down. In this way real social understanding and sensitivity can be helped to develop. These situations can be used to nurture our young "social engineers."

A great deal of meaningful cultural transmission can take place in the way the school experience is lived. The values that govern human relationships and guide human action, the way the teacher and the school reward and punish, the role that is extended to or denied children all determine in a very significant way the kind of social education that takes place. A stronger program in citizenship education results from the combination of a well-conceived program of social studies and the conscious use of the total school living experience itself in the direction of desired social behaviors and strong individual democratic personalities.

RECOMMENDED READINGS

AMBROSE, EDNA, and ALICE MIEL. *Children's Social Learning: Implications of Research and Expert Study.* Washington, D.C.: Association for Supervision and Curriculum Development, 1958.

AMERICAN COUNCIL OF LEARNED SOCIETIES AND THE NATIONAL COUNCIL FOR THE SOCIAL STUDIES. *The Social Studies and the Social Sciences.* New York: Harcourt, Brace & World, Inc., 1962.

CLEMENTS, H. MILLARD, WILLIAM R. FIELDER, and B. ROBERT TABACHNICK. *Social Study: Inquiry in Elementary Classrooms.* New York: Bobbs-Merrill Company, Inc., 1966.

ESTVAN, FRANK J., and ELIZABETH W. ESTVAN. *The Child's World: His Social Perception.* New York: G. P. Putnam's Sons, 1959.

FENTON, EDWIN. *The New Social Studies.* New York: Holt, Rinehart and Winston, Inc., 1967.

HANNA, PAUL R., and others. *Geography in the Teaching of Social Studies.* Boston: Houghton Mifflin Company, 1966.

JAROLIMEK, JOHN. *Social Studies in Elementary Education* (third edition). New York: The Macmillan Company, 1967.

JAROLIMEK, JOHN, and HUBER WALSH. *Readings for Social Studies in Elementary Education.* New York: The Macmillan Company, 1965.

JOYCE, BRUCE. *Strategies for Elementary Social Science Education.* Chicago: Science Research Associates. Inc., 1965.

MASSALIAS, BYRON G., and FREDERICK R. SMITH. *New Challenges in the Social Studies*. Belmont, Calif.: Wadsworth Publishing Company, Inc., 1965.

MICHAELIS, JOHN. *Social Studies for Children in a Democracy* (third edition). Englewood Cliffs, N.J.: Prentice-Hall, Inc., 1963.

———— (editor). *Social Studies in Elementary Schools* (Thirty-Second Yearbook). Washington, D.C.: National Council for the Social Studies, 1962.

RAGAN, WILLIAM B., and JOHN D. MC AULAY. *Social Studies for Today's Children*. New York: Appleton-Century-Crofts, Inc., 1964.

SCOBEY, MARY-MARGARET. *Teaching Children about Technology*. Bloomington, Ill.: McKnight & McKnight Publishing Company, 1968.

SHAFTEL, FANNIE R., and GEORGE SHAFTEL. *Role-Playing for Social Values*. Englewood Cliffs, N.J.: Prentice-Hall, Inc., 1967.

Healthful Living: Physical and Health Education  13

Today's elementary school accepts health and physical education as important objectives of education. It will be remembered that in the 1938 statement of the Educational Policies Commission, entitled *The Purposes of Education in American Democracy,* the position is taken that the educated person "understands the basic facts concerning health and disease . . . protects his own health and that of his dependents . . . works to improve the health of the community . . . and is participant and spectator in many sports (and other pastimes)."[1] The more recent study of objectives for elementary education, carried on by Kearney and others for the Russell Sage Foundation in 1953, was quite explicit as to the responsibilities the elementary school was typically accepting in these two areas of the curriculum. Noted were responsibilities to physical development, health, and body care—including individual health, elementary aspects of public health, safety, physical education, grooming, and understanding of growth.[2]

More recently the Project on Instruction, after noting that priorities for the school included instruction in health education and physical education, had this to say about these two curriculum areas:

> Health education and physical education have become increasingly important in the general education portion of the elementary and secondary school curriculum in the last half century. Urbanization, changed social conditions, and technological advances have created new health problems as well as benefits, both for individuals and

[1] Educational Policies Commission, *The Purposes of Education in American Democracy* (Washington, D.C.: NEA, 1938), p. 50.

[2] Nolan Kearney and others, *Elementary School Objectives* (New York: Russell Sage Foundation, 1953), p. 52.

for the community. . . . The school, as the only social institution that reaches all children and youth, has responsibility for teaching the basic information and for helping young people develop the habits and attitudes essential for healthful living. Effective health education begins in early childhood and continues as a cumulative program though the elementary and secondary school years. The need for a systematic school program of physical development has also been intensified because of conditions created by urban living and technological change. Today most children and adolescents do not engage in the vigorous muscle-building activities that were a part of daily living for earlier generations. . . .[3]

These and other statements make it quite clear that the elementary school does have responsibilities in the areas of health and physical education. The extent of these programs, and the effectiveness of the effort expended, varies from one school system to another. In increasing numbers of school systems, a well-conceived set of experiences is guided by clearly stated and well-understood purposes. In others, purposes are less clear and the school's efforts in health and physical education are vague and correspondingly less effective. The nature of a complete effort in the areas of health and physical education is coming to be understood, and the elementary school moves ever closer to the development of programs that accept a full share of responsibility for contributing to the health and physical well-being of children.

FACTORS AFFECTING PROGRAM DEVELOPMENT

As the elementary school has moved to strengthen its efforts in health and physical education, several fundamental matters have had to be considered and resolved. Most important among these have been the following.

The Shared Nature of the Health Responsibility

In the area of health, it has taken considerable study and discussion to clarify the way in which the school might and should share in the maintenance and improvement of children's health. The primary responsibility for the health of children rests, in the main, with parents. At the same time, society has taken steps to protect itself; and the local, state, and national communities have accepted certain responsibilities in the area of public health. For example, doctors are required to report

---

[3] Project on Instruction, *Deciding What to Teach* (Washington, D.C.: NEA 1963), pp. 102, 113–114.

contagious diseases, communities exercise the right of quarantine, and various community health agencies provide both education and service to the general public. The particular way and extent to which the school, as a specialized social institution, could and should participate in the area of health has been of concern. This matter is clarified considerably when the school is asked to take on major responsibilities consistent with its basic purposes as a social institution—that is, to provide for health instruction. While family and community both instruct to some extent, the school is looked to for the greatest part of this burden. That other responsibilities for the total health effort are shared is clearly recognized.

A Clear Rationale for Physical Education

By the end of the American Revolution in 1783, it was generally agreed that the schools should help to insure that each generation would be physically fit and possessed of physical strength. This was of special importance insofar as the males in the population were concerned, with the motivation arising from the demands of military service. A soldier needed to be strong and to have considerable powers of endurance; his physical education was almost synonymous with military education. This idea is still with us to the extent that students at the college level may be exempt from required physical education experiences if they are taking military training.

From this beginning, it has taken time for people to recognize the basic importance of physical fitness in all aspects of life—in one's personal, family, and vocational-professional activities—and to want a varied school program of physical education, accordingly. With recognition of the way in which physical fitness contributes to success in all undertakings, personal and social, have come extensively developed physical education programs. Along with them has also come a more specific question: Is there really a need for a formal physical education program in the elementary school? This question has been answered affirmatively by educators who have allocated to the elementary school certain responsibilities for which it is peculiarly fitted. The school can be provided with adequate space, both indoors and outdoors, and with necessary equipment and personnel to carry on the kinds of experiences that are basic to physical fitness in childhood. The reciprocal relationship between in-school and out-of-school activities has become obvious. Skills and abilities learned in school have application in the child's life away from school. And, of course, out-of-school experiences provide considerable reason and motivation to participate in the organized program of the school.

The fact that a new definition of health has recently emerged has had an effect on the development of elementary school programs in health and physical education. The older definition described the healthy person as one who was without sickness. The new definition is more dynamic and inclusive. In the words of the World Health Organization, "Health is a state of complete physical, mental, and social well-being, and not merely the absence of disease."[4] Such a definition does not deny the importance of being without sickness and disease; it goes beyond these considerations in important ways. It suggests a goal not only to keep children free from sickness and disease, but also to provide them with the knowledge, the attitudes, and the habits that will help them to maintain a continuing state of well-being. They must "feel good" physically and they must "feel good" about themselves.

Increased insight into the conditions that contribute to this well-being has called attention to the general way in which the school environment itself instructs and educates. The human element, especially the teacher, and the school plant combine with the intellectual and emotional elements in the school situation to provide both the setting for health education and health education itself. Thus, to realize the purposes of the program calls for an all-out effort at school that differentiates between the formal and the less formal aspects of the health curriculum, and recognizes the general comprehensiveness of the health effort.

Thus, the modern elementary school educator realizes the basic importance of efforts in health and physical education. He accepts as a major responsibility the provision of sound and effective instruction in health and physical education. Armed with increased insight into human development and more dynamic concepts of health and physical fitness, he strives to provide healthful school living conditions for their contribution to children's well-being. In addition, the school provides a program of health services that recognizes health education as a cooperative effort and is conceived to operate in agreement with and in support of this shared responsibility.

PROVIDING FOR HEALTH INSTRUCTION

The instructional phase of the health education program seeks to develop lasting health interests, wholesome attitudes toward health, and adequate health information. Most importantly, the program aims at the development of proper health habits and practices on the part of chil-

---

[4] From a publication of the World Health Organization, a special organ of the United Nations.

dren. Unless the health interests, attitudes, and information developed culminate in sound health practices, the school will have fallen short of its intended objective. The curriculum is designed on the assumption that it will be primarily the regular classroom teacher's responsibility to develop the learning experiences necessary in health instruction. He may also call on certain specialized personnel employed by the school, such as a school nurse or a school physician, or he may utilize similar community people as resource persons on special occasions to increase the effectiveness of his efforts.

Basis for Selecting Health Experiences

Health education experiences for the elementary school are determined chiefly by the basic health needs of children. These health needs are, of course, not much different from those of any other age group. The fact that the years from five to twelve are growing and developing years of great importance does add elements of special concern for health in childhood. Children's basic health needs, insofar as physical health is concerned, center around proper nutrition, adequate rest and sleep, cleanliness, opportunities for physical activity, protection from disease and accidents, and the understanding and appreciation that lead to proper care of the body. In the area of mental health, the basic needs of children for acceptance, security, love, success, recognition, intellectual stimulation, and a basic sense of personal worth must be recognized and dealt with. These basic health needs give direction to the selection of appropriate subject matter for the curriculum in health. At the same time they furnish the basic information that influences the way in which the school plant is designed, the school day is organized, and the teacher-pupil relationship is established.

The Scope of Health Education

The scope of the health instruction program, following as it does from the basic health needs of children, is broad. It provides for learning experiences focused around areas of concern that are directly related to children's health. A nationwide examination of health instruction in the schools completed in 1963 reported the following as health content areas emphasized in the first eight years of the public school system, or in the elementary school:[5]

---

[5] *School Health Education Study: A Summary Report 1961–63,* sponsored by the Samuel Bronfman Foundation, New York City, pp. 33–35.

Accident prevention	Posture and body mechanics
Cleanliness and grooming	Rest and sleep
Dental health	Vision and hearing
Food and nutrition	Communicable diseases
Exercise and relaxation	

All of these are important to the individual who would protect and conserve his own health and, in the larger setting, that of his fellows in the community. While it is not too difficult to reach agreement on the fact that the scope of the health education curriculum must be broad, it is somewhat more difficult to gain agreement on certain other related questions.

The relative value of various areas to total health instruction. All areas of health education are not equally vital in the elementary school program, and therefore each must take its proper place. In planning the health curriculum most school systems find it helpful to obtain the assistance of medical personnel and health education experts.

Byrd, an authority in the field of health education, has called attention to this point by commenting on "good grooming" as a topic in health education. He wrote as follows:

> Virtually every physician has rendered medical service at one time or another to unkempt, poorly groomed, untidy and even dirty patients who possessed the vigor and vitality to give them a long life at the high level of energy. Such physicians have also treated neat, well-groomed, fastidious, clean and attractive persons who were suffering from tuberculosis, mental illness and a host of other serious diseases. Grooming does not make a fundamental contribution to high levels of vitality, endurance and length of life. There *are* certain relationships to health in the field of good grooming, but these should not be overemphasized. A person can learn to wash his hands as a part of his training in cleanliness, food sanitation and control of communicable diseases. This may also be a part of the process of good grooming. It is likewise true that to be well groomed is to give a person an added measure of confidence and self-respect. These factors have mild relationships to mental health. It is only when teachers and those who develop a health curriculum have the misconception that "good grooming" makes a major contribution to health education that the total development of the school health curriculum suffers.[6]

Implicit in this quotation is the kind of studied and enlightened choice which must be made as health instruction is planned for in the elemen-

---

[6] Reprinted by permission of the Association for Childhood Education International, 3615 Wisconsin Avenue, N.W., Washington, D.C., 20016, "School Health," by Oliver E. Byrd, M.D., from *Childhood Education,* Vol. 35, No. 9 (May 1959), pp. 394–397.

tary school. All of the earlier listed topics are of some value; but some may be considerably more important than others.

Selection of subject matter. Another difficult question met in planning the health curriculum has to do with the selection of subject matter to be taught in relation to each of these general areas. Content selected for study must be appropriate; it must meet certain criteria for selection. Proper learning situations are more likely to be provided and appropriate subject matter is most likely to be selected when the elementary school is very clear as to the objectives of the program. This point is well illustrated by Byrd in this statement on health education:

> Many health textbooks and health courses have been constructed under the mistaken concept that learning about the structure and function of the human body is health education. Anatomy and physiology are long-established sciences, predating hygiene and health education by many years, but the content of these fields is different and should not be confused with health education. To illustrate this distinction among anatomy, physiology and health education, we may postulate that a classroom teacher falls to the floor in a classroom, breaks the humerus and severs the brachial artery. A person well versed in anatomy might view this unfortunate teacher and observe accurately: "This teacher has broken her humerus and has severed the brachial artery." A second observer, well versed in the field of physiology, might observe: "This teacher will empty the circulatory system within a few minutes if the bleeding is not stopped." A person qualified in first aid or health education, without knowing the name of the bone that has been shattered or the name of the blood vessel that has been severed, might conclude: "I must apply a compress to stop this bleeding if this person's life is to be saved." The latter might then proceed to save the life of the patient without knowing anything about the patient's anatomy or physiology.[7]

Now, obviously, this is not to say that there is no place or need for providing information to children concerning the anatomy and the physiology of the human body. In the illustration above some knowledge of physiology is necessary in order to know where to apply the vital compress. But the need to make choices about the subject matter to be included in the health education curriculum becomes clear. Generally speaking, the health curriculum aims at healthful living. The knowledge the school attempts to develop, as well as the way in which it attempts to develop it, must meet the fundamental test of its contribution to enlightened and effective health practices. Recently in health education, too, the interest in identifying basic concepts as a guide to the selection of subject matter has been evident. In 1962 a project was activated which

---

[7] Byrd, pp. 394–397.

was to give priority to the identification of the crucial health problems of the 1960's and the 1970's as these related to school-age children, and to the determination of basic health concepts which represented "what a health educated student should know at the completion of health instruction in the elementary and secondary grades—K–12."[8]

Together, these references vividly call attention to the preparation an elementary school system must make if effective health instruction is to be offered. It will not suffice to operate in the classroom at the level of "hold up your handkerchiefs, and now let me see your nails." Rather, the elementary school must be continuously alert to relate the content of its health instruction to the goals it is trying to achieve.

Placing Health Education in the Curriculum

If the health education program is to be effective, it must find its proper place in the total elementary school curriculum. Time, a most precious thing in the classroom, must be found for health instruction. Generally, instruction in health is carried out in the elementary school in three ways.

Relating health instruction to other curriculum areas. A good deal of the instruction in health is related to or developed in conjunction with broad studies that are pursued in the social studies or the science areas of the curriculum. In the social studies, for instance, attention to family and local community living can effectively deal with matters of health. Things that families do or do not do in order to live healthfully can be noted. Studies of local community living can direct attention to the persons and the facilities in the community that are there to safeguard the health of all concerned. Field trips can be made to the local public health office; a doctor may visit a class and describe the work of a local health clinic. In these and many other ways, health education may find a meaningful place in a social studies unit of work.

Similarly, work in science may be related to health education. Studies of living things, of plant and animal life, of bacteria, or of basic food content may furnish the setting in which to call attention to the human need for fresh air and sunshine, to practices that help to control the spread of communicable diseases, or to the desirability of a balanced diet.

Some classroom studies, as noted elsewhere, are so broad as to become social studies–science–health units of work at one and the same time. For instance, a comprehensive study of the way in which a

---

[8] Study undertaken by the Curriculum Commission of the Health Education Division of the American Association for Health, Physical Education, and Recreation, 1962.

community is supplied with fresh, safe drinking water will deal with local government, municipal and private services, minerals, bacteria, chemical processes, bodily functions, human uses of water, and so on. The "related study" setting is one in which much health instruction is accomplished.

Direct instruction in health education. It is necessary in addition to provide certain opportunities for direct instruction in health matters. All of the things that must be considered in the health program cannot be treated in relation to other ongoing studies, or cannot be as profitably treated in such a setting. At times it is better to start with a direct effort in health education. This effort may be an attempt to understand communicable diseases and the sorts of living habits that are basic to their control. Or the school's and the teacher's objectives may suggest a direct study of accident prevention in all of its ramifications. Or again, to accomplish the necessary understandings about the rest-exercise-sleep relationship, the way in which the body expends and recovers energy may well be treated in a direct instructional setting. Use of planned health units is the most usual way to deal with health instruction after about grade three.[9]

A functional setting for health instruction. The school has another opportunity that it can and does utilize for health education: the broad school living experience in and of itself. With the ultimate ends of the program being healthful practices based on adequate understanding and positive health attitudes, the idea of using the ongoingness of the school living experience *in toto* as a setting for health instruction is sound. Understandings can be developed and practices can be strengthened by utilizing the lunch period in relation to instruction about foods and nutrition; certain playground activities or planning for field trips can be seen in relation to efforts to educate for safety and accident prevention; regular weighing and measuring schedules can be seen in relation to understanding growth and development; vision screening tests can be related to proper education for care of the eyes; and so on. Once the possibilities for health instruction in such situations as these are grasped by the elementary school and the teacher, some very meaningful health education takes place.

Guarding Against Fears and Anxieties

Enthusiasm to provide sound and adequate health education in the elementary school must be tempered with great sensitivity for and understanding of the children with whom the school is working. It is possible, and usual, for the results of instruction in health to make quite

---

[9] School Health Education Study, p. 19.

positive contributions to children's learning. It is not unknown, however, for such teaching to lead in some instances to the development of fears and anxieties on the part of some children. Instruction in this area must be offered with a great deal of awareness of the situation in which particular children find it necessary to try to live healthfully. If goals are put forth absolutely, with certain "or else" implications, and children realize that these goals are beyond their reach at the present time, the negative results in terms of mental health may overshadow any gains that might have come from the instructional effort. A way of living that calls, for instance, for a bath each day is simply not realistic in certain situations. A fixed number of glasses of milk or particular balanced formats for meals are daily goals that some children cannot meet. Neither should the school provide false or incomplete information. A range of healthful living practices must be accepted. Information about bodily cleanliness may indicate that a daily bath is most desirable; it may also indicate that something less than this is acceptable and not to be feared. Similar information may indicate that meals balanced in particular ways with respect to food content are most desirable; but it may also show that eating in these ways is to be done as often as possible and that "bad things" are not going to happen immediately to one who does not have such a diet regularly. Often, children are simply powerless to control certain aspects of their living experience, such as the place in which they live, the adequacy of facilities to be shared among a number of people, or the long-established eating habits of parents. They must be helped to live as healthfully as possible in their present situation, and they may form attitudes about healthful living which will cause them to want to live differently as the situation permits. This is a far more acceptable result of instruction than is the development of fears and anxieties based on wondering "what will happen to me since I don't live that way." Sometimes, a family may recognize the soundness of some health knowledge or practice brought home by a child and try to revise some aspect of their living accordingly. More often patterns of living cannot be altered until a person is independent enough to be establishing his own way of life.

PROVIDING FOR PHYSICAL EDUCATION

Companion to the instructional program in health education in the elementary school is the program in physical education. These two aspects of the curriculum support each other. Clearly, a definition of *health* as "a state of well-being" calls for a person that is physically strong, possessed of sufficient stamina and strength to carry on both work and recreational activities without undue fatigue. Too, a certain degree of physical skill and dexterity is demanded by many aspects of daily living. Control over and coordination of one's physical self is important.

From what has been said earlier in this chapter, it is clear, too, that it is just as important for children to learn how to play properly as it is to work properly. The need for a person to have ways of relaxing and recreating is well accepted. Many will find a source of relaxation in the area of physical activity.

Actually, a very basic developmental task for children in our culture is to be able to handle the body efficiently. This most often means that girls and boys must be able to handle themselves with a high degree of poise and coordination as they participate in various individual and group activities appropriate to their sex. It means they must be able to run, jump, and throw with speed, agility, and accuracy. Such skills are combined into many individual and team sports in our society, and we expect great numbers of our people to participate in them. The pressure for boys to develop physical skill to some degree is quite strong; for a boy, to be a successful athlete is to be admired and approved by the majority of our people.[10]

Additionally, the possibilities that physical education activities hold for the accomplishment of certain general objectives of education should be noted. Many of the dual and team activities in which children participate in the physical education program make a contribution to the development of such personal traits as loyalty, responsibility, and fair play. They help a child to sense what it means to be a good team member and what teamwork is all about; they make their contribution in helping a child become a good winner and a good loser. All of these characteristics are admired and sought in our society, and the setting that much of the physical education program provides for their development should not be overlooked.

For all of these reasons, physical education is an integral part of the curriculum of the elementary school. Its purposes include:

1. Physical development—the building of physical power
2. Motor development—the performance of physical movement
3. Mental development—knowledge of physical activities
4. Personal development—the development of the self
5. Social development—participation with others in physical activities

The Distribution of Time and Effort

Physical education is usually provided as a daily experience for all children. Teachers believe that all students need this experience, and most states require it as a part of their state legislation pertaining to education. Almost all children will be able to participate in whatever

---

[10] See Robert J. Havighurst, *Human Development and Education* (New York: David McKay Company, Inc., 1953), p. 28.

regular program of physical education is provided. Some children will need to participate in a modified program. These children, handicapped physically in some way, must be identified, and the program must be adapted for them so that they can participate to some degree with their classmates. But at times a very special program is necessary to meet the needs of certain pupils.

Physical Education as Instruction ·

Physical education is an instructional program. The major goals of this aspect of the curriculum, no less than of others, can be realized only by teachers who perceive the activities provided as guided experiences, or as teaching-learning situations. It *is not* physical education simply to release children from their classrooms to spend a fixed period of time on the playground, with certain basic equipment and apparatus at their disposal. It *is* physical education to guide and assist in some specific activity, with the purposes for which the experience is provided clearly in the teacher's mind.

Physical education and school recreation. The school must provide recurring opportunities for use if physical skills, once developed, are to be maintained and refined. If these skills are to be used in the ways intended by the purposes of the program, the school should provide typical situations in which to practice them. There may be noon-hour intramural sports programs and folk dancing opportunities. Day-long play days may be organized to bring larger groups of children together for recreation; or the school may join hands with the community in operating an after-school recreation program centered in the elementary school plant and grounds.

Physical education and recess. Recess periods, usually required for about ten minutes out of every hour, are related to the health and physical education effort in its broadest sense. These short periods of time provide a few minutes of relaxation and exercise, fresh air, a chance for toileting, and an opportunity for conversation. They make their contribution to the physical and mental health of pupils. But they are not to be confused with the program of physical education.

The bulk of the total time and effort devoted to physical education in the elementary school is divided between the physical education class and the school recreation program. Some elementary schools, especially those that include seventh and eighth grades, will have teams competing in interscholastic sports, and in these instances some additional time and effort must go to this aspect of the program. The approximate distribution of time, effort, and pupil involvement can be shown in the diagram.

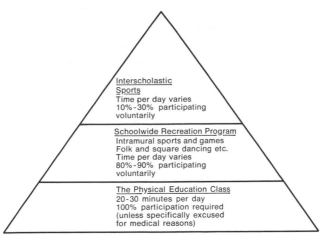

THE PHYSICAL EDUCATION PROGRAM

The physical education class is expected to include all children as participants. It is usually scheduled for about twenty minutes daily in the primary grades, and for from twenty to thirty minutes daily in the intermediate and upper grades.

The recreational program of the school, including intramural sports and games, folk dancing, and the like, is usually scheduled for noon times, or for the last part of the school day on certain occasions. It is hoped that from 80 to 90 percent of the students will participate voluntarily in these activities, and the program is designed to involve such numbers.

Some elementary schools have an organized interscholastic sports program. Some communities develop such an intensive interscholastic sports program at the secondary school level that the elementary school is seen as a potential "feeder" for high school teams, and efforts are made to identify and develop the athletic potential that might be found in elementary school age children. Where such an interscholastic sports program is found in the elementary school, some 10 to 30 percent of the children are expected to be participating voluntarily in it. More is said later in this chapter as to the advisability of interscholastic ventures in the elementary school.

The Scope of Physical Education

The broad purposes of the physical education program call for a broad and varied scope of activities. The following paragraphs give a more detailed picture of this breadth, and some insight into the nature of the experiences that each aspect of the program is expected to provide.

Coordination and control activities. These experiences are provided to help children to develop proper uses of the body. In the main, these uses are concerned with locomotion and playing skills. The experiences in locomotion are focused on learning to move the body in various positions and at various speeds appropriate to particular activities. The experiences with playing skills are focused on helping children to learn to throw, catch, jump, and the like, with the idea that these skills will be applied, singly and in combinations, in various work and play activities in which children engage.

Quickly organized activities. These activities do not demand highly refined skills for participation. In the main, these are games and relays that operate from simple line, circle, or scatter formations. They are adaptable to almost any number of participants, to almost any available play area, and to almost any block of time. They are designed to include everyone in a class or group, providing vigorous activity, use of physical skills, and some feeling for team effort in a situation that is relatively simple to learn and to conduct.

Rhythmic activities. Experiences in this area are related to the basic impulse of human beings to move to rhythm. A variety of situations are made available for children, extending from opportunities for individual self-expression to music and rhythm, to more organized and systematic responses such as are found in folk and square dancing. Provision is made for creative expression, and for increased efficiency and control in bodily movement. A by-product is the gain for children in social grace and social experience.

Individual and dual activities. This area of activity consists of games that pit one person against another, or two people against two others. These experiences contribute heavily not only to the general goals of the physical education program, but especially to the recreational aims of the program. Such activities as tetherball, foursquare, and shuffleboard fall into this general category, setting the stage for eventual participation in such games as handball, bowling, tennis, and golf.

Self-testing activities. These are experiences that have as their purpose the development of the individual child's strength, coordination, balance, and endurance. They are typically organized and administered in such a way as to help a child to gain insight into his ability at a certain time in the school year, and to check on this improvement at a later date. Such activities as balancing, chinning, doing push-ups, running, and jumping are typical of those used for these self-testing purposes. In the past few years this sort of thing, under the banner of *physical fitness,* has enjoyed a great deal of attention in the school program, and more time has been used for such activities than has heretofore been true. Some educators see these activities as timely and necessary for development; others believe that they are being overemphasized and are taking time away from other valuable physical education experiences. The seriousness of this issue is reflected in this excerpt from a recent publication that reviewed current curriculum developments:

> Physical education, on the other hand, seems locked in a titanic struggle for dominance or priority of aim—between the "physical fitness" or physical training concept and that of the more meaningful and holistic concept of physical education. . . . Fitness "scores" and muscular strength have dominated recent evaluation of the physical education curriculum.[11]

Athletic team games. This is an area of experience in which children come into contact with more highly organized games, usually seasonal in nature, and traditional in our culture. The age and the general development level of particular children have a great deal to do with the degree to which and the manner in which such games are presented in the elementary school. Games like kickball, catchball, modified volleyball, modified soccer, and touch football are played in prelude to regulation football, basketball, baseball, volleyball, and soccer as played later by youths and adults.

That these games provide an opportunity to develop physical skill and endurance, to have fun and enjoyment in playing, and to develop some of the desirable personal and social traits mentioned earlier is undoubtedly true. That they must be used with discretion and reason in the elementary school is equally true. This is especially clear when the matter of interscholastic team games is considered.

Almost every study that has ever been made, by separate or combined groups of elementary educators, physical education specialists, and medical doctors, has recommended against the participation of elementary school age children in interscholastic sports competition.[12] They suggest that such contests, if held at all, be held infrequently and under very informal auspices. The length of the contest, the rules under which it is played, and the spectator situation should be arranged with the age level and the maturity of the participants clearly in mind. Reports such as these point out the dangers inherent in highly organized interscholastic team sports for both the physical and the mental health of children. With

---

[11] Delber Oberteuffer, "Health Education and Physical Education" in *New Curriculum Developments* (Washington, D.C.: Association for Supervision and Curriculum Development, 1965), p. 39.

[12] American Association for Health, Physical Education, and Recreation, Joint Committee Report, *Desirable Athletic Competition for Children* (Washington, D.C.: The Association, 1952).

the strong cultural value placed on athletic prowess in our country, this is not always a popular or easy position for the elementary school to try to take. However, the impact of such evidence is persuasive, and there is only a small amount of such sports competition in the six-year elementary school, and a fairly reasonable approach to such contests in the eight-year elementary school. Of course, much of this kind of activity has of late become a community-wide enterprise, subject to control and regulation from groups other than school.

This, then, is the scope of the program. It is broad and varied, and must be so if it is to accomplish the goals set for physical education in the elementary school.

Sequence in the Physical Education Program

The matter of sequence in the physical education program is based primarily on the rate at which, and the ways in which, the child grows and develops. Readiness is a concept that is particularly applicable to this aspect of the curriculum. Children are not able to profit from certain kinds of instruction in physical education until they have matured physically in certain ways. While instruction in physical education is committed to the development of physical skills and coordinations, effort is not expended wisely until the body has developed to the point that it will respond efficiently to such instructional effort. Some of the earliest basic studies in readiness were focused on physical and motor development. An educational psychologist summed this matter up recently as follows: "Both observation of children's learning of such complex skills as ball playing, skating, swimming, or writing and an experimental investigation of the hypothesis indicates that for complex skills, training makes a relatively greater contribution to improvement than for simple skills. But for complex skills, neither uninstructed practice nor teacher-guided training can make up for limitations in maturity. . . ."[13]

Sequences within the physical education curriculum are also based on the ultimate setting in which physical skills are to be used. Young children are taught to run properly, to hop and to skip, to jump and to throw. Preliminary activities precede attempts to combine these various physical skills into an organized game. Throwing, catching, and running games, for example, precede attempts to play organized softball or baseball. Similarly, touch football as an organized game is preceded by chances to learn to throw, catch, and kick a football. Simple folk and square dances that contain most of the basic steps are learned before the more intricate and involved dances are attempted.

---

[13] Arden N. Frandsen, *How Children Learn* (New York: McGraw-Hill Book Company, Inc., 1957), pp. 72–73.

Thus, a cut across the physical education curriculum at any particular point should reveal activities and experiences designed with both the readiness of the child to profit from the instruction and the ultimate ends of the program clearly in mind.

Staffing for Physical Education

In most elementary schools, the regular classroom teacher is expected to handle the instruction in physical education, as in all other areas of the classroom program. Some elementary schools provide a special consultant in this area to work with classroom teachers as they strive to grow in ability to handle physical education. Some few schools are staffed with a special physical education instructor, assigned probably to the intermediate grades. Most of the physical education at the seventh and eighth grade levels is handled by special teachers.

Mastery and the Development of Physical Skill

As in other areas of the curriculum that demand high skill, so in physical education does the concept of mastery have to be dealt with. The school must answer the question of how much physical skill it should try to exact from each child. A number of facts must be kept in mind as this question is answered.

Individual differences. The fact of individual differences is probably more obvious in the physical education area than in any of the other strands of the curriculum. We can easily see the differences in height, strength, weight, and so on, and can predict with considerable effectiveness which children will run faster, jump higher, and throw farther than others.

Personal choice and motivation. More difficult to appraise, and certainly more difficult to reflect in our practices, are the differences that are based on personal choice and motivation in the area of physical accomplishment. A child may obviously possess the physique to accomplish more or perform better in certain areas of physical activity. But both his choice of areas in which he desires to participate and the level of skill development acceptable to him in those areas are highly personal things. In the elementary school, where physical ability and outlets for physical prowess are being explored for the first time in any systematic way, the school will do well not to mistake timidity, lack of personal security, or lack of information concerning certain physical activities for a considered choice to be a nonparticipant. Without undue pressure, children should be helped to meet and accomplish certain physically oriented developmental tasks while they are young, at the ages where the culture tends to expect this of them. However, as children move on through the intermediate grades and into the upper grades, and the school can be relatively sure that a child is choosing to pursue or not to pursue physical activities as an area of interest on the basis of some personal experience with them, this preference must be recognized and respected. And, with evidence that the acceptance of a level of skill in any such activity is made as a personal considered choice, the school will do well to allow for a very flexible and individualized definition of mastery in this area. Some children will be motivated to develop a level of skill beyond their physical endowment, and they will need to be counseled and guided sensitively. Others will be highly motivated and possessed of a high degree of physical skill. This they should be helped to appraise and exploit to their best interests, too. Surely no precise or rigid definition of mastery will do.

Sex differences. Lastly, the level of skill which the elementary school will seek to develop in children is related to sex differences, both biological and cultural. Differences in rate of physical development between girls and boys make for some differences in accepted levels of achievement and skill at various age and grade levels. Although boys tend to develop in height and weight a little more rapidly than girls in the earliest years, this gap tends to close by the end of elementary school. At the same time, the physical strength of boys continues to be greater. While girls compete on fairly even terms with boys during most of the early elementary school years, they no longer do so in the last years of the intermediate grades and in the upper grades of schools that include the seventh and eighth years. Though many girls may be taller and heavier than boys at that time, they will not be as strong physically.[14]

Culturally, too, there are different expectancies set in this area for boys and for girls. These expectancies influence the acceptance of particular levels of skill development as satisfactory. The female role does not require or demand as much physical strength, endurance, and skill as does the male role. In fact, girls with high levels of interest and potential in physical activities sometimes find it extremely difficult to reconcile these with the expected female role. Boys find the opposite to be the case, with the cultural expectancy being set for high interest and skill in physical things, and certain levels of achievement more or less expected of them. The work of Havighurst on the developmental tasks of middle childhood puts it this way:

> Boys are expected to learn these [physical] skills to a higher degree than girls. A girl can do rather poorly on them and still hold

---

[14] L. Cole and J. B. Morgan, *Psychology of Childhood and Adolescence* (New York: Holt, Rinehart and Winston, Inc., 1947), pp. 4–5.

status in the peer group, while a boy who does poorly is called a "sissy" and loses status. Boys of all social classes are expected to acquire physical skills.[15]

Thus, attention to the idea of mastery in physical education must include consideration for physical endowment, personal choice and motivation, and sex differences both physically and culturally based.

HEALTH AND PHYSICAL EDUCATION
AND THE SCHOOL ENVIRONMENT

In agreement with the evidence in the field of physical and mental health concerning the importance of the total environment in which a person spends his time, the elementary school gives considerable attention to the provision of a healthful and safe school environment for children. If the school experience is to contribute as completely as it might to a total state of well-being this provision is quite necessary. The school plant and the school grounds, the provision of certain special facilities therein, the general way in which the school day is organized, and the relationship the teacher tries to establish with his class and among the children in his charge all come to be seen as parts of the school's effort to provide for the health of children. Let us consider each of these briefly here, to grasp the sense in which the total environment provides for and helps to insure effective health education.

The School Plant and Grounds

Site selection and school building design are carried out with a direct concern for providing a safe and healthful place for children. Every effort is made to place the school in a safe place, safe in the sense that children can come to and from the school without undue fear for their personal safety. Also, the site should be large enough so that several hundred children can live healthfully on it, without undue crowding and limitations on physical activity. Most states now have recommended minimum standards for the size of an elementary school site, and communities strive to procure ground accordingly. Our very large cities have difficulties in getting sufficient land, especially in the center-city areas, to follow this space requirement for school building design, and they must develop plans that are realizable in the setting in which they must build.

The building itself is designed with children in mind, and the sort of living that should go on in an elementary school is reflected in the way in which space is arranged. The typical new elementary school is a one-story building, so that children do not have to climb up and down stairs. Such

15 Havighurst, *Human Development and Education*, p. 28.

a building simplifies living for individual children, and increases the safety of the large groups of children that must move from one part of the building to another at particular times. The building is designed not only to be functionally adequate, but also to be attractive. The general outside appearance of the building is pleasant, and the grounds are usually landscaped. Colors used to decorate both the outside and inside of the modern elementary school are selected to add to the general pleasantness of the school environment. Proper lighting, heating, and ventilating systems make their contribution to a healthful school environment. Classrooms are equipped with running water and drinking fountains to make it easier to practice certain desirable health habits day by day. Toilet facilities are increasingly placed in classrooms so that children can take care of physical needs in a more natural and efficient way than the former group facilities made possible.

School furniture has undergone drastic change in the past ten years. Comfort, attractive design, and the use of color have been welcome additions in the classroom. The changes that have come about all contribute to the physical and mental health of students.

Special Equipment and Facilities

Providing ample play space. Outdoor play space, divided with the safety of children in mind so that young children and older children can participate with satisfaction in games appropriate to their ages, continues to improve. Also, the kinds of special equipment and apparatus placed at the disposal of children on the playground are increasingly designed and selected with greater sensitivity to the kind of play in which different age groups want to participate. Even the general surfacing of playground space, and the special surfacing that is provided under certain kinds of equipment, more often is selected with the health and safety of children clearly in mind. It is encouraging to see recently the more frequent provision of an adequately covered play area for elementary schools. If the physical education program is to operate successfully the year around, such a facility is badly needed.

Providing adequate lunch facilities. Elementary schools must provide suitable noon lunching facilities for children who find it necessary to have their lunch at school. In some instances all that is necessary is to arrange for a proper place for eating for those children who bring their lunch to school from time to time. Many elementary schools, however, must have a lunching facility for practically their complete student body. In such situations the elementary school is usually equipped with kitchens, serving facilities, and ample eating space to prepare and serve a hot lunch at school at a low price. The direct contribution which such a service can make to sound nutrition is obvious. Additionally, the indirect educational benefits which accrue from such a facility must be noted. The opportunity to impress upon children the necessity for taking enough time to eat a relaxed lunch, the advisability of eating a balanced meal, and the satisfaction which comes from eating varied lunches can be exploited. The chance for children to participate in the preparation and serving of the lunch again adds to the significance of this special facility for the overall goals of the health education program.

Organizing the School Day

In present-day elementary schools teachers organize the school day with the physical and mental health of children in mind. The length of the school day itself is adjusted in the elementary school with an eye to the well-being of children of various ages. Five-year-olds usually attend kindergarten for about two and one-half hours. Children in the primary grades have a shorter school day than do children in the intermediate grades. Homework assignments are made sparingly during the elementary school years. Decisions as to the length of the school day and the amount of work to be done away from the school are made with the intent to help children to live healthfully. Planners try to take into account the twenty-four-hour day of the child, with attention to time for work, play, relaxation, personal interests and hobbies, and family experiences.

Within any one of these school days we find teachers planning their program to provide a proper balance among work experiences, play and physical exercise, rest and relaxation. Every effort is made to instill variety into the school day and to dispel feelings of boredom and fatigue. Teachers speak often of "pacing" activities in the school day. They are indicating that they plan the work of the day so that a quiet activity, such as a sitting and listening experience, is followed by some more lively activity in which the children may participate in a different way. Recesses which come each hour are a part of this same attempt to pace the school day. Then, too, the length of time children are asked to concentrate and work on certain tasks varies with the nature of the task itself. An attempt is made to guard against nervousness, daydreaming, and tension, and to keep children at given tasks for periods of time commensurate with their staying powers.

The Teacher-Pupil Relationship

The nature of the relationship a teacher establishes with his pupils, individually and collectively, makes its contribution, good or bad, to the total well-being of children. A wealth of testimony from pupils indicates the positive contribution that comes from working with a teacher who is kind, friendly, firm, consistent, impartial, understanding, and patient in his dealings with them. Abundant testimony is available, too, as to what happens when the opposite sort of circumstances prevails. Teachers know this, and they do their best to create the sort of psychological climate in their classrooms that will support, and not thwart, the emotional well-being of their pupils. There are times, of course, when it is difficult for a teacher to find something about every child in his classroom that he can honestly admire. But, this is the goal that he must work toward to help to bridge the distance that otherwise might stand between teacher and pupils. The reverse is equally true, of course; children come to school wanting to like their teacher, and there are times when they have to look hard for the link that can join them in a satisfying working relationship.

As teachers work with their class group they keep a number of things in mind. They know that each child must see himself as one of the group. They know that children must all find a way of participating in the activities of the group. Further, they know that this participation must be reasonably successful, and that children must be given recognition for this successful participation. Finally, they know the security that comes to children from knowing that their future is secure in the group, too. These concerns suggest the efforts the teacher must make for the mental health of his pupils. This is a large task, but one of fundamental importance.

Teachers are aware, too, of the natural competition found among children when they are associated together in any close way. Competition is accepted and used as positively as possible for motivation to learning. But every effort is made to do away with intensive competition that leads to anxiety. Every effort is made to insure fair competition for the children in the class. Grouping, rotating classwide responsibilities, balancing committee memberships, and the like are all a part of the work of the teacher who would guard and strengthen the mental health of children.

HEALTH SERVICES AND HEALTH EDUCATION

The health program of the elementary school extends into the area of health services. The services offered by the school are related to very specific purposes. Some health services are provided by the elementary school so that the welfare of the pupils in attendance may be protected. Others are designed to enable the school to work cooperatively with parents, community medical personnel, and community health agencies to help insure the physical and mental well-being of the children of the school community. It is clear that elementary school teachers are not expected to practice medicine in any sense of the term. In fact, most states have very explicit legislation stating the limits on the activities of school teachers in the area of health service. Many elementary schools have a nurse as a regular staff member, and some have a school doctor and dentist who work in the district full time, making regular visits to individual elmentary schools, or otherwise providing service to children. Others use public health nurses on a part-time basis, and contract similarly for the services of a doctor who will spend some agreed-upon amount of time in the school district. Classroom teachers do assist in certain ways as the service program operates, but the total effort is guided by persons qualified to do so. Let us consider in some detail the exact nature of this health service responsibility, and the service activities that are provided.

Determining Health Needs

Encouraging periodic health examinations. The health of the child is of concern to many people. It is to the benefit of each child that his developing health profile be determined as completely as possible. Such health data as are needed to determine this profile must come from a number of sources. Information comes from parents and from children themselves, from examinations made by private or school medical personnel, from the daily observations of classroom teachers as they work intimately with children, and from the regular screening and recording programs related to height, weight, vision, and hearing that the school typically carries on. Clearly, only a part of this evidence is appropriately collected by the school itself. But, as a community institution, it can act as a strong protagonist with individual families and with community groups to encourage the development of a broad program for determining the health needs of children. For instance, school and community may join together in developing a plan for periodic health examinations, medical, dental, and psychological, for children. Often such programs provide that examinations are to be held at school and on school time. Parents are not forced to use this service, but its convenience is difficult to resist and the result is usually that more children receive regular health examinations than would normally be the case. The school is also in a position to urge parents to have children examined when the day-to-day contact at school seems to reveal some deviation from the normal that should be investigated and explained. Referral routines and channels can be established that make it easy for parents to follow through on such suggestions, and the realization of the ends of the school's health program is helped accordingly.

Maintaining a health record system. A part of a continuing assessment of the health status of the child is to make data available to concerned persons. When information is recorded systematically and housed in a convenient place it is much more likely to be referred to and used. To some extent, the elementary school can provide another needed service in this regard. Information on the health status of each child can be brought together on a cumulative health record form, and can readily be made available to appropriate school personnel, parents, and family physician. All of these persons need access to this information and an interpretation of it at different times for different purposes. Parents and children, obviously, need to become increasingly aware of the pattern of development that is unfolding in these data. Teachers need to be well informed, too, on this matter, if they are to understand certain aspects of the pupil's performance properly, and are to adapt the classroom experience realistically to specific health conditions. The family physician may find these school-centered data a useful supplement to whatever health records he maintains on a given child. School and community health personnel can work together to develop a valuable health record service.

Assisting in Disease Prevention and Control

The elementary school is also given certain responsibilities to meet in the area of the prevention and control of disease. Part of the responsibility is related to the protection the school must extend to the children in attendance. Operating as it does in the place of the parent in matters such as this, the elementary school must have an ongoing service program designed to identify and isolate the sick child. Children who exhibit symptoms of illness must be immediately separated from the larger group until the illness can be properly diagnosed. While teachers are expected to be alert to such warning signs, they are also expected to call for assistance from school or community medical personnel for a final determination of the child's condition. The school's responsibility for action is greatest when the illness is diagnosed as a contagious disease. In such instances its responsibility extends beyond the ill child. Parents of other children who may have been exposed need to be informed so that they can procure preventive treatment for their children, and can be alert to symptoms of the disease that may develop.

In discharging these responsibilities the school has an opportunity for health service instruction activities. Contacts with parents provide an occasion for encouraging the use of effective preventive health measures with children. An effort can be made, for instance, to help parents to see the wisdom of providing for regular immunizations for their children. In fact, this effort may provide the motivation for a community-wide immunization program, cosponsored by the school, community medical personnel, and community health agencies, that will operate in and through the school system.

It also provides an opportunity for the school to develop a more realistic position for all concerned on the matter of regular school attendance. Some parents, and even some schools, seem to feel that a child should be in school, no matter what. Undue emphasis on perfect attendance can often work to the detriment of the child who is ill but comes to school anyway, and to the rest of the children in his class and school who are thus unnecessarily exposed to disease. A realistic policy on attendance urges the parent to keep the sick child at home.

Caring for Emergencies at School

Because the school acts in the place of the parent, each school must have a planned program for the care of emergencies, such as sickness and personal injury. The school must provide immediate care in all such situations. A sick child must be moved to a safe place and made as comfortable as possible. An injured child must be administered proper first aid. Teachers, in conjunction with school health personnel, are expected to be able to handle such occurrences safely and wisely. Parents are to be notified immediately of such happenings; they should be told the extent of the injury and what action would seem to be necessary. Perhaps he should be taken to a physician's office; perhaps the physician should be summoned to the school because it may appear unwise to move the child. Anticipating occasions when parents cannot be contacted, the elementary school must take the initiative in working out procedures for meeting sickness or injury in the absence of direct parent contact. Thus, names of physicians to be called, neighbors to be notified, and the like, are kept on file at the school to insure that the service program will be able to meet emergencies efficiently under any and all conditions.

Through these various programs of service, the elementary school rounds out its total program in health and physical education.

RECOMMENDED READINGS

BRESLOW, LESTER. *Building America's Health*. Raleigh, N.C.: Health Publications Institute, Inc., 1955.

FRASER, ELLEN D., JOHN B. BRANSFORD, and MAMIE HASTINGS. *The Child and Physical Education*. Englewood Cliffs, N.J.: Prentice-Hall, Inc., 1956.

HAAG, JESSIE HELEN. *School Health Program*. New York: Holt, Rinehart and Winston, Inc., 1958.

HALSEY, ELIZABETH, and LORENA R. PORTER. *Physical Education for Children: A Developmental Approach*. New York: Holt, Rinehart and Winston, Inc., 1958.

IRWIN, LESLIE W., JAMES H. HUMPHREY, and WARREN JOHNSON. *Methods and Materials in School Health Education.* St. Louis: C. V. Mosby Company, 1956.

JOINT COMMITTEE ON HEALTH PROBLEMS IN EDUCATION OF THE NATIONAL EDUCATION ASSOCIATION AND THE AMERICAN MEDICAL ASSOCIATION. *Healthful School Living.* Washington, D.C.: NEA, 1957.

JONES, EDWINA, EDNA MORGAN, and GLADYS STEVENS. *Methods and Materials in Elementary Physical Education.* New York: Harcourt, Brace & World, Inc., 1958.

NEILSON, N. P. E., and WINIFRED VAN HAGEN. *Physical Education for Elementary Schools* (revised edition). New York: The Ronald Press Company, 1957.

PRESIDENT'S COUNCIL ON YOUTH FITNESS. *Youth Physical Fitness: Suggested Elements of a School-Centered Program.* Washington, D.C.: U.S. Government Printing Office, 1961.

SCHNEIDER, ROBERT E. *Methods and Materials of Health Education.* Philadelphia: W. B. Saunders Company, 1958.

School Health Education Study: A Summary Report. New York: The Samuel Bronfman Foundation, 1964.

Aesthetics and Creativity: The Fine Arts

14

To think creatively and to express in words, pictures, music, dance, or other media some of his emotions has been a need of man throughout time. Every cultural group has produced rituals of song and dance, crafts relating to a mode of living, and other means of expression through the manipulation of raw materials, sound and bodily movement. Man has utilized creative thought to produce scientific invention and mathematical formula, and to increase the use of his growing fund of knowledge.

CREATIVITY

The concept of creativity is a complex one, defined variously by different authorities and only recently becoming better understood. The term may be applied to individuals, processes, or products. Frequently it is erroneously or loosely employed; it may be applied to ideas or actions indirectly related to the creative act.

Creativity is a human response that has qualities of ingenuity, spontaneity, or uniqueness. It is a manner of expressing ideas or thoughts in an original way as opposed to conformity, to imitativeness, to the commonplace process of production, or to the less purposeful, free thinking of reverie. It is a restructuring of ideas or things resulting in newness or novelty, divergent from the obvious, tested, or safe. Spontaneity, flexibility, insight, imagination, interpretation, fluency, and inspiration do not in themselves represent creativity. Creativity involves a personal feeling or response as well as mental activity resulting in a concrete product.

One general interpretation of creativity implies talent or possession of various types of giftedness. This notion of creativity has traditionally been related to the artist who paints a picture to express experience, the musician who composes a lovely bit of harmony as an expression of his inner feeling, or the poet who selects appropriate words and puts them together creatively to express a thought. The idea includes the formulation of an aesthetically pleasing product.

But the complexity of creativity and a new approach to the term is demonstrated by ways in which authorities try to identify kinds or levels of creativity. Taylor[1] distinguishes five levels at which an individual may be creative. The first level, *expressive creativity,* involves independent expression where skills, originality, and the quality of the product are unimportant. This is exemplified in the spontaneous drawings of children. Taylor notes that creative experiences at this level are prerequisite to later, more advanced, and more highly controlled creative achievement. His second level, *productive creativity,* is distinguished by the fact that the individual gains mastery over some portion of the environment and produces an object. The object produced need not be discernible from the products of others. *Inventive creativity,* the third level, is marked by the presence of ingenuity. New uses of old parts are involved, though there is no contribution of new basic ideas, as in the accomplishments of inventors, explorers, and discoverers who seek new ways of seeing old things. Those who make significant alterations in the basic foundations or principles of a theory have achieved Taylor's fourth level, *innovative creativity.* Such accomplishments are made by the very few who have highly developed abstract conceptualizing skills. *Emergentive creativity,* the highest level, is rare. It requires the ability to absorb the experiences which are commonly provided and from this produce something that is quite different. The formulations of Einstein, Freud, Picasso, and Wright are cited as representative of this level of creativity.

Maslow[2] interprets two kinds of creativity. That creativity labeled *primary creativity* is the production that is new and different from the currently existing, and is likely to stem from the unconscious. *Secondary creativity* involves a deliberate and studied approach to a rational creation.

Eisner[3] identifies four types of creativity. The first he calls *aesthetic organizing,* or the ability to organize ideas, qualities, and actions into pleasing or harmonious relationships. Highly aesthetic contributions in visual arts, music, and poetry may fall into this category. Second, Eisner

---

[1] Taylor, I. A., "The Nature of the Creative Process," in P. Smith (editor), *Creativity: An Examination of the Creative Process* (New York: Hastings House, 1959), pp. 51–82. Quoted in Morris I. Stein and Shirley J. Heinze, *Creativity and the Individual* (New York: The Free Press, 1960), pp. 38–39.

[2] A. H. Maslow, "Emotional Blocks to Creativity," *Humanist,* Vol. 18 (1958), p. 239.

[3] Elliot W. Eisner, *Think with Me about Creativity* (Dansville, N.Y.: F. A. Owen Publishing Company, 1964), pp. 29–35.

identifies *boundary pushing,* or the generation of original ideas that push away from culturally defined boundaries that surround common objects or ideas, escaping from conventional stereotypes, such as different uses for established inventions, as installing an electric shaver outlet in an automobile. Boundary pushing is the extension of ordinary objects or ideas, or redefining or uniquely combining established objects. Third is *inventing,* or the construction of essentially new objects or devices by combining existing materials and ideas to produce a new product. Thomas A. Edison was such a creative inventor. Fourth is *boundary breaking,* the rarest of all creativity types, which is a conception of entirely new, fresh, dramatic assumptions which are opposed to traditional concepts. Einstein, Freud, and Galileo were such boundary breakers. Theirs was the ability to reject or make problematic major organizing ideas previously accepted as fact.

The Creative Individual

Recent studies by psychologists and educators have identified a number of characteristics of the creative individual. A creative person may demonstrate many of these traits but not necessarily all. Summarizing these characteristics, we find that the typical creative person is as follows:[4]

Intelligent beyond the average but not necessarily gifted.

Not necessarily interested in high marks in school.

Often discouraged by parents, teachers, and classmates, and sometimes is a problem to them.

Not a satisfied student, may drop out of school.

Less concerned about financial success; has low interest in economic values.

Lacking a well-rounded personality.

Energetic.

Independent in thought and action.

Flexible, permissive, tolerant.

Able to change, be different.

A nonconformist, "bohemian," not a joiner.

Apt to react in varied and unanticipated ways.

Accepting of innovation.

Willing to take larger than usual personal risks.

---

[4] Adapted from Marie Mehl, Hubert H. Mills, Harl R. Douglass, and Mary-Margaret Scobey, *Teaching in Elementary School* (third edition) (New York: The Ronald Press Company, 1965), pp. 295–296.

Often able to turn disorder into something meaningful.

Rather intuitive, has the ability to sense the implicit.

Sensitive but not easily hurt.

More imaginative than the average person.

Possessed of broad interests.

Humorous and playful.

Agile in mind; moves rapidly from one thing to another.

Attracted to complexity.

Not repelled by risks and the uncertainty of the unknown.

Apt to have a strong sense of destiny.

Likely to possess high opposite-sex characteristics.

Sometimes a slow starter but a quick finisher.

More likely to experiment with a variety of media.

Troubled by things generally but able to handle his own problems adequately; not afraid to act alone.

A self-possessed dreamer.

Elementary school teachers do not expect to make all children highly creative. From the above traits, however, we can derive clues for the creative characteristics desirable in human beings. Lowenfeld and Brittain[5] identify eight basic aspects of creativity emerging from studies in the arts and sciences. These are characteristics toward which teachers work with all children. Note how they reflect some of the traits listed above: *sensitivity* to problems, attitudes, and feelings of other people and the experiences of living; *fluency* in producing ideas and thinking freely; *flexibility* in adjusting to new situations; *originality* in responses; *ability to redefine or reorganize* ideas and things; *ability to abstract* by analyzing or seeing the relationship of various parts of a problem; *ability to synthesize* or combine several elements into a new whole; *ability to organize* by putting parts together in a meaningful way.

Creative Thinking

The creative individual engaged in any level of creative endeavor becomes involved in mental activity. The purposeful and orderly process of creative thinking is the process of deriving new meaning, new interpretation, or new relationships, or of developing new combinations and new patterns from experience and known facts. The process of consideration, of mental exploration, of ingenious and imaginative reasoning is the method whereby the new emerges from the old through thought.

---

[5] Viktor Lowenfeld and W. Lambert Brittain, *Creative and Mental Growth* (fourth edition) (New York: The Macmillan Company, 1964), pp. 7–9.

For this reason, some authorities use *creativity* synonymously with *creative thinking*.

Four stages in the process of creative thought were first identified by Wallas in 1926 as he analyzed the formation of a new thought.[6] *Preparation* occurs when the individual sets himself to the work of creation. He feels the need or the urge; he identifies the task; he utilizes all his resources of accumulated experience and skills to explore and analyze the medium of his problem. *Incubation* may be the stage in which the creator is not consciously working upon the solution of the problem. This may be a time of frustration, restlessness, brooding, withdrawal, or apparent indifference. During this period the subconscious is maturing the idea. *Illumination* is that unpredictable, happy point at which the insight occurs or the idea is consciously recognized. Emotion may be released, multiple ideas may follow in rapid succession. *Verification* is the final period during which the product is analyzed, tested, modified, or elaborated to the exact form of the finished product. All the creator's increased knowledge, skill, and experience, as well as a critical attitude, are needed.

In order to think creatively the individual needs competence in two areas. First, he must have some knowledge about the subject. Whether the desired end is the drawing of a house and barn, a poem about the first spring crocus, or a theorem within physics, the creator must have some knowledge about the topic that will guide his thinking. Second, the creator needs some skill in the manipulation of his medium. Without skill in the use of the pencil, the construction of a poem, or the thought processes of physics, the creator cannot complete the product though his knowledge about the subject and his talent for creative thinking related to the project may well modify the need for skills utilizing the medium.

Process and Product

In the creative process, the creator manipulates materials or ideas according to his experience and knowledge, seeing something new and unexpected or aesthetically beautiful, a resulting creative product.

Which is more important, the process or the product? Lowenfeld emphasized the creative factor as being a mode of expression, not content; the *how*, not the *what* of a product.[7] Surely we would agree that if creative thinking is important to the education of children, the creative process assumes much value. This process involves the identification of a

---

6 See G. Wallas, *The Art of Thought* (New York: Harcourt, Brace & World, Inc., 1926).

7 Viktor Lowenfeld, *Creative and Mental Growth* (revised edition) (New York: The Macmillan Company, 1952), p. 4.

feeling or an idea that needs to be expressed through some medium. Also involved is the direction of activity toward the completion of the product; decisions, manipulation, and ongoing evaluation become part of the process. All of the maneuvering an individual does, alone or in a group, in the act of creation becomes a part of the person and influences the development of his creative potential. The delineation of the problem, the sharing of ideas, the development of a concrete expression of an abstract feeling, is a process through which growth takes place and character is formed. Even if the product is entirely unsuccessful, the creator may sense satisfaction from the procedure and involvement that produced the end result. A child who has created a song that may be technically inferior has learned much about the process of creating.

The product created may sometimes assume more importance than the process developing it. The playwright, for example, is especially concerned about his creative product and its effect upon theater patrons. The process that the author goes through assumes less importance than the message held within the finished product. Perhaps a group of children who develop a rhythm pattern may also receive more value from the performance of the final activity than from the experiences in developing it.

We cannot indicate that either the process or the product will assume greater importance. Both are necessary in an aesthetic program. Generally a balance may be found, though different media may demand different emphases. The challenge to the teacher is to help children achieve ever more effective processes of creation and higher levels of production.

Valuing the Creative Product

Creativity involves a process yielding some concrete results or tangible product that represents communication between the creator and his audience. Authorities generally agree that the product should be useful, defensible, or satisfying to people. This means a social judgment is related to the value or degree of creativity (uniqueness and/or aesthetic harmony) assigned to the creative product. The judgment is usually made by experts in a particular field. In working with children this latter idea about the creative product at Taylor's level of expressive creativity is most important. To demonstrate creativity a child need not produce something that has never been done before or something always aesthetically expressive. Rather, he should demonstrate ability at his own level to produce or express in an individual way, to communicate feelings and ideas from a different point of view or with some amount of unique modifications arising from his own personal reaction.

Some people believe that creativity can be important because of the individual satisfactions of the creator, because the product created satisfies the personal purposes of the creator. The young child who models a pot of clay may produce a result of little social worth or aesthetic value. Only the child and his mother are delighted by the crude work. Even adults engaging in various arts as leisure time activities seldom produce something that will arouse the intellect or emotions of others. But the mere act of creating, of producing something that is one's own creation, is important to developing the creative potential of all people.

Children and Creativity

One of the problems related to the school's program for aesthetic development lies in the lack of understanding about *who* possesses the creative potential. Authorities agree that there is creative potential in all individuals; the difference lies in degree. Even within one individual, differences occur in the degree to which he may be creative in various fields. Most children in school possess more latent creative ability than most teachers suspect.

Creativeness is apparently dependent upon both hereditary characteristics and environmental factors. That some inherited ability influences creativity is suggested by the life of Mozart, who composed at the age of four years. On the other hand, studies have shown that artistic ability can be influenced by experience, for environmental factors may promote or delay the development of creative ability. It is generally agreed that, with encouragement, creativeness within an individual may be improved.

Very young children seem to demonstrate greater freedom of expression than older people. As children grow older, social pressures—especially group standards and social criticism—discourage originality or individuality. Children who make up their own songs or who dance "senselessly" meet adult ridicule, part of the stern reality of life. Imaginative stories may be met with derision. Schools themselves insist upon social conformity. Even television and advertisements influence child behavior and its natural spontaneity by demanding some kind of conformity. It is understandable that as the child grows older his behavior falls in line with socially acceptable attitudes and ideas. We cannot assume, however, that younger children will be the most creative; in spite of social pressures, many individuals make important creative contributions at mature ages. Such men as Victor Hugo and Beethoven produced original, lasting material when they were over fifty years of age.

The task of the teacher is to develop and encourage a psychological atmosphere within the classroom that accepts spontaneity, individuality, freedom of expression, creativity. A fine balance must be achieved between the creative behaviors and social conformity. The teacher must also remember that while creative potential is inherent in the individual, it is not a characteristic that can easily be turned on and off, as water in a faucet. Aesthetic expression is the result of all experience. A teacher cannot conduct a rigid and directive program most of the day and then expect to be successful in a nondirective art lesson. Creativity must be nourished—fed by many aesthetic experiences, cultivated by many opportunities to create, and fostered in a consistent atmosphere of flexibility and constructive teacher guidance.

Upon that ability common to problem solving and creative thinking, civilization has been developed, and man has changed his manner of living throughout history. It is this creativity, this expertness, that produces new ways of doing things that advance a culture; without it, the culture would stagnate. Our democracy in particular is dependent upon creative minds and the flow of new ideas that bring desirable change.

Elementary school teachers are giving serious consideration to the development of creativity as a result of extended researches, to the identification of creative characteristics, and to the definition of instructional techniques that will release creativity in children.

THE FINE ARTS PROGRAM

Teaching in the fine arts area has gone through a cycle of different approaches, beginning with the traditional method of exposing children to the products of experts and encouraging them to copy the work. Later, as the appreciation-imitation approach was modified, children were stimulated to free expression in the arts without much direction or guidance. Today the program seeking to achieve creativity and appreciation offers a variety of experiences. Some of these experiences deal with music, dance, and rhythms; some with arts and crafts; and others with dramatics, poetry, literature, and creative writing. Each of these areas has its characteristic activities.

Purposes: Two Directions of Communication

Aesthetic ideas necessitate a two-way communication just as language does; one must be able to express himself, but he must also be able and willing to receive, appreciate, and understand the expressions of others. Therefore the broad program that develops aesthetic responsiveness in children tends to emphasize two directions.

The *expressive* direction seeks to develop within each individual his own creative potential and the ability to recognize and use that potential. It involves experiences encouraging creativity, the self-assigned creative enterprise, and the development of skills (lessons in techniques and aesthetic principles) promoting greater satisfaction in creation. Also part of this direction are skills like musical and dramatic reproduction that enable individuals to recreate the creative product of another. Both skilled technique and creativity are essential for interpretation, meaning, and artistic reproduction.

The *receptive* direction seeks to help children appreciate and enjoy aesthetic qualities around them. Its purpose is to develop sensitivity and appreciation for the beauty of nature, for efforts of other cultures, for the aesthetic heritage of our society, and for current artistic contributions.

The purposes of the fine arts program are related to these two dimensions, and might include the following ideas:

1. To develop the individual creative potential, the unique personal expression in both intellectual and manipulative abilities, by the following:

    Providing experiences for self-expression with many media

    Developing skills and abilities in the manipulation of various media

    Promoting satisfaction and fulfillment in creation

    Encouraging emotional release through communication of feelings and ideas, and through freedom of expression

    Providing recognition for individual achievement

    Fostering interests for recreation and leisure time activities

    Encouraging creative thinking and willingness to modify and adjust to social arrangements in a democracy

2. To develop an aesthetic sensitivity and response to beauty and creativity, an appreciation for the creative efforts of others, by

    Developing a capacity for aesthetic response on the feeling and verbal levels

    Developing understanding of the aesthetic heritage of our society

    Developing sensitivity to beauty in all facets of life

    Encouraging participation in aesthetic social activities as group singing, dancing, symphony

    Fostering understanding and enjoyment of the aesthetic efforts of peoples of other cultures

    Understanding principles of good taste which make for more efficient consumers of manufactured products

Content

The content of the program in most schools is an outgrowth of curriculum units, other subject matter, various holidays and seasons, and other specific needs for art activities. The kinds of experiences that teachers provide are determined by the curriculum and the aesthetic needs and desires of the children as they live and work in the school and community. However, the *scope* of the fine arts program must be determined by the perspective that is placed on the content—the depth to which the content is explored. Children should have the opportunity to deal with various kinds of content activities within a frame of reference including these elements:

Observing, or looking and seeing things with sensitivity.

Exploring, in which children satisfy their natural curiosity by going beyond the routine path of life to find out about things.

Experimenting, or discovering and testing ideas and materials.

Appreciating, or being aware of and perceiving the worth of a thing.

Correlating, or determining the relationship or systematic connection between two things or two parts of one thing.

Evaluating, or judging the value of a thing.

Sharing, or communicating about an object, idea, or performance.

Enjoying, or feeling more than mere satisfaction in achievement or production.

Designing, or producing something with a scheme or plan in mind.

Organizing, or bringing together several parts into a meaningful whole.

Arranging, or determining proper order, position, or plan.

Constructing, or making a three-dimensional piece.

These elements are closely related and in certain situations may be difficult to distinguish. However, it is important that children have the opportunity to operate in all these approaches to art.

Time for Fine Arts Experiences

Three questions are of concern to teachers who want to provide aesthetic and creative activities in the fine arts: When should the activities be engaged in? How can they be related to the overall program? How much time should be allotted to each activity?

Usually courses of study or other school district bulletins help teachers arrive at a reasonable distribution of time. Definite allotments are commonly made for music and art; some musical activities such as rhythm and dance may be part of the physical education period; poetry and literature may be included with language arts. These time allotments are usually flexible and should be used with discretion.

Several methods of allocating time can be utilized. If twenty minutes a day are allotted for art, it may be wise to add together the twenty minutes of two or three days so that adequate time is available for an activity. If the creation of a cooperatively composed song runs over the usual time for music, the next period is simply cut short or the time is made up the next day. Time can be used flexibly for some subjects. Work on choric verse is a justified use of the language arts hour. Practicing a folk dance or painting a mural may well be part of the social studies hour, if the activity is related to the major topic being studied. This kind of flexibility is easily worked out in the self-contained classroom of the elementary school.

The teacher needs to recognize the amount of time necessary to complete the activity. Some activities may well be extended over a number of days; others necessitate completion in one day. To develop a lesson well, the teacher should allot enough time to prepare, to do, to clean up, and to evaluate. The introduction, motivation, or planning periods may vary in length according to the previous experiences of the children. The time for the activity must be predetermined and understood by all children. Preferably, the teacher warns the class a few minutes before the closing of the work period. The time for evaluation may also vary in length. If children do not complete the work they have undertaken in the period allotted, the teacher should schedule additional time so that the satisfaction of completion may be realized.

Another problem is how the aesthetic activities are to be made a part of the overall program. Some teachers believe that all activities should be integrated as part of the unit. Others believe that all aesthetic experiences should be presented regularly as special lessons and unrelated to other curriculum areas. The type of curriculum planning that utilizes both of these ideas is perhaps most effective.

Within the social studies unit all types of aesthetic activities are used, and apparently for two purposes. First, they allow the children to express their own ideas about the central topic in pictures, murals, creative songs, or stories. Second, some activities help the children better understand the cultural group being studied. Authentic songs and dances, study and use of realia, designs, and literature help the children understand the creative expression of others. Such activities are frequently made an integral part of unit study.

Aesthetic activities provided only in the context of the unit may not give the variety of experiences and skill development deemed valuable for children. Some special lessons that are unrelated to the units are needed. Activities associated with holidays, special auditorium programs, or other events such as unusual thunderstorms, the first spring flowers, or frost on the windows might well be motivation for special experiences. Or a teacher might plan a delightful hour of work with aluminum wire sculpture just to add variety of media, to provide another kind of creative experience for children.

Another way to bring aesthetic activities into the overall program is to make them part of the regular ongoing daily program. Opening exercises bring an opportunity to sing. Rest periods give an opportunity to listen to music played quietly. Many teachers find that some of the art experiences become excellent independent activities when children have completed other assignments. Easel painting, clay modeling, weaving, or finishing other uncompleted projects related to unit work may be continued quietly and individually with a minimum of teacher supervision.

Guidance in Basic Techniques

A constant controversy exists over teaching basic techniques versus providing basic experience, or freedom of uninhibited expression. Should children be provided with materials and allowed to manipulate them in their own way or should they first be given some guidance in the basic techniques for the use of the medium?

Educators today rather widely agree that persistent and formalized drill on the use of a paint brush, the mixing of colors, or any other technique usually should *not* precede more informal experiences with a medium. Both children and adults need to experience a period of exploratory manipulation before they can create or before they can understand specialized techniques. For example, the child who first uses calcimine paint will play with the brush on the paper just to see what happens to the paint. The child who handles clay for the first time will pound and push and pull experimentally before he produces a definite shape. All individuals seem to go through this exploratory phase to some degree, though the length of the period may differ among individuals or according to the material involved. Teachers therefore should allow time for free manipulation of some materials before they give much guidance in technique.

Generally speaking a child should first be provided with many kinds of experiences in many kinds of creative expression. Then as he himself expresses a desire for technical help, or as the teacher helps him to discover a need for it, the basic techniques are taught to help him gain greater satisfaction from the medium. Consciousness and insight will give children greater benefit from the formal teaching of skills.

Part of the rationale that suggests some manipulation prior to training in technique is the expectation that the child will be creative, that he will express some ideas in his own way. Ideas emerge from experience, and the experience may be the manipulation of a material or some other activity that develops and clarifies ideas so that they may be expressed in concrete form. For example, if children dramatize pioneer family life, they need much information gleaned from reading, talking, studying relics, and looking at pictures. For a dramatic production, this kind of knowledge is much more logical than instruction in the use of gestures, voice control, or how to move on the stage. If children are writing poetry, they may need to try out many phrases to see how they sound before the structure of the poem will develop.

The general rule of experience before technique cannot always be followed. In the case of some craft activities, the child needs instruction before he can participate. Before asking children to weave a basket, for example, the teacher will need to explain the procedure for weaving. Or if children are to do paper sculpture, they might first need some techniques in how to handle the paper. In these cases the teacher makes sure he demonstrates only technique and does not present materials in such a way that the children's creativity is influenced.

The presentation of techniques is not to be confused with a teacher's method of organizing the experience. When he helps children arrange the paper for finger painting and guides the distribution of the paint, he uses good common sense to avoid confusion and disorder. Once plans are made and material is distributed, the children are free to use the medium as they wish.

Evaluating the Arts

Instructional guidance which moves forward in terms of growth necessitates evaluation. However, work in the aesthetic area can be neither right nor wrong as it is in arithmetic; nor can it be labeled good, satisfactory, or poor as it is in handwriting. Evaluation in the aesthetic area must be flexible, must be designed to inspire children to freedom of expression and ever finer levels of creativity. Therefore all levels of creativity must be accepted in a way that will preserve the dignity of the individual and the intrinsic worth of the product.

Every opportunity should be taken to help children find satisfaction in the expression of their own ideas in widely varied responses. Satisfaction is the major criterion in both individual and group activities. Because satisfaction is a part of growth, evaluation helps children reach for ever more satisfactory levels of production. Arbitrary standards are generally avoided.

Evaluation for aesthetic activities takes several forms. In the primary grades, the art activities are provided as a means of expression, free from restraint or a great deal of criticism. Evaluation may be asking the simple question "Do you like it?" Children evaluate their art work in terms of the stories they tell or the purposes for which the project was made. They share reasons why they like a product, and point out the particularly pleasant aspects of it. A little more mature evaluation of this type involves answering questions from children and teacher about the picture. With the very young children part of the evaluation process is to encourage verbalization, or talking about the idea that has been concretely expressed. The teacher develops the atmosphere of acceptance without ridicule or judgment. As children become more sophisticated in their creative efforts, the teacher provides stronger guidance, helping the children use the art to decorate the classrooms, and helping them to understand some of the basic principles of art. They begin to identify the reasons why certain pictures or three-dimensional pieces are more pleasing than others. As curiosity is aroused in dealing with the art activities, teachers explain and help children identify such points as line, center of interest, mass, unity, subordination, variety, and color. The teaching of principles comes as a part of a well-thought-through plan to help children understand our cultural ideas of beauty.

For longer projects, ongoing evaluation is important. The group painting a mural is constantly studying it to be sure that all ideas are included, that the various parts hang together well, that color, proportion, and size are consistent. Self-evaluation as well as cooperative evaluation is encouraged.

Young children seem to use naturally and unconsciously some of the principles of art. For example, they create large centers of interest, subordinate lesser details, and produce effective contrasts. When a child creates a good example of a principle, the teacher may wish to point out the effect to the whole group. A compliment from the teacher may encourage others to try something similar.

Teachers who know the sensitivity of the individuals in their groups will be careful about evaluation given publicly. Frequently a private word or two will help a youngster without the embarrassment that might be caused by a group evaluation.

Teachers for the Fine Arts

The majority of the children in the nation are provided aesthetic experiences by the regular classroom teacher for two reasons. First, elementary schools have been traditionally organized around one teacher for one group of children. Second, there is neither money nor personnel available to provide specialists to teach the various arts in all schools.

There are several advantages to having the regular teacher responsible for the aesthetic program. He is more likely to know the interests and needs peculiar to his own group than is a teacher who teaches a single subject to a number of groups. He can more adequately integrate various aesthetic and creative experiences into the overall program, for creativity should be a part of all activity rather than limited to a special time and place. He can make special emphases when the situation calls for it. He can provide instruction to small groups at the moment they need it rather than wait for a special lesson when the whole group expects guidance.

On the other hand, it seems rather unrealistic to expect that every classroom teacher can be highly skilled in all areas or have the training and expertness demanded for some instructional situations. Special teachers with talent and ability in many ways can bring greater resources to the fine arts program. Because administrators recognize the need for some specialists, many schools are finding the means to provide them, particularly for instrumental and vocal music and for general arts and crafts.

Special teachers may operate in many ways. Some teach lessons at designated hours that may be enrichment lessons entirely unrelated to other activities. In this case the classroom teacher must assume responsibility for other types of creative experiences. Some specialists work closely with the teacher in planning and teaching lessons that not only enrich creative experiences but also are suggested by other curriculum areas or previous activities of the children. When a special teacher works with the regular teacher, or acts as a consultant, it is important that the teacher not leave the room when the specialist conducts a lesson.

The problem of special help is solved in some schools by the provision of services of special supervisors or consultants. Such consultants may conduct workshops to extend the skills of the teachers, prepare written materials for teacher and child reference, or gather materials for use in the classroom. They may visit classrooms regularly to find ways in which they may help improve instruction, or they may encourage teachers to call upon them when specific help is needed. Experts are very helpful in enriching aesthetic and creative experiences for children.

Patterns of teacher education also help to alleviate this problem. Some institutions give minors in special subjects, others help each young teacher develop strength in a particular area. In this way, a teacher may teach a regular class and act as a resource teacher in a special area to other teachers.

SPECIAL COMMENTS: MUSIC EDUCATION

Today most Americans can enjoy the music of symphony orchestras, small instrumental groups, soloists, operettas, ballets, marching bands, popular bands, etc., on television, radio, and in community concert series. Background music pervades shopping centers. Meetings may involve community singing. Neighborhoods organize groups that dance to folk music.

Because our modern society produces music, rhythm, and dance in many kinds of situations and in many modifications of form, the young child needs school experiences that will help him develop appreciation, discrimination, and ability to participate. The teacher must be sensitive to each aspect of music that stimulates the interest of individual children. Some may enjoy singing a melody, others may delight in rhythm or bodily movement, still others may prefer to listen passively, and others may enjoy playing an instrument.

Techniques of Music

Many music educators question the importance of teaching staff structure, music reading, and theoretical principles of music at the elementary school level. How many pupils will need and use such skills? How many gain real satisfaction from their use? How many thoroughly understand the theoretical principles of music that are taught within a heterogeneous group? Some music educators, however, believe that elementary children should develop literacy in the language of music just as they do in the mother tongue. Since many children have no contact with music in high school, they should learn the fundamentals of reading and writing music by the end of the eighth grade.

The teaching of mechanical techniques, therefore, is usually delayed. Since children cannot read with ease in the primary grades, the use of music books is easily postponed until the late third or fourth grade. Very little formal drill is used. Gradually, and as individuals can comprehend, children learn to find the key of a song, distinguish the time values of notes, and gain insight into other technical knowledge that in the past has been presented in formal drill periods.

Listening

Children should understand that music may demand various kinds of listening. The background music in the market may be listened to with less conscious effort than the formal performance of the chamber music group. In live programs of music, dance, or opera the reactions of the audience are a strong influence on the effectiveness of the performance, and enthusiasm on the part of the audience can only be generated through some understanding of the demands of the art form.

Today's teacher provides many situations for listening to music of various kinds. Children listen to simple, familiar songs. They learn melodies that are a part of the historical life of the American people and their world neighbors. They hear popular tunes, classical themes, and descriptive melodies. Children learn to identify the sounds of musical instruments, relating them to the melodic parts and to the total production of a number. When children learn to sing the various parts of a choral melody, they learn to distinguish the elements of harmony.

Children learn to listen for differences in rhythm; they learn early that music will tell them to skip and walk. Later, they distinguish between a waltz and a march, and the fun is not only in the listening but also in moving to the music.

Singing

Simple songs for children have improved over the years; they are really singable and the stories behind the words are interesting. As the songs for each grade level increase in complexity, they continue to interest children.

Beginners learn songs by rote. When children can read words they will look at songs written in books and follow the notes to sing up or down as the music indicates. As they gradually learn more of the mechanics of music, they become able to sing a new song from the notes without much previous listening to or study of the song.

Teachers encourage children to sing in sweet, unstrained tones. The aim is to develop true voices that are clear and flexible. The ability to carry a tune comes from the child's opportunity to listen to simple tunes, his efforts to sing, and the teacher's guidance. The monotone is rare. Children who do seem to have difficulty finding the pitch and singing the tune accurately need time and patient encouragement, and sometimes just the physical nearness of the teacher's or another strong singer's voice.

Usually part singing is taught in the intermediate grades. The background for part singing is set when the children sing rounds in first grade. Later the children sing descants, melodies that are sung above other melodies. By fourth grade children are ready for two-part singing; three parts may be introduced as boys' voices begin to change at the end of the sixth grade.

Frequently children are introduced to singing games in which the action is limited. Children sit in their seats or stand quietly so that the quality of singing is not influenced by energetic movement.

Recordings

The teacher who does not play the piano or who lacks talent for singing can easily procure records or tapes for accompaniment, appreciation, dancing, rhythms, and identifying musical instruments. Listening to stereophonic sound is a splendid aesthetic experience for children.

Instruments

As early as kindergarten children learn to use rhythm instruments to accompany marked rhythmical music or bodily movement. Intermediate and upper-grade children are taught to recognize size, shape, and tonal quality of individual instruments, and some children have the opportunity to learn to play them. Frequently musical groups are formed in second and third grades to teach use of harmonicas or other simple musical pipes. Older children become participants in bands or orchestras as an enrichment activity.

Producing Music

An important part of the aesthetic program is the way in which the teacher helps the children to be creative about producing music. Creativity comes through much experience and real enjoyment. After many musical experiences children may indicate the desire to create their own songs, rhythms, and dances. The teacher is sensitive to his need when it arises. His attitude must be free and flexible so that he may help the children learn to communicate through the language of music. He helps children develop their musical imagination as they consciously keep in mind sequence of melody, harmony, sounds, and tonal quality.

SPECIAL COMMENTS: ARTS AND CRAFTS

The art program seeks to achieve the general objectives of the aesthetic program through its emphasis on manipulation of and appreciation for many kinds of materials and products. The program is neither an inflexible pattern of preselected activities nor free expression without guidance or structure. Rather, a great variety of activities are employed, and all clues from children's needs, work, and interests are utilized to plan these experiences. Teachers find that painting or drawing or the graphic arts alone do not satisfy all aesthetic desires. Therefore the craft activities that involve many kinds of materials and three-dimensional products are introduced into the program.

Materials of Art

A trend that is both encouraging and creatively acceptable is the more efficient use of a greater variety of materials. For painting and drawing there are increasing numbers of crayons, calcimine paints, chalks, charcoal, and pastel crayons. The use of pencil for drawing is not encouraged in primary grades, and watercolors as a single medium are introduced only in the upper grades. Variations with these materials are achieved through the use of different textures and colors of papers, wet or dry papers, and combinations of media.

Crafts materials are as endless and varied as the imaginations of the children and their teacher. Clay, textiles, wood, and paper may be used in many kinds of craft projects and modeling. Scraps, such as bits of yarn, wire, metal, rubber, glass, shells, and colored paper, can be used for making baskets, dioramas, mobiles, and collages. The imaginative child can utilize many of the materials he has in his home (the plastic berry baskets, cardboard boxes, and used Christmas wrappings) to make numerous three-dimensional pieces.

To develop the children's creative use of materials, the teacher first helps the child understand the intrinsic nature of the materials. Demonstration and manipulation lead to skill development, appropriate use of materials, and conscious consideration of the various forms they may take. Standards for workmanship and appreciation of good workmanship are valued. The aim is to help the child think creatively about materials and be experimental and versatile using them.

Printing and lettering are important parts of a well-balanced art program. Children learn manuscript writing in the first grade, so if this skill is maintained throughout the grades, the matter of lettering is not difficult. Teachers help children to use Speedball pens, felt brushes, crayons, pencils, charcoal, and chalk for various kinds of labels and charts. Printing is worked out when children use potato stencils, silk screens, and linoleum blocks to make booklets, posters, and decorative papers.

Art in the Classroom Environment

The environment of the classroom reflects the children's art activities through attractive displays of paintings and drawings, child-planned bulletin boards, and exhibits related to other studies.

Children who have developed a sensitivity to beauty and who are proud of their classroom are eager to make it a pleasant place to live. They will bring flowers, knickknacks, bits of scrap to be arranged into displays of color and beauty. To illustrate their studies, they will collect articles and pictures to be placed on bulletin boards. They like to display their art work and will help make frames for paintings or arrange necessary space for a mural or illustrated timeline.

The excellent prints of art masterpieces that are now available add another dimension of appreciation when frequently referred to and enjoyed.

Art and the Curriculum

The development of creativity and the appreciation for it cannot be achieved in one or a series of art lessons that are unrelated to anything else in the classroom. The form, shape, color, and texture of all things children experience are not limited to art lessons. All beautiful objects must be considered and appreciated at the time and place and in the context in which they are found; children are guided to develop a sensitivity to the world around them. Thus art is an integral part of the curriculum. Just as we cannot logically isolate a people's art from their religion, leisure time activities, technology, and other elements of culture, we cannot isolate the school's art program from other subject areas that contribute to aesthetic and creative development. Creativity must be encouraged in every aspect of daily activity and over an extended period of time.

SPECIAL COMMENTS: LITERATURE

The teacher shows the importance of experience with fine literature by providing time and materials for children to explore, enjoy, and develop appreciation for the creative writing of others. Teachers know that appreciation for literature, and poetry, can be taught and becomes something that the spirit incubates. Delightful, happy, and stimulating experiences with literature and poetry reflect the teacher's own love for and appreciation of fine writing.

Characteristics of Good Literature

One of the first things a teacher or a child notices about a book is its appearance. The jacket, the binding, the format or arrangements of print and pictures on the page, the type of print, and the kind and quality of pictures are important to the attractiveness of the physical makeup.

Good literature has emotional appeal, a readable style, and content that stimulates child interest. Except for fantasy tales, literature should have the quality of being true to life. Good literature also demands ideas and activities as well as moral implications that are socially acceptable. Literature available for children is of great quantity. Stories include folk tales, fables, myths, epics, modern fanciful tales, stories of the here and now, stories of other times and places, animal stories, and biographies related to almost every corner of the world. Poetry can be found about everything: nature, fantasy, adventure, and all sorts of people.

Authors present ideas on life and living through humor, fantasy, or realism; and the resulting literature will vary in structure, tone, and appeal. Artistic writing is pleasing and in accordance with cultural standards that determine choice of words, phrases, and sentence structure, and is charming by the mental picture it evokes. Not only the ideas but the style reflect the creativity, personality, and thinking of the author. Actually there is little difference between prose and poetry; the experts themselves have a hard time defining them.

Satisfaction through Literature

Reading or listening to good literature gives the child knowledge about the characters of the story and mental pictures of them; in effect it helps the child "live with" the characters. Identification in this way helps the child meet a number of emotional needs; he experiences personal security, belongingness, the feeling of loving and being loved. He gains a sense of satisfaction through knowing about people and the things that make their lives different. Children develop appreciation for change and variety in the products of civilization and in the style of living. They find aesthetic satisfaction in realizing that other people enjoy the products of creativity. Insight into other people's problems and ways of living may well give guidance to children as they develop into mature and well-balanced individuals. Literature can develop within the reader an appreciation for moral and spiritual values and a desire for beauty; it can provide an avenue of escape from the monotony of daily life.

Poetry in Particular

No longer is poetry a problem to children because of forced memorization. The appreciation of poetry comes in the feeling for vigorous and colorful vocabulary, the beautiful sequence of words, and the singing quality rather than formal analysis of meter and related structural elements. Children enjoy appealing ideas and the humor and beauty of a poem rather than the moral lesson it teaches. The successful teacher whose pupils really love poetry has created a mood each time the children experience a poem. His introduction is simple and to the point. He waits for reactions of the children rather than asking formal and pointed questions.

Creativity, as an individual trait, is increasingly being recognized by educators as a necessary part of the curriculum which seeks to develop a humane person. In a computerized, impersonally urbanized culture, children need elementary school experiences that will free them to think creatively and develop skills in several kinds of creative production. They also need opportunities to understand and appreciate the creative products of others. Teachers are giving considerable thought to the kinds of experiences, not only in the fine arts program, but in other areas of the curriculum, that will help children to be sensitive, appreciative people, enjoying the efforts of others, and able to engage in the kind of thinking and action that will result in creative endeavor.

RECOMMENDED READINGS

ANDERSON, WARREN H. *Art Learning Situations for Elementary Education.* Belmont, Calif.: Wadsworth Publishing Company, Inc., 1965.

GARRETSON, ROBERT L. *Music in Childhood Education.* New York: Appleton-Century-Crofts, Inc., 1966.

GETZELS, JACOB W., and PHILLIP W. JACKSON. *Creativity and Intelligence.* New York: John Wiley & Sons, Inc., 1962.

KAPLAN, MAX, and FRANCES J. STEINER. *Musicianship for the Classroom Teacher.* Chicago: Rand McNally & Company, 1966.

KAUFMAN, IRVING. *Art and Education in Contemporary Culture.* New York: The Macmillan Company, 1966.

KNELLER, GEORGE F. *The Art and Science of Creativity.* New York: Holt, Rinehart and Winston, Inc., 1965.

MARKSBERRY, MARY LEE. *Foundation of Creativity.* New York: Harper & Row, Publishers, Inc., 1963.

MC FEE, JUNE KING. *Preparation for Art.* Belmont, Calif.: Wadsworth Publishing Company, Inc., 1961.

MERRITT, HELEN. *Guiding Free Expression in Children's Art.* New York: Holt, Rinehart and Winston, Inc., 1964.

NYE, ROBERT E., and VERNICE NYE. *Music in the Elementary School: An Activities Approach to Music Methods and Materials* (second edition). Englewood Cliffs, N.J.: Prentice-Hall, Inc., 1964.

SHUMSKY, ABRAHAM. *Creative Teaching in the Elementary School.* New York: Appleton-Century-Crofts, Inc., 1965.

SMITH, JAMES A. *Creative Teaching of the Creative Arts in the Elementary School.* Boston: Allyn and Bacon, Inc., 1967.

SWANSON, BESSIE R. *Music in the Education of Children* (second edition). Belmont, Calif.: Wadsworth Publishing Company, Inc., 1964.

The Changing Role of the Teacher

Part 3

Change in the curriculum inevitably leads to change in what the teacher does in the classroom. The considerations that each teacher must deal with in ordering the classroom environment and in implementing instruction with pupils are dealt with here. The new curriculum brings with it new challenges to the use of time and space, to skill with teaching materials, to plans for teaching, and to the assessment of the results of teaching. Because the teacher is important as an individual, ideas about human relationships and self-understanding are included in this part.

Implementation of Teaching: Planning

15

These last chapters are addressed more directly to the teacher and to teaching than are those in Parts One and Two. Much has been said and even more implied about teaching in earlier chapters, but here the focus is to be more directly on the teacher as a professional person, and on teaching as a set of professional decisions and actions.

The curriculum has been defined as the school's plan for the intentional modification of pupil behavior in the direction of agreed-upon educational goals. That plan must be implemented in the classroom. Instruction is the totality of actions taken to realize or implement the plan. Teaching is the presentation of the plan to pupils, and learning is the pupil's responses to the presentation. Admittedly this description is an oversimplification, but it does help to convey the nature of these closing chapters.

Thus far attention has been directed primarily to the changing curriculum of the elementary school. A variety of forces at work have been identified which press for change. There has been discussion in general terms of the responses, conceptually and ideationally, which people who work with the elementary school and its curriculum are making to the changing school. Chapters have been devoted to each of the several areas of the elementary school program in a further and more specific effort to portray the current and emerging nature of curriculum plans. Now we turn to a more direct focus on the teacher and his teaching. For it is through teachers that we come to have, operationally, elementary education. Teachers work with pupils in the school. This is not to deny the realities of children learning without recourse to teachers. But in the elementary school we look to a teacher to guide and direct and insure learning. The earlier cited statement from the Education

Policies Commission on issues in elementary education makes this statement in its concluding paragraphs:

> Many of the contemporary issues in elementary education will persist. New issues will arise. One element, however, is common to all issues in elementary education. This is the central role of the teacher. The teacher, more than any other factor, determines the quality of elementary education. There is no substitute for a person of high integrity, sensitive to children and professionally trained, to perform the teaching function. . . .[1]

Thus, these closing chapters are devoted to teaching and to the teacher. The remainder of this chapter concerns itself with the planning and carrying out of teaching plans and strategies. The chapters which follow look at the selection and use of materials, at living with children, at the evaluation of teaching and learning, and at the teacher himself.

PLANNING FOR THE TEACHER

One kind of planning for teaching is usually done *for* the teacher and takes place at the school system level. This planning encompasses a great many things such as decisions on general goals to be achieved, a choice of overall curriculum organization, implied and stated preferences for methodology, extent of materials of instruction to be made available, a general plan for evaluation and for recording and reporting the progress of pupils, and so on.

At one time the influence of the system was quite complete and specific. Teaching plans were handed to teachers, and teachers were expected to follow them in their work in the classroom. This method was considered to be a way of monitoring what was happening and of insuring a certain quality of teaching in all schools and classrooms in the system. However, this method gradually came to be viewed as a way of working which placed too great a constraint on the teacher. As professional training improved, teachers were seen as very legitimate sources of teaching ideas themselves. Too, it became increasingly clear that any general set of teaching plans and procedures developed for a total school system called for modification and adaptation for specific building units in the system where pupil populations differed greatly from the assumed "norm."

What has followed in more recent times has been an extension of autonomy to the individual elementary school building, and to the individual teacher. In most instances there are limits on this autonomy, of course. A school system does have an existence as an organization in

---

[1] Educational Policies Commission, *Contemporary Issues in Elementary Education* (Washington, D.C.: NEA, 1960), p. 25.

which there will be rather general agreement on goals to be sought, and the system will make every effort to inform teachers of these goals, to win their acceptance of them, and to assure itself that classroom instruction is oriented toward their realization. Similarly, there will be general agreements as to what will transpire in any given area of instruction, including usually an overall year-by-year framework statement of work to be accomplished.

Instructional guides. These systemwide agreements are usually made known to teachers through a series of published instructional guides. Typically these are developed by levels within the school system. That is, there will be a guide for elementary school science, or perhaps one for science in the primary grades and another for science in the intermediate grades. These guides attempt a concise but clear and complete description of what the school system expects will be done at various levels of the organization, including units of work to be developed, topics to be studied, skills to be mastered, and other topics.

Resource units. As an accompaniment to these instructional guides, many school systems furnish teachers with resource units. These resource units contain a wealth of information and suggestions for the development of a given series of learning experiences in the classroom. They describe things which teachers might do with their classes; they direct attention to materials of instruction available for use in conjunction with suggested experiences; they contain directions for building objects or processing materials when called for; they include suggestions for evaluating what has happened. A resource unit is a catalog of ideas from which a teacher might draw in his efforts to bring a part of the curriculum to life in the classroom.

Teaching sequences. Usually, resource units have not been organized around particular or preferred teaching sequences. A common practice has been for the teacher to develop an anticipated sequence of learning experiences, using the resource unit for help in so doing. This sequence is altered, then, in ways that become appropriate after the study is under way in the classroom. Thus, there could be many acceptable sequences through a particular learning unit as a function of the dynamics of a given classroom group.

PLANNING THE SCHOOL YEAR

The classroom teacher must look longitudinally at the school year itself as a unit for planning.

Planning over the school year. The teacher is wise to lay out at the beginning of the year a tentative time plan for dealing with the complete range of responsibilities for teaching that he is expected to encompass. In such a plan, the weeks and months that school will be in session would be tentatively allotted to the various broad topics or units of work, to the kinds of skill extension and refinement, to desired aesthetic experiences, and so on, that are considered to be legitimate expectancies. Clearly, once the work of the year actually gets under way and the teacher begins to be more intimately acquainted with his class, adjustments will need to be made in this long-range time plan. There is a great deal of truth in the idea that "plans are made to be departed from." However, when departures are made on the basis of an anticipated use of the school year, the teacher is clearer in his mind as to just what it is that he is extending, or cutting down, or omitting entirely from the original plan.

Planning for learning units or enterprises. Within this year-long time plan the teacher needs to make other anticipated longitudinal choices. He must estimate how long a given learning enterprise, such as a unit of work in social studies or science, or an initial experience with long division, or a unit on liquid measurement, is likely to continue in the classroom. Sometimes such choices are made wholly or partially at the system level. A teacher may be required to spend nine weeks on each of four social studies units suggested for his grade and six weeks on each of six science units. Or the system may simply suggest what are considered to be most appropriate time spans for various learning units at different age and grade levels. In art the time may be tentatively divided in terms of the various media a teacher wants his class to experience; in physical education the time may be divided according to games that are appropriate on a seasonal basis. Of course, any such decisions must be held as tentative ones, for once the actual classroom experience is under way any number of things may cause the teacher to shorten or to lengthen the anticipated block of time. Child motivation may be extremely high or low in relation to particular enterprises, and adjustments in time will have to be made accordingly. Unforeseen developments on the social scene may make it wise to carry certain experiences to points not originally called for at all. Again, the plans may often be departed from, but the choice involved is more likely to be seen as the choice that it really is when such a tentative kind of time division among learning units in all areas has been made.

Time Plans and Unanticipated Teaching Opportunities

Questions are often raised with respect to the teacher's exploiting unanticipated teaching opportunities that arise during the school year.

Obviously, this is not a simple question of time, but a more involved matter related to curriculum planning generally. If the reader has learned his lesson well from the earlier chapters in this book, he will realize that a commitment to one point of view in curriculum suggests one answer to this situation, while allegiance to another suggests a different approach. This becomes a time question when it is interpreted in time terms. That is, does a teacher have time to lay aside previously made plans when such unanticipated opportunities arise? Needed immediately is some interpretation of the phrase *lay aside*. Does this mean to lay aside for a day or for a few days—or does it mean to drop some ongoing study completely in favor of this more important opportunity for teaching? This matter calls for sound professional judgment on the part of the teacher. No doubt certain "golden opportunities" will develop; teachable moments arise almost every day. In each instance there will be several avenues for action open to the teacher, ranging from completely ignoring the opportunity to using it to launch a major learning enterprise.

It is difficult to set down general criteria to use in making such decisions. We can agree that no teacher should be so saddled with prior plans that he must let all such teachable moments pass by. At the same time, it may be unwise to cast aside certain well-thought-out but only partially developed learning situations too readily. Some things that must be kept in mind can be pointed out. Small projects that arise can often be worked into the time plan for a few days without really dropping anything when the class is highly motivated to pursue the matter. Time allotments may simply be cut back here and there to make room for this venture. Also, a teacher must be careful in making an assessment of the extent of pupil interest in certain unanticipated developments. Often only a few students are really concerned about the happening or could profit from the additional learning opportunity. In such cases, time can usually be found for these students to pursue the matter without drastically altering the ongoing program of the total class group. Another consideration that teachers might well apply in such decisions relates to the need for children to have opportunities for carrying on a learning enterprise "all the way" at times, starting with the unexpected but nonetheless wholehearted identification of an area of concern to them. Such opportunities should not be withheld from pupils completely. There is a certain kind of enthusiasm and satisfaction that comes from identifying something important and carrying through a study plan accordingly. A good many school systems recognize this and try to plan for it accordingly by assigning a learning load to a particular grade level that makes a place for some pupil-teacher selections of this kind if they develop. These become program elements along with the standard units of work that are to be covered each year.

There are certain elements, as we will show, that must be planned for in a good school day or week. These elements grow out of the total commitment which the elementary school has to the education of children, and they must be combined into a teachable classroom program. There are many ways to develop a teaching schedule; we shall indicate what seems to us to be most defensible and feasible at this time. The school week is the most useful and realistic time span for the teacher to try to deal with in his programming, in our judgment. It is more efficient to think of balancing the "educational diet" for children over the span of a week than of a day. Some things should undoubtedly occur daily in the classroom program, but all things need not and cannot. This is true for program areas as such, like health and science, and it is even more true for the nature of the experience provided within any one program area. It must be remembered that the emerging curriculum calls for time for experiences with subject matter and time for experiences with various intellectual skills. Thus, while the social studies may be scheduled daily, pupils may construct something one day, do research on another, and discuss together on still another. The teacher may include aesthetic experiences on a regular schedule in the program, having music on one day and art on another, or having personal production at one time and appreciation at another.

The school day may seem the most logical unit for planning, and certainly it is a time unit the teacher must deal with, but we see this more as a vertical experience within the space of one week. A teacher is faced at the close of one day with decisions as to what shall be done the next, and so it is on through the week. Day-to-day planning decisions become adjustments within the weekly plan that are necessary and possible as the class attempts to accomplish what has been set for them to do in that week.

Planning the Classroom Program

The following types of experiences must be planned for in a balanced classroom program. Time must be found weekly and/or daily, depending on the particular circumstances at hand, for these elements:

1. Time for a comprehensive and somewhat leisurely experience centered on some significant aspect of the social, natural, or technological environment.
2. Time for direct and systematic help in the extension and refinement of language and arithmetic skills.

3. Time for aesthetic experiences, both creative and appreciative, and very broadly defined to include music, art, poetry, literature, and the dance.
4. Time for exercise and for rest and relaxation.
5. Time intermittently to participate in schoolwide activities.

Following are two examples of classroom programs developed with these five points in mind, for primary and intermediate grade groups.

A Possible Plan for a Primary Group

9:00–9:15	Getting the day started (sharing and planning)
9:15–10:15	Developing the unit of work (exploring some aspect of the social, natural, or technological environment)
10:15–10:30	Recess
10.30–11:50	Time for work with language and arithmetic, in groups and individually (a recess period would come from about 11:15–11:25)
11:50–12:00	Preparing for lunch (some will eat at school; some will go home)
12:00–1:00	Noon hour (lunch and recreation)
1:00–1:30	Aesthetic experiences of various kinds
1:30–1:50	Physical education
1:50–2:00	Preparing for dismissal (including an informal look back at the day's work in anticipation of tomorrow)
2:00	Dismissal

A Possible Plan for an Intermediate Group

9:00–9:15	Getting the day started (sharing and planning)
9:15–11:00	Developing the unit of work (exploring some aspect of the social, natural, or technological environment; a recess period would come from 10:00–10:15)
11:00–11:10	Recess
11:10–11:50	Flexible time for work with language and arithmetic (in groups and individually)
11:50–12:00	Preparing for lunch (some will eat at school; some will go home)
12:00–1:00	Noon hour (lunch and recreation)
1:00–2:00	Additional time for work with language and arithmetic
2:00–2:30	Combined recess and physical education time
2:30–3:20	Aesthetic experiences of various kinds (perhaps a class club one day a week)
3:20–3:30	Preparing for dismissal (including an informal look back at the day's work in anticipation of tomorrow)
3:30	Dismissal

Obviously, any such attempt to indicate a possible schedule for using time obscures the dynamics that are so much a part of the classroom situation. It is impossible to call attention to all of the shifts and changes a teacher and a class may decide to make in any given week or any particular day in such an arrangement in light of the situation at hand. Periods of time normally allotted to certain kinds of experiences may become much longer or shorter in order to get particular jobs started or completed. Unit-of-work experiences, which usually come in the early part of the day, may be shifted to the afternoon in order to take advantage of a particular resource visitor (Mr. Brown, the city recreation leader, can leave his office at 1:30 to talk with us about plans for the new park), or a field trip (the postmaster suggests that we come about 2:00 in order to see the big pile of mail that arrives at the post office for distribution the next day). The time for aesthetic experiences may shift according to the availability of facilities (we can get the all-purpose room at 11:00 this morning for our dancing), the weather (there are such beautiful clouds to sketch this morning), or the general mood of the class (let's sing for awhile; it may make us all feel a little brighter).

Maintaining balance in a changing program. It does follow that a shift in any one part of the weekly or daily anticipated work plan calls for shifts in other parts of that same day's program or in a general rearrangement of work expected to be done over the week. In our view, the teacher has a continuing responsibility to insure balance and comprehensiveness in the child's learning experience at school. Therefore, shifts and changes are made with this responsibility in mind. For instance, no matter how exciting and crucial the unit of work experience may become, it is hard to defend taking more than a given amount of time each day for it, except under very unusual conditions. When such occasions present themselves, as they will intermittently, and it seems to be important to stay with some situation for a period of time extending over several days, the teacher has a responsibility to help the class to sense what is happening to the rest of their educational "diet" and to project some plans beyond these immediate crucial days for bringing a semblance of balance back into the program. It must be remembered that balance is not something that must or will occur on a daily or even a weekly basis. Balance will usually emerge over a longer period of time than that. What is important is that the teacher and the class can look back over a balanced and comprehensive classroom program from time to time during the year.

Time for schoolwide activities. The time that is wisely invested in intermittent schoolwide activities, such as programs, assemblies, school safety drives, and the like, must inevitably come out of the schedule. Knowing ahead of time that such an activity is to take place enables a teacher and class to plan their work accordingly. These experiences are usually rather well spaced throughout the year, and the time they take away from class activities seems justified in light of the experiences themselves.

Current Views of Decisions about Teaching

At the present time the intricacies and complexities of developing effective teaching plans are recognized more than they have been in the past. It is not possible here to discuss the development of specific teaching strategies for particular subjects or types of pupils. We can call attention to variables to be dealt with and to tasks which are inherent in the development of most teaching plans, no matter the focus of the study or the children to be taught, and this will serve as a reminder of the complex nature of the job.

Any plan for teaching must take into account several variables. These have to do with the subject matter to be taught (including both content and process), intellectual skills to be taught, pupils to be taught, and the person who will do the teaching. Each variable in its own way sets limits on and opens up possibilities for ways of working. Furthermore, the more completely we come to understand these variables the more careful, deliberate, and demanding looms the job of developing effective teaching strategies. For instance, as we have come to accept the idea of structure, both conceptual and methodological, in subject matter we have had to accept differences in structure from one subject area to another. There are differences in the way in which one subject matter is best learned and taught in comparison to another. Learning and teaching in the humanities are not the same as they are in the sciences; learning and teaching in the natural sciences are not quite the same as they are in the social sciences. Therefore the nature of the subject matter to be dealt with has a direct bearing on the development of the teaching plan.

The same is true when including goals in teaching that have to do with thinking and with intellectual skills. Evidence accumulating suggests that the growth of thinking power broadly conceived is developmental. That is to say that success with a given way of thinking is dependent on earlier success with other ways.

Ideas from Piaget about the necessary balance between assimilating experiences (the taking in of information) and accommodating experiences (time to alter present schema to new information) suggests a necessary pacing and alternating of kinds of experiences in a teaching plan as it extends over time. Plans, too, should reflect a shift for the teacher to more question asking and less question answering.

Little need be said concerning the way in which pupils affect plans.

General knowledge about all children and learning (each child is unique, learning is individual, learning is an active process, cultural background affects learning, and so on) combines with specific knowledge about particular pupils with whom the teaching plan or strategy is to be used. This pupil variable alone can make a plan that is superbly suited to one group of children and most unsuited to another.

The teacher himself is a variable to contend with. Perhaps the way to treat this variable is to say "know thyself" and "to thine own self be true." There is such a thing as a personal teaching style; any teacher does some things very well and other things not so well. To assume that the teacher's talents should not affect a teaching plan is to overlook an important detail.

Thus, generally, teaching plans must include the following:

1. The transposing of subject matter into elements that can be learned.
2. The specifics of the things which pupils will do, and the order in which they will do them.
3. The actions which the teacher will take to make certain that pupils are able to do what they must.
4. Ways of knowing at the outset, during, and after a learning episode the status of pupils (what they have learned and are learning) with respect to it.

All of this presupposes a level of professional competence on the part of the teacher; he must understand the content and the processes to be taught and the ways in which they can be taught.

At the present time there are some people who wonder if the regular classroom teacher should be expected to handle adequately all of these variables in his planning. They suggest that better overall plans and more efficient sequences of experiences for carrying the class to learning goals would eventuate in the classroom if they were predesigned for teachers. They have in mind the development of empirically tested arrangements for learning which become literally instructional "systems" which the teacher would activate. The extemporaneous in teaching would be decreased, the predetermined increased. A good deal of predesign is actually happening in the context of the experimental programs in various areas mentioned earlier. In these, investigators are trying to ascertain the consequences to the pupil of going about things one way or another in terms of the goals which are held for the curriculum. As investigators determine that a given thing can, with some assurance, be accomplished in a particular way, they tend to urge teachers to follow the pretested plan. Keep this in mind as you read on and we will return to it later in this chapter.

Useful at this point is a closer look at each of the program elements included in the specimen daily programs referred to above.

THE UNIT OF WORK: A PLAN
FOR TEACHING

The unit of work is a scheme considered by most elementary educators as a preferred way of getting at problems and developing understandings, especially in the social studies and science aspects of the curriculum. The unit makes great demands on the classroom teacher, calling for a broad informational or subject matter background, considerable understanding of and empathy for children, and a varied set of teaching skills. But the results that follow from a well-developed unit of work are most satisfying.

In the elementary school, the units of work developed at various grade levels assume a strategic importance in the overall scheme of things. Whether they are separate social studies units and science units or joint ones, they play a central role in much that happens in a classroom. In addition to the specific social studies or science study goals to be achieved, the unit experiences typically provide motivation and inspiration for activities in other areas of the curriculum and a setting in which learnings from other areas can be functionally applied. As we consider the unit of work idea be especially alert to the dynamics of the strategy for teaching which is the essence of good unit development and try to anticipate the challenge to this strategy which may come from current curriculum improvement efforts. Reflect specifically on the issue of pre-design versus the extemporaneous in teaching.

The label "unit of work" has been put on a variety of ways of working in elementary education. Some teachers use the phrase as a term synonymous with a given block of subject matter, and many textbooks are no longer made up of chapters but contain a list of units. Another use of the label stems from the earlier days of project teaching in connection with a learning activity that is, in the main, child originated and child consummated. Units of work have also been categorized as being "subject matter" and "experience" or "activity" units. These labels differentiate between units that would be highly prearranged or more emergent in the classroom, and the balance that will be sought between subject matter and the learning process itself as the unit takes form.[2] However, these labels are only partially meaningful and useful. In our view, all well-

---

[2] See William H. Burton, "Implications for Organization of Instruction and Instructional Adjuncts," *Learning and Instruction*, Forty-Ninth Yearbook, National Society for the Study of Education (Chicago: University of Chicago Press, 1950), p. 218, for a discussion relevant to this matter.

developed units of work are concerned with subject matter and with experiences and activities of many kinds. Similarly, the teacher is concerned about both the content and the process aspects of the developing learning enterprise. The use of such seemingly contrasting labels has grown up in attempts to call attention to matters of emphasis, or of degree, rather than of kind. It is in this sense that they may be useful as points of reference.

Defining the unit of work.   Growing out of what has been said here, the unit of work can be defined as a series of highly related learning experiences of various kinds, all focused on some significant aspect of the social or scientific-technological environment, and having as its purpose the development of understandings, attitudes, values, appreciations, and skills that lead to modifications of behavior that are important to the children involved and to the wider society.

Selecting units of work for development.   Most often the elementary school teacher is able to exercise some choice over the selection of specific units to be developed in the classroom. While some school systems may still stipulate units to be covered, the more general tendency is to include a place for teacher determination to play its part.

Particular school systems will not only develop a broad curriculum framework, but will also develop rather extensive lists of units of work that are related to the theme at each grade level and that stand the test of general significance. In such situations the teacher is asked to select units from the list prepared for his grade; thus there is some element of choice involved.

School districts will expect the teacher to determine the specific units to be developed over the year. Thus, if the general theme for the year is one of "exploring the local community" in a primary grade, the teacher is free to approach this theme in whatever way seems to make most sense to him and to his class. Specific units may eventually be developed on "supplying our community with water," or on "working in our community," and so on. Similarly, if the general theme at an intermediate grade level is one of "becoming acquainted with the development of the United States," the teacher is free to do what he will with Colonial America, the Westward Movement, and so on.

Selecting when there is no predetermined framework.   Should a teacher find himself working in a school where there is no predetermined framework at all for the curriculum, he will need some criteria by which units of work will be selected, and some guidelines to help him in the planning that he may do by himself and with his class. In this connection a number of things readily come to mind. Such a teacher will need:

1. To make himself aware of units of work already experienced at school by the pupils with whom he will be working.

2. To know something of the general nature of the group of children that will be in his class.

3. To assure himself of the social significance of any units of work he might contemplate developing over the year.

4. To assure himself that the pupils in his class will find the units suitable to their abilities and maturational level.

5. To know something of the local community in which the school is situated and the kind of life that children there generally lead, because it might bear on the unit to be selected.

6. To consider his own background of knowledge, skill, and experience, and satisfy himself that he can now handle the contemplated unit successfully or can prepare himself to handle it.

7. To assure himself that there are sufficient material resources, such as reading material, audio-visual aids, construction materials, and the like, in the school district and community resources to be utilized to make it possible to develop the contemplated unit efficiently and comprehensively.

Developing "supports" for unit teaching. The importance of the seven points listed immediately above and the time that it takes to follow through on them have had considerable influence on the decisions of school systems to develop both an overall framework in curriculum and lists of possible units for development within the framework.

It is important that individual units selected are appropriate for particular age levels of children involved. Also children should experience a cumulative series of socially significant unit studies over the elementary school years. These are considerations that cause many school systems to develop broad curriculum designs for their total elementary school program. The earlier noted selection of key concepts and generalizations to be developed in the social studies and in science is an effort to insure that subject matter dealt with is of significance. The task for the teacher then becomes one of planning units in which these concepts and generalizations can be dealt with.

Along with these concerns over significance come some others that are quite close to the classroom teacher. It has been mentioned that unit teaching is demanding; it calls for the use of a variety of approaches to learning, fed by a variety of instructional materials and resources. Many school systems have found that teachers, if they are to do a good job of unit teaching, need help in locating materials, in having materials made available to them, in knowing what to utilize in the community in the way of learning resources, and so on. Such assistance extends to the matter of helping teachers to broaden their own backgrounds of knowledge, skill, and experience to make possible the kind of unit teaching envisioned here.

It is out of this general "need" setting that the already mentioned concept of the "resource unit" has developed. Many school districts not only list a great many possible units of work that might be brought to life in the classroom, but they furnish the teacher with a catalog, literally, of ideas for the unit, of materials found in the district and in the community that are useful in the unit, and of suggestions for broadening their own backgrounds, and so on. This catalog gives the busy classroom teacher a kind of support and security in approaching the development of a new unit of work. It enables him to anticipate some of the problems that may eventually develop in the unit; it directs him to materials and resources, and to techniques and procedures for solving these problems when they do develop. Certainly such supporting arrangements are commendable, in our view.

THE UNIT OF WORK AND THE EDUCATIVE PROCESS

As a way of organizing classroom activities, the unit-of-work method is consistent with what we know about children and the learning process. Let us take a look at some of the characteristics of the unit that lead to this conclusion.

Teacher-Pupil Planning

The unit of work makes a place for a great deal of teacher-pupil planning. Children will be involved from the outset, sometimes as a part of the unit selection itself, as active partners in developing the learning enterprise. Thus, the teacher utilizes the psychological information that describes the child as an active, goal-seeking individual who will be more likely to understand and accept learning tasks and to carry through on them with enthusiasm if he has helped to select and plan them. By doing a great deal of planning with the class the teacher is much more likely to keep the unit experience close to the children. Although original unit selections are made with an eye to child maturity levels, they must be constantly assessed in terms of the particular children with whom the teacher is working. Some years ago, Jersild commented on the social studies curriculum thus, ". . . the problem becomes one of scaling to size the ideas and concepts that go into the social studies curriculum and of harnessing these to projects that have meaning in the everyday lives of children"[3] The task of making these ideas meaningful to children is a

---

[3] Arthur T. Jersild, *Child Development and the Curriculum* (New York: Bureau of Publications, Teachers College, Columbia University, 1946), p. 115.

perennial concern, not only in the social studies but in other areas of the curriculum as well. The use of teacher-pupil planning techniques can do much to keep this concern before the classroom teacher. The teacher still preplans but all such planning has a kind of anticipatory focus and is subject to change.

Planning between teacher and pupils covers a wide variety of things related to the unit, with the teacher quite active as a guide and participant in these sessions. Theman does a good job of helping teachers to sense some aspects of their role in these sessions. She suggests that the teacher help children to remember such factors as:

Balance. What else do we need to do?

Sequence. What ought we do first?

Time. Will we have time to do all these things today?

Consideration for others. Will a work period at that time bother others?

Permission. We need to have our parents' written permission to take a trip. How can that be done?

Course of study. This is a topic we are required to study. . . . How and when can we include this topic in our plans?

Sharing opportunities. Should we always select the boys who can do the best work with tools or should the girls be given a chance?[4]

Other questions come readily to mind. Some would be attempts to satisfy the teacher that material covered up to a certain point in the unit has been understood by the children. Thus, these planning sessions make their contribution to the teacher's effort to evaluate what has been happening. As the teacher grows in skill and security with teacher-pupil planning, unit teaching improves.

Units and Subject Matter Divisions

Since the focus in a unit of work is usually on some significant aspect of the social and/or scientific-technological environment, the teacher's job becomes that of exploring and investigating the area as completely as possible with his class. Accepting this, the matter of subject matter divisions has to be reckoned with. Over the years the point of view has developed that there are advantages to teaching units of work with little or no attention to subject matter boundaries. Whatever the unit may be—the study of a foreign culture, an analysis of the air age, or a systematic look at local community life—the teacher and the class are free to make their way through the unit in terms of the questions and concerns that develop, utilizing organized subject matter as appropriate and necessary. An illustration will make this advantage clear.

---

[4] Viola Theman, *A Good School Day* (New York: Bureau of Publications, Teachers College, Columbia University, 1950), pp. 38–39.

Suppose that a third grade group is developing a unit of work focused on studying the supply of water to the local community. In the process the teacher and class take a field trip to the local water purification plant. Once back in the classroom, the teacher will try to exploit this experience to the fullest in furthering the development of the unit. In a planning session, pupils ask questions such as the following:

1. What is in the water that makes purification necessary before it can be used in the community?
2. What is put into the water to make it safe for use?
3. Who owns that big plant that we visited?

A little reflection, in terms of organized subject matter, will indicate that answers to the first two questions will lead the class into the natural sciences, while the third question will lead into the social sciences. What is the teacher to do? The most widely accepted interpretation of the unit of work idea tells the teacher that the class is to be helped to follow these questions through to their answers, with no cause for concern as to the subjects that are being studied. The teacher has an opportunity to help the class to begin to sense the differences in their questions, and to increase their awareness of and skill in using organized subject matter. Children can begin to see, with some teacher help, what "natural science" as a large learning area encompasses and to contrast "social science" with it. Their understanding of large divisions in organized knowledge would be a by-product of the unit enterprise and not a dividing line along which it would be developed. The focus of some units causes them inevitably to be more science than social studies, or vice versa—but they are not so labeled at the outset.

Over the years there have been teachers who have contended that the unit, properly conceived, can encompass the full day of teaching and learning at school. We tend to doubt the feasibility of trying to attach so much responsibility to it. Clearly, the unit of work must have a considerable amount of time assigned to it. There must be time to think, to reason, to contemplate, to experiment, to plan, to evaluate, and so on. Time is needed for what might be profitably characterized as leisurely learning. Language and mathematics skills of various kinds will inevitably need to be used in the experiences that develop within the unit. Attempts to express one's thoughts and feelings about the unit, or to appreciate fully some aspects of it, will call for the utilization of art, dramatics, and music of various kinds in various ways. But it is to be remembered that the learning takes place within a sharply focused unit of work and as direct means of making that particular venture more successful.

Thus, a part of the teacher's responsibility is to protect the integrity of the unit experience by not trying to make it the carrier of all learnings that are vital and important for children at school. True situations of use will emerge in the unit in which language will function as the strategic individual and social tool that it is. Quantitative situations will be met from time to time in the unit, and out of these children will have a chance to use much of the arithmetic they are being asked to learn and to see the number system as an important social invention. For the teacher to decide to teach all of his language and arithmetic within the unit of work is too often to destroy the setting that provides the dynamics of good unit teaching. The unit becomes strained and artificial as attempts are made to get this or that into it, and many of the values of unit teaching are lost. In fact, the teacher will have his hands full keeping the unit focused as it is. Such an experience will usually cause children to think of many interesting things and to raise a variety of provocative questions. The teacher will do well to keep the class from being led down too many byways in the process. Burton, in writing on the introduction of certain subject matter into the unit on logical grounds or activities only superficially related to the real purposes of the unit, comments as follows:

> The point here is that, regardless of whether the local emphasis is upon subject matter or upon the experiences of the learner, only subject matter and experiences should be included with an instructional organization which relate to and support the central purpose, thus enhancing the integration within the learner.[5]

A Dynamic Concept of Method

It is in the area of method that the unit of work is both most demanding on the teacher and most rewarding in terms of results. The central focus is on problem solving, with most of the dynamics that carry the unit forward coming from the children themselves. The teacher nevertheless plays a decisive role in all of this.

Relation to drives present in children. The basic methodology of unit teaching relies heavily on the drives exhibited by children for much of its form. From psychology we know that children have strong inclinations to find things out, to create, to experiment, to build, to dramatize, and to feel the security that comes from knowing. All of these can be used directly in the approach that the teacher takes to develop the unit of work, step by step, with his class.

Focus on problem solving. The central focus in developing the learning sequence in the unit is on problem solving. The teacher's role is that of helping the class to be explicit about concerns they have that should be resolved and questions they have that need to be answered in relation to the general theme of the unit at hand. The teacher's role extends to

---

[5] Burton, "Implications," p. 222.

making available to the class or arranging with the class the particular learning experiences that are necessary to follow through on these identified interests, concerns, and questions. It is anticipated that as particular interests, concerns, and questions are dealt with in the classroom they will lead to the identification of still others and that this process will repeat itself until the area of the social or natural environment on which the unit is focused has been completely explored.

If one could imagine a second grade class studying the postal system in their community, the following sequence might develop as a part of the unit:

Desires, Questions, Concerns, Problems	Experiences Provided
To find out about the job of the postman	Reading an informational story that tells about the work of the postman
	Interviewing the postman who comes to the school
	Getting permission for the class to sort and deliver the mail received at the school
	Deciding to write letters to friends in other grades
To know how to write a letter and address an envelope	Studying a model letter that the teacher has prepared on a chart
	Studying a model addressed envelope that the teacher has prepared
	Discussing the importance of accurate addresses on envelopes
	Learning about the dead letter office
To know something about postal rates	Reading about the first class, second class, air mail, etc.
	Examining samples of these different types of mail
	Establishing the relationship between the weight of a letter and the cost of mailing it
	Relating stamps to classes of mail; reading about regular and special issue stamps.
To know more about special types of mail service	Listening to or reading teacher-prepared stories about registered letters, parcel post, special delivery, C.O.D., money orders
	Discussing the use of these various types of mail service and situations in which they would probably be used

	Discussing jobs that they know about in the post office
To know more about special jobs in the post office	Viewing a film that calls attention to a variety of jobs in a city post office
	Visiting the local post office to find out about special jobs there

Or, perhaps a sixth grade class studying something of the air age and the impact of air travel in the world today might spend a portion of their unit time as follows:

Desires, Questions, Concerns, Problems	Experiences Provided
To find out why the newest airplanes do not need propellers	Discussing the use of engines in airplanes
	Determining the properties of air that make aviation possible
	Looking at a wing diagram showing how the shape of the wing affects the passage of air over it
	Looking at a chart that shows the four forces acting on a plane
	Reading an informational story, *Airflight*, which discusses the function of the propeller, among other things
	Looking at a diagram of a jet engine, showing the lines of thrust exerted by it
	Viewing a film that discusses jet propulsion
	Discussing their findings in relation to their questions
To know more about man's early attempts to fly	Reading mythological tales of man's early attempts to fly
	Painting pictures of what those early attempts may have looked like
	Viewing pictures of some of the earliest successful heavier-than-air craft
	Learning the difference between lighter-than-air and heavier-than-air craft
	Becoming aware of man's early attempt to fly with balloons
To make a timeline of the history of man's successes with flying	Reading to find accounts of famous flights of the past
	Writing reports (each student one flight) of these most famous flights

> Deciding to make both a timeline and a world flight map showing historical achievements
>
> Viewing a bulletin board, prepared by the teacher, of pictures of early famous planes and flyers
>
> Reading about and discussing the Wright brothers
>
> Planning to visit a nearby museum where an old plane is exhibited

At times, of course, the next general area of concern in the unit will not readily emerge from the dynamics of the situation. The class will reach a "dead end" in the questions and concerns they can express. At these times the teacher must make a careful assessment of the development of the unit of work up to this time, determining whether or not there are still significant areas within it that ought to be made known to the class. If there are, the teacher will make plans for a kind of "priming" experience that may provide the momentum needed to help the class to take this first step. This might be a special field trip, a carefully chosen resource visitor, some printed material that the teacher shares with the class, or an exhibit of pictures and artifacts. It will be carefully chosen with an eye to the kinds of questions the teacher would like the class to raise concerning the undeveloped portions of the unit at hand. If it is deemed important enough, and the questions do not come from the class, the teacher will suggest some key questions himself in an attempt to move the unit along.

The teacher's assessment of the situation, as the process begins to be sluggish and mechanical, may lead to the conclusion that the unit had best be terminated. It may indicate that the class has really become aware of most of the significant aspects of the area and that to force it beyond this point is neither wise nor efficient. If this be the case, steps will be taken to plan for the culmination[6] of the unit, and the teacher will begin to anticipate the next unit that will be treated in the program.

Structure built around four types of activities. An analysis of the experiences that take place in the classroom during the course of the development of a unit of work will indicate that the teacher tries to provide time and opportunity for four types of activities:

---

[6] In discussing units of work, the terms *initiation, development,* and *culmination* are usually used to refer to the beginning, the major portion, and the termination of the unit respectively.

1. *The development of research skills*—Children need opportunities to consult a wide range of materials, such as books, maps, charts, graphs, motion pictures, encyclopedias, people, places, and so on, to gather the information needed to handle the questions and concerns that arise in the unit of work. Along with this seeking comes attention to the development of skills and techniques for using these various sources, for organizing material from them, for making judgments concerning the accuracy and authoritativeness of the material, and so on.

2. *The development of problem-solving skills*—Children need opportunities to come face to face with problems that are real and important to the children in the class and that are significant in terms of the unit being developed. The intent is not only to realize some gain in the unit from the end product of the problem solving undertaken but also to grow in the ability to sense a problem, to bring past experiences to bear on it, to gather and apply new evidence to it, to test various satisfactory solutions to the problem in the process, and finally to select the most appropriate solution or response that leaves the children ready to face a new problem situation.

3. *Opportunities to dramatize*—Play is a serious business to children, seldom recognized as such by adults. But teachers use a technique most often referred to as *dramatic play* in developing units of work, which gives children an opportunity to explore an area of human experience by reliving a past happening or simply re-creating a current situation. Under teacher guidance they bring to bear the understanding and insights they have as they dramatize the situation. They may use costumes and props to make their dramatic play more realistic, but their actions are improvised out of their fund of information related to the situation, and they are limited accordingly in what they are able to do. Dissatisfaction with dramatic play can lead, obviously, to discussion, research, and so on in the unit. Too few teachers sense the value of this technique.

4. *Opportunities to construct and to process*—Capitalizing again on the desire of children to construct, and to process raw materials into various finished products, the teacher will provide opportunities for children to make and build things that are needed in the unit as it is developing. Not only do the children gain things for use in the unit; they also gain in opportunities for problem solving, for making plans, for following through on them, for evaluating along the way as well as at the point of completion. Too, they gain in general insight and understanding of the ways in which man processes raw materials of many kinds in the satisfaction of his basic needs.[7]

Together these four types of activities indicate the large areas into which the many experiences and approaches to learning in the unit group themselves.

---

[7] See Lavone A. Hanna, Gladys L. Potter, and Neva Hagaman, *Unit Teaching in the Elementary School* (revised edition) (New York: Holt, Rinehart and Winston, Inc., 1963), Chapters 8, 9, 11, and 12 for excellent detailed discussions of these four types of activities.

Relation to democratic group living.   There are two virtues of the unit-of-work approach to learning that make it a desirable experience in relation to the larger concern to provide experiences at school in democratic group living. One of these is that the unit of work is a cooperative venture in learning, with both individual and group achievements contributing to the final success of the unit. The other is that individual differences among children can be used to promote the success of the venture, helping children to assess this phenomenon in society more realistically.

The unit of work is adaptable to both individual and small-group work. The learning enterprise is, first and foremost, a total group experience. The large group, however, finds it necessary and wise to delegate certain tasks from time to time to either small work groups or to individuals. Responsibilities of various kinds are assumed, in the interests of the total group enterprise, by these small work groups or by individual children, and the fruits of their labors then contribute to the progress of the total unit of work. Thus, in the classroom the children can participate in a learning experience that reflects many of the dynamics of democratic living. The tenet of democracy related to "the cooperative solution of common problems" becomes a reality in this learning venture. Democratic insights and skills of important kinds can be developed in the process.

The unit of work is adaptable to individual differences. Differences in the group become a valuable asset rather than a classroom liability. Children who have interests and strengths of particular kinds can usually find a place and a way of contributing to the progress of the enterprise. Things must be built, reports must be prepared, murals must be designed and completed, discussions must be led, and so on. In each instance there are children who are able to do these things with ease and security.

At the same time, of course, the teacher is anxious that all children have a chance to construct, to dramatize, to read and report, and to participate in other ways in the enterprise. For this reason, he will make sure (1) that his shelves hold a wide range of reading materials, all useful in the unit but some more simply written than others, (2) that construction tasks range from simple to complex so that all may find an opportunity to participate at the level their skill will allow, and (3) that roles in dramatic play are assigned thoughtfully and in the best interests of the children participating as well as in the interests of the success of the play session.

A child is more likely to be realistic about the variations in his ability and aptitude, and more willing to work to strengthen areas where progress might reasonably be made if he has at the same time areas in which he realizes that his contribution to the unit's success is an important and vital one. Similarly, the group will assess its "differences" and will realize that its strength comes in great part from its diversity. Thus, the teacher who can see the positive side to the individual differences factor will find in the unit approach a challenging but rewarding opportunity to deal with it.

TIME FOR TEACHING THE SKILLS

Time must be reserved in the classroom program for more than a major unit of work. The development of understanding and proficiency in the areas of language and mathematics remains a primary goal for the elementary school years, and teachers will need to use time in their daily and weekly programs for these areas. Time so reserved will make possible direct and systematic attention to the progress that children are making in these areas. The teacher will carry on rather distinct instructional programs to extend and refine the developing skills. In certain instances the teacher can work with the class as a whole. Often, however, the teacher will be working with individuals or small groups of children who have particular needs or who are ready for certain more advanced instruction in reading, written expression, or arithmetic.

There will be many occasions for children to use language and arithmetic skills in the unit-of-work setting. Most often they will be practicing skills already developed to some point. At times unsuccessful efforts on the part of some children to use these skills in such a setting will provide some additional motivation for them to try harder in the skill programs as such. Similarly, pupil success or lack of it in attempts to use language or mathematics in such situations will provide the teacher with an additional kind of evaluative evidence as to the quality of learning which has taken place in the instruction provided in these curriculum areas. Out of this evaluation can come decisions to reteach particular items, or to review them, as the situation seems to call for. But the unit of work does not take the place of deliberate programming to advance learning in language and mathematics.

TIME FOR AESTHETIC EXPERIENCES

It is necessary for the teacher to provide time for aesthetic experiences that are completely removed from the unit-of-work experience. While the arts, broadly defined, are to be used by teacher and children to enhance the study taking place in the unit in whatever manner or means appears to be appropriate, the arts should not be restricted to this role. This has been made clear in an earlier chapter that dealt with aesthetic experiences in the curriculum (see Chapter 14). To implement the policy endorsed here calls for time in the daily and weekly program for such opportunities. Children ought to read and enjoy poetry at times for the values that come purely from the experience, not because it will help them to understand the unit. Children ought to be invited to sketch clouds on a beautiful day apart from a unit focused on weather. Children should sing and dance apart from using these activities to help them to understand some given period in American history. Aesthetic experiences, both creative and appreciative, can be justified on many counts that relate to the direct contribution that they make to the developing child in addition to the use that may be made of them in a unit of work.

Teachers will get some cues for the type of aesthetic experience that may be most appropriate at given times from the unit. If the unit experience has been such as to motivate the class to do a great deal of drawing and painting, it may well be that a poetry reading session is in order for that week. Or, if the unit has utilized songs and dances to help children to "feel" a given culture or a past happening, it may be a good time to work with some art media during the week. As in other matters, the teacher's professional judgment will be most important here. What is sought is obvious—ample time and opportunity for children to have aesthetic experiences in light of their direct contribution to human development.

TIME FOR REST, RELAXATION, AND EXERCISE

Little need be said about the provision for opportunities for rest, relaxation, and recreation during the school day. This is time that must be taken, and it is time well invested. Part of this comes, of course, in the regularly scheduled physical education program. The remainder comes in recesses and other breaks in the day. Arrangements for operating elementary schools cause these periods of time to fall at regular, predetermined time intervals. This regularity is often necessary to assure the proper sharing of playground and other facilities around the school, and in most instances this kind of schedule takes care of the need very well. There are occasions, however, when the need for relaxation does not appear by the clock. To the degree that the local situation permits, it is often wise to commit time to this need at points other than those that the fixed time schedule would allow. In some instances extra time will be needed for relaxation; in others time for relaxation will be taken when it is needed, and one or more of the scheduled rest periods will be ignored.

TEACHING PLANS AND NEW CURRICULA

Current curriculum reform projects tend to run counter in part to the position that has been taken in this chapter. Science is now usually separated from social studies in the curriculum. As a result, certain constraints are put on the development of units of work. They become identified with one or the other of these broad divisions of knowledge and are to be seen as science or social studies units. Thus they are aptly labeled subject matter units in a more delimited way than they would have been in the past. Some classroom teachers see this limitation as putting undesirable restraints on the development of unit experiences and on the pursuit of wide-ranging questions that may come before the class.

More to the point is the practice in some of the new curricula of presenting the teacher with predesigned sequences to be followed in the development of the classroom experience. This practice runs quite counter to the dynamic sort of sequencing that has characterized unit teaching for some time. Such sequencing relies heavily on teacher-pupil planning for the determination of next steps in the unit experience. Some of the new programs purport to make available to the teacher experimentally derived predesigned sequences for pupils to follow in developing concepts, generalizations, and thinking skills. It may be that such predesign is necessary recognition of the care with which plans for teaching must be designed if the goals to which teachers aspire for pupils are to be achieved. It may also constitute somewhat of a restriction on authentic problem solving and inquiry at a time when these activities are coming to be valued highly as a part of learning. The job of the teacher shifts to one of presenting the predesigned sequence as interestingly as possible, attempting to find ways for pupils to genuinely involve themselves with it. The teacher seeks feedback to ascertain who has learned what before the next already-determined step is taken into the sequence, rather than using feedback to decide what the next step should be. This procedure is quite a shift from what many elementary educators have considered "best practice." Teachers do not reject predesign altogether. Most teachers do their own anticipatory preplanning. But they are aware of the dynamic nature of the teaching-learning encounter itself once it commences in the classroom, and the way in which plans are revised and reconstructed in that setting. It may be that this extemporaneous dimension of teaching will have to be curtailed in the interests of improved pupil learning. But if it is curtailed too much, it may have just the opposite effect. This trend needs to be watched very carefully for its consequences on teaching and learning. It could easily become too prescriptive and not in the best interests of either the teacher or his pupils.

CLASSROOM PROGRAMMING, UNGRADED SCHOOLS, AND TEAMING FOR TEACHING

A word needs to be said concerning the added tasks that are involved in developing classroom programs in schools that adopt an ungraded arrangement and a teaming organization for teaching. The same elements as have been identified earlier (subject matter to be taught, intellectual skills to be developed, pupils being taught, teachers available) will have to be dealt with. And in an ungraded, teamed school the possibilities for dealing with them are increased. At the same time it is imperative that plans be arrived at jointly. All teachers involved with a particular group of children must be a party to the programming that is done. And all must be guided in their teaching by this agreed-upon programming. Any adjustments that might appear to be useful in tomorrow's schedule in light of today's experience must be made in consultation with all of the team, especially if the adjustment involves taking more or less time, or doing something in the morning instead of the afternoon, for example. If two or more teachers work with any given child it becomes their responsibility to share information about the progress he is making. For example, the teacher working with a particular pupil in the social studies unit must let the pupil's reading teacher know something of the ease or the difficulty with which he reads social studies material. The shared planning for teaching that follows from the teaming of teachers is in fact seen as one of the most attractive aspects of the idea. This is one of the points at which new arrangements for work call for new ways of accomplishing the classroom programming task.

RECOMMENDED READINGS

ALMY, MILLIE. "Are They Too Young for Problem Solving?" *Progressive Education,* Vol. 27 (March 1950), pp. 143–148.

ASSOCIATION FOR SUPERVISION AND CURRICULUM DEVELOPMENT. *Creating a Good Environment for Learning.* Washington, D.C.: NEA, 1954.

———. *Toward Better Teaching.* Washington, D.C.: NEA, 1949.

———. *The Way Teaching Is* (Report of a Seminar on Teaching). Washington, D.C.: NEA, 1966.

BEAUCHAMP, GEORGE A. *Basic Dimensions of Elementary Method* (second edition). Boston: Allyn and Bacon, Inc., 1965.

HANNA, LAVONE A., GLADYS L. POTTER, and NEVA HAGAMAN. *Unit Teaching in the Elementary School* (revised edition). New York: Holt, Rinehart and Winston, Inc., 1963.

MC KIM, MARGARET, CARL W. HANSEN, and WILLIAM L. CARTER. *Learning to Teach in the Elementary School.* New York: The Macmillan Company, 1959. (See especially Chapters 5, 6, and 12.)

MIEL, ALICE (editor). *Creativity in Teaching: Invitations and Instances.* Belmont, Calif.: Wadsworth Publishing Company, Inc., 1961. (See especially Chapter 6.)

PETERSEN, DOROTHY G. *The Elementary School Teacher.* New York: Appleton-Century-Crofts, Inc., 1964. (See especially Chapter 7.)

SHUMSKY, ABRAHAM. *Creative Teaching in the Elementary School.* New York: Appleton-Century-Crofts, Inc., 1965.

THOMAS, R. MURRAY. *Ways of Teaching.* New York: David McKay Company, Inc., 1955.

Tools for Teaching:
Materials and Technology

16

The aids to learning that the teacher selects and the considerations he makes as he plans their use are the focus of consideration for this chapter. A standard variety of equipment and materials are usually ready in the school. Countless other instructional materials are available from varied sources. Materials are used to develop concepts, raise questions, facilitate problem solving, allow practice in skills, effect experimentation, and permit observation. The selection of these materials, their sources, and the relationship between them is discussed in this chapter.

DEVELOPING INSIGHT INTO
INSTRUCTIONAL MATERIALS

Instructional materials facilitate communication. They make new ideas lively and meaningful. Their use helps the teacher illustrate the spoken word, provide variation in the repetition of facts, and practice in the skills. They bring to the sight and the minds of the children wonders of far-off places and past eras. They help the teacher manage the rapidly accumulating new knowledge. Through variety instructional materials make teaching more effective; they help to raise the level of learning from verbalism and out of the rigid structure of the textbook.

Kinds of Materials and Techniques

It would appear to be a simple matter to define the term "instructional materials." In reality it is not. It is easy to form a vague idea as to what one has in mind when this term is used, but authorities who try to differentiate among various terms related to materials find little agreement, and many of the terms are used synonymously. Differentiating between kinds of materials represented by a textbook, a chalkboard, a pair of scissors, and a motion picture becomes important to the teacher who selects and uses them, to the child who learns from them, and to the administrator who must order them. The following definitions are outlined to clarify this differentiation, and will be used consistently in this chapter.

Instructional materials is a broad, general category to indicate all material that will facilitate or help the teaching-learning process. Thus, instructional materials may include a piece of chalk, a chalkboard, or a film.

Audio-visual materials is a term best defined as encompassing those multisensory materials specifically provided by an audio-visual center. Originally conceived, "audio-visual" was limited to films, slides, filmstrips, and recordings and was typified by audio-visual "gadgets." Educational usage has broadened the term, and at present it includes both materials and services related to all areas of learning. Authorities frequently use words like "sensory devices" and "perceptual experiences" when referring to audio-visual procedures. One definition exemplifies the broad meaning and relates techniques integrally to materials:

> [*Audio-visual*] is a generic term referring to experiences, equipment, and materials used for communication in instruction. [It] implies techniques based upon practices utilized in education and training.[1]

The term audio-visual materials, then, is an inclusive term and represents items ranging from magnets for bulletin boards to sound filmstrips and implies specialized techniques for their use.

Instructional supplies refers to materials that are expendable and are therefore constantly reordered. Such items are chalk, pencils, paper, art materials, and workbooks. These are the "raw materials" of instruction, usually facilitate an activity, and in this way contribute to meaning of the learning.

Instructional equipment, the term most generally standardized in meaning and use among authorities, refers to permanent or nonexpendable materials such as the apparatus or furnishings in a school. Frequently these are mechanical materials, but not always, for under the category of equipment are listed chalkboards, bulletin boards, and screens as well as projectors, mimeographs, and other machines. Equipment helps in the presentation of information.

Source materials, resource materials, and instructional resources are terms that may be used synonymously. For purposes of definition we will

---

1 James W. Brown, Richard B. Lewis, and Fred F. Harcleroad, *A-V Instruction: Materials and Methods* (second edition) (New York: McGraw-Hill Book Company, Inc., 1964), p. 565.

use the single term *source materials*. Included among them are textbooks, documents, realia, people, films, and community settings that help children answer questions, clarify and broaden concepts, organize thinking, and solve problems.

Instructional devices are materials that are devised or especially constructed to help with specific tasks. In the elementary school a device may be teacher-constructed, school-constructed or commercially prepared. Examples are charts, flannel boards, pocket charts, mock-ups, and arithmetic counters. Such devices are another means of furthering understanding or imparting knowledge.

Instructional aids are not synonymous with materials. The term *aid* implies something supplementary, something that is a help and furthers the teaching act. Some persons think of an aid as a gadget or crutch. Because of this confusing connotation, the term is not used in this book.

Instructional techniques are the teaching methods utilized for the most efficient use of the materials. They require knowledge about the content and manipulation of the material. Techniques involve broad skill in planning, organizing, and timing that will relate one material to another effectively in the experiences of the children. For example, pictures may need the supporting evidence of books or maps. Transcriptions may need the supplementary information provided by pictures, resource people, or documents. Such materials are not effectively provided at random or in unrelated situations. Nor is children's experience with them unstructured.

The table here demonstrates the relationship between materials and techniques as well as the differentiation between them. In this representative listing, we see in the top row the special group of instructional materials that are the sources of information. The second row indicates the particular places where the materials are produced, collected, and made available to the schools. The third row lists the broad techniques of presentation, and the fourth row lists the kinds of activities demanded of the children for participation.

Materials	Books, documents, periodicals; Films, pictures; Maps, graphs; People; Places; Radio, television; Realia; Records, transcriptions.
Found in	Catalogs, bulletins; Community; Museums; Organizations, agencies, associations, industry.
Organized for use through	Demonstrations; Dramatic plays; Exhibits; Experiments; Field trips; Interviews; Programs; Research.
Learning accomplished by	Creating; Feeling; Listening; Observing; Reading; Talking; Thinking.

The vital need for audio-visual materials in the teaching-learning situation is demonstrated by several roles played by audio-visual technology. The roles are presented by Erickson,[2] but it is noted that not all of the materials play all of the roles and that some media may play more than one role at the same time or at different times.

1. Audiovisual technology provides the teacher with a means for extending the horizon of experience.
2. Audiovisual technology helps the teacher provide meaningful sources of information.
3. Audiovisual technology provides the teacher with interest-compelling springboards into a wide variety of learning activities.
4. Audiovisual technology assists the teacher in overcoming physical difficulties of presenting subject matter.
5. Audiovisual technology provides the teacher with a kit of tools to carry out diagnostic, research, and remedial work demanded by up-to-date instructional purposes.
6. Audiovisual technology provides the teacher with rich resources of pupil purpose when communicative materials are produced jointly by pupils and teachers.

Categorizing Instructional Materials

Instructional materials are the tools of the trade. The teacher must know well their inherent possibilities and their limitations. Clear insight into instructional materials leads to a more precise use of them. The teacher, knowing the capabilities of one instructional tool as opposed to another, is more likely to choose a certain one when it is available, or will adjust his expectancies for success in the learning situation in the light of the material with which he has to work.

The individuality of various instructional materials is evident when one begins to categorize those that are available. Several meaningful categorizations have been developed in an attempt to introduce some relationship to the materials that are available. Two are commented upon here.

The cone of experience. Dale has offered a most useful device for helping us to obtain some perspective on instructional materials through a diagram he calls "The Cone of Experience." This configuration indicates the extent, variety, relationships, and techniques from which we can identify two important factors. First, each material holds a relative position between the points of concreteness and abstraction. Second, the role

---

[2] Carlton W. H. Erickson, *Fundamentals of Teaching with Audiovisual Technology* (New York: The Macmillan Company, 1965), pp. 12–27.

THE CONE OF EXPERIENCE [3]

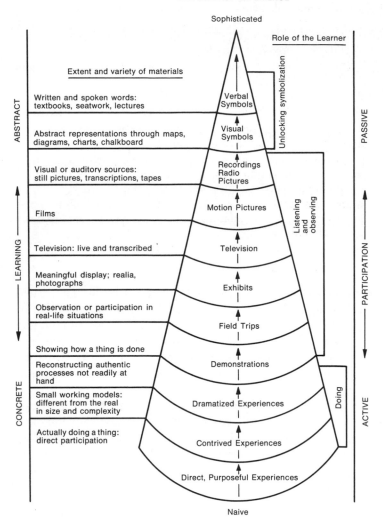

[3] Modified from Edgar Dale, *Audio-Visual Methods in Teaching* (revised edition) (New York: Holt, Rinehart and Winston, Inc., 1954), pp. 42–56.

of the learner ranges from active participation to rather complete passivity in the use of the various materials. Near the base of the cone the learner experiences directly; near the point he must resort to skill with some system of symbols, as in reading or in map work, in order to derive meaning from the material.

A longitudinal projection of categories. Barnes has provided us with a slightly different concept of categories for instructional materials, using a longitudinal idea rather than a vertical one. Again this concept relates materials between points of concreteness and abstractness, but Barnes relates abstractness directly to learning theory. He lists four operational assumptions for using his model to guide learning in desirable directions:

1. In situations where the pupil is naïve, learning proceeds best from concrete, direct experiences and materials.
2. In situations where the pupil is mature, learning proceeds most efficiently from symbolic materials.
3. Continuity in school learning may be found in the pupil's directional growth from naïveté to maturity.
4. The continuity factor is of prime importance both in relatively short-range, specific learning situations and also in general, long-range maturing toward adult levels of performance.[4]

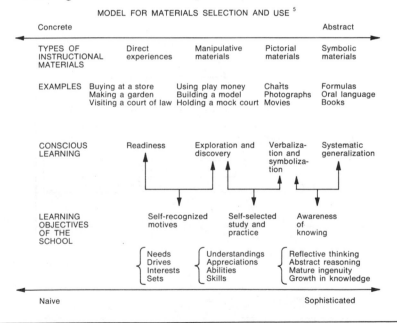

MODEL FOR MATERIALS SELECTION AND USE [5]

Concrete				Abstract
TYPES OF INSTRUCTIONAL MATERIALS	Direct experiences	Manipulative materials	Pictorial materials	Symbolic materials
EXAMPLES	Buying at a store Making a garden Visiting a court of law	Using play money Building a model Holding a mock court	Charts Photographs Movies	Formulas Oral language Books
CONSCIOUS LEARNING	Readiness	Exploration and discovery	Verbaliza-tion and symboliza-tion	Systematic generalization
LEARNING OBJECTIVES OF THE SCHOOL	Self-recognized motives	Self-selected study and practice	Awareness of knowing	
	Needs Drives Interests Sets	Understandings Appreciations Abilities Skills	Reflective thinking Abstract reasoning Mature ingenuity Growth in knowledge	

| Naive | | | | Sophisticated |

---

[4] Fred P. Barnes, "Materials of Learning—and Learning," *Educational Leadership*, Vol. 9 (April 1952), pp. 402–408.

[5] Modified from Barnes.

One other factor is related to Barnes' assumptions: children must be helped to relate abstract ideas to concrete situations.

Today's Typical Practice

Most teachers rely heavily on verbal symbols in books, workbooks, seatwork, and spoken words. Next most frequently used are visual symbols as found in maps, charts, and diagrams. Both are at the far reaches of Dale's cone in terms of abstractness, and to the far right of Barnes' outline in the same way. Today's most common practice would be more accurately shown by inverting Dale's cone to indicate the most commonly used materials at the base and the amount of use of each medium represented by the widest part of the cone. Note that the verbal and visual materials, used more today than the others listed, are shown on the pyramid as diminishing only a partial step. From then on, the materials seem to decrease in use to the direct, concrete experiences that are the most difficult to provide for children.

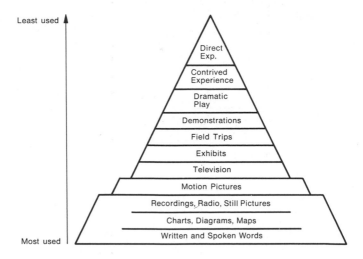

Barnes' model, showing the same diagrammatic scheme for today's common practice, would invert symbolic materials to the left:

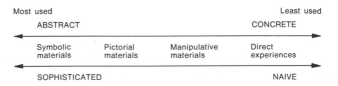

If present teaching procedures were more in agreement with evidence in learning, teachers would provide more experiences with instruction materials that are closer to the concrete end of the continuum, and not concentrate so heavily on abstract situations to facilitate learning. If children could receive more of their instruction from actual experience the effectiveness of much of what teachers do would undoubtedly be improved. Especially would this be true for young children and for children who are limited in the kind of ability that we refer to as "intelligence," since intelligence is focused on verbal ability in great part. Teachers cannot always provide as much concrete experience as we would like and still meet the goals that they are asked to achieve in the classroom. Yet one of the greatest achievements of human beings is the ability to learn from the experience of others and to develop symbol systems so that they may deal with things in the abstract. Thus, for children not to be proficient with symbol systems is for them to be deprived of a great human invention. There does not seem to be any real reason, however, why teachers could not change the shape of "typical practice" in the way shown, using Dale's cone as an example.

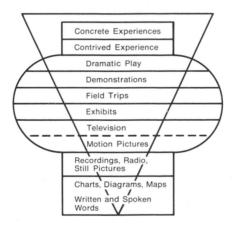

From this bulging, lantern-shaped diagram we can see that modified practice might include less of concrete and contrived experiences and more of recordings, charts, maps and written symbols so that each type of experience is offered equally. Balancing these activities at either end of the concrete-abstract continuum, teachers would provide greater numbers of experiences in the center, represented by techniques that combine several materials for the learning process.

Throughout elementary school years, however, the shape of this "learning lantern" will need modification because of the characteristics of children and the purposes of the educative experiences provided. In the first grade, for example, more concrete experiences are necessary because of the limited verbal skills of the children; in their preschool years direct experience has been the vehicle for almost all their learning. Pupils in sixth, seventh, and eighth grades may require more abstract experiences to bring a necessary sophistication to their education.

Erickson[6] suggests a system of principles that calls for creative teacher action with the entire range of audio-visual materials:

1. *The Principle of Selection:* Teachers should base their selection of high quality audiovisual materials upon valid teaching purposes (objectives) and upon the unique characteristics of a specific group of learners.
2. *The Principle of Readiness:* The use of audiovisual instructional materials should be preceded by the development of adequate learner readiness for effective participation.
3. *The Physical Control Principle:* Details relating to physical facilities for using audiovisual materials should be handled or arranged by the teacher in a manner that safeguards material and equipment and provides for economy of time and optimum learner attention.
4. *The Action Principle:* Teachers should guide the learner in the important processes of reacting to and taking appropriate action as a result of audiovisual experience situations.
5. *The Appraisal Principle:* Teachers should subject both the audiovisual material and the accompanying techniques to continual evaluation.

Selecting and Evaluating Instructional Materials

Why select? The foregoing section has pointed out the great variety of materials available to teachers and something of the difference in their possibilities and limitations. Because he cannot ignore these materials, or even use them all, the teacher is faced with the task of selecting the proper materials for the job he has to do. Such selection includes evaluation that precedes selection and evaluation that follows use.

How select? If materials are to be selected with consciousness of purpose, selections must be made in line with certain principles that can be understood and accepted by the teacher. The following are examples of guiding principles that give us a basis for selection and evaluation of materials.

1. The materials selected must be those needed in terms of the purposes sought in the program. The *reason* for using the materials must be found, in part, in the established goals. One does not organize the program around the materials available, but rather seeks materials appropriate to the goals set.
2. Materials selected to aid learning are an important part of the means to the desired end. They are means to raise questions, to provide information, and to stimulate thinking. In fact, the use of a

[6] Erickson, *Fundamentals,* pp. 95–136.

given material, such as a textbook or a map, serves as a means to two ends when we realize that the children not only are gaining content, but are also learning to gather information. Thus, the material selected is a vehicle to carry two kinds of learning: content gained from it and skill in the use of it.

3. The materials selected should be appropriate to the specific learning situation. These considerations become important: Does the material provide new and important information, or does it extend existing knowledge? Is it related directly to the unit, lesson, or problem? Is it worth the time and expense involved? How well does it perform its intended function? Is the teacher's guide helpful? Does it work well with other instructional materials to achieve the desired learning purposes?

4. Materials selected must provide valid learning. The content must present information that is authentic for the time and place represented; the ideas must be presented with integrity and must contribute to the study topic in a realistic, meaningful manner. If the teacher cannot determine the accuracy of the material, he must depend on authorities that do. Many materials are authenticated by educators in the field who endorse them. This is a particular problem today because of rapidly changing knowledge in areas like science. Textbooks and encyclopedias can become easily outdated. In a different vein models used need to be authentic in design, working principle, and materials lest they be miseducative for pupils.

5. The materials selected should be appropriate to the individual differences of the learners. The intellectual or verbal ability of the group influences the selection as to vocabulary, abstractness, and general understandability; materials need to challenge mental powers but not go beyond them. Prior experience will influence understanding, motivation, acceptance, and interest. What has gone before determines in great part the kind of learning the material will produce. For example, teachers frequently use the spelling workbook without modification when some children need more limited lists of words, others need augmented lists, and all need to include some key words specifically related to the ongoing classroom program.

6. Materials selected should represent variety in kind and function. Differences in interests and abilities demand a variety of approaches to learning, hence materials should provide numerous kinds of interrelated experiences for children—the use of all the senses, active and passive participation, concrete and abstract ideas, black and white or color, sound or silent, moving or still, real or represented. One does not use the motion picture, for example, to the exclusion of other materials. The best use of materials is made when more than one kind are used to supplement and reinforce each other, such as a model and a series of still pictures that illustrate a historical story or episode related to the log cabin.

7. Selected materials should make possible either overt or covert participation on the part of the learner. This participation may be physical, mental, or emotional; the child may be doing, listening,

watching, or making interpretation from language symbols. Every learning experience is proportionately effective to the amount of involvement for the learner. One child may react well to a movie, another to a tape, still another to a resource person. One child may participate in varying degrees for each of these. It is important that most of the children in the group be able to involve themselves in the experiences, or the material may not be valid for use.

8. Materials selected should promote cooperative learning, help children recognize and accept both individual and group research, and develop problem-solving skills. The materials children work with provide ideas for sharing and questioning or defending. The ideas from interrelated materials are woven together to form a generalization or to broaden a concept. Pictures, for example, need photographic content readily understood by children so that discussion and debate may take place. After the material is selected for its content, the teacher makes sure his method of using the material is appropriate to cooperative learning.

9. Materials selected should approach a high standard of mechanical excellence. Organization, format, length, sound, photography, color, and vocabulary should be technically satisfactory. Poor fidelity on a tape or record or crowded or cluttered composition of a poster distracts the children's attention and limits the amount of learning.

Who selects? Interestingly, evaluation of materials exists at the national, regional, state, and local levels, and is a kind of screening process carried on by a variety of groups. On the national and state levels, various professional associations such as the National Education Association and its affiliated groups select and review materials in their journals. Magazines such as *The Instructor* and *The Grade Teacher* devote regular columns to the evaluation and use of new materials. Audio-visual journals are an excellent source for evaluation and current listing of materials. Other periodicals, such as the *Saturday Review*, provide critical evaluation of books, films, and other materials. Commercially prepared catalogs contain evaluated listings of audio-visual materials. Several universities issue similar bulletins. All of these have some influence on the selection of materials at the local level.

Within the school district, selection responsibilities are frequently divided. The school board, as a policy-forming group, recognizes the importance of instructional materials by providing the budget for purchase. The superintendent, working with the board, assures recognition of the need and provides means by which teachers know about materials and their availability and use. This may be accomplished by the addition to the staff of a director of curriculum or a materials coordinator, either one with the responsibility of leadership in the materials area. He may, while doing other types of inservice training activities, publish appropriate bulletins, establish a selections committee, and procure adequate supplies, equipment, and source materials for classroom and district use.

Teachers, administrators, technical personnel such as the librarian or materials coordinator, and sometimes parents or community representatives, are members of the local selection and evaluation committee. This committee examines the materials and the guidebooks accompanying them, relates materials to established school objectives, considers the manner in which various materials supplement each other, and relates material to the school's curriculum outline. Selections are made and recommendations forwarded. Teachers involved in this kind of responsibility are well informed about new materials and can pass this information along to others in their buildings.

Faculties in individual buildings normally arrange discussions about materials. This sharing of ideas and information helps individual teachers become familiar with exactly the materials and services available, and how to procure them. Development of policies and techniques for classroom use also result from these discussions. Thus the teacher keeps up to date and gains information and understandings that will help him and the children in his group make the final selection of materials used in the learning situation.

SOURCES OF INSTRUCTIONAL MATERIALS

Choices for instructional materials used in the elementary school curriculum must be carefully made by type, and also the sources from which they will be procured must be carefully considered. Four categories of instructional materials are often referred to in the effort to indicate sources of supply. These are:

1. Materials from educational publishers.
2. Free and inexpensive materials.
3. Community resources.
4. Teacher-made materials.

Let us consider each of these groups of materials, remembering that instructional materials overlap any classification of this sort since some commercially produced materials may also be teacher-made, and some free and inexpensive materials are also available from the immediate community. Our discussion will enter these items in the most appropriate classification, and only mention their use elsewhere.

Materials from Educational Publishers

A great many of the materials used in the elementary schools are produced commercially and purchased by schools. Available from this source are an infinite variety of supplies, precisely constructed equipment, and carefully prepared, authoritative source materials. In the matter of supplies, though quality of materials may vary, the selection and procurement is usually accomplished in the school district at the system level. The teacher has only to choose among the supplies available. Equipment is usually screened and purchased by a staff member with technical knowledge. The teacher's responsibility lies in knowledgeable operation and use. Some ideas about use will be presented in this chapter as we discuss space utilization. Of source materials and instructional devices, the teacher makes more complete selection. A few comments on trends and problems concerning these should be helpful here.

Commercial materials are improving. It is not difficult to understand, even for the most unsophisticated observer, that materials the schools use today are much better than those of just a few years ago. Commercial houses are utilizing improved techniques of printing, of color reproduction and binding. Paper, ink, and illustrations are of increasingly finer quality. The raw materials of industrial production are being organized into an artistic design and a dramatic format that reflects clarity and practical function.

Producers are also acquiring professional help for the planning of materials. Not only specialists in education, but experts in such areas as cartography, science, photography, history, and engineering are being consulted. Studies of teacher use to determine curriculum needs are also influencing the planning and sale of materials. In all, producers are making every effort to use technical progress and professional help to produce materials that are effective and appropriate.

Books: text and reference. Books as instructional materials have been historically important to the school and probably will continue to be. High competition in the use of other kinds of materials has brought about improved quality of textbooks and a trend by publishers to supplement them with materials such as workbooks, tests, films, filmstrips, tapes and transcriptions, as well as teacher's guides. Greater numbers of supplementary books are also being published to augment the textbook series.

The advantages of textbooks are obvious. They may be used and reused and are therefore economical. They present a logical arrangement of subject matter that is carefully organized, arranged in graded sequence, and supplemented with teaching suggestions. These very advantages have long been the subject of heated debate, however. Some educators feel that preselected material is limiting, that added supplementary materials may further influence rigid teaching according to prearranged plans. It is also felt that use of textbooks fosters learning centered about recall. Content is considered to be too highly compressed in one book. Who can understand the Civil War after three pages of reading? Also, textbooks are criticized because they may be quickly out-dated. Change in method has been to a differentiated use of the textbook plus the use of other materials to facilitate learning.

In an article discussing the textbook, Barnes points out the three common uses of textbooks that are highly related to curriculum develop-ment and methodological procedure.[7] First is the use of the single text-book, followed rather rigidly as it is planned by the authors. The effect of such use is dependent upon the teacher, tends to be rather formal, and may have limited adaptability. The textbook outlines what to teach and the sequence in which it is to be taught with little adjustment for the individual differences of children or local conditions. The second is the multiple textbook method in which different books are used by different groups of pupils in the classroom. This method provides wider adjust-ment to individual needs but may introduce problems concerning differ-ent sequence and vocabulary among the various textbooks. The third method is to use textbooks as references only. Barnes further indicates that very little research is available on the best use of textbooks, and implies that educational leaders have provided little information as to the best use of textbooks as instructional material.

Our textbook dilemma, according to Barnes, is the result of two opposing camps, one claiming textbooks as a panacea, the other as a cause of pedagogical problems.

> On the one hand, the publisher and his authors defend the text-book, while being constantly alert for necessities to modify or replace it. Implicitly, this group recognizes specific flaws in the product and the developing threats to its continued dominance. The publisher also has a set of values and ideals concerning the educative process. With-out doubt he is much closer to his market intellectually than are most other industrialists to consumers of their products. Finally, the pub-lisher may be expected to act in terms of enlightened self-interest. The role of printed materials in school learning has been altered greatly since the time of the McGuffey brothers. Their books did not compete with sound-films, radio, television, and attractive trade books. The *Eclectic Readers* were not used during a period of profound change in pedagogical theory.
>
> On the other hand, protagonist educators have denounced the textbook in terms of frontier educational concepts and philosophies. Professional pressures force educational leaders to live on the cutting edge of the culture. From this elevation the textbook has appeared far distant and obsolescent. Considered in relation to changing culture patterns and new knowledge of what the best-conceived schools can do, these educators' views appear quite logical. But even horizon-pushing professional educators admit, quietly, that most schools and

---

[7] Fred P. Barnes, "The Textbook Dilemma," *Teachers College Record*, Vol. 55 (April 1954), pp. 369–383.

most teachers in practical situations would have to close up shop were they suddenly to be deprived of the textbook. The admission has to be made that the textbook, as it is, has a logic in most circumstances.[8]

Trade books are those that are not designated as textbooks and that are sold in bookstores to the general public. They include such types as fiction, biography, travel, and science books. In the classroom, they are frequently used as supplementary reference books and recreational reading books. They are helpful because they are colorful and intriguing, they get at various points of view, they are usually less condensed, and they are suitable to different interests and reading levels.

Reference books play a definite role in the elementary school curriculum as sources of information on particular topics that may not be adequately handled in textbooks. These include the student encyclopedias that are written in simple language and with a multiplicity of illustrations. Dictionaries are also published for use by children at various levels of ability. Adult references such as almanacs and atlases are also useful in the classroom. All of these materials demand special skills of research and interpretation to facilitate their use.

Current reading materials, such as newspapers and magazines, have been especially produced for children, and some strictly for school use. *Reader's Digest*, for example, publishes a special school edition. Such papers as *My Weekly Reader* and *Current Events* are commonly used so that children may read about current human affairs.[9] Other materials frequently utilized by children are pamphlets and brochures.

Another type of commercially published material, the comic book, has been highly controversial. Because of the pictorial type of communication, these booklets intrigue youngsters and tell a vivid story with few words. Criticisms have been directed at their questionable moral standards, language, art, and emotional appeal. Comic books have proved their worth, however, and many are now accepted in schools.

Michaelis presents a checklist for evaluating social studies textbooks that is helpful for the consideration of texts and references:

As an instructional resource

Is it related to the content of the program?

Is it accurate and up to date?

Can concepts and understandings be grasped by children who will use it?

Is level of reading difficulty—vocabulary, style of presentation, sentence structure—appropriate for children who will use it?

---

[8] Barnes, "The Textbook Dilemma," pp. 382–383.

[9] For a complete list of magazines and newspapers, see George D. Spache, *Good Reading for Poor Readers* (Champaign, Ill.: The Garrard Press, Publishers, 1958), pp. 92 ff.

Will it contribute to problem-solving skills?

Do illustrative materials—maps, pictures, drawings—contribute to the meaningfulness of the content?

Are study aids, suggested activities, and related references adequate?

Physical features

Is it attractive and appealing to children?

Are margins and page arrangements adequate?

Are size, spacing, and type size adequate?

Major emphases

Does the book inspire loyalty to American ideals and institutions?

Does it contain material that can be used to develop positive attitudes?

Are generalizations supported by facts?

Are controversial issues handled fairly and objectively?

Does the book emphasize movements and trends rather than isolated events?

Does it stimulate interests that lead to further study?[10]

Maps and globes. Teachers and children construct maps as one way of organizing information, but because most of the maps used in the elementary school are prepared commercially, we include them in this section. Next to books, maps are perhaps the most used instructional materials. Recent social and cultural events, development of a highly mobile population, and space age transportation have placed a greater emphasis upon maps.

Although maps are historically tied to geographic study, their current use is not limited to any one curriculum area. Classroom situations of all kinds call for constant references to maps. No longer are maps used only to locate places or facilitate the memorization of place names. Today the map is considered a vehicle for understanding the contemporary affairs of people and their cultures.

Reading a map involves interpretation of such abstractions as color, shading, outline, and scale. The pupil must be able to find and follow the map legend, or information data, and understand the semipictorial form symbolically indicating items such as rivers and mountains. To gain an adequate concept of the map's representation, he must also understand the various types of projections used to construct maps.[11]

Producers make maps available at three levels for the interpretation

---

[10] John U. Michaelis, *Social Studies for Children in a Democracy* (third edition) (Englewood Cliffs, N.J.: Prentice-Hall, Inc., 1963), p. 317.

[11] For an excellent description of map projections, see Brown and others, *A-V Instruction*, pp. 132–133.

of symbols: a simple map for beginners, a more advanced map for inter-mediate grade pupils, and maps of standard complexity for advanced students. Maps are also produced in a multiplicity of types. Content is available from physical or topographical maps; economic maps showing products, resources, or industry; political maps with location of cities and countries; cultural maps that present information about population or war. Forms of maps vary; they may be outlines, wall maps, atlases, decorative maps, globes, three-dimensional maps, and slides for projec-tion.

Dale lists some standards that may be used in selecting maps:

Visibility. Can students see and read the map without eye strain?

Detail. Is there too much detail?

Scale. Are the scale markings clear, dependable, and easily interpreted?

Symbols. . . . are there too many symbols to be remembered by the students?

Color. Is the color a genuine aid or an end in itself?

Accuracy. Is the map accurate in terms of its specific purpose?

Grade level. Is the map suited to the abilities of your students?

Point of view. Does the map help students to think of the world from points of view other than their own?

Durability. Will the map survive steady use in the classroom?[12]

Filmstrips, photographs, and photographic slides. These materials are increasingly available as free and inexpensive materials and can be teacher-made, but most come from commercial sources.

Filmstrips, photographs, and photographic slides are attention-focusing still pictures, studied by prints or projection. They have their limitations because they are a still form, but they can suggest motion. Their advantages lie in the ease with which they can be manipulated, their adaptability to all areas of the curriculum, their use in overcoming problems of space and time, and the way in which they reproduce reality. Skill is required to "read" or interpret the picture. The child's maturity, ability to notice details, or previous experience may influence the number, depth and validity of the clues received from the picture. The teacher's responsibility lies in selecting pictures appropriate to the children and helping them gain the skills of interpretation.

Flat pictures are a medium to which children respond naturally. Personal identification, too, is easily made with a good photograph. The greatest advantage of photographic flat pictures lies in the flexibility of use. They can be used to introduce subjects, provide information, moti-

---

[12] Dale, *Audio-Visual Methods,* pp. 341–342.

vate learning, correct impressions, or review subject matter. One picture may be used for a number of learning situations. Some of the problems in their use lie in mounting, display, appropriateness to time, and the possibility of ambiguous presentation.

Types of pictures are greatly varied. There are originals or reproductions of photographs, line drawings, paintings, and posters. Their function varies from those that demonstrate or explain a structure or operation to those that are documentary, that candidly present information about ways of life or phenomena. Also, there are the aesthetic interpretations of artists that serve more than informational functions.

Dale's standards for judging still pictures are helpful:

1. Will it achieve my teaching purpose?
2. Does the picture convey a generally true impression?
3. Does the picture give an accurate impression of relative size?
4. Will the picture add to the student's fund of knowledge?
5. Will the picture stimulate the imagination?
6. Is this a good picture technically and artistically?
7. Does the picture focus attention upon one main idea?
8. Does the picture have a proper amount of detail?[13]

A *filmstrip* is a group of pictures organized in a related sequence on a transparency for projection. When accompanied by a transcription, it is called a *sound filmstrip*. These materials are helpful because they are easily projected, require little storage space, can be used in a semi-darkened room, may be observed on the screen for as short or as long a time as necessary, and present information in a logical sequence. Some teachers feel this orderly sequence is inflexible and something of a limitation. In evaluating a filmstrip the teacher notes the suitability of the captions; the effectiveness of the sequential organization; the relevance and the timeliness of the material dealt with; the ways in which photographs, drawings, and diagrams are effectively related; and the ways in which discussion and other activities will result.

Transparent slides are usually in 2″ × 2″ and 4″ × 4″ dimensions. Slides can be shown in any order, and present many kinds of graphic representations: cartoons, graphs, diagrams, tables. Though they are slightly more costly and require a more fully darkened room, they have great usefulness in the classroom.

Several other types of equipment are designed to project materials. The opaque projector will project any nonopaque picture. The overhead transparency projector is designed so that the teacher may face the class rather than the screen as he draws or inserts pictures for projection. The

---

[13] Dale, pp. 269–274.

stereographic projector contains twin lenses so that a three-dimensional projection results. The tachistoscope is used for a timed exposure so that recognition of words, phrases, or pictures may be controlled. Microprojection is the projection of material from a microscope. Microfilm is a transparent picture in reduced size that may be projected. Each of these types of projection has advantages for particular situations.

Motion picture films. "Movies" bring both reality and imagination into the classroom. Their advantages are great in that they depict motion and sound, contain a minimum of titles to be read, and present a continuity of action. Films related to any area of the curriculum are available and may be presented at the convenience of the teacher and the children. Their production utilizes techniques so that real things may be reduced in size for an overall view, or things usually unseen by the human eye may be enlarged for studying. Microphotography, telescopic photography, X-ray photography, slow motion, fast motion, and animation help to overcome ordinary problems of time, size, and distance that would occur if the real things were observed. Movies have become invaluable records of actual events, and techniques of production facilitate documentation that is dramatic and authentic. Other types include fictional drama, religious information, travelogues, and training films. Innumerable films of increasingly high quality are being produced by governmental agencies, educational organizations, and commercial producers.

Though films are becoming more and more popular with teachers, a few limitations are discernible. When time and size are reduced or enlarged, children may form incorrect concepts. Films are being adapted to various age levels, but they may not always be adequate to the maturity of a special group. They are utilized for group instruction; individual use is difficult to arrange. Frequently mechanical difficulties occur in projection. Because films are so expensive, schools usually arrange to borrow them from a central source; there may be difficulty in ordering and length of time the films may be kept. Gradually teachers are understanding that films are not merely for entertainment, and that careful study, involving preparation and follow-up, is necessary to film utilization. Generally speaking, however, the educational value of films outweighs their limitations so that their use is encouraged. In evaluating films teachers use three criteria. First, the information presented is considered in terms of the age of the children, the direct interest appeal, the authenticity, and the direct relationship to the topic being studied. Second, the technical characteristics are important. One notices the color, sound, photography, organization, and good taste of the production. Third, the teacher is concerned with the educational quality, that is, the amount and kind of learning that it produces for the children.

Exhibits, objects, specimens. The "real things," such as objects, models, specimens, and samples that are three-dimensional, are commonly termed *realia.* With the modern improvements of packaging and plastic-embedding, and the engineering accomplishments of mock-ups, cut-aways, and models, some splendid materials are available. Their advantages stem from the fact that children can handle and manipulate these materials; they work *with* the things, not just study *about* them. Children can become familiar with the unfamiliar or extend understandings of the familiar. They can assemble and disassemble, care for, organize, classify, mount, and display these realia.

Samples may be living or preserved, in kits or in prepared exhibits, and either natural or man-made. Models may be enlarged or reduced from the original size to be made more useful for study. They may display working parts, or merely authentic structure and design, as ship models. They may be stationary, mechanical, or power driven.

The use of realia is most helpful but, like some "busy" window displays or pictures, too many such things can detract rather than add to a learning situation. Realia must be convenient in size, durable, simple, easy to find, inexpensive, and safe to have in the classroom.

Children and teacher find many means for displaying realia, but the primary methods are the exhibit and the specially arranged room environment. Social studies and science activities frequently call for such arrangements of materials, and particular ideas in language arts or arithmetic often need emphasis through a carefully arranged display that includes a number of related source materials. Dale lists several standards for exhibits that are worthy of note: An exhibit should (1) have one central idea, emphasizing simplicity; (2) be placed where it is certain to be seen; (3) be seen and not read—the message is received at a glance; (4) contain labels that are short and simple; (5) utilize labels that are uniform and legible, with careful lettering; (6) sometimes use motion to attract attention, such as a turning vase or waving flags; (7) be well lighted; (8) add interest and attractiveness with color; (9) add sound for emphasis as music or speech; (10) be worth looking at.[14]

Free and Inexpensive Materials

More and more public and private agencies, profit and nonprofit organizations whose business is not primarily education, are making available materials and services for the teacher's use. Among these free and inexpensive materials are books, pamphlets, cartoons, charts, comic books, samples, specimens, diagrams, pictures, maps, exhibits, films, and recordings.

---

[14] Dale, pp. 184–186.

Problems concerning use. The use of free and inexpensive materials has in some instances been questioned, and the major issue has apparently been concerned with the amount and quality of advertising accompanying the materials. Also, several years ago a number of materials were available that seemed poorly organized from an educational point of view. Too many ideas were displayed on one chart; materials were issued on the adult level and so had little meaning for many children; only one short sequence in a film would be relevant to the children's problem. Some school boards, in an attempt to screen materials that contained too much advertising and were educationally poor, set up strict policies concerning the use of free and inexpensive materials. Because of the criticism, organizations producing them have in recent years made an appreciable attempt to produce acceptable materials.

Sources. Business and industry and other types of organizations have found that it is good business to inform teachers, children, and parents about their products. Airline companies, oil companies, lumber and paper companies, and almost all large industries now have educational departments organized as part of their public relations programs. Excellent films, exhibits, and loan materials are commonly available, and in some situations personnel will be sent to talk with children and demonstrate materials.

Some industries have developed cooperative organizations that place education as one of their major purposes. The National Dairy Council and the American Association of Railroads are two examples of these. Governmental organizations also plan materials for school use. The United States Printing Office makes available for small sums many informational bulletins. Chambers of commerce, consuls, tourist bureaus, and other groups will send either free or for small sums many kinds of descriptive publications.

Commercial materials are varied and many, but finding them is made easy by the numerous catalogs that list free and inexpensive materials and are revised each year. Following is a list of the most popular of these catalogs:

Educators Progress Service. *Elementary Teachers Guide to Free Curriculum Materials,* Randolph, Wisconsin.

George Peabody College for Teachers. *Free and Inexpensive Learning Materials.* Division of Surveys and Field Services, Nashville, Tennessee.

Kenworthy, Leonard S. *Free and Inexpensive Materials on World Affairs.* Public Affairs Press, 2153 Florida Avenue, Washington, D.C.

Miller, Bruce. *Sources of Free Pictures. Sources of Free and Inexpensive Teaching Aids. Sources of Free and Inexpensive Pictures.* Box 368, Riverside, California.

National Education Association, Association for Supervision and Curriculum Development. *Using Free Materials in the Classroom.* 1201 16th Street N.W., Washington, D.C.

Salisbury, Gordon, and Robert Sheridan. *Catalog of Free Teaching Aids.* P.O. Box 943, Riverside, California.

Criteria for selecting free and inexpensive materials. As teachers evaluate free and inexpensive materials preliminary to using them, they will consider several factors. Grambs has developed a check list for selection of current materials that will serve as standards for evaluation.

1. Is the agency that produced the materials clearly stated?
2. Are sources given for quoted facts? If so, are the sources reputable and authoritative?
3. Is the date of publication given? Is the material recent, when usefulness of the data depends upon recency?
4. Are any particular groups or individuals singled out for derogatory portrayal that is likely to give offense?
5. Is the cost, if any, commensurate with the educational value of the material?
6. Can materials be filed for future use?
7. Are the films and filmstrips reviewed in standard guides to films? If so, is the review favorable for the use contemplated?
8. Do commercial aspects of the material outweigh the educational contribution?
9. Does the material support a special-interest point of view without due regard to objectivity?
10. Does use of the material obligate the school in any way?
11. Is the material in accordance with school policy regarding the use of textbook material?
12. Are the reading level and the idea content within the range of ability of the class?
13. Would any of the community mores be offended by use of the materials?[15]

Community Resources

The community in which the school operates, in which the children live, is one of the most valuable sources of instructional materials.

The community-school concept. There can be no doubt that the close interrelationship of school and community makes the school a more effective social institution. The community-school concept places primary importance upon viewing the school as a part of the human affairs that

---

[15] Jean D. Grambs, *Using Current Materials to Study Current Problems* (Stanford, Calif.: Stanford University Press, 1952), p. 27.

surround it, as knowing the community, serving it, and using it as a source for learning.

The teacher who knows the community utilizes it as a rich source for instructional material. He finds people and things to bring to the classroom, and places to which to take his pupils. He uses the community as a laboratory that furnishes opportunities for both concrete direct experiences and the means of exploring more abstract social processes.

The contributions of community resources to classroom learning include access to the realities of life itself. Through observing, listening to, and talking to people, and visiting places, children learn more about the world around them. They come to understand more about work and the interdependencies of people's jobs. They learn something of the variety of problems facing the local community, and the way solutions are developed and applied. They can be helped to develop a sense of history in relation to local community life that is useful not only in that setting but in the several wider community contexts which they must come to understand and in which they must learn to live effectively.

In utilizing the community the teacher is careful to maintain accepted social amenities. Preplanning facilitates the orderly handling of children and helps to guarantee full use of time. Common courtesy is demonstrated in every situation. Letters of request are sent to places one would visit, of invitation to persons sought for classroom visits, of thanks to both after the visits have been made. When materials are borrowed for use in the classroom they should be labeled for prompt and accurate return to the owner. Children should learn to handle and use such material carefully and correctly.

Kinds of resources available. Usable as sources for learning are local libraries of all kinds, museums, industries (such as a newspaper plant, oil refinery, airport), governmental agencies (such as the courthouse, the post office), hospitals, service organizations (such as Red Cross, chamber of commerce), and so on.

In industry, libraries, governmental offices, and other community agencies are found valuable *published materials:* census reports, courthouse records, telephone books, city directories, weather reports, industrial and other organizational reports, advertising, brochures, pamphlets, pictures, and films. Samples, specimens, and other realia available from community services have already been discussed under free and inexpensive materials.

One question arises in the consideration of using sources of information. How does the teacher find them? He, of course, utilizes the usual references such as the district source files and published catalogs. (See list at the end of this chapter.) Also the wise teacher consults the children. Thirty sets of eyes, ears, and questions are more effective than one. Children who help to gather materials have a greater interest in classroom activities, higher motivation for learning, and a stronger feeling of belonging, having made a contribution to the group.

Field trips. Field trips are a widely used method of instruction. Entering kindergartners and first graders are often oriented to the school and its immediate neighborhood by taking short walks to see the houses, the busy street, the shopping center, or the fire station. This will help children know their neighborhood and the activity within it. Field trips to factories, museums, zoos, government agencies, and other community institutions are accepted in most schools as important ways to understand the local area and to enrich curricular content.

Taking the children out of the school on a trip involves administrative procedure that varies with each school district. More and more community organizations are cooperating with the schools as they seek to build public understanding of their functions. Most frequently the teacher arranges for an expert to guide the children during the trip. The teacher first ascertains if the factory or business is willing to cooperate, what facilities they will exhibit, how the tour will be conducted, and to what extent the information gained will contribute to the educational purpose of the trip. The date and time are carefully prearranged. In some districts, school buses are readily made available; in others, parents or other means must be used for transportation. Usually the trip is preceded by the careful formulation of questions the pupils need to have answered. Follow-up includes evaluating the information received in relation to prestated questions as well as recording information and pursuing activities that have emerged from the trip.

Consultants. Another method of bringing the school and the community closer together is to ask members of the community to contribute to the program. From the community and its various agencies and organizations come people that can be used as consultants: teachers, "old-timers," postmen, businessmen, travel agents, government officials such as the county agricultural agent, representatives from industry, and parents.

A most valuable source of information is direct contact with people who are "experts" on the topic under study. The policeman, the judge, and other community helpers are frequently invited to the classroom to tell the children about their responsibilities. A pilot, a grocery man, a ticket agent, and other businessmen can serve as consultants at every school level. Children can help to find the aunt or the neighbor who can make Mexican tortillas, the friend who has traveled in Canada and taken pictures, or the engineer who worked on the big dam and has personal experiences to tell about it. Many large businesses employ men who deal with public relations and educational services; they are happy to talk to the children and bring materials for them to use.

Preparing for a consultant involves more than inviting him according to the accepted social custom. Michaelis lists the following guidelines for use with consultants:

1. Through group discussion determine whether or not the use of the visitor is the best way to secure required information on existing needs and problems.

2. Clarify and list the specific needs and questions on which help is desired.

3. Select a resource person who can make a rich contribution.

4. Plan with the visitor, giving attention to timing and the needs, questions, interests, and age level of the group. Give special attention to vocabulary and illustrative materials that may be used.

5. Make plans with the children for receiving the visitor, introductions, expression of appreciation, behavior standards, and recording procedures.

6. Both the teacher and children should be ready to raise questions and state problems.

7. The teacher should guide the discussion and stimulate group thinking as needed.

8. Use the information to solve problems and to further expression through reporting, art, writing, dramatization, and so forth.

9. Evaluate the effectiveness of the use made of the information secured.

10. Write a letter of appreciation including (if possible) material showing how the contribution was used.

11. Continue the unit, moving on to new needs and problems that have arisen.[16]

Radio and television. Mass media provided by community enterprises cannot be ignored as instructional material. We have already said a little about newspapers and magazines; radio and especially television are growing in importance and have a number of characteristics in common. Both are utilized at home more often than at school. These media have a great influence upon the opinions and ideas of the people of our country; children come to school expressing these opinions and behaving accordingly. The tunes they hum, the advertisements they quote, the programs they discuss that have been heard or viewed at home become part of school life. Both radio and television produce planned programs that are arranged according to public demand and sponsor need. It is difficult to know how much the programs influence what people want and how much what people want influences the programs presented.

---

[16] Michaelis, *Social Studies,* p. 517.

Both radio and television can broadcast events at the time of origin and can record these events for later presentation. Sports, political meetings, and special events such as election returns and space launchings are listened to and viewed by millions. One hundred years ago important news took months or years to reach the far corners of the world.

Radio is the older of the two media, and since the advent of television it has cut back the kinds of presentations it offers for the public and for the schools. Radio programs have been helpful to teachers because children can listen in some cases more easily than they can read. The uniqueness of the medium is in itself an influence upon learning. One disadvantage stems from scheduling. The science or music program must be heard when it is scheduled, whether at recess time or arithmetic time. Also, some excellent programs worth using for school purposes are scheduled during out-of-school hours, and the teacher must accordingly make modifications in the teaching procedure. Another disadvantage is the limitation of one-way communication. The teacher on the radio can only tell his audience. Questions and discussions are possible only with the local teacher after the broadcast. Some programs have attempted to overcome this problem by preparing in advance materials that are sent to participating schools, and by receiving questions that may be discussed in later broadcast lessons.

Television is a new and constantly improving medium, and its advantages for education seem to be mounting. Some research information is now available but we still need to know more about the effectiveness of television. We do know that children spend many out-of-school hours watching it.

From eleven studies made from 1958 to 1960 Schramm and associates come to these conclusions:

> A child who has begun to use television by age three typically uses it about 45 minutes a weekday (Monday through Friday). By age five his viewing has increased until, on the average, it is a little over two hours a day. From age six until about the sixth grade, when the child is entering adolescence, viewing time is on a slowly rising plane between two and two and a half hours. Then viewing time rises rather sharply to a high of a little over three hours a day. This hump usually occurs somewhere between the fifth and eighth grades. Then it enters upon a slowly falling slope until by the twelfth grade (about age seventeen) it is again between two and two and a half hours.
>
> These are weekday figures. Sunday viewing averages from one-half to one hour longer.[17]

[17] Wilbur Schramm, Jack Lyle, and Edwin B. Parker, *Television in the Lives of Our Children* (Stanford, Calif.: Stanford University Press, 1961), p. 30.

Television has greatly broadened experiences for today's children. Their vocabulary, their ideas, and their play reflect these experiences. Interest in various curriculum areas has been stimulated because of television. The elementary school teacher needs to watch the children's programs once in a while just to understand their language and their ideas. It is well to remember that the programs designed for the general public are produced by showmen, not educators. Some of Walt Disney's programs, for example, have much educational worth, but their primary purpose is entertainment. It is no wonder that youngsters are more interested in subjects like "Beaver Valley" than in subjects found in the basic textbook. The problem of content in television programs, especially those used in classrooms, is of great concern to educators.

Several kinds of television programs are emerging that can be helpful to the teacher. More and more educational channels are being established that present both national and local programs of educational interest. Most programs now are on the adult level, but a number are especially designed for children. The *kinescope,* or photographically recorded transcription of TV programs, is being increasingly used. *Videotape* (television recording on magnetic tape) is used similarly. Special events and other appropriate programs that have been recorded are available for school use. *Closed circuit television* is gaining such acceptance that some schools are purchasing the expensive equipment necessary for it. In the closed circuit, a broadcast is made only to the sets that are connected directly. Use of closed circuit TV has demonstrated great possibilities for classroom instruction and for inservice and preservice teacher education.

The consensus is that television can teach. The training of instructors for television is not complicated, and the teaching is good because careful preparation is made. Teaching done over television is not "off the cuff" as it sometimes is in the classroom. Part of the success is that many kinds of instructional materials are used on television, such as pictures and charts, chalkboard illustrations, and demonstrations serving to point out and relate the small details of a topic. Such techniques have been worked out because of the limitations in time and in the scope of the picture. Some educators believe that oversimplification could result, at the cost of effectiveness. Television programming must be understood by the classroom teacher so that the classroom time used for preparation and follow-up may be modified to make the best use of the medium.

The disadvantage of one-way communication in television or in radio has been identified and some steps are being taken to overcome it in the classroom follow-up. Though television can bring specialists to the children, the teacher must follow through on the ideas and provide for participation for the children other than listening and watching the program.

Teacher-Made Materials

Finally, we discuss the kinds of materials that are prepared by the teacher or, under his guidance, by the children themselves. Though this section is titled "teacher-made materials" the term will include both.

The need for teacher-made materials. Not all materials necessary to teaching are available from outside sources. Schools make every effort to procure adequate and varied materials of instruction, but it is well understood that these prepared materials are supplemented by the teacher. Often because of special circumstances, very special materials are demanded. For example, they may be needed to provide reading material for slow readers or to make readily available otherwise obscure information needed in an ongoing unit of work. When children can help to prepare such materials they have a valuable experience in organizing information and in devising appropriate ways of communicating it to others.

Kinds of teacher-made materials. Almost all the materials discussed thus far here may be designed and prepared by the teacher. Models, maps, posters, cartoons, booklets, charts, graphs, recordings, pictures, slides—all can be produced completely or partially by the teacher.

Teachers collect and organize picture files. They make flannel boards, pocket charts, number lines, and flash cards. They make simple barometers, rain gauges, and electric switchboards. Over the years the typical teacher comes to have an extensive and varied collection of materials he has prepared for his own use in the classroom.

Skills needed for teacher-made materials. The production of teacher-made materials requires certain skills in design and construction. Familiarity with layout and lettering, skill in the use of such tools as lettering pens, simple carpenter's hand tools, measuring and cutting tools, and an understanding of the techniques of mounting, scoring, and spatter and spray painting—all will help the teacher achieve more usable teacher-made materials.

PROGRAMMED LEARNING MATERIALS

Programmed learning materials have assumed a strategic importance in recent years and must be discussed here. Essentially such materials organize subject matter in a particular way enabling a learner to instruct himself. The use of programmed materials today is additional evidence of the educators' constant search for more effective methods of instruction.[18]

Programmed learning is not a completely new idea. Some would say that Plato was the first programmer, because his tutorial type of teaching progressed from fact to fact, and insight to insight, through continual stimuli and responses involving teacher and student. First suggestions and designs for a machine that would "teach" came from Sidney L. Pressey in 1926,[19] but Pressey's machines involved primarily a method of testing for information or arriving at a correct response through repeated choices. The "father" of the present teaching machines is B. F. Skinner of Harvard University who improved upon Pressey's ideas in 1958 to produce a more versatile machine.[20] Automated procedures or "teaching machines" advanced the popularity of programming in the early 1960's. In the last few years, however, the machine has lost much of its importance, and emphasis has shifted to the program itself and to the theory and practice of programmed instruction. The character of materials has changed from a test that determines how much a student already knows to a method of presenting new material. In 1964 it was estimated that five hundred programs were available for school use either in textbook or machine format.[21]

Types of Programming

Several types of programming systems have emerged as the materials have been developed. One is the *linear program* in which a correct response leads directly to the next problem or frame in the sequence. Pressey's linear program used a multiple-choice format in which the learner was to recognize the answer from a set of alternatives. From a stimulus the learner makes a response by selecting an answer. If his choice is incorrect, he goes back into the program until he finds the correct answer and only then proceeds to the next item.

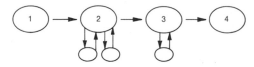

[18] Fund for the Advancement of Education, *Four Case Studies of Programed Instruction* (New York: The Fund, June 1964). 94 pages.

[19] For details of his ideas, see Sidney L. Pressey, "A Simple Device Which Gives Tests and Scores and Teaches," *School and Society*, Vol. 23, pp. 373–376.

[20] See B. F. Skinner, "Teaching Machines," *Science* (Oct. 1958), pp. 969–977.

[21] NEA, Division of Audio-Visual Services, *Selection and Use of Programed Materials* (Washington, D.C.: NEA, 1964), p. 8.

Skinner's linear program emphasizes a "constructed response" in which clues link the correct answers so the learner can compose his own response. Recall is more important than recognition in this system.

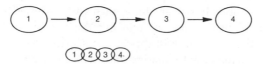

Crowder was the first to introduce the *branching program* in which a pupil's response may lead to any one of several related responses before progressing to the next level. He believes that in this kind of program it is possible to deal with opinions and therefore to teach about abstractions as well as more straightforward information.

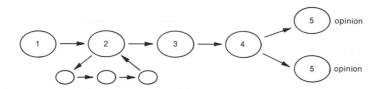

Characteristics of Programmed Materials

All programs, no matter what the form, have certain characteristics in common:

1. The information is presented in a careful logical sequence.
2. Sequence is designed in small segments or steps gradually increasing in level of difficulty.
3. The material demands active, overt response at each step by the learner.
4. There is a constant interaction between the learner and the program.
5. The learner is immediately informed of the accuracy of his response; therefore he has constant knowledge of his progress.
6. The degree of advance is so small, and continuity and previous learning are so well integrated with clues to the next new situation, that the learner's response is almost errorless, correct about 95 percent of the time.
7. The learner responds to each idea many times and in different contexts.
8. The material is self-pacing, designed so that the learner may progress at his own rate.
9. The learning situation is individual; one is not in competition with other learners.

Special advantages and related problems. At present programmed materials are being used on a largely experimental basis for instruction in several subjects throughout the country. Already it seems apparent that some subjects are more adaptable to programming than others. At the present time more has been done with programmed materials in the elementary school in the area of reading than in any other part of the curriculum. At the same time it appears that other parts of the language arts and a great deal of mathematics may well be successfully adapted to programming.

Some leaders in elementary education look upon programmed materials with suspicion and doubt their value. They react negatively to ideas of *automatic teaching, mechanical learning,* and the like. At the same time a number of advantages are pointed out by the proponents of programmed materials. One lies in the fact that work is done at the student's own pace. The child goes as fast or as slow as necessary to assure satisfactory responses. The result is individualized instruction. Some liken it to the tutorial system in which teacher and student work in a one-to-one relationship.

Programs immediately reinforce correct responses, too, or indicate wrong ones as the case may be. Progress through a program seems to assure "mastery" at every level. The immediate feedback furnished to the student in this programmed context gains considerable support from present-day psychologists.

Some authorities maintain that programmed materials will relieve the teacher of much that is repetitive in teaching, allowing him more time for the creative details of teaching, for those more personally inspiring aspects of the job, and for the "personal touch" that programs cannot provide. In fact, some observers believe that the use of programmed materials will drastically change the role of the teacher.

Despite the seeming advantages of programmed materials, questions continue to arise concerning their use. Some of these questions center on the very important matter of ensuring that high quality programs are developed. And these questions lead to concerns about the proper combination of persons to develop programmed materials. What cluster of competences is needed for this task? Another set of problems has to do with the way the teacher will use available programs, including the type and kind of student most apt to profit from their use. Some educators feel that the repetitive and redundant style of such materials will make them seem dull and boring to other than slow-learning children. They need evidence that bright children will maintain interest in such materials.

Still, the programmed materials from which the teacher could select continue to multiply. And teachers are trying to develop appropriate criteria for their selection and use in the classroom. Matters of curricular relevance, cost, restructured use of teacher time, utilization for remedial, review, or enrichment purposes and similar concerns are important to these criteria.

Computer-assisted instruction. While it was indicated earlier that there is somewhat less excitement over the machine or "hardware" part of programmed materials now than was true some years ago, there is one important qualification that must be invoked. It has to do with the extent to which the computer is being linked with programmed materials in what is referred to as a computer-assisted instructional system. We are all becoming increasingly aware of the impact of the computer on our lives. One estimate suggests that computer-affiliated activities—that is, the designing, manufacturing, programming, and servicing of computers— will constitute the world's leading occupation by 1970.[22]

Computers are already in experimental use as instructional aids for teaching in the areas of reading and arithmetic in the elementary school. Some of this work centers on the provision of drill and practice exercises in classrooms. Appropriate exercises are selected by the computer and transmitted via telephone lines to teletype terminals in classrooms. As pupils type their answers to the exercises presented, the computer responds, letting them know if they are right or wrong. And, depending on their performance each day, the computer selects appropriate exercises for each pupil to work on the next day. It also furnishes each day to the teacher a record of what each individual pupil did in his time at the teletype and a composite of the performance of the total class.

Even more engaging are the computer-assisted instruction systems which are being tested to provide instruction in reading and arithmetic to children in the elementary school. A project at Stanford University, under the direction of Professors Suppes and Atkinson and focused on teaching first grade pupils to read and to do beginning arithmetic, is at the forefront in this area.[23] Industry is investing a great deal of money in the development of prototype systems that can be used in this way. The work in this area at the present time must be seen as tentative and experimental. But already the results are exciting, and it would seem that we are but on the threshold of understanding the potential that may reside in the combination of the high-speed computer and programmed materials of instruction. Many elementary educators are reluctant to embrace this development hurriedly. They have reservations about the possible effects on pupils of computerized instruction. They see in this development a

[22] Shirley Thomas, *Computers* (New York: Holt, Rinehart, and Winston, Inc., 1965), p. 9.
[23] Richard Atkinson and Duncan Hansen, "Computer-Assisted Instruction in Initial Reading: The Stanford Project," in *Reading Research Quarterly* (Fall 1966), Vol. II, No. 1 (International Reading Association, Newark, Delaware), pp. 5–26.

dehumanizing move in the education of children, and they are skeptical of it. Others are more concerned lest such instructional systems be used before they have been perfected to the extent that they must be, if they are to do the job which many see them being able to do. These persons especially are fearful that the "hardware" part of such systems will be satisfactory before the "software" or program part is, and that somehow the American penchant for technology will demand their use before they really are ready. Be that as it may, the potential of such systems to provide individualized instruction for pupils will assure their further development and use in the years ahead. They seem to us to have much to offer.

THE CURRICULUM MATERIALS LABORATORY

A center for services to teacher and students alike is rapidly gaining importance in design and function. The curriculum materials laboratory may be identified by various terms throughout the country: instructional materials center, audio-visual center, instructional technology center, multi-media instructional laboratory, communication media center, learning resources center. The term *curriculum materials laboratory* refers to that central place designated to provide access to the variety of materials that will enhance the teaching-learning situation and the services of personnel trained as materials specialists.

It has been well said that a "resources or instructional materials center provides the life blood of a man-machine educational system, and through it the developing technology finds its expression. It is the subsystem for information processing, not for administrative efficiency alone, but for promoting learning, the main function of the whole system."[24]

Most often the curriculum materials laboratory is organized at the district level to provide services for all schools. The pooling of materials, equipment, and personnel is more economical and makes possible a wider variety of resources. The center, whether at the district or local school level, has a dual function as a resource center and as a learning center.

The curriculum materials laboratory stores and distributes all materials and equipment that is considered practicable to purchase and use. Trained personnel base the selection of materials upon their technical knowledge, local curricular programs, and teachers' demands.

One would expect to find in the laboratory a full line of audio-visual equipment: movie, filmstrip, slide, and overhead projectors, television

---

[24] William Clark Trow, *Teacher and Technology: New Designs for Learning* (New York: Appleton-Century-Crofts, Inc., 1963), p. 126.

sets, tape recorders, record players, and electronic copying machines. Also stored there are the filmstrips, records, tapes, motion pictures, slides, transparencies, and transcriptions needed for use in the machines, and instructional manuals related to them. Files of books, pamphlets, and mounted pictures are organized for ready use. Realia of infinite variety, instructional kits, and complete self-contained packages of instructional materials on specific topics are available. Mobile projection stands for single or multiple use of communication media may be there. Specialized materials, such as wood, nails, and chip board, may also be kept in the laboratory or are procured for teachers through the laboratory.

Also at hand is information that will help the teacher go beyond the resources of the laboratory. Catalogs, source books, and indexes to free or rental libraries call attention to many audio-visual products. Other catalogs list free and inexpensive materials from business, industry, and governmental groups from across the nation. Files of community resources, and lists of possible field trips or resource personnel in the locale may be part of the information available to the teacher.

Effective use of the laboratory as a resource center depends on the ease with which teachers can use it. Various means are employed to help teachers and students find the needed material. Most district level centers offer regular delivery services to schools. Where the center is a part of an individual school, procurement is very simple, of course.

RECOMMENDED READINGS

BROWN, JAMES W., and KENNETH D. NORBERG. *Administering Educational Media*. New York: McGraw-Hill Book Company, Inc., 1965.

DE BERNARDIS, AMO. *The Use of Instructional Materials*. New York: Appleton-Century-Crofts, Inc., 1960.

DIAMOND, ROBERT M. (editor). *A Guide to Instructional Television*. New York: McGraw-Hill Book Company, Inc., 1964.

FRY, EDWARD. *Teaching Machines and Programmed Instruction*. New York: McGraw-Hill Book Company, Inc., 1963.

HALACY, D. S., JR. *Computers: The Machines We Think With*. New York: Harper & Row, Publishers, Inc., 1962.

KINDER, JAMES S. *Using Audio-Visual Materials in Education*. New York: American Book Company, 1965.

LAIRD, DONALD, and ELEANOR C. LAIRD. *How to Get Along with Automation*. New York: McGraw-Hill Book Company, Inc., 1963.

THOMAS, R. MURRAY, and SHERWIN G. SWARTOUT. *Integrated Teaching Materials* (revised edition). New York: David McKay Company, Inc., 1963.

WILLIAMS, CATHERINE M. *Learning from Pictures*. Washington, D.C., Department of Audio-Visual Instruction, NEA, 1963.

WITTICH, WALTER ARNO, and CHARLES FRANCIS SCHULLER. *Audio-Visual Materials: Their Nature and Use* (fourth edition). New York: Harper & Row, Publishers, Inc., 1967.

For lists of sources of textbooks, periodicals, films, recordings, equipment, three-dimensional materials, maps, globes, pictures, graphics, free and inexpensive materials, see the appendices of the following books:

BROWN, JAMES W., RICHARD B. LEWIS, and FRED F. HARCLEROAD. *A-V Instruction: Materials and Methods* (second edition). New York: McGraw-Hill Book Company, Inc., 1964. Pp. 571–584.

DALE, EDGAR. *Audio-Visual Methods in Teaching* (revised edition). New York: Holt, Rinehart and Winston, Inc., 1954. P. 534.

EBOCH, SIDNEY C. *Operating Audio-Visual Equipment.* San Francisco: Chandler Publishing Company, 1960. P. 73.

KINDER, JAMES S. *Audio-Visual Materials and Techniques* (second edition). New York: American Book Company, 1959. P. 592.

SANDS, LESTER B. *Audio-Visual Procedures in Teaching.* New York: The Ronald Press Company, 1956. P. 670.

THOMAS, R. MURRAY, and SHERWIN G. SWARTOUT. *Integrated Teaching Materials.* New York: David McKay Company, Inc., 1963. P. 545.

Evaluation: Determining Progress Toward Goals

17

The point has been made on several occasions that elementary school education is formal education. Everything is done that can reasonably be done to minimize the factor of chance in the education of children. Goals are established, and the educational enterprise is brought to bear on their accomplishment. It will be remembered that the curriculum has been viewed as the school's plan for the intentional modification of behavior in the direction of agreed-upon educational objectives. The commitment of the school to evaluation is obvious in this statement. An agency that would intentionally modify behavior must know from time to time how successful or unsuccessful it is being at the task. As for the classroom teacher, McDonald, an educational psychologist, makes a strong point when he says:

> . . . a practitioner who cannot measure reliably and validly the behavior he tries to produce and control is helpless. He does not know when he has succeeded or failed. He cannot estimate progress. He cannot revise instructional strategies to fit the present acquisitions of learners.[1]

Here we will be concerned primarily with evaluation from the standpoint of the classroom teacher. Much of what will be dealt with has carry-over value for thinking of a total elementary school program, or for a total system of schools. Evaluation must occur at all of these levels; we choose here to emphasize the classroom teacher as such.

---

[1] Frederick J. McDonald, *Educational Psychology* (second edition) (Belmont, Calif.: Wadsworth Publishing Company, Inc., 1965), p. 580.

Consistency of Evaluation with Stated Objectives

Evaluation begins with the objectives which the school and the teacher are trying to achieve—with the behavior modifications and changes which they seek to bring about in pupils. At this point it would be wise to review the material on educational goals in Chapter 4. Note especially the concern expressed there for more specific and less general statements of these goals. That plea was made so that teachers would know more assuredly what it was that they were really to try to accomplish with their pupils. The more specific and concrete the expression of the goal the more likely that the actions taken by the teacher, and the responses sought from pupils, would be consistent with it. In that chapter elementary educators were urged to give due thought to the behavioral expression of goals as an aid to clarity and as a way of reducing ambiguity in instruction.

Here we must consider the same set of propositions again, but this time from the standpoint of ascertaining whether or not goals stated have been achieved. When goals are not stated well and are thus understood only partially by teachers, what follows is that evaluations are made against goals other than those agreed upon—not so much in the intentional sense of doing something else, but in the unintended sense of not realizing the difference. A consequence is that the pupil is asked to do on a test things only obliquely related to central purposes. In the process he is reinforced and rewarded for learning accordingly, again on matters only tangentially related to the goals which are really intended to be the focus of effort.

Coverage of the Totality of Objectives

An evaluation program must cover the full range of objectives to which a particular elementary school and classroom is committed. The cognitive goals must be considered as well as the affective goals, the subject matter goals as well as the personal-social goals. That progress toward all of them, not just some of them, must be judged is overlooked more often than would be expected. Schools and teachers often place priority on intellectual goals, to the point that a disproportionate amount of attention may be given to their evaluation. Also, the instruments available for measuring progress in the areas of attitudes, values, interests, appreciations, and many personal-social goals are not very satisfactory.

For this reason schools shy away from their use and teachers shy away from attempts to construct such instruments themselves. Still there must be evaluation that is related to each of the broad areas within which goals are stated. One simply cannot defend spending time in school on behavior changes of whatever kind and then not try to evaluate the results of the effort. What is called for is the development of more adequate instrumentation to get at some of these less tangible goals.

The Focus on Immediate and Not Ultimate Objectives

Evaluation by the teacher in the elementary school classroom usually focuses on the attainment of immediate objectives, and is concerned little with the evaluation of ultimate ones. The classroom teacher plans week by week, provides learning experiences for his class, and wants to evaluate the results. What he does next at any given time is a function of what this rather immediate evaluation tells him. Yet a teacher always has a sense of the ultimate. It gives a kind of direction to his efforts and adds importance to them. But the task of prediction when dealing with the ultimate is difficult and uncertain. To move from a positive evaluation of a child's work in a civics unit on primary elections to any very strong statements about the way in which he will participate in a political party as an adult is impossible. To conclude that a child who computes accurately in simple arithmetic will not make errors in maintaining his check book account as an adult is to stretch the point. Predictions can be made only after studies have been conducted which follow children into adulthood and establish a relationship at some level better than chance. Only then is prediction against ultimate goals very fruitful.

TEACHING AND EVALUATION

Evaluation is an integral part of the total teaching act. Any paradigm on teaching will start with goals and end with evaluation. Through evaluation the teacher is provided with feedback about his teaching and about his pupils' learning. It is on the basis of what this feedback is that next steps are contemplated and next actions taken. Viewed thus, evaluation becomes a continuing process. It is not an event that takes place only once every six or eight or ten weeks. Summaries of evaluations are pulled together at spaced intervals and are usually coincident with the sending home of report cards or the convening of parent-teacher progress conferences. Sometimes a special summing-up evaluation takes place at the end of a major unit of work or an extended sequence in mathematics. But evaluation has also been going on while the unit was being developed or the sequence accomplished. It is not only an integral but a continuing aspect of teaching.

EVALUATION AS PROCEDURE

Evaluation as procedure includes several things It includes agreement on the behavior that teaching is to develop (the matter of goals). It calls for some measure of behavior change on the part of the pupil. It requires a standard of some sort so that the measured amount of change can be referred to for evaluation. And this must include some orientation to a range of behavior around the standard along some "outstanding–barely satisfactory" or "acceptable–unacceptable" continuum. Think about this in terms of states a pupil can name, countries a pupil can locate on a map, addition facts a pupil can recall, art media with which a pupil can work. How would you evaluate his naming thirty-seven states? What if he can locate all of the countries in South America? What if he can locate a country on that continent when asked to by reference to a map which shows boundaries only? Let us consider some other matters that will help us to understand this whole procedure more completely.

Evaluation and Measurement

Evaluation, assuming goal agreement, begins with measurement. The teacher must have some way of determining whether or not the behavior change sought has actually taken place, and to what degree or extent it has taken place. That is, a teacher is measuring pupil performance all the time as he finds himself reflecting on the way in which Bill can do something but Joe cannot, or the ease with which Mary relates to her peers but the difficulties Arleen has in relating. While this informal measurement is important, it is not sufficient for the teacher's overall purposes. Some children may be overlooked, and some learning goals may be missed almost entirely. To prevent such omissions, a more systematic and regularized approach to measurement becomes necessary.

The observation of children. The teacher can observe and describe children in typical situations which call for the use of the behavior with which the teacher is concerned. Such a way of measuring has much to recommend it. A real situation is more accurately measured than a contrived situation. There are, however, some real limitations on the use of observation by the teacher for measuring purposes. One of these has to do with the problem of obtaining a representative sample of any pupil's behavior. The pupil may not naturally use the behavior under scrutiny, especially in anything approaching the full range of it, at the time when he can be observed. What the teacher sees may not be an adequate sample for evaluation purposes. Secondly, there is the problem of recording what has been observed. Usually the teacher cannot simply sit down and observe, recording data in the process. Typically there is a lapse of time between the observation and the recording of it, and the record often becomes incomplete and inaccurate as a result. The teacher records what impressed him most, and other less impressive but potentially more important parts of the observation are lost to the evaluation. Teachers can work to become more skillful and efficient with observations, and undoubtedly they will improve in their use of them.

Teachers may keep *anecdotal records* on children in their class. Such a record should contain complete, nonjudgmental, systematic descriptions of typical samples of behavior for a given child. The record should note what a child did, and it should not contain attempts to explain why he did it. If such a record is held to descriptions of behavior only, and if it extends over a sufficient period of time and over an adequate number of different behavior settings or categories (on the playground, in class, and so on) it can eventually lend itself to evaluation. But, if the record itself becomes judgmental in its choice of words and phrases, and if anecdotes are few in number and erratically collected, they suffer all of the weaknesses of ongoing child observation as noted above.[2]

Tests and children's performances.   Most teachers use tests to measure behavior change in pupils. Tests can help the teacher to determine the present status of pupil performance, and some tests lend themselves to prediction about future performance on the basis of present status. A test is a contrived situation. In a test every effort is made to require pupil responses that are consistent with goals sought. Tests merely sample performance. It is not possible to ask pupils to do everything that they might be able to do if time were available. Therefore, the sample of behavior taken by a test must be a representative sample of the totality of behavior which could be measured and about which the teacher is concerned. It is assumed that the pupils being evaluated have had an opportunity to learn whatever the test includes. As contrasted with natural observations, children know when they are being tested. Tests take place at specified times, and they are usually announced ahead of time so that children may prepare themselves for them. The test situation is the same for the whole class or for a particular subgroup of the class. If the test is timed, all pupils are given the same limited amount of time. If it is a power test, all pupils may work as long as they want to. All must either write their reponses to test items, or give them orally, or actually

---

2 See A. E. Traxler, *The Nature and Use of Anecdotal Records* (New York: Educational Records Bureau, 1939).

perform tasks, or do some combination of all of these. In the test situation more control is exercised over the behavior under study, with the result that information from it is usually seen as being more dependable for evaluation purposes.

The Preparation of Tests

Some tests are prepared commercially and others are prepared by the teacher. Both kinds of tests have their place in the classroom, and both are used. Before they are considered here, let us define two terms used in conjunction with tests and note the kinds of tests available.

Test validity. Test validity is the extent to which a test actually provides a measurement of that which it purports to measure. This quality is more accurately referred to as *content* validity. The tester wants to be assured that whatever is included in the test is consistent with what the school and the teacher have been trying to accomplish with pupils. The test would be invalid and unfair for evaluation purposes if it sampled behaviors other than those which the teacher has been trying to develop. There is a different kind of validity, referred to as *predictive* validity, which has to do with conclusions that a teacher will make about future performance, on the basis of present status. Readiness tests, for example, must include a kind of predictive validity.

Test reliability. Test reliability is the consistency with which a test measures. If a test is reliable, a pupil would make about the same score if he took the test more than one time.

Kinds of tests. Tests in one large category are concerned with achievement, with the attainment of objectives set for pupils. Some of these are designed to serve certain diagnostic purposes as well, that is to help the teacher to ascertain the reasons for inadequate performance, in light of which teaching procedures may be adjusted. Tests in a second large category are concerned with the measurement of pupil characteristics other than achievement. These tests focus on intelligence, on aptitudes, on interests, and on other personality factors. These are useful in evaluation. For example, decisions about the adequacy of a child's performance are made with an eye to the ability to perform which he possesses.

Commercially Prepared Tests

Testing is an important and extensive aspect of the operation of schools with the result that tests are prepared and sold commercially for the use of teachers. Almost any type of test known is available on this commercial market. Since this discussion is necessarily limited, most of the attention will be given to the standardized tests of achievement about which one hears so often.

The meaning of standardization. A standardized test is one that has been prepared carefully over a considerable period of time by people who are expert at the task. In the process of being standardized, the test is administered to a very large number of pupils (thousands usually) and their scores on the test are computed. These scores are then reported in the form of "norms" which are organized around the typical performance in the pupil group that took the test, and which show the distribution of performances above and below this typical performance. Later, when a pupil takes the test, his *raw* score, that is the actual number of right or wrong responses, is usually translated into a language of *age norms, grade level norms,* or *percentile ranks.* The group of pupils who took the test originally and whose scores provided the norms for it are referred to as the *standardization group.* In the manual which comes along with such a test this group is carefully described. This is imperative information, for when a teacher uses a standardized test to evaluate pupils' performances he is comparing them with the standardization group. If his class is different from this group, that is more able or less able, or small town rather than big city, or in the Northeast rather than the Southwest, the reasonableness of comparing his class's performance with the test norms is open to question.

The possibility of comparison is one of the major purposes for which standardized achievement tests are used. Usually the tests that are used are part of a systemwide evaluation program. Individual classroom teachers help in the selection of the tests to be used frequently. Once the selection is made all teachers abide by it. In fact, testing periods are regularized and the whole operation is coordinated at the system level.

It is important for the school and the teacher to examine the content of the standardized achievement tests they intend to use. They need to determine the *curricular validity* of the test in relation to the local school program. No matter how well a test may have been standardized, if it does not sample pupil behaviors that have been objects of teaching in the classroom it is not a good test to use.

This matter of curricular validity assumes rather special significance in this era of curriculum change. It takes time for the test makers to revise their instruments to fit many of the new instructional programs. In the interim a school must be careful to recognize the incongruities that may exist between standardized tests which they have used successfully over the past several years and the changed nature of the curriculum of the school. For this reason a number of the curriculum improvement projects are including in their work the development of testing instruments and procedures that fit their curriculum plans.

The use of norms. Norms are derived in the first instance from what was, in the standardization group, the most typical performance. Other children's performances are then compared to this most typical score, with some matching it, some not reaching it, and others exceeding it. The use of grade level norms can be especially bothersome in this respect. It must be remembered that to be "at" grade level is to make the same score that the typical student in the standardization group made. To be "above" grade level is to make a score higher than was typical; to be "below" grade level is to score lower. Illustratively, if a fourth grade pupil in the third month of school makes a score which is translated by a grade norm table into a grade level score of 4.3, he has attained the typical performance of fourth graders who took the test when it was standardized. If the table shows a grade level score of 5.3 for his raw score it means that he has exceeded the typical performance by a considerable amount. It does not mean that he has done as well as a fifth grader would do on the same test in the third month of the fifth grade. It is simply a way to denote his position relative to the typical fourth grade score, and it must be interpreted by the school and to the pupil and his parents accordingly. The same reasoning must be applied to scores below the grade level norm.

Grade level norms are always tied to what was the typical performance of some group of pupils. They are measures of what actually was the case, not of what it ought to be or possibly could be. These norms must not then become the standards to which a teacher aspires for educational effectiveness. At best they simply tell the teacher that his pupils' learning (and in a sense his teaching) is about as effective as is others. But the scores may be a reflection of ineffectiveness, relatively speaking. It may be that in light of the ability of the pupils a much better job can be done and needs to be done. Norms, if overstressed, can lull a teacher or a school into an unwise sort of complacency about teaching efforts. A school system that aspires to having all of its pupils "at grade level" may be in fact a very confused operation. The grade level score will be much too low an expectancy for some pupils; it will be too high an expectancy for others; only for some will it be appropriate. These individual differences may be overlooked in the use of norms.

Administering standardized tests. Standardized tests are to be administered to pupils under the same conditions that were present for the standardization group. The teacher is provided with a set of printed instructions which include all that he must know. The directions to be given to pupils are printed out for the teacher and are to be read to the class. The time available for the completion of the total test and for any of the subtests must be held constant. The way in which the test is scored must be the same. All of these factors together make the comparison of performances possible. Some tests which try to get at pupil characteristics such as intelligence are to be administered, scored, and interpreted by persons especially trained to do so.

Teacher-Made Tests

Almost every teacher makes up his own tests from time to time to be used in the classroom. It is essential that he do this job and that he do it well. There are several reasons for the use of teacher-made tests. They can be constructed in light of local conditions, both as to curriculum and pupils, assuring high content validity. They can be held to the coverage of more limited amounts of subject matter or skill learnings than can most commercially prepared tests. They are somewhat more readily used for diagnostic purposes as well as for a check on current performance status.

To construct a test is a demanding job, and something that must be done as carefully and as skillfully as understanding and competence will allow. Matters of reliability and validity are important for teacher-made instruments as well as for commercially prepared ones. The teacher must choose item style in light of what it is that he wants to test for and what the capabilities of a particular item style are for getting at it. A test item evokes some kind of behavior from the students, and it must be the behavior which the teacher is interested in trying to measure.

Suppose a teacher wants to find out whether a pupil knows when the Pilgrims landed at Plymouth Rock. The pupil will be asked to recall a certain piece of information. Notice the way in which item style can vary the recall situation for the student. He might meet the item in this style:

The Pilgrims landed at Plymouth Rock in the year _____.

Here the student is asked to recall a particular date and to place it in the blank space provided. But suppose the teacher designs the item in this way:

The Pilgrims landed at Plymouth Rock in the year (select one)
(a.) 1606, (b.) 1590, (c.) 1620, (d.) 1492.

Now the task for the student is considerably different. He must recall, yes, but he is helped by being asked to identify one of four given dates as the correct one. Recall is combined with recognition. There are other ways to vary recall and recognition type items, too. They can be styled as true-false items. The teacher can make up two lists, one of events and the other of dates and ask pupils to match them correctly. The teacher can make a matching test more difficult by including more events than dates, or vice versa. Still all such items as these get at recall.

If the teacher wants to test for understanding, he must use a different kind of test item. With young children the teacher will often resort to a list of words that stand for certain objects plus pictures of these objects along with some others. Children are asked to draw lines that match the appropriate picture with a given word. A correctly drawn line is evidence that a concept has been developed or is developing. Such an item might look like this:

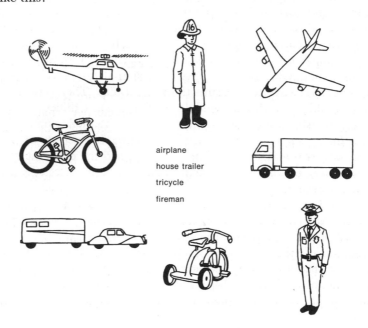

airplane

house trailer

tricycle

fireman

More pictures than words have been included to add to the complexity of the choices which the pupil must make.[3]

A teacher might test older children for understanding of capital letters and items of punctuation in this way:

Directions: Below is a group of statements which you are asked to read and correct insofar as capital letters and punctuation marks are concerned. In some examples capitals and punctuation marks are used incorrectly; in others they are omitted incorrectly; in some both conditions may exist. Mark through capital letters that should not be so;

[3] See J. R. Gerberich, *Specimen Objective Test Items* (New York: David McKay Company, Inc., 1956). Also see R. Ebel, "Writing the Test Item," in E. Lindquist (editor), *Educational Measurement* (Washington, D.C.: American Council on Education, 1951), Chapter 7.

mark out punctuation used incorrectly. Place capital letters over small letters wrongly used; put in punctuation where there is none but should be.

1. Jim Smith and mary jones went to the store together?
2. The boy and his Father took a trip to new york on April First 1966.

A teacher can design items that measure the ability of a student to reason from certain given information and to draw conclusions and establish generalizations on the basis of the information and in relation to questions asked. Such items are styled as attempts to get at higher levels of cognitive functioning than recall, recognition, or even understanding. For this reason, they are somewhat more difficult to construct, but they are essential if some of the thinking behavior teachers seek to develop in pupils is of this kind. A great value is put on thinking ability at the present time. Only recently have professional test developers begun finding effective ways to measure thinking ability. Therefore classroom teachers should not be discouraged if they find the task difficult.

Essay questions are not used as much in the elementary school as they are in higher levels of the school system. The essence of an essay question lies in the fairly long and complete written response which it requires. Young children are not skillful enough with written language to write such a response, and many children of intermediate school age find it difficult. It is more common to find the middle grade teacher resorting to the use of short-answer questions that are essay-like in nature. A pupil may be asked to compare two things in a brief written statement, he may be asked to describe some phenomenon briefly, or he may be asked to summarize what he sees as the advantages and disadvantages of some course of action. Whatever the question, the teacher does not expect as complete an answer as he would from a student in the secondary school.

Scoring Tests

Tests given must be scored, and both ease and accuracy of scoring become important matters to the teacher. Most extensive batteries of standardized achievement tests are machine scored, and teachers are furnished with the results for their study and analysis. What they reveal influences teaching plans, and provides information for pupils about their performance status. Machine scoring does mean that the style in which items appear must lend itself to the machine. Thus, essay questions, some kinds of reasoning questions, and even some understanding questions are extremely difficult to design in ways that can be machine scored and still reveal the kind of pupil behavior the teacher wants to measure. Of course, teacher-made tests are to be corrected by the teacher.

A question arises: How objectively can a test be scored? What is the extent to which two or more people would arrive at the same score on a test that each has examined? Because of this question much use has been made in the recent past of so-called objective tests, those with items which call for matching, or are true-false, multiple choice, and the like. They are easily scored, and it is almost impossible for two people to differ on the rightness or wrongness of such responses. In items like essay-styled questions, the scoring of an answer can become highly subjective. One person might score the response one way while another person might score the same response very differently. This has been one reason for teachers avoiding the use of the essay-style item. It accounts, too, for the care with which one must prepare such questions and then prepare himself to score them. Some sort of model response must be worked out ahead of time and applied against each answer as consistently or as objectively as possible to help overcome the subjective variability of personally preferred answers.

Measuring Social Structure

Sociometric devices are techniques for trying to appraise the social relationships within a given classroom group. One such technique is the sociogram. To implement it, the teacher must pose to the total class some question which calls for an indicated preference on the part of each pupil. This might be: "Who would you prefer to sit by in the classroom?" or "Who would you like to sit next to on the bus on our field trip?" The teacher assures the pupils that only he will see their responses, and implicit in the technique is the promise that something will be done in arranging seats in light of the collected information. Teachers then analyze the choices of pupils to identify isolated children, extremely popular children, and other categories. Since social structure shifts and changes such a technique must be used more than one time before any very useful generalizations can be drawn about the group or any individuals in it.

Another sociometric technique is the "guess who" questionnaire in which children match their peers by name with a list of behavioral statements provided them, such as "best thinker," "big talker," "best groomed," "best athlete." Still another device is the social distance scale. This instrument lists the names of all children in the class and then each child checks names of children he would like to be with as the teacher describes various possible social situations, work situations, and so on. The number of times a child's name is checked is some evidence of his relative position in the group, and some evidence of the way in which his peers see him.

No doubt these are useful and helpful devices. We would suggest, however, that the novice use them with particular care. Such questions as are asked touch on some very private and sensitive matters within any child's social group. The information must be treated with the utmost confidence. In some situations where the teacher is committed to act on the information (rearranging seats) the confidence is hard to keep. In our judgment sociometry should be used only after very careful study of what it can and what it cannot do, and of ways to use it and still protect children. If one is unsure either of why he is using it, or of his competence to use it, he probably should not use it at all.[4]

Pupil's Self-Measurement and Self-Evaluation

Most of us would agree readily that one hallmark of maturity is the willingness and the ability to undergo self-evaluation. Some elementary school teachers are most skillful in devising rating scales, progress charts, and records to help children to begin to learn to keep account of their own behavior in relation to some goal that they are trying to accomplish. Some of these are as simple as growth-graphs over several weeks of scores on spelling quizzes, or graphs for the number of library books read. If a teacher wishes to encourage and support self-evaluation, he will undoubtedly have to find time to hold individual conferences with pupils as well. In these he has a chance to demonstrate the importance he attaches to self-evaluation, to give some indication to the child of how it might be accomplished, and then to give assistance to the child in developing a predisposition to doing it and skills for doing it. What a teacher attempts depends in part on the age of the children with whom he works. Older children can do more than can younger children. The teacher will not expect all children, no matter their age, to respond to this as well or be as successful with it as will some.

Evaluation, Grades, and Reports

Early in this chapter it was noted that an evaluation procedure called for (1) clarity as to the behavior to be developed, (2) a defensible and valid measure of the extent to which the behavior is or is not present in a pupil, and (3) the application of some standard against this measured amount of behavior that leads to judgments about how well the child is doing or how acceptable or unacceptable his performance is. The last part of the procedure takes us to the heart of evaluation. In a sense the measurement (the test) yields only quantitative information

---

[4] For suggestions on uses, see H. Jennings and others, *Sociometry in Group Relations* (Washington, D.C.: American Council on Education, 1948).

about the extent of behavior change. Whether or not it is adequate calls for evaluation. Acceptability of performance is related to many and varied things. In part it is a function of what the teacher wants children to be able to do and strong feelings he may have as to the age at which they should be able to do something. This sort of thinking is not unrelated to the discussion in Part 1 of Havighurst's developmental task concept. Acceptability is also related to the teacher's knowledge of the ability and aptitude of any given child. Performance is clearly related to the potential of the pupil to perform. The realities of individual differences show up in the varying levels and qualities of performance that the school will find in the behavior of its pupils. Generally speaking, teachers recognize differences and think about pupils accordingly as they work with them. There is not yet an acceptable resolution of the fact of difference from the standpoint of grades and marking systems used by schools to record and communicate pupil performance status to the child and to his parents.

The Problem of Individual Differences

One part of this problem in evaluation is to decide how to allow the realities of human variability to reflect usefully in the grades and marks assigned to pupils. Grading has a long tradition of competitiveness. The teacher has decided on some high level of quality in performance and labeled it "A" work; slightly lower is "B" work, and so on down whatever marking system may be in use. This system has long been seen as penalizing the pupil with limited ability who may work very hard but achieve very little. Such a pupil would be destined, in the above system, to earn only C, D, and F grades no matter how hard he might try to do better. One solution attempted has been to do away with the use of grades, but they seem to persist in some form. Another approach to the problem has been to say that any grade given is a joint function of the effort expended by the pupil, the ability he is purported to have, and his actual performance. Thus, a child with superior endowment, who works hard, and who performs well can receive an A. So can a child with only average endowment, who works hard and performs as well as he can be expected to perform. The confusions that such a rationale can cause are evident. In spite of the essential soundness of the system, it has proved to be most difficult to operate. Thus, the school and teacher still face a problem in evaluation when it comes to putting some reasonable and acceptable mark on a given pupil's performance.

In the main, schools still try to sum up and communicate their evaluation of pupil progress through the use of a symbol system. It may be a series of letter grades such as A, B, C, D, and F. It may be S (for superior), P (for passing), N (for needs to improve), and U (for unsatisfactory). Whatever the system may be, it is next to impossible to sum up all of what a teacher needs to say about a child as a reader, or as a mathematician, or as a scientist, or as an artist, by using just one symbol. Thus, no matter how adequate the evaluation that has been carried out, much of it is lost in the use of an inadequate way of communicating it. The teacher is not really sure what he finally means when he records the single letter, and the parent attaches his own meaning to it from whatever set of biases he may hold or insights which he thinks he has into the whole affair. Schools, teachers, and parents are well aware of the problems involved. Attempts have been made to use individual descriptive statements prepared by the teacher about each child, with no mention of grades at all. These are generally successful at first, but fall of their own weight because of the demands they make on a teacher's time and skill. The most successful arrangement at this time, used either to replace report cards or as an adjunct to them, is the parent-teacher conference. Here face-to-face meeting, preferably at school, is made possible and both interested parties have a chance to exchange information and improve the communication that needs to take place.

Cumulative Records

The elementary school collects a wide variety of information on each child enrolled. This information is filed in a *cumulative record* to be used by the teachers to understand the child better. Begun when the kindergartner first enters school, the record usually contains not only factual information about the child and his family, but health records, test scores, anecdotes, subject matter progress records, unit experiences, and activity lists. Schools that schedule regular parent-teacher conferences frequently have an outline to direct the discussion, and copies of this outline placed in the cumulative folder help to reveal not only the progress of the pupil but the nature of the relationship of the family to the school.

The cumulative folder is a professional record, and should be treated as such. Some teachers use records frequently and others do not. Teachers prefer to use complete, up-to-date, accurate records. Folders filed in the classroom where they are readily available encourage more frequent use and facilitate ease of entry of material on the records. The teacher or other persons may make pertinent entries during the year, and at the end of the year one of the teacher's final responsibilities is to put the record into a form that will be most useful for the teacher with whom any given pupil will be working next year.

The teacher who is familiar with the records of his group of children will gain insights into the background, experience, strengths, and weaknesses of the group as a whole. He will note special interests, abilities, and problems of individual children. He will find clues as to what books he may use with profit; he will be able to anticipate necessary groupings of pupils in light of both interest and achievement. He will find information to guide the expectations he can hold for pupil learning and the "place" at which to begin the year's work. Special entries about individual pupils can help him to be effective with them from the outset. Only one caution is necessary, and this is that the teacher tries not to let the past record have too much influence on his attitude toward a child. For this reason many elementary school teachers unfortunately do not seek out the cumulative records. If the record is up-to-date and complete at all it can help the teacher very much in anticipating what his next group of pupils will be like. We would urge teachers to take the cumulative record system seriously—enter data therein regularly to keep records current, and develop an objective attitude toward the records in order to use them and not be used by them. Just as a physician refers to a patient's past medical record, so the teacher can make use of the child's past educational record.

THE SOCIAL CONSEQUENCES OF TESTING

It is well known that some people, both lay and professional, have doubts about some of the school's uses of tests. Achievement tests are not questioned as much as some other kinds of tests. The major targets are the instruments that measure other types of pupil characteristics, such as values, intelligence, and personality. Some persons find it difficult to decide whether a teacher has asked for information which he needs in order to do a better job of teaching a pupil, or whether he has asked for information that borders on an invasion of privacy, with only an obscure relevance of the information to teaching.

The classroom teacher will do well to take this question seriously. It is his responsibility to try not to misuse a test. There are poor tests and there are good tests. The teacher must know them well enough to endorse the use of the good ones and to question seriously any use of the others. Tests are never perfect measures. Persons who devise tests must resort to sampling procedures, and to inferences about the whole of a performance from the measurement of only part of a pupil's behavior. Certainly test data should be supplemented by direct observational data. In addition, the quality of work done day by day by a pupil in the classroom needs to be considered in the evaluation of his performance. No single set of test data, or any other single item of information should be used as the basis for drawing broad conclusions about any child or group of children. The crux of the matter turns on the ability and willingness of teachers and of the school systems in which they are employed to use tests thoughtfully and with good judgment. Teachers would be handicapped seriously without their measuring devices, both those that center on achievement and those that get at other more complex personal variables. A classroom teacher needs to inform himself well on this whole matter and use what he learns carefully and profitably.

RECOMMENDED READINGS

ADAMS, GEORGIA S., and THEODORE L. TORGESON. *Measurement and Evaluation in Education, Psychology, and Guidance.* New York: Holt, Rinehart and Winston, Inc., 1964.

AHMANN, J. STANLEY, MARVIN GLOCK, and HELEN WARDEBERG. *Evaluating Elementary School Pupils.* Boston: Allyn and Bacon, Inc., 1960.

AHMANN, J. STANLEY, and MARVIN GLOCK. *Evaluating Pupil Growth* (second edition). Boston: Allyn and Bacon, Inc., 1964.

ASSOCIATION FOR SUPERVISION AND CURRICULUM DEVELOPMENT. *Evaluation as Feedback and Guide,* Yearbook of the Association. Washington, D.C.: The Association, 1967.

DAVIS, FREDERICK B. *Educational Measurements and Their Interpretations.* Belmont, Calif.: Wadsworth Publishing Company, Inc., 1964.

EBEL, R. I. *Measuring Educational Achievement.* Englewood Cliffs, N.J.: Prentice-Hall, Inc., 1965.

GREEN, JOHN A. *Teacher-Made Tests.* New York: Harper & Row, Publishers, Inc., 1963.

GRONLUND, NORMAN E. *Measurement and Evaluation in Teaching.* New York: The Macmillan Company, 1965.

HOFFMAN, B. *The Tyranny of Testing.* New York: The Crowell-Collier Publishing Company, 1962.

LINDVALL, C. M. *Measuring Pupil Achievement and Aptitude.* New York: Harcourt, Brace & World, Inc., 1967.

NATIONAL SOCIETY FOR THE STUDY OF EDUCATION. *The Impact and Improvement of School Testing Programs* (Sixty-Second Yearbook, Part II). Chicago: University of Chicago Press, 1963.

REMMERS, H. H., N. L. GAGE, and J. FRANCIS RUMMELL. *A Practical Introduction to Measurement and Evaluation.* New York: Harper & Row, Publishers, Inc., 1960.

THOMAS, R. MURRAY. *Judging Student Progress* (second edition). New York: David McKay Company, Inc., 1960.

Human Relations: A Vital Dimension in Teaching

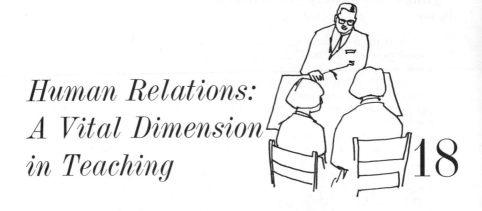

18

It is important that this book not close without addressing itself directly to the teacher as a person and to the network of interpersonal relations that are so much a part of teaching. One statement that attempts a behavioral description of teacher competence lists the following as roles which the teacher must be able to fill as a part of the job:

1. Director of learning.
2. Guidance and counseling worker.
3. Mediator of the culture.
4. Link with the community.
5. Member of the school staff.
6. Member of the profession.[1]

The discussion in earlier chapters has made clear the way in which a grasp of subject matter and psychological and sociological information serves the teacher in filling these roles. Personal characteristics and the quality of interpersonal relations also play a part in these roles. We agree with Fraser when he says:

> [Teaching] is a profession that demands a human touch and an ability to inspire young people to achieve great things. . . .[2]

We believe that the "human touch" referred to makes it mandatory that those who would teach realize the way in which the "teacher as a person"

---

[1] California Teachers Association, *Teacher Competence: Its Nature and Scope* (San Francisco: California Teachers Association, 1957), p. 48.

[2] George W. Fraser, *An Introduction to the Study of Education* (New York: Harper & Row, Publishers, Inc., 1951), p. 18.

idea intrudes into the teaching-learning situation and bears on the teacher-pupil relationship in the classroom.

Hughes has this highly personal dimension in teaching in mind when she says:

> A teacher interacting with children is confronted with the new meanings they are building and the meanings they are expressing. Each response of the children has a freshness that says it has not occurred previously, at least not for them. No matter how many children of the same age one has met, lived with, or taught, this one and the next one are new, and the new formulations with which they are responding must be met with new formulations on the part of the teacher. *Responsiveness* is the material with which the teacher creates; the *product* is the meaning that emerges from the interaction. One is instantly aware that the product is not something that one can hold, taste, measure, hang on the wall, or otherwise exhibit; instead, what can be seen is the smile, the renewed vigor with which the problem is attacked, the sage nod of the head, the light in the eye. What is heard is the next question, the statement of insight or understanding, and the boast to a classmate of now knowing and understanding.[3]

Trow, in recognition of the many different roles the teacher is asked to assume suggests that their fulfillment grows out of individual personal characteristics and demands certain skills of social integration. His thesis is that "quality of teaching is a function not only of the degree of development of skill but also of the intrusion of personality and role factors into the teacher's classroom behavior." He identifies the several roles of the teacher in light of this "skills–personality–role" construct as follows:

Extraclass Roles of the Teacher

> *Faculty member:* placed close to the bottom of an organizational hierarchy, one now to be judged, not so much by what he knows as by what he does.
>
> *Community liaison officer:* utilizing community resources and establishing and carrying on parent-teacher relationships (patterns of community relationships differ widely among schools).
>
> *Learner:* learning from children and from formal sources to make up for weaknesses in his own education and to keep abreast of new discoveries.

Administrative and Executive Roles of the Teacher

> *Disciplinarian* (policeman): deciding what to do about discipline and control as a part of the total instructional process.

---

[3] Marie Hughes, "Integrity in Classroom Relationships," in Alice Miel (editor), *Creativity in Teaching* (Belmont, Calif.: Wadsworth Publishing Company, Inc., 1961), pp. 79–80.

Measurer and record-keeper (clerk): keeping systematic records necessitating specific skills in this matter.

Learning-aids officer (librarian): selecting and preparing learning aids that provide varied sensory referents to build new concepts.

Program director (planner): directing all activity taking place in the classroom and involving the techniques of decision making and maintaining desirable group climate.

Instructional Roles of the Teacher

Motivator: discovering whether pupils are emotionally ready to learn and if not to take such steps as may be necessary to develop that readiness to learn.

Resource person: telling or supplying information, explaining or clarifying, demonstrating with various media to guide child performance.

Evaluator: determining the level of performance of pupils in comparison with expectations based upon age, grade, intelligence, and previous experience; judging and recognizing abilities, handicaps, and talents.

Adapter: adapting instruction and materials to various interests, abilities, aptitudes, and needs; creating best climate for learning that will challenge all students.[4]

Following in this general vein, we want here to consider the teacher as a person, and his interactions with his direct client group, his pupils. Teachers work with and through children first and foremost; the realization of educational goals and objectives is to be found in the modified behavior of them. Certainly the consideration of a range of highly "personal" things is most appropriate.

THE TEACHER—THE PERSON

"Know thyself." "To thine own self be true." In all probability the inescapable point of departure in considering teaching and human relations is with oneself. Teaching calls for a considerable measure of self-understanding. In Chapter 3 the psychological construct referred to as the "self-concept" was mentioned as having importance for teaching to the extent that school experiences contribute to the developing self-concept of the pupil and to the degree to which the teacher can be more effective with pupils whose self-concept she is able to understand. The teacher too has a self-concept. The extent to which any teacher understands his own purposes and behavior will be related to his success in filling the several roles required of him in teaching.

---

[4] William Clark Trow, "Role Functions of the Teacher in the Instructional Group," in National Society for the Study of Education, *The Dynamics of Instructional Groups,* Fifty-Ninth Yearbook, Part II (Chicago: University of Chicago Press, 1960), pp. 30–50.

Jersild gives a comprehensive definition of *self* in one statement that includes the ideas of a number of authorities:

> The self is a composite of thoughts and feelings which constitute a person's awareness of his individual existence, his conception of who and what he is. A person's self is the "sum total of all that he can call his." The self includes, among other things, a system of ideas, attitudes, values and commitments. The self is a person's total subjective environment. It is a distinctive "center of experience and significance." The self constitutes a person's inner world as distinguished from the "outer world" consisting of all other people and things.
>
> The self is "the individual as known to the individual." It is "that to which we refer when we say 'I.' " It is the "custodian of awareness"; it is the thing about a person which has awareness and alertness, "which notices what goes on, and . . . notices what goes on in its own field."
>
> The self has also been described as the nucleus of personality.
>
> The self is both constant and changeable. It includes the ". . . constant nature of an individual plus all that is conditioned by time and space and that is changeable." It provides a "nucleus on which, and in which, and around which, experiences are integrated into the uniqueness of the individual." In the process of experience, the healthy self adds, assimilates, and integrates within its own system that which is essential and authentic, while renouncing what is "unessential, strange, and harmful."[5]

Jersild's definition pictures the self as a subjective, complex being or image, a composite of experience, reaction, integration. The self-concept is the consciousness of this composite being, the awareness and interpretation of one's own powers, ideas, behavior. McDonald defines a person's self-concept as "the way he sees himself; the set of characteristics he associates with himself; the set of inferences, drawn from self-observation in many different situations, that describe his own characteristic behavior patterns."[6]

The self-concept may be influenced by several factors: (1) one's own desire or willingness to observe and examine himself; (2) the sum total of one's experience; (3) one's perception of the judgment of others and one's acceptance by society; (4) the balance of homeostasis, or how one maintains himself inwardly; and (5) the differentiation one perceives, or the recognition of differences between one's own purposes and the intentions of others.

---

[5] Arthur T. Jersild, *In Search of Self* (New York: Bureau of Publications, Teachers College, Columbia University, 1952), pp. 9–10.

[6] Frederick J. McDonald, *Educational Psychology* (second edition) (Belmont, Calif.: Wadsworth Publishing Company, Inc., 1965), p. 433.

Willingness to examine oneself. A self-concept grows, matures, and changes just as any other concept develops through increased knowledge and understanding over a period of time. However, one cannot have an accurate self-concept unless he consciously and willingly studies himself. Too many people take experiences of life for granted. They are blind to themselves just as they may be blind to the beauties, joys, and sorrows of the world about them. Some people consciously or unconsciously avoid an introspective examination of the causes for their own behavior. Some may attempt to conceal their real natures either inwardly, to themselves, or outwardly, to others. Most people learn about themselves a little at a time, building and developing self-concept gradually.

> . . . [the teacher] will again and again find himself in a process of self-examination. To a person who is insecure such self-examination can be painful and threatening. The more insecure a person is, the more desperately he will feel a need to remain rigidly set in his ways. But to one who is secure enough within himself to face his thoughts and feelings when the opportunity arises, the process is challenging and rewarding.[7]

Experience. Every person is a product of his experience. His family, his childhood, his school experience, his friends past and present, all make him what he is. His thoughts and ideas on life and living and his feelings about people and things are a result of his accumulated life experience. Many teachers need to broaden their experience, their liberal education, and their contact with different kinds of people, for the broadened self-concept that will reflect that experience.

Judgment of others. Part of one's feeling about himself is how he thinks others are judging him. Man needs the moral and physical support of other people in all types of life activities. So many of our individual behaviors, such as manners, fashion of dress, and habits of speech, are developed because of what others may think about us. The teacher who feels accepted by his students works more easily with them. Methods of teaching, selection of curriculum content, management of classroom activities are influenced in part by what the teacher thinks the principal, the parents, and other teachers expect him to do.

Traditionally, teachers have been "put on a pedestal" by society. That is, people have felt that to be a "good" teacher a person must be almost perfect. The good teacher did not drink or smoke; his was the "right" religion; he had no unpopular prejudices; he was always in good mental and emotional health. Only recently have people allowed themselves to think of teachers as normal human beings, with joys and sorrows, with problems, and with the strengths and weaknesses of other people. Teachers can now understand more clearly that they may be

---

[7] Jersild, *In Search of Self*, p. 119.

"models" of a kind to the children but that they are also human. Their self-concept is strengthened in the knowledge that the community is more understanding and more accepting of the humanness of each teacher.

Homeostasis. Usually, the normal, well-balanced self maintains an internal balance, or constancy, an equilibrium termed "psychological homeostasis." Because of this, the individual "seeks to preserve the self of which he is aware."[8] In other words, human beings may tend to resist change unless a sound self-concept can justify and condone change. One may not wish to do something different unless he is sure he is capable of successfully accomplishing the task. An idea may not be accepted easily if it is in conflict with the self-concept.

Differentiation. Any individual's behavior, influenced by what he thinks and feels about himself, will be similar to or different from the behavior of those about him. In some situations the individual is expected to act the same as others, but in other situations to act the same would be entirely unacceptable. For example, a mother may come to school in a pair of slacks, but a female teacher would not do so. The self-concept is influenced by the degree to which the individual recognizes the differentiation between his own purposes and those of others interacting in the same specific situations. That is, a teacher decides upon the appropriate role in various situations through his understanding of himself as a teacher.

The Self-Concept of the Teacher

Jersild makes three points in support of his thesis that teachers must know themselves:

1. An essential function of good education is to help the growing child to know himself and to grow in healthy attitudes of self-acceptance.
2. A teacher cannot make much headway in understanding others or in helping others to understand themselves unless he is endeavoring to understand himself. If he is not engaged in this endeavor, he will continue to see those whom he teaches through the bias and distortion of his own unrecognized needs, fears, desires, anxieties, hostile impulses, and so on.
3. The process of gaining knowledge of self and the struggle for self-fulfillment and self-acceptance is not something an instructor *teaches* others. It is not something he does *to* or *for* them. It is something in which he himself must be involved.[9]

---

[8] Donald Snygg and Arthur W. Combs, *Individual Behavior* (New York: Harper & Row, Publishers, Inc., 1949), p. 56.

[9] Arthur T. Jersild, *When Teachers Face Themselves* (New York: Bureau of Publications, Teachers College, Columbia University, 1955), pp. 13–14.

The teacher who is secure within himself, who knows himself and feels no consistent inadequacy, is most likely to be a well-balanced, stable teacher. If he knows that he is doing his best, and that his best brings positive results, he will teach with more ease and efficiency. If he feels he "belongs" he can accept and work more readily with differing motives and characteristics of others. He can help children to help themselves.

Because of his self-concept, each teacher's interpretation of the teaching role varies. The manner in which he guides children will reflect his concept of himself as a teacher, of what he thinks a teacher should be, and of the behavior expected of a teacher. If a teacher feels he will establish better relations by being permissive with children, he will behave accordingly. On the other hand, if he feels a teacher's role necessitates firm control, he will picture himself in that role to be most successful.

Self-examination requires consciousness of one's own behavior in all the varying situations of teaching. On the playground, within a small study group, during total class discussion, in the activity period, throughout the quiet work-study period, the teacher needs to be conscious of his interaction with children. He determines why he asks a certain series of questions, why he speaks to a child in a special manner, why he ignores the behavior of another. And during these situations what are his feelings: depression, exhilaration, confusion, satisfaction, success?

> Self-understanding requires something quite different from the methods, study-plans, and skills of a "know-how" sort that are usually emphasized in education. . . . What is needed is a more personal kind of searching, which will enable the teacher to identify his own concerns and to share the concerns of his students.[10]

A teacher needs to relate the acts of teaching to his own notions of meaning, anxiety, loneliness, emotion, conformity, sex, hostility, and compassion.[11] He needs to examine his ideas of the meaning of existence, of life and living, of the work he is doing. He needs to understand his inner problems, realize his own limits. What is important in life for him? He needs to define his anxieties, to realize that anxiety is shared by all mankind, and that anxiety may cause one to be industrious, impulsive, competitive, or a perfectionist. He needs to identify his own limits of loneliness, and know that this may be a barrier, a real cause of acceptance, rejection, or fear of others. He needs to understand that emotion is frequently present and that people need freedom of emotional expression. He should know of the burden of conformity. He needs to comprehend that sex roles, as prescribed by society, change, and that one's

---

[10] Jersild, *When Teachers Face Themselves*, p. 3.

[11] Jersild. These ideas are listed and described in detail in several chapters of the book *When Teachers Face Themselves* and modified here.

own interpretation of the sex role greatly influences behavior. He needs to know the pain of anger and the inner causes and effects of hostility. And he especially needs to understand that true compassion is a mature feeling and a quality among mankind that is not to be avoided or ignored.

The Self-Concept and a Teaching Philosophy

Too often teachers work with children without a real understanding of the reason why they take certain actions. They have never carefully thought through their educational goals or the basic philosophy upon which their teaching rests.

> The techniques are important, but in the last analysis the techniques used by a teacher will be determined by his concept of himself, of his duties, and of his students. . . . No matter how thorough his training in skills and techniques of teaching, those skills and techniques will not be used if they do not conform to his personal philosophy of life and serve his immediate ends. If the results he wishes to secure are not those which can be secured by the approved methods, the methods will be distorted or abandoned.[12]

The following questions may help a teacher to define his philosophy of education:

1. Do you want to help each child become a truly effective individual, behaving according to democratic standards? What does democracy mean to you? What democratic standards should children achieve?
2. Do you feel you should help children in their adjustment to and participation in a technological culture? Do you understand (and help children understand) the relationship between the realities of life and the curriculum they encounter, such as arithmetic, physical education, science, and the social studies?
3. Are you thoroughly accepting of the facts of individual differences? Do you teach children from the point at which learning will take place? Do you understand and use several methods in dealing with individual interests and abilities? Do you help children develop self-direction and use self-evaluation? Do your relationships with children convince each child that he is important to you as an individual?
4. Are your purposes also influenced by principles which define a good learning experience? Do you understand the importance of stimulating favorable working conditions? Are you convinced of the necessity for learners and teacher to plan and develop work cooperatively? Are you aware of the continuity of experience? Do the children's learning experiences lead to basic understandings, fundamental concepts, or generalizations? Do you provide for balanced

---

[12] Snygg and Combs, *Individual Behavior,* p. 324.

development? Do you believe in variety of experience as an aid to learning?

Concise answers to questions such as these provide a basis for sound teaching practices.

THE TEACHER AND HIS PUPILS

Teachers spend most of their time in a web of interpersonal relationships with pupils. Some transactions take place on a one-to-one basis with the teacher working with a single student; others occur in small groups; a great many times the teacher is called upon to relate to the total classroom group. This set of relationships can start with the pupil as well; the dynamics involved run both ways. Pupils relate to teacher just as teacher relates to pupils. Any situation that involves a leader and a group calls for social organization to facilitate getting important and necessary work done and to make being together more pleasant. In an elementary school classroom the ability of the teacher to establish wholesome personal relations with his pupils and to bring about sufficient social organization to allow the pupils to function effectively as a group assumes major importance. The teacher-pupil relationship is a valued one in our culture.

Democratic Relationships

Because the American teacher operates within a democratic value system the relationships he develops with pupils must reflect those values. Graham identifies the American style of democracy through six tenets:

1. *The intrinsic worth of the individual* irrespective of his race, religion, or socioeconomic level. Man has dignity. He has the right to and the responsibility for self-direction. His independence assures him both freedoms and obligations. This belief is the core of the democratic philosophy because herein lies man's right to liberty, freedom, and equality of opportunity. We believe in "Liberty, Equality, Fraternity" because we respect man and judge him capable, in concert with his fellows, of making wise decisions.

2. *Equality of opportunity.* The equalitarian emphasis in the United States is such that equality of opportunity deserves the status of a separate belief. Americans aspire to political, social, legal, and educational rights for every person. In the more stratified European countries where equality of opportunity has been stressed less than in this country, this belief would probably be subsumed under the belief in the intrinsic worth of the individual.

3. *Cooperation* in solving the problems of general welfare. Each man, no matter how humble, can contribute to a discussion that relates to his and the group's common good.

4. *The use of reason in solving problems.* Man is a rational being who uses evidence and reason in reaching decisions.

5. *The improvability of man.* Although man may view his past with pride, he looks to the future with confidence that even greater human progress is possible. This belief and the belief in cooperation and the use of reason in solving problems add great strength to our democracy because they make provision for orderly change. It is significant that Jefferson referred to our government as an experiment.

6. *Government by consent.* Government is a tool, an agency, a device, a means to an end created by man to serve his purposes. The government's powers are prescribed; its use of force is limited by law.[13]

Putting these into practice in the classroom, the teacher develops and maintains a situation that does the following:

1. Values the dignity of each individual pupil as he demonstrates his own interests and abilities in academic endeavor in the context of the classroom group; fosters mutual respect and acceptance between and among pupils.

2. Encourages freedom of thought and action that is restricted only by responsibility to the group and to oneself and by the obligations of self-direction.

3. Provides varying kinds of experience so that a pupil will have equal opportunity to learn consistent with his ability to do so.

4. Provides many situations in which cooperation is essential for completing the activity, and out of which cooperative behavior comes to be valued and learned.

5. Encourages the development of cognitive processes including problem solving and critical and creative thinking.

6. Includes shared, ongoing evaluation that makes possible modification in and orderly change of plans and action.

7. Maintains an atmosphere and posture about the future that will foster optimism about mankind.

Thus the teacher tries to develop in his classroom a microcosm of the larger society. The hope would be to live a satisfying life in the limited environment of classroom and school the better to insure such a life being lived in the unlimited environment away from school.

The Teacher and the Child's Self-Concept

The idea of the self-concept adds to both the possibilities and the responsibilities of the teacher as he works with pupils. Having been made

---

[13] Grace Graham, *The Public School in the American Community* (New York: Harper & Row, Publishers, Inc., 1963), p. 39.

aware of the self-concept in all of its subtleties and complexities, he seeks to appeal to it in part to help the child to sustain his efforts to learn while at the same time he tries to guide the child to a realistic and positive perception of himself. It is not possible to "teach" a self-concept to a child, of course, nor is it possible to instruct him in methods of developing a self-concept. But a teacher sensitive to the self-concept idea is in a better position to help children come to grips with the ongoing process of self-realization. The teacher contributes to psychological, social and academic security that makes it possible for children to be introspective. He provides a broad range of experiences and encourages pupils' self-evaluation while they take part in a variety of situations. He supports children so they may develop healthy attitudes of self-acceptance. He assumes that it is extremely difficult to feel good toward others until one is able to feel good toward oneself. He helps the child see himself as others see him.

Several postulates related to this educational process are outlined by Bower.[14] These necessary conditions of learning can give us clues to the aspects of self of which a child should become conscious. Opposite each postulate listed below are some ideas for the teacher to contemplate as he helps the child develop his self-concept in school.

Postulate	*Ideas*
1. The school has become a major primary or key integrative agency for children. All children need to undergo successfully the expressive social and content demands of the school. One cannot skip blithely through this system with a kind face and a bland smile and emerge "educated."	1. As an individual operating in various kinds of learning groups, the child recognizes his ability to communicate, the status of his own interactions, and the continuing needs of his own content mastery.
2. Learning "school" skills is the basic business of children in school. A child who fails to learn these skills "has given hostages to fortune." His ability to function as a child and as an adult is increasingly limited.	2. The child has opportunity to evaluate himself in the several "school" skills and to understand his own rate of progress in them.
3. Schools are transmitters and generators of symbolic lore and symbolic skills. The essence of education is learning to use symbols effectively as representation of ob-	3. The child recognizes the symbols substituted for things and ideas and appreciates his increasing ability to utilize them.

[14] Eli M. Bower, "The Achievement of Competency," in Association for Supervision and Curriculum Development, *Learning and Mental Health in the School*, Yearbook (Washington, D.C.: NEA, 1966), pp. 26–27.

jects, events and relationships in creative and interpersonal activities.

4. Education is a cognitive-affective mediation of content by a student. The mediation or processing of the content is done by that part of the personality called ego processes.

5. To be educationally successful, students must learn to develop competent and effective mediational or ego processes.

6. Information which is not mediated or acted on by ego processes becomes a kind of intellectual shellac which often serves to give a high gloss to an empty house.

7. The process of learning involves the development and utilization of five distinctive but overlapping ego processes. These are:

   a. The processes of experiencing a wide variety of objects (including self), events and feelings and attaching symbols to them (differentiation)

   b. The processes of binding objects, events and feelings with accurate symbols in a firm but not untieable knot (fidelity)

   c. The processes of managing heavy or light cognitive-affective loads via regulation of informational inputs and the discharge of stress (pacing)

   d. The processes of taking on new metaphors and matrices or revising old metaphors and matrices in perceiving oneself and the world (expansion)

   e. The processes of assimilating new information and integrating it within appropriate layers of the personality (integration).

8. Meaningful learning involves a student, learning content and a

4. Not only does the child utilize opportunities to plan, evaluate, analyze, experiment, and solve problems, he realizes the part that these experiences play in his own attitudes and behaviors.

5,6. With increasing use of thought and action as educational facilitators the child judges the effectiveness of these techniques in his own individual use of them and as the group uses them. Recognition and evaluation are guided to positive attitudes of ongoing improvement.

7. The child experiences a feeling of satisfaction and growing power as he progresses through the five ego processes.

8. The child recognizes the guiding and supporting functions of the

Postulate (Cont.)

mediator-teacher. For students, all learning is undergone in personality matrices which not only give direction to the meaning of the content to the learner but determine its eventual use. Knowing is a conglomerate of cognitive-emotional symbols which get attached to experiences but stay on in ego processes.

Ideas (Cont.)

teacher and is conscious of the human interrelationships involved in the learning process.

Another statement points to six general conditions essential to individual development as follows:[15]

1. *Stimulation.* Well-taught subject matter is the school's chief instrument for stimulation because knowledge increases response to the environment and academic challenge can contribute to self-enjoyment and self-discipline. How much opportunity does each child have to react freely and vividly to a rich texture of greatly varied stimuli?

2. *Responsible Freedom.* Development of individual freedom is not license to do as one wishes, for one always must assume responsibility for his own actions and activities committed in a context of social orderliness. Freedom is another means of stimulation. Is each child taking increasing command of his own life space with his maturing years?

3. *Support.* If a child is to grow to his full individuality he *must* be living in an environment where he feels he belongs, where he is wanted and respected. He *must* know that his rights, his inherent personal privileges, are highly regarded and will be protected. Though school people cannot commit themselves to love in the parental sense, they can commit themselves to a kindly warmth and acceptance and a climate of sunny affection.

4. *Success.* School provides opportunities for new successes and making positive gains from inevitable failures. A long balanced build-up of success upon success releases energy for the next bigger try. Does the youngster go home from school most days, with the feeling of at least some little success lingering in his memory?

5. *Commitment.* It is hard for anyone to grow to full stature until he can come into full and free communication with the people and the world about him, until he can invest his full energy in something outside himself, taking all the risks of rebuff and failure. In his years of schooling how much is each youngster helped to reach out beyond himself, to perceive some ideal, and throw himself into working for it?

---

[15] Joint Project on the Individual and the School, AASA, ASCD, NASSP, Department of Rural Education, *A Climate for Individuality* (Washington, D.C.: NEA, 1965), pp. 30–39.

6. *Self-Insight.* Under the five foregoing conditions the child has much opportunity to learn about himself, and will have gained the assurance to look at himself and all around him with a clear eye. As he moves through the curriculum, how much does each child find that helps him understand himself and build a valid self-concept of what he is and can be?

In the final analysis the teacher helps each pupil see himself as a person interacting in many kinds of situations at school. The pupil takes part in self-discovery, analysis of anxieties, overcoming fears, learning the value of mistakes, and becoming a fully functioning person who thinks well of himself and of others. According to Hughes, "The maintenance of 'wholeness,' of confidence, of self-acceptance in the individual, makes it possible for [the pupil] to relate himself to the world in an open manner. He is freer to take in more from his environment and to risk the giving of more in terms of ideas, solutions to problems, artistic products, inventions, and so forth. He can become concerned and involved with people, objects, and situations. It is with personal commitment that he gives of himself enough to be creative."[16]

The Teacher and Classroom Organization

It is necessary to have order in a classroom if work is to be accomplished. There must be rules of behavior which members accept and use to guide their actions. Consistent with the wider society of which the school and classroom are a part, and in consideration of the age and maturity of a particular group of children, the teacher should make an effort to involve pupils in the formulation of these rules and to gain their acceptance of them as guides to classroom and school behavior. The classroom need not be and should not be a heavily rule-laden place. Rules should be sufficient only to get the work of the group accomplished in an orderly and efficient way. The teacher's goal should be for internal rather than external controls over behavior. All children must learn self-control, and the elementary school and classroom are places where such learning can take place.

Self-Direction and Self-Management

The ultimate goal is the gradual development of a self-directed, self-reliant, self-critical, self-managed individual. Self-direction is the ability to guide one's own behavior in a socially acceptable manner. It involves judgment between right and wrong and consequent control of one's

---

[16] Marie Hughes, "Integrity," pp. 105–106.

feelings and actions. It involves an attitude of self-examination that seeks improvement of one's own conduct. It necessitates enough confidence in oneself and regard for one's own character to act independently.

Self-direction is a learned behavior. The human being is not born with an intuitive ability to direct his own affairs in a complex society. At each level of maturity the child behaves in a specific situation within his perception of the situation. He does what he thinks best, what he thinks might be expected of him, or what he thinks he can "get by with." His perception of any situation is directly related to his experiences in similar or related situations. Thus we realize that children need to be *taught* the skills of self-control, and helped to recognize their own increasing ability in self-management. This means the teacher provides opportunity for children to assume gradually the responsibility for their own behavior. Also he teaches the skills and attitudes necessary within an environment compatible with self-direction.

Goals for self-direction. Bernhardt describes four adult characteristics related to mental health and self-fulfillment that the teacher can use as overall goals for self-direction.[17]

1. Physically, he will have learned to adjust his personal appetitive satisfactions to his needs with free enjoyment and gratification. He will accept the responsibility of observing reasonable care of his health, avoiding the dangers of self-indulgence. He will be able to gauge his strengths and limitations. And he will be able to manage his affairs so as to avoid the ill effects of stress and be able to relax at will.

2. Mentally, he will gradually learn his potentialities and limitations and temper his aspirations in accordance with this knowledge. He will slowly build up judgment in terms of his successes and failures, adequately evaluating both. As he accumulates knowledge he will also develop the ability to weigh, discriminate, and choose. He will learn to arrange his decisions so as to reduce anxiety to a minimum. He will learn to feel at home in the world of ideas, opinions, and beliefs, and he will reduce to a minimum the tendency to be prejudiced. He will value accomplishment irrespective of its relationship to the achievement of others. He will learn to distinguish clearly between his work with its responsibilities and his leisure time activities with their infinite possibilities for variety and enjoyment. He will learn to be open-minded, welcoming new ideas but not necessarily adopting them as good or true. He will be characterized by reason and reasonableness.

3. Emotionally, he will have learned self-control, neither denying nor inhibiting his emotions but channeling them into acceptable and useful behavior. Thus no temper tantrums will interfere with his

---

[17] Karl S. Bernhardt, *Discipline and Child Guidance* (New York: McGraw-Hill Book Company, Inc., 1964), pp. 5–6.

efficiency. And fears and insecurities will lead to sensible caution and effective learning. He will never be ashamed of being afraid, nor will he allow his fears to keep him from acting in accordance with his standards. His emotions will find their outlet in enthusiasm, sustained effort, appreciation, and admiration without envy or resentment. He will develop a degree of aesthetic appreciation which will enhance his enjoyment of living. In fact, his enjoyment of living, learning, experimenting, and exploring will be boundless.

4. Spiritually, he will formulate a philosophy of life and find some answers to the purpose of living and this will aid him in achieving a measure of serenity.

Teaching the skills of self-direction. Self-direction is learned in the context of the total school experience. It is impossible and impractical to devote an independent lesson or a unit to the development of self-discipline skills. Rather, the teacher tries to contribute to each individual's growing power of self-direction through his choice of teaching method, his approach to classroom organization, and his wise guidance of human relationships.

The Relation of Work Habits to Self-Direction

Implicit within self-direction is being able to choose between alternatives, knowing the limits within which choice can be allowed, and being able to assume responsibility for choices made. In the classroom situation, then, the young child needs opportunity to make decisions about work plans and act independently within certain limits of freedom or established procedures.

> A disciplined person is efficient in the way in which he carries out a responsibility. He displays self-control and good judgment in performing the tasks he has undertaken. Helping children and youth to develop effective work habits is another important goal in building toward self-discipline.
> The individual with disciplined work habits can set up and carry out plans for himself. He is able to outline his own goals clearly, and he can lay out a series of proposed steps to reach these goals. He knows how to budget his time and energy in order to keep several responsibilities moving ahead simultaneously. He is able to settle himself to work without undue procrastination and waste of time.[18]

The teacher who seeks to develop in each pupil a degree of self-direction promotes the development of work habits carefully. He allows the children to help plan ways of getting work done. He discusses with

---

[18] Margaret C. McKim, Carl W. Hansen, and William L. Carter, *Learning to Teach in the Elementary School* (New York: The Macmillan Company, 1959), p. 136.

them the need for and reason for establishing certain working arrangements so that children can cooperate through understanding and can execute work plans accordingly.

Establishing Routines in the Classroom

Young children find it helpful in beginning to be responsible for their own behavior at school to have certain routines established in the classroom. Routines are procedures for doing things in an agreed-upon way that is known to all. They become customary ways of meeting rather repetitive situations and once agreed upon they require minimal supervision by the teacher. Actions can be taken quickly, without discussion, and with the security of knowing that one is acting in an acceptable way. Examples of such routinized actions are these:

1. Setting an established format for opening the school day.
2. Using a standardized way of distributing such materials as paper and books.
3. Developing a procedure for leaving the classroom to go to the playground.
4. Having set ways for sharpening pencils, for toileting, and other actions.
5. Providing a way to use time when an assignment is finished early.

The establishment of such classroom procedures is an ongoing process. The teacher lends positive leadership to the planning, development, and evaluation of them. He is consistent in assisting his class to maintain them. He anticipates situations that may call for some revision in procedures, such as passing out special supplies, and helps the children plan a means of achieving an orderly system for coping with them. He has the children join him in assuming responsibility for understanding tasks to be achieved and identifying procedures for so doing. He emphasizes the responsibility of each individual to adhere to agreed-upon procedures. With teacher guidance children are able increasingly to direct their own efforts, to make their own plans, and to evaluate their efforts accordingly.

The Teacher as Disciplinarian

It is true that, in spite of the goals of self-direction, some children will need to be disciplined for misbehavior frequently and almost all children will need to be disciplined at some time. In most instances misbehavior is simply a manifestation of "growing up." It is a testing of limits on acceptable behavior; it is an expression of protest over and reluctance to accept rules; it is a sign of frustration over work to be done. Sometimes misbehavior is a means of gaining attention either of classmates or of teachers. Whatever may be the cause, there are times when the teacher is called upon to control the behavior of a child or of a class. Some teachers find that this requirement poses a kind of threat to them. They see it as an unpleasant task and are not really sure that they can carry through effectively with it. Others simply do not like to have to discipline children, believing that external control runs counter to the goals of self-management and self-direction; such teachers accept all but the most serious instances of pupil misconduct as simply struggles on the road to "becoming." Most teachers resist an authoritarian approach to the problem, with a teacher-imposed set of rewards and punishments used to control pupils. Yet most teachers are aware that a *laissez-faire* approach —that is, a situation in which there is no imposed guidance or direction— leaves much to be desired. Most come to accept a more democratic perception of classroom discipline. They begin to see it as necessary social control, helpful to group members in pursuit of valued goals. The teacher comes to be seen as an organizer and director who helps the group to function at its highest level of efficiency.

Discipline, in the positive sense, is a necessary ingredient to instruction. No group can operate without order; children as individuals find security in standards. Mental hygiene, also necessary to effective learning, is helped by the quiet supportive atmosphere of good discipline.

Developing and maintaining good discipline is not a special skill and cannot be separated from all aspects of good teaching procedures. Children who are busy, happy, and satisfied with their own school achievement will for the most part be well-disciplined individuals. Effective discipline is another result of competent teaching. The teacher who is committed to a positive approach to discipline will manage learning situations so that misbehavior is avoided rather than merely corrected. There is a constant progress toward responsible, self-directed behavior.

It is not appropriate for us to try to go into great detail on this matter in a book on curriculum and teaching. It is enough to say that discipline is a part of teaching, however, and it must be anticipated and dealt with as constructively as possible. There is useful literature to which one can refer in child psychology and in counseling psychology that treats this matter directly. You will find that a "praise and approval" approach to children's efforts to come to grips with themselves is preferred. Children thrive on recognition and appreciation of their endeavors. Given encouragement they try harder; with recognition comes greater desire for accomplishment.

There are services that the teacher may use to help him to deal with "exceptional" children. Teachers do meet pupils from time to time that they are not able to cope with. Most school systems make available the services of a school psychologist to assist in the diagnosis and treatment of children whose behavior is most atypical and for whom special arrangements of one kind or another have to be made. The most severe cases are referred to psychiatrists for consultation and assistance, with either the parents or the school assuming responsibility for so doing. To some extent counselors are assigned to the staffs of elementary schools but this is not yet common practice. Teachers must recognize the limitations on their own abilities in working with some children and use the special services which the school system makes available to them.

CREATIVITY IN TEACHING

Two prerequisites to creative teaching, that is teaching that is ingenious, unusual, and inventive, are a high level of professional competence and skill in human relations. Knowing that one is good at the job and being at ease with others enables a teacher to create an environment that is relaxed, free from anxiety, unhurried, and open to ideas. In such an environment children can ask questions and seek answers freely. There is an atmosphere of mutual respect, trust, and expected justice. Channels of communication between teacher and pupils are open; children are listened to appreciatively. The whole approach to learning is open, spontaneous, original, experimental, and highly personal—not closed in the sense of being restrictive, conforming, and controlled. But, let us consider what some others have had to say about this matter of creativity both for the teacher and for the pupil.

Zirbes suggests that the teacher can move forward to creativity by directing his efforts as follows:

> *from* stereotyped conformity *toward* free expression
>
> *from* passive compliance *toward* active identification
>
> *from* imposed direction *toward* cooperative planning
>
> *from* coercive requirements *toward* voluntary commitments
>
> *from* mass handling *toward* individual guidance
>
> *from* extrinsic motivation *toward* intrinsic value concerns
>
> *from* submissive acquiescence *toward* wholehearted involvement
>
> *from* restictive domination *toward* responsible self-direction
>
> *from* stultifying repression *toward* spontaneity
>
> *from* the fixing of habits and skills *toward* the cultivation of flexible adaptive responses to life-related situations.[19]

Eisner makes five suggestions for encouraging creative thinking in children:

---

[19] Laura Zirbes, *Spurs to Creative Teaching* (New York: G. P. Putnam's Sons, 1959), pp. 26–27.

1. Encourage children to deal with alternate solutions to problems, to put off formulating answers until they have explored a range of possibilities.
2. During idea sessions, participants are made to feel as comfortable as possible and criticism is not allowed.
3. The student needs to have experience and skill in the subject area itself.
4. A person must be able to control the syntax and techniques of the discipline within which he is working if he is to use the discipline in a creative way.
5. Creative behavior should be rewarded when it occurs.[20]

Torrance suggests that, to reward the creative behavior of pupils, the teacher should do the following:

1. Treat unusual questions with respect.
2. Treat unusual ideas with respect.
3. Show children that their ideas have value.
4. Provide opportunities for self-initiated learning and give credit for it.
5. Provide periods of nonevaluated practice or learning.[21]

The personality of the teacher has a great deal to do with creativeness in teaching. The way in which he relates to his pupils and they relate to him is seen by Hughes to be determined by the quality of integrity. She calls attention to the following as being fundamental to this relationship:

1. Maintaining the active quality of integrity in human relationships facilitates the process of integration within the individual and the group. Through cultivation of respect, mutuality, and unity children have courage to expose themselves and share feelings.
2. Openness to experience means that children encounter the world with their full senses, develop increased awareness, and learn to trust and respect their own reactions. This necessitates a teacher's flexibility and sensitiveness to the meaning for children, lack of threat, and responsiveness to the diversity of meaning a situation may have for children.
3. Fostering courage and risk, one condition of openness to experience, helps the children explore, try things out, and be themselves. The child must perceive the teacher-learner situation as one that furthers a goal or purpose he has accepted for himself.

---

[20] Elliot W. Eisner, *Think with Me about Creativity* (Dansville, N.Y.: F. A. Owen Publishing Company, 1964), pp. 38–40.
[21] E. Paul Torrance, *Education and the Creative Potential* (Minneapolis: University of Minnesota Press, 1963), pp. 56–57.

4. Encouraging alternatives and problem solving lies in the teacher's response to the child's intellectual explorations and purposes. It is to permit the seeking of several positive solutions to a problem as opposed to complete adherence to a preconceived answer or way of doing things. The teacher's response to diversity in ways of working problems, offbeat questions, and better ways to meet individual differences are also important.

5. Dealing with the process of consultation, or acceptance of an expression of feelings and points of view within the framework of social responsibility, requires teacher guidance in the examination of the consequence of a rule or a solution to a problem in terms of all who are affected by it.[22]

All of this seems to harmonize with the need to recognize the importance of today's children, tomorrow's citizens, being able to face a myriad of unforeseen sets of circumstances. There is a very real limit on the extent to which teachers can provide children with a fixed repertory of responses for an unpredictable future. But teachers can try to induce a posture toward the future that includes a willingness to come to grips with the unexpected. Individuality becomes a matter of concern for the learning situation, too. Teachers must find a *modern* way of nurturing the special character and unique strengths of each individual in a world in which that individual will be highly involved in groups. Teachers must find ways of handling group situations so that even they contribute to the individuality of each member. As a society we need unity, yes, even a certain conformity; but we need diversity too. We must learn to combine both, in a new harmony.[23]

There are no certain formulas to follow in bringing creativity to one's teaching and to the learning of one's pupils. However, the following ideas may be worth thinking about in this regard:

An attitude toward teaching. Probably most important in the desire to teach creatively is the teacher's attitude about teaching. He cannot be content with what he knows. He understands that both his scholarly and professional competence are improvable. He grasps the extent to which man's knowledge expands and he realizes he must continue to study lest his own background become obsolete. He understands, too, that teaching procedures and practice change and that he must continue to be alert to improve on his own pedagogical skill. He realizes that his education as a teacher is a continuing, career-long requirement.

Thoughtful action. Creative teaching results from reasoned and purposeful action. This kind of action emerges from careful thinking; rarely

---

[22] Hughes, "Integrity," pp. 80–100.
[23] Joint Project on the Individual and the School, *A Climate for Individuality*, p. 10.

is an unplanned, spur-of-the-moment action effective. What appear to be spontaneous ideas can usually be traced to some previous consideration. In general, creative teaching is based upon well-evaluated perceptions that are related to specific situations or problems.

Treating children as individuals. When a teacher treats all children as individuals and devises means for respecting individual differences, there is a greater demand for creative teaching. The planned program must be flexible and accepting of differences in pupil ideas and actions as well as differences in pupil pace and progress. Patterns of growth and development in children are fostered and guided so that progress is maximized for each. Conditions should be favorable for active pupil participation in selecting and initiating activities; planning and evaluating experiences should be encouraged.

Taking advantage of every opportunity for variety. The creative teacher is alert to discover ways of bringing variety and interest to the learning situation. Ideas can be taken from the local community, from the cultural backgrounds of the children, from unique regional characteristics, from current world affairs, or from the teacher's own experiences and those of his colleagues. Variety in organization, materials, activities, and teaching procedures strengthens and supports creative teaching. It is important, though, that such variety be reasonable and appropriate, rather than a conglomerate of unrelated or confused situations.

Providing opportunity to enjoy creativity of others. One dimension of creative teaching encompasses the means by which the teacher provides pupils with opportunities to meet and recognize creativity (see Chapter 14). Children need to appreciate not only their own creative acts and endeavors, but those of others as well.

Enjoying and making the profession more satisfying. A final consideration for the development of creative teaching is the teacher's own enjoyment of the role. Problems occur and not all teaching experiences are truly enjoyable, but among the routines and the difficulties are the moments of light, the times when teacher and children are delighted and gratified by observable results. The more creative the teaching, the more often appear the really satisfying moments that make teaching worth while.

RECOMMENDED READINGS

BAY, MARY A., and LOIS V. JOHNSON. *Classroom Group Behavior.* New York: The Macmillan Company, 1964.

BLACKHAM, GARTH J. *The Deviant Child in the Classroom.* Belmont, Calif.: Wadsworth Publishing Company, Inc., 1967.

GNAGEY, WILLIAM J. *Controlling Classroom Misbehavior.* "What Research Says to the Teacher" Series, #32. Washington, D.C.: NEA, 1965.

LANE, HOWARD, and MARY A. BEAUCHAMP. *Human Relations in Teaching.* Englewood Cliffs, N.J.: Prentice-Hall, Inc., 1955.

LIFTON, WALTER M. *Working with Groups.* New York: John Wiley & Sons, Inc., 1966.

MIEL, ALICE (editor). *Creativity in Teaching.* Belmont, Calif.: Wadsworth Publishing Company, Inc., 1961.

SMITH, JAMES A. *Creative Teaching in the Elementary School.* Boston: Allyn and Bacon, Inc., 1966.

Author Index

Italicized numbers indicate references found in Recommended Readings at the end of chapters.

Van Hagen, Winifred, *322*

Wagner, Eva Bond, *158*
Wallas, G., 327
Walsh, Huber, *295*
Wann, Kenneth, 293
Ward, Morgan, *241*
Wardeberg, Helen, *425*
Washburne, C. W., 214–215
Welch, Ronald C., 233–234
Wesley, Edgar B., 267
Wiles, Kimball, *94*

Williams, Catherine M., *407*
Wilson, Dorothy W., 212
Wilson, Guy, 212
Wise, C. T., 212
Wittich, Walter Arno, *408*
Wolfe, Dael, 252–253
Woody, Clifford, 216
Wooton, William, *241*
Wrightstone, J. Wayne, 29, *41*
Wynn, Richard, *118*

Zirbes, Laura, 444

Subject Index